THE ECONOMIC DEVELOPMENT OF THE TERRITORY OF

Papua AND New Guinea

Report of a Mission Organized by the
International Bank for Reconstruction and Development
at the Request of
the Government of the Commonwealth of Australia

THE ECONOMIC DEVELOPMENT
OF THE TERRITORY OF
PAPUA *AND* NEW GUINEA

PUBLISHED FOR

The International Bank for Reconstruction and Development

BY The Johns Hopkins Press, Baltimore

THE MISSION

Kenneth R. Iverson,	Chief of Mission
Marinus van der Mel,	Chief Economist
Philip C. Chambers,	Adviser on Agricultural Production
Leonard H. S. Emerson,	Adviser on Education
Richard J. Lund,	Adviser on Industry, Mining and Power
Campbell P. McMeekan,	Adviser on Agriculture and Livestock
Dr. Lawrence O. Roberts,	Adviser on Public Health
James A. Simmons,	Economist
Konrad Studnicki-Gizbert,	Adviser on Transport and Communications
Horst von Oppenfeld,	Agricultural Economist

This is the report of an economic survey mission to the Territory of Papua and New Guinea which was organized by the International Bank for Reconstruction and Development at the request of the Government of the Commonwealth of Australia. The basic objective of the Mission, as agreed by the Government and the Bank, was to undertake a general review of the economic potentialities of the Territory and to make recommendations to assist the Australian Government in planning a development program designed to expand and stimulate the economy and thereby raise the standard of living of the people.

The Mission consisted of ten members from six countries. Four members of the Mission were from the permanent staff of the Bank. In addition, Mr. Eric Schaefer of the Bank staff spent some two weeks in the Territory and in Australia in connection with technical and organizational matters of highway construction and maintenance. The Mission's Adviser on Public Health was borrowed from the staff of the World Health Organization (WHO).

The Mission assembled in Washington in May 1963, was in Australia, Papua and New Guinea from early June to early September of that year, and started the preparation of its report at the Bank's headquarters in Washington during the latter part of September 1963. A draft of the report was presented to the Australian Government in June 1964 and the Mission Chief, Chief Economist and Adviser on Agriculture and Livestock returned to Australia in July to discuss the report; high ranking officers of the Territory Administration also were present.

Statistical data in the report have, wherever possible, been brought up to date as far as June 30, 1963; with few exceptions, no attempt has been made to include information beyond that date.

The Territory of Papua and New Guinea consists of the Trust Territory of New Guinea (following World War II it was placed under the trusteeship system provided for in the charter of the United Nations) and the Australian Territory of Papua; they are administered by Australia in an administrative union. Article 76 of the charter of the United Nations spells out that: "The basic objectives of the trusteeship system, in accordance with the Purposes of the United Nations laid down in Article 1 of the present charter, shall be: (a) to further international peace and security; (b) to promote the political, economic, social, and educational advancement of the inhabitants of the trust territories, and the progressive development toward self-government or independence as may be appropriate to the particular circumstances of each territory and its peoples and the freely expressed wishes of the peoples concerned, and as may be provided by the terms of each trusteeship agreement; (c) to encourage respect for human rights and for fundamental freedoms for all without distinction as to race, sex, language, or religion, and to encourage recognition of the interdependence of the peoples of the world; and (d) to ensure equal treatment in social, economic, and commercial matters for all members of the United Nations and their nationals, and also equal treatment for the latter in the administration of justice, without prejudice to the attainment of the foregoing objectives and subject to the provisions of Article 80."

It is the Commonwealth Government's declared aim to help the inhabitants of both Papua and New Guinea to become self-governing as soon as possible. The report was prepared during an important phase in the country's political evolution. Early in 1964, elections took place for a House of Assembly with a clear majority of elected, indigenous members; this House met for the first time in June 1964.

The Mission gratefully acknowledges the wholehearted cooperation it received from the Department of Territories and other departments of the Commonwealth Government, the Reserve Bank of Australia and the Commonwealth Banking Corporation. The Prime Minister met with the Mission Chief and other members of the Mission both before and after the Mission was in the Territory. The Australian National University was helpful on numerous occasions. In the Territory the officials of the Administration cooperated to the fullest extent and were most helpful to the Mission's work. The Mission also wants to mention the special effort made by the Department of Territories in the preparation of statistical data.

While in the Territory, Mission members traveled extensively, visiting 14 out of the 15 districts, where they received substantial assistance from the District Commissioners and their staff. Discussions were held with representatives of private groups such as the planters, taxpayers' associations and chambers of commerce, with private agricultural, industrial, commercial, banking and religious interests and with a large number of private individuals, both in the Territory and in Australia. The Mission also had the opportunity to talk with members of Native Local Government Councils, members of the Legislative Council (now the House of Assembly) and with other political leaders.

In the report which follows, the first chapter is intended to provide general background knowledge about the Territory. The second chapter gives a summary of the major objectives, principles and conditions for implementation underlying the Mission's program for economic development, the main sector recommendations and the budgetary implications of the program. The other six chapters contain the detailed analysis of the major sectors examined by the Mission.

In transmitting the report to the Australian Government, the President of the Bank noted that, since the Executive Directors and the management customarily do not review the recommendations of economic survey missions in detail, the report as transmitted represents the views of the Mission rather than those of the Bank. The letter of transmittal added, however, that the Bank believed that the findings of the report deserved the most careful consideration and discussion. Similarly, while other international agencies were given an opportunity to comment on the portions of the report of particular interest to them, responsibility for the recommendations of the report is to be regarded as that of the Mission alone.

The currency of the Territory of Papua and New Guinea is the Australian Pound (£A). The pound is divided into 20 shillings (/-) and the shilling is divided into 12 pence (d).

£A1 = US$2.24.
US$1 = .446 of £A1 (8 shillings and 11 pence).
£A5 = £ Sterling 4.

STATISTICAL CONVENTIONS

Figures are rounded to the last significant figure shown. Due to rounding, components in a table may not always add exactly to the total indicated.

UNITS

Timber: the volume unit used is the super foot (su. ft.), which is the equivalent of 144 cubic inches; plywood and veneer sheets are recorded in square feet of specified thickness ($\frac{3}{16}$ths or $\frac{1}{16}$th of an inch).

CONTENTS

THE REPORT

ANNEXES

STATISTICAL APPENDIX

LIST OF MAPS

LIST OF CHARTS

THE REPORT

PAPUA AND NEW GUINEA

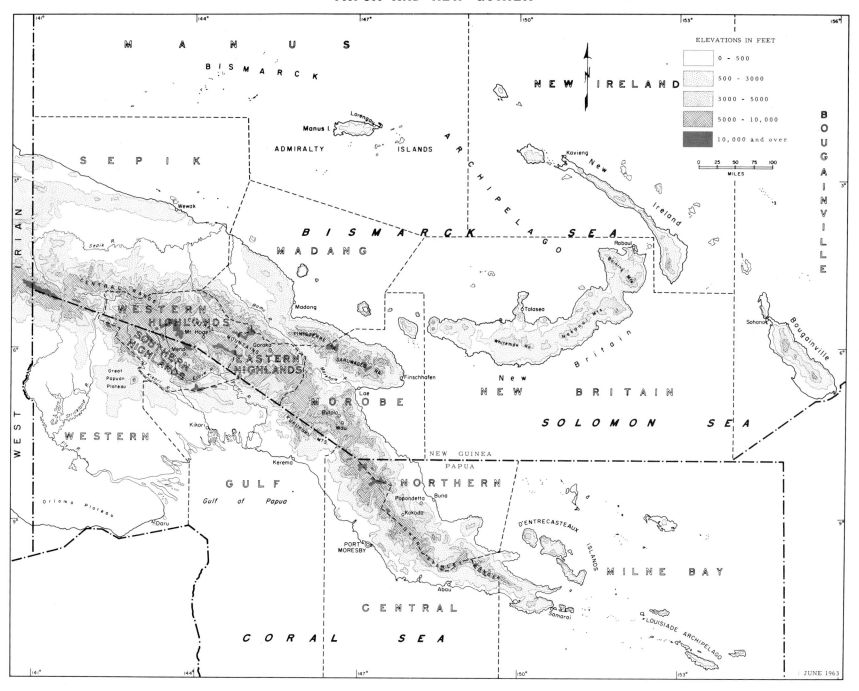

ELEVATIONS IN FEET

0 - 500
500 - 3000
3000 - 5000
5000 - 10,000
10,000 and over

MILES
0   25   50   75   100

JUNE 1963

CHAPTER 1 *THE SETTING*

The Territory of Papua and New Guinea with its large mainland and outer islands is located in the tropics about 100 miles to the north of the mainland of Australia. It is an area of unusual variety with rugged mountain ranges, fertile valleys, great rivers, extensive forests, vast swamps. It is truly underdeveloped.

The indigenous[1] people are, for the most part, primitive. However, some have become a part of a small modern economy. Others are only now emerging from the Stone Age. Development has been guided and directed by the European administrators, missionaries and residents, who account for slightly more than 1 percent of the population of 2 million. The people are being influenced by the process of change. For them health programs which overcome the ravages of disease, farm programs which help to produce crops that bring cash to buy useful goods, schools teaching modern concepts and the "secrets" of the European, religious teachings, law and order, and the lessening of fear of the unknown are developments which are becoming meaningful and assuming new importance.

HISTORY, GOVERNMENT AND POLITICAL DEVELOPMENT

For an understanding of the objectives of Australian policy, and the potentials for economic development of the Territory of Papua and New Guinea, it is essential to review briefly the background of the Territory.

Little is known about the origins of the indigenous people, or about their history prior to the arrival of the European. Portuguese and Spanish navigators first sighted the island of New Guinea in the early part of the sixteenth century. The Spanish named it Isla del Oro (Island of Gold) but later called it New Guinea as the natives of the island seemed to resemble those of the African coast. Various European powers explored the coasts and islands for some two hundred years before territorial claims were made. The Dutch claimed the western part of the island of New Guinea early in the nineteenth century. A British protectorate over the south

---

[1] The Administration has adopted "indigene" to identify the native people. The Mission in this report uses both "indigene" and "native."

coast of Papua was proclaimed in 1884. At almost the same time Germany annexed northeastern New Guinea. In 1906, the Commonwealth of Australia assumed responsibility from the British for the Territory of Papua.

With the outbreak of World War I, Australia occupied German New Guinea and after the war continued its administration under a mandate from the League of Nations. Separate administrations were maintained for the Territory of Papua and for the mandated Territory of New Guinea. Following World War II, the Territory of New Guinea was placed under the trusteeship system provided for in the charter of the United Nations. Australia undertook to administer the Trust Territory of New Guinea and the Australian Territory of Papua as an administrative union known as the Territory of Papua and New Guinea. Administration headquarters were established at Port Moresby.

The introduction of European administration led to the gradual establishment of law and order. Finding few hereditary chiefs or formal political organizations through which they could administer their territories, the colonizing powers established systems of direct rule. The coastal areas of the mainland and the outer islands, where Australians and Germans first settled, were under control and largely secure by the turn of the century. It was not until the early 1930s that Europeans first penetrated into the great mountain ranges of the New Guinea mainland and discovered the relatively dense populations of the highland valleys. The early explorations were followed by government patrols; administrative posts were set up; airstrips were built; medical aid posts were organized and usually roads were built to facilitate the administration of the area. Inter-tribal fighting was gradually suppressed and law and order established.

During this early period, Christian missions made a noteworthy contribution as a civilizing influence in general, and specifically through the establishment of schools and medical services. Today there are over 2,400 missionaries of various denominations in the Territory.

World War II marked a turning point in the history of the Territory. Major engagements had been fought with Japanese forces over the Kokoda Trail, at Buna, Milne Bay, Lae, Bougainville, Manus and other places. The Japanese forces had been stopped in the Territory and prevented from reaching Australia. After the war, stress was placed on the need to preserve the Territory as an area friendly to Australia. As a related phenomenon, there were for the first time a large number of Australians with a knowledge and feeling of interest in the area and its people. Also with the post-war era came the rapid march to independence of colonial people in Asia and Africa. These events inevitably were reflected in the attitude and interest of Australia particularly, and the world generally, in the fact that here was a primitive area with a considerable number of people living in a state of tutelage.

Australia re-examined its policies toward development of the Territory and adopted a policy predicated on its commitment under the Trusteeship Agreement and its decision to treat Papua and New Guinea as one unit to promote the political, economic, social and educational advancement of the indigenous people.[2] Australia made it clear that it intended to produce, as soon as practicable, an opportunity for complete self-determination and that it would defend the freedom of choice and respect the wishes of the people of the Territory. In effect, Australia assumed the responsibility to administer the Territory in the best interest of all the people until such time as they would be able to conduct their own affairs.

The administrative, judicial and legislative structure for the Territory is based on the Papua and New Guinea Act of 1949 and later amending legislation.[3] Executive authority in the Territory rests with the Administrator. He was first assisted by an Executive Council but after 1961 an Administrator's Council was established with six members over which he presides. The executive functions of government are carried out under his direction by 16 functional departments.[4] The Territory is divided into 15 administrative districts, each with a District Commissioner responsible for the general administration and coordination of the activities of all departments within the district. The act also provides for

[2] In addition to carrying out the basic objectives of Article 76 of the U.N. charter (see Preface), the Trusteeship Agreement provided that in the discharge of its obligations Australia would, in accordance with its established policy:

a. Take into consideration the customs and usages of the inhabitants of New Guinea and respect the rights and safeguard the interests, both present and future, of the indigenous inhabitants of the Territory; and in particular ensure that no rights over native land in favor of any person not an indigenous inhabitant of New Guinea may be created or transferred except with the consent of the competent public authority;

b. promote, as may be appropriate to the circumstances of the Territory, the educational and cultural advancement of the inhabitants;

c. assure to the inhabitants of the Territory, as may be appropriate to the particular circumstances of the Territory and its peoples, a progressively increasing share in the administrative and other services of the Territory;

d. guarantee to the inhabitants of the Territory, subject only to the requirements of public order, freedom of speech, of the press, of assembly and of petition, freedom of conscience and worship and freedom of religious teachings.

[3] The Act is administered by the Minister of State for Territories through the Department of Territories at Canberra. Under the Act the Governor-General has authority to appoint an Administrator to administer the Territory on behalf of the Government of the Commonwealth of Australia.

[4] See Organization Chart on page 4.

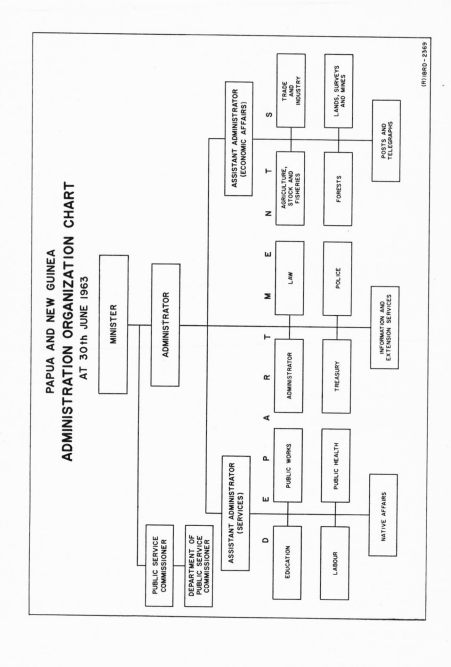

PAPUA AND NEW GUINEA
ADMINISTRATION ORGANIZATION CHART
AT 30th JUNE 1963

(R) IBRD - 2369

a Supreme Court with jurisdiction in civil and criminal matters as provided for by or under ordinances and for appeal therefrom to the High
Court of Australia. Under the Act other courts and tribunals can be
established by ordinance. A Territory Public Service, separate from the
Commonwealth Public Service, was created.

A Legislative Council, subject to the assent of the Administrator or, in
certain cases defined by the act, of the Governor-General, was given
legislative power in regard to the peace, order and good government of
the Territory. The Commonwealth Parliament retained the right to
legislate directly.

The Commonwealth Government adopted a threefold approach to
expanding the part to be taken by the indigenous people in the processes
of government. It increased the representation of the indigenous people
in the legislature, it established a system of local government, and it laid
the foundation for increasing the role of the indigenes in the Administration both by expanding educational facilities generally and by establishing
specialized institutions to train indigenes for the public service.

Prior to World War II, there were separate Legislative Councils in the
two Territories but the indigenous people were not represented. The
Legislative Council for the combined Territory met for the first time in
1951; of 29 council members, three were natives. In 1961, 12 natives, six
appointed and six elected, were included in an enlarged council of 37
members which for the first time contained a non-official majority, but
the indigenes voted only for indigenes and the Europeans voted only for
European candidates.

In 1964, the Legislative Council was replaced by a House of Assembly
of 64 members with a clear majority of elected members. The election
procedure was also changed. There are 44 members of any race elected
on the basis of universal adult suffrage, ten non-native members elected
on the same basis, and ten official members appointed by the Governor-
General on the nomination of the Administrator. With the creation of
the new House of Assembly there will be a majority of indigenous members in the body that makes the laws and appropriates the money for the
Territory, although the Australian Government remains responsible for
its defense and for the economic, social and political advancement of the
people. The Administrator's Council was also reformed, with three
official and seven elected members being appointed to it.

The establishment of Native Local Government Councils was also
provided for by the Papua and New Guinea Act of 1949. Prior to that
time, indigenous participation in local government consisted of the
election of native village councilors to assist local officials appointed by
the Administration. These councils had no financial powers, and with

little authority were virtually discussion groups. The Native Local Government Councils were intended to extend the administration from the single village to an area of a number of villages and thus increase the resources and make possible the undertaking of larger development activities. Wider powers, including powers of taxation, were given to the councils.

The first such council was established in 1950. The expansion of the council system was at first very slow. In many areas there was a reluctance to join. In other areas passive or even active resistance was encountered. But progress was made. By 1956, ten councils had been formed, all in coastal areas. In 1959, the first Highland Council was organized. Thereafter, the pace quickened and by mid-1963 a total of 77 councils had been set up, covering a population of about 700,000. At the time of the Mission's visit at least one council had been formed in every administrative district. They ranged in size from 2,500 to 43,000 members, the majority being in the 7,000 to 14,000 group.

The councils have taken an increasing role in development efforts at the village level. They have wide authority to take measures for the peace and welfare of their communities, subject to the approval of the Administration. Their principal source of revenue is a head tax (council tax). Besides establishing their own governmental organizations and facilities, the councils have built or maintained roads and bridges, health centers, medical aid posts, schools, markets, wells and water tanks. Some, notably the councils in the Gazelle Peninsula on New Britain which operate cacao fermentaries, have participated in business ventures. New legislation envisages a greater devolution of authority to the councils in the management of their finances without prior approval of the Administration.

The councils have also promoted among the people of neighboring areas greater realization of common problems. This has led in some cases to the amalgamation of neighboring councils, as in the Gazelle Peninsula, where four councils combined to form one council representing some 40,000 people.

The emergence of these elected political bodies has been an important step toward giving increasing numbers of indigenous people experience in handling the political, social and economic problems arising in the areas for which the councils have responsibility. The councils have provided the structure through which the participants can begin to obtain an understanding of the democratic processes of government. In the short time the councils have been in operation, remarkable progress has been made. But the effective history of the councils has covered only a few years; almost two-thirds of them have been organized since 1959. Thus the process of learning the ways of modern government has only begun.

Indigenes have participated also in the Town Advisory Councils which have been set up in most urban centers. The urban centers are, however, relatively small and widely scattered. Only three towns have more than 5,000 people, Port Moresby with 33,500, Rabaul on New Britain with 8,500 and Lae on the eastern shore of the mainland with 6,500.

In the Auxiliary Division of the Public Service, established primarily as a training division to prepare the indigenes for positions requiring greater competence, there were more than 900 indigenes in training by July 1963. At that time, 125 natives had been appointed to higher classifications, namely 14 to the Second and 111 to the Third Division.[5] In addition, there were some 19,000 indigenes employed by the Administration outside the public service, including about 10,000 Administration servants in semi-skilled technical, manipulative and clerical occupations, about 6,000 as laborers and some 3,000 with the police and corrective institutions. Natives were also receiving training and experience as members of the Administrator's Council, District Advisory Council and other local groups.

No national indigenous political parties have been organized and among the population at large there is as yet no feeling of a national identity. For the most part the indigene continues to be tied by custom, tradition and family to the area of his village. Few have traveled and most of these but limited distances. Natural and linguistic barriers have restricted communications. While English is the official language, it is spoken by few.

Communications on a national level are thus restricted and have been a barrier to political and economic development. The paucity of educated native leadership has been another serious barrier. At the time of the Mission's visit less than 100 indigenes had received a full secondary education. No single indigene had completed a university education.

However, as will be seen in the following sections, the process of change is being carried forward on all fronts, political, economic and social. The Mission was impressed by the remarkable progress made since the last world war under the direction of the Australians.

[5] The First Division is composed of departmental heads, other than Commissioner, and such other officers as the Minister determines. The Second Division includes all officers whose duties are of an executive, professional or clerical nature and the Third Division those officers not included in other divisions. The Auxiliary Division comprises native officers only; it is composed of many school teachers and technicians, clerical assistants and tradesmen. Under the Public Service Ordinance 1963, all positions in the Auxiliary Division will lapse as soon as the ordinance is brought into force. Serving Auxiliary Division officers will be absorbed into the Third Division and future recruitment at this level will be directly to the Third Division. Also, suitably qualified Administration servants will be transferred to the Third Division.

THE LAND

The Territory comprises the eastern half of the island of New Guinea, the Bismarck Archipelago of which New Britain, New Ireland and Manus are the largest islands, Bougainville and Buka in the northern Solomons and the Trobriand, Woodlark, D'Entrecasteaux and Louisiade island groups to the east of Papua. In all, there are about 600 islands stretching for more than 1,200 miles from east to west and some 750 miles from north to south. The total land area of the Territory is 183,540 square miles, and compared with States in Australia is twice the size of Victoria, and half the size of New South Wales.

The eastern portion of the New Guinea mainland accounts for about 85 percent of the land area. A complex system of mountains extends from the eastern end of the island to the western boundary. Precipitous slopes, knife-sharp ridges, great height variations up to more than 15,400 feet and broad upland valleys characterize this mountain area. Large rivers with great volumes of water flow to the south, north and east. Few of the rivers are navigable except by small boats in the lower reaches. But the largest river, the Fly, which rises in the mountains of western Papua and flows over 700 miles through the great southwestern plains, can be navigated for nearly 500 miles by shallow draft vessels drawing less than eight feet. The same is true of the Sepik River, which rises in the central cordillera close to the headwaters of the Fly but flows first northward and then eastward into the Bismarck Sea. Between the northern and the massive central ranges of mountains is the Central Depression, comprising the valleys of the Sepik, Ramu and Markham rivers. In the Fly and Sepik river valleys, and to a lesser extent in others, are great areas of swamp.

In the islands, mountains also cover much of the area, with peaks rising to 8,500 feet. Along large portions of the coasts there are lowlands and rolling foothills of varying width.

The Territory lies wholly within the tropics with its northern islands almost bordering the Equator. The lowland and coastal areas are generally hot and humid but the altitude of the mountains makes for progressively lower temperatures and generally a moderate climate.

It is outside the tropical cyclone area but it has northwest and southeast monsoons which are heavily laden with moisture. Most areas have an average rainfall of 80 to 90 inches a year, while in some rainfall exceeds 200 inches. In the several rain shadow zones, the rainfall is much lower. As an example, the rainfall around Port Moresby is only 40 to 60 inches per year.

Despite the luxuriant vegetation, large areas of the Territory are infertile. The heavy rainfall gives rise to continual leaching of the soil under the rain forest. There are, however, considerable acreages of high and medium fertility. While land resource studies have covered only a portion of the Territory, available information suggests that there are extensive areas of unused lands in the upland valleys, the coastal areas and to a greater or lesser extent in the large river valleys which are well suited to the production of crops characteristic of the wet tropics. Extensive grasslands are suited to livestock although in some areas the climatic conditions impose limitations to some forms of animal production. Dense forests covering three-quarters of the Territory have a large commercial potential.

The heavy rainfall in the mountain ranges provides a substantial hydroelectric potential. A wide range of minerals has been discovered, including gold, silver, platinum, manganese, copper, lead, zinc, nickel, bauxite, iron and thin seams of low-grade coal. However, most of the deposits discovered to date have been of no economic value. The main exception is gold, which for many years was the Territory's principal export. Extensive drilling in western Papua has led to the discovery of potentially large quantities of natural gas but, as yet, of no significant quantity of oil.

THE PEOPLE

The indigenous people have a great diversity of physical types. The predominantly dark-skinned, woolly-haired Melanesians who occupy the greater part of the western Pacific are in the majority. Based on a physical difference in stature, hair texture, nose form and other characteristics, a distinction has sometimes been made between a Melanesian type and a Papuan type. In this context, the Papuan type is representative of the interior and the Melanesian of the coastal and island areas.

A few Negrito groups have been reported in the mountain areas. In the northwest islands of the Manus group, people bear a physical resemblance to the inhabitants of the area commonly called Micronesia. The Polynesians are few in number and are confined to the Tauu and Nukumanu islands of the Bougainville District.

When the European came, the people were at a Stone Age level. Living in the rugged mountains and in dense jungle and swamp lands, they comprised numerous hostile groups, intermittently feuding with their neighbors. Some were cannibals and head-hunters. Fear of their neighbors and the possibility of surprise attack, coupled with the extremely difficult terrain, restricted movement much beyond the lands belonging to the group.

One of the outstanding characteristics of the people was its fragmentation into small communities, usually numbering 100 to 200, and sometimes only a few families, each speaking a language generally unintelligible to neighboring groups. With at least 700 dialects or languages being spoken, communication between European and native, as well as among natives, has been most difficult. Gradually, however, there developed a language which was a combination of Melanesian and English (Pidgin English). This became the lingua-franca in New Guinea and was also spoken in Papua, where Police Motu, the vernacular of the natives living in the immediate vicinity of Port Moresby, became the lingua-franca. Nevertheless, the fragmentation of languages continues to be a major obstacle. Writing was unknown prior to the introduction of European script.

Within the villages, hereditary leadership was practically nonexistent except in the Trobriand Islands, where hereditary rank had an important part in determining leadership. Elsewhere, valor in war, the number of wives, the possession of know-how and skills such as in hunting, gardening and canoe-making were keys to leadership.

Religious beliefs and practices have played an integral part in the indigenous cultures, and magic and the propitiation of the spirits still exercise a potent influence upon the lives of indigenous people. There is one movement that deserves mention: the Cargo Cult. Sparked by the desire for European goods, the natives place their faith on the intervention of ancestors and deceased spirits to obtain their desires. Generally, a central figure or a small group of men claim to have been visited in dreams by ancestral spirits and promised that if the people make certain preparations the ancestral spirits will return bringing cargoes of European-type goods. When the promised cargo does not arrive, confidence in the central figures evaporates and the particular movement crumbles.

Prior to the arrival of the European, metals were not used. The indigenes were dependent upon primitive implements such as the stone axe, spear, bow and arrow and digging stick to provide their subsistence. Needs were few and for the most part easily satisfied. Food came from subsistence gardens—sweet potatoes, yams, taro, cassava, bananas, maize, sugar cane and leafy vegetables. Edible nuts and fruits such as the coconut, breadfruit, pandanus and betel nut came from wild or planted trees. Wild sago and nipa palm provided the bulk of the diet in some areas. Small animals (no large game animals except a few deer exist in the Territory), fish from the sea and the rivers, and domesticated pig added to the diet. But the quantity of meat was small and the diet was generally deficient in protein. Before law and order was established, cannibalism was practiced in various areas of the Territory.

In traditional society, each individual is taught to carry out all the duties considered suitable for his or her sex. Besides domestic duties in the home, women usually maintain the gardens, while the men do initial clearing and such heavy work as fencing. Planting, harvesting and maintenance is generally the work of both sexes. Houses are built of poles, sticks, grasses and palm fronds from the jungle. With the mild climate, little clothing is worn. Even in the colder higher elevations the limited garments usually are made of grass, bark or leaves. The few furs have been used primarily in colorful headdresses.

Trading was limited in traditional society. Some coastal and inland peoples exchanged salt, food, pottery, stone axes, wood carvings and shells. Sea voyages were undertaken by canoe fleets to places where goods and food could be exchanged, but these voyages may have had more religious than commercial significance. Nevertheless, trade was carried on and some of these exchanges still continue.

In most areas, ownership of land traditionally has been vested in the community, with usufructuary rights granted to individuals or families by agreement of all members of the owning group. Inheritance has followed two patterns: the matrilineal in some groups, the patrilineal in others. Often inheritance patterns were complex, with a large number of people claiming rights in a given piece of land. Also complex were the social obligations existing among the members of kinship groups. Each member could claim the assistance and support of other members in case of need and this could not normally be refused. Where necessary, the support of the young, the old and the sick was a group responsibility. In these ways traditional society provided a measure of social security for its members. The system of group responsibility makes many natives reluctant to leave their old environment to obtain employment elsewhere on a permanent basis. Once detached from the old environment completely, it may be difficult to obtain re-acceptance as a member of the former group.

Today the pattern of life for the majority of the people is not greatly changed. Subsistence production is still the principal means of livelihood; land is with rare exceptions still owned communally; patterns of inheritance and social obligations are largely unchanged. Notwithstanding the economic progress of recent years, less than 2.5 percent of the native people live in towns, only 80,000, or 4 percent, are in wage employment, and of these nearly 30,000 are migrant workers who will in most cases return to their villages after a two-year absence.

The indigenous population is currently estimated at about 2 million—it was much smaller when the Europeans arrived. Only gradually as Administration control was extended over the Territory was it possible to establish records of the population. Even today, part of the indigenous population is estimated, but this probably amounts to less than 5 percent of the total, and the population statistics are, therefore, reasonably comprehensive. The official estimate of the present rate of population growth is 2.3 percent per annum. As health services spread, it seems reasonable to expect that this rate of growth will rise. Estimates prepared within the Administration project a population of 2.45 million by 1970 and 3.44 million by 1980. These are based on the expectation of an annual rate of growth of population rising to more than 3.5 percent in the late 1970s.

The over-all population density is low, with only 11 persons per square mile. There are large areas of country with both favorable and unfavorable climate and terrain where the population is very thinly spread, and other areas which are quite densely populated. The Western District of Papua, covering 40,000 square miles or 22 percent of the Territory of Papua and New Guinea has only 3.4 percent of the population and a population density of 1.7 persons per square mile. By contrast, the Eastern Highlands District with less than 4 percent of the land has 18 percent of the population and a density of 51 persons per square mile. Within the Eastern Highlands District there are small areas, in particular the Chimbu region, with population densities reaching 500 per square mile, and in the Gazelle Peninsula in New Britain centers of population exceed 100 per square mile though the total population of the area is small. Other dense population areas are the Wabag area in the Western Highlands and the Maprik area in the Sepik. The greatest concentration of population is in the highlands on the mainland of New Guinea, where there are more than 800,000 people or 40 percent of the whole population. The outer islands, New Britain, New Ireland, Bougainville and Manus have about 230,000 people, and the bulk of the remainder of the population is in the Sepik, Madang and Morobe districts of New Guinea and the Central district of Papua.

Besides the indigenous population, there are about 27,000 non-natives of whom 21,000 are Australians, some 2,700 Chinese and the balance mostly people of mixed race. The majority of the Australians come to the Territory to work in the Administration, on plantations, in business and the professions, and generally regard Australia as home and intend one day to return. There are, however, other Australians who own and operate plantations or have business interests and consider the Territory their home. The Chinese on the whole have deeper roots in the Territory, many families having lived there for several generations. Most are engaged in commerce but some have expanded into coastal shipping and the operation of plantations.

POPULATION DISTRIBUTION

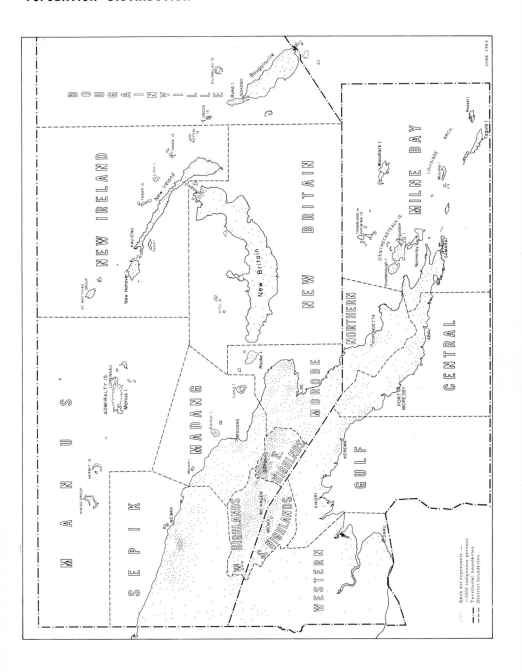

JUNE 1963

The Chinese community has grown quite slowly since the end of World War II. With the expansion of the economy and the great increase in governmental activity the Australian community has grown from less than 6,000 in 1947 to 21,000 in 1963.

THE ECONOMY AND ITS DEVELOPMENT

While the great majority of the indigenous people are still engaged in subsistence production, a small money economy has developed over the past 80 years under European stimulus and direction. Until World War II, the growth of the money economy depended primarily on the expansion of export production. Since then, exports have continued to expand, but the principal generator of growth has been the rapid rise in government spending.

The Export Sector

The beginnings of commercial contacts between the Territory and the outside world were the occasional stops of passing ships along the coast of New Guinea in the early 1800s when items such as trinkets and simple tools were exchanged for coconuts and shell. But it was not until the 1870s that the first trading stations in the Territory were established and regular commercial transactions with the outside world began.

Copra was the product of principal interest to European traders. Supplies from native growers proved to be unreliable and limited in quantity, and the advantages of organizing a steady and dependable supply on the basis of plantations under European management were soon realized. The first plantation was established in New Britain in the early 1880s. Thereafter, most of the increase in production came from European owned plantations, though the authorities in Papua and New Guinea encouraged and even compelled the indigenes to plant coconuts on their own behalf. Copra was virtually the only product exported from New Guinea. In Papua, gold mining was the principal attraction for the Australians in the early years, though output was very small. A few coconut and rubber plantations were established before World War I.

In both Territories, the pattern of development was essentially the same: the expansion of the market economy was the result of the establishment of European owned and managed enterprises with the indigenes supplying the unskilled or semi-skilled work force, often as indentured labor. Only to a very limited extent did the indigenes produce for the market on their own account. This continued to be the pattern until after World War II.

During the 1920s, copra production, almost all from plantations, increased rapidly. In the early 1930s when copra prices collapsed, the market economy continued to expand following the rapid development of the Bulolo gold fields, stimulated by devaluations first of the Australian pound and then of the United States dollar. No estimates of the output of the economy are available for this period, but between 1920 and 1940 the Territory's exports rose in value from roughly £A1 million to £A4 million of which almost £A3 million was gold.

Since the end of World War II, the export sector has continued to expand and has become more diversified. Exports have risen in value to an average of more than £A15 million in recent years. Output of copra and rubber has expanded steadily. From the mid-1950s a new development has been the fast rise in production of coffee and cocoa. These four commodities now account for more than 70 percent of total marketed agricultural production, and since 1950, when copra production had recovered almost to its pre-war level, marketed production of the four commodities together has almost doubled in volume. Prices have in most years been favorable. Copra and rubber prices have shown marked fluctuations but on average have been much above the immediate pre-war and post-war levels. The quality of the cocoa and coffee produced is good and coffee especially has commanded high prices in overseas markets.

The accompanying charts show the change in the composition of exports since 1921/22 and growth in the volume and value of commodity exports excluding gold since 1948/49. Except for the sharp rise and fall in value between 1958 and 1961 associated with fluctuations in copra prices, the value and volume of commodity exports have kept pace with each other over the post-war period, and the effect of the sharp decline in copra prices since 1960 has been largely offset by the rapid growth in exports of higher priced commodities, notably coffee and cacao.

Native farmers have contributed increasingly to the expansion of output of the principal export crops. Spurred by the example of European growers and stimulated and assisted by the Administration, they have become important producers of copra, coffee and cocoa. However, more than two-thirds of the total output of the four major export crops still comes from European plantations.

Almost half of the 500,000 acres of coconut palms have been planted by native growers, though production marketed by them is only about a third of that from European plantations. The natives use the coconuts for food and sell only the surplus. They do not fully harvest the crop due to transport difficulties in some areas and to an apparent lack of incentive as their need for money is often quite small. Nevertheless, their marketed production has almost tripled since 1950 and the prospects are that native

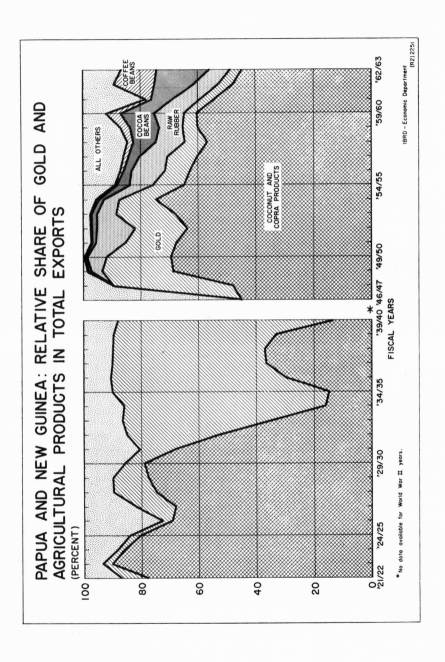

PAPUA AND NEW GUINEA: RELATIVE SHARE OF GOLD AND
AGRICULTURAL PRODUCTS IN TOTAL EXPORTS
(PERCENT)

COFFEE BEANS

ALL OTHERS

COCOA BEANS

RAW RUBBER

GOLD

COCONUT AND COPRA PRODUCTS

* No data available for World War II years.

FISCAL YEARS

'21/22   '24/25   '29/30   '34/35   '39/40   '46/47   '49/50   '54/55   '59/60   '62/63

100   80   60   40   20   0

IBRD – Economic Department

(R2) 2251

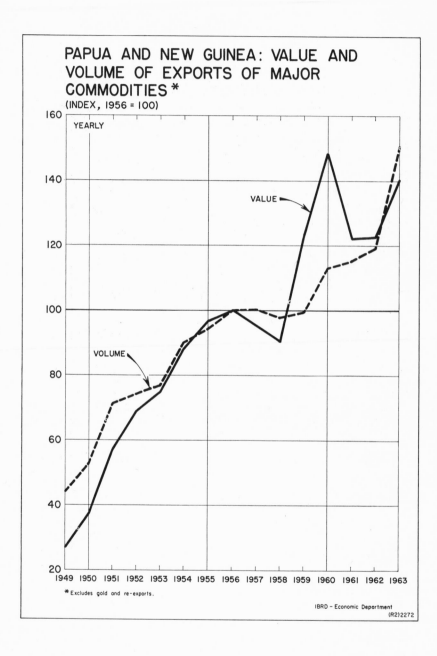

PAPUA AND NEW GUINEA: VALUE AND
VOLUME OF EXPORTS OF MAJOR
COMMODITIES *

(INDEX, 1956 = 100)

YEARLY

VALUE

VOLUME

*Excludes gold and re-exports.

IBRD – Economic Department
(R2)2272

production will increase faster than the European in the next few years because a higher proportion of native plantings are immature. The total output of copra is now in excess of 110,000 tons, an increase of about 45 percent since 1950.

Cocoa, introduced by the Germans shortly after 1900, remained of little significance until after World War II. Since then, plantings have expanded rapidly, the greatest concentrations being in New Britain, Bougainville, New Ireland, and the Madang and Northern districts. By 1961/62, European plantings approximated 98,000 acres and some 5,000 indigenes had planted over 20,000 acres. The fast expansion in European plantings was due in part to the leasing of new land by the Administration to planters, particularly in the Northern District, but more importantly to the interplanting of cocoa and coconuts on existing coconut plantations. The fact that the acreage of immature trees in 1962 equaled that of mature trees is indicative of the rate of planting. Exports of cocoa reflect the dramatic increase in cocoa plantings, having grown from 1,000 tons in 1954/55 to over 14,000 tons in 1962/63. The indigene now produces about a quarter of cocoa exports.

Both Arabica and Robusta coffee are grown, but over 90 percent is the Arabica type with plantings concentrated in the Eastern and Western highlands and Moroba districts of New Guinea. From the late 1940s, European plantings expanded rapidly as new land was leased by the Administration to planters. From about 1954, indigenous plantings, again spurred by the European example, have grown even more quickly, and by 1962 about 60 percent of the 23,000 acres planted to coffee and over 40 percent of production was under indigenous control. Exports have grown from just over 30 tons in the early 1950s to more than 4,800 tons in 1962/63, and it is estimated that production from existing plantings could about double within the next three or four years.

In contrast to the other major export crops, rubber production has been confined almost exclusively to European plantations, mainly located close to Port Moresby. Rubber production is technically more difficult than coffee and cocoa, and indigenous plantings have not been encouraged by the Administration. Production is now close to 5,000 tons annually, almost double the level of ten years ago.

Of other exports, gold production recovered rapidly after World War II, but with the depletion of the deposits at Bulolo and rising costs, production has fallen to about £A650,000 worth, a drop to about 70 percent of the post-war peak reached in 1953.

Only a small export industry has to date been developed from the Territory's great forest resources. Most of the annual cut of about 80 million super feet is used to meet domestic needs. Plywood, however, has become an important export. Production was started at Bulolo in 1953 by a company owned almost equally by the Commonwealth Government and private investors. The main market has been Australia. About three-quarters of all timber exports, valued at £A1 to £A1.5 million in recent years, have been plywood. The balance comprises logs and sawn timber, for which the main markets have been Australia and Japan. In 1962/63, log exports to Japan increased sharply (at £A319,000 they were nearly seven times greater than in 1961/62) and the prospects for increased sales to Japan are good.

Small quantities of peanuts, passion fruit juice, crocodile skins and shells have also been exported, together amounting in value to about £A700,000 in recent years.

The growth of export production has been assisted by special marketing arrangements for important Territory products in Australia. Australian importers are encouraged by duty rebates to buy the Territory's rubber and coffee, and rubber also enjoys a price support varying inversely with the market price. Duty-free quotas have been fixed for imports into Australia of the Territory's plywood and passion fruit juice. Australia takes about 40 percent of copra exports, all the rubber and most of the passion fruit juice, two-thirds of the coffee, and 85 to 90 percent of plywood. Exports of coffee to Australia have increased in volume by almost eight times in the past five years to almost 3,000 tons. Although Territory cocoa does not enjoy any preferential arrangements in the Australian market, as free entry is accorded to all Commonwealth cocoa, the volume of cocoa exports to Australia at 2,500 tons has doubled in the same period. Over-all, Australia is the Territory's principal market, taking roughly half of total exports.

Agricultural Credit

The expansion of agricultural production for export has been achieved despite little organized provision of development credit. The bulk of the finance for European plantation development has come from private sources. Most of the cocoa has been interplanted with coconuts on established plantations, with finance provided largely by the reinvestment of copra profits. To finance coffee plantings, some private capital was brought from Australia, profits from other ventures in the Territory were used, and as plantings matured, profits from coffee were reinvested.

The trading banks, which are branches of four Australian banks, lend normally on overdraft and these loans are legally callable on demand. In practice, loans have been made available for periods ranging up to seven or eight years, but for the most part they are essentially short term, used to finance working capital. At June 30, 1963, the trading banks had outstanding loans of about £A920,000 to agriculture, livestock and dairying, virtually all to European farmers and planters. Lending by the Commonwealth Development Bank, though for longer periods, has until recently been very small. A source of some long-term finance was the Ex-Servicemen's Credit Scheme, which was started in 1958. Funds were provided by the Administration and the total of loans granted, for periods ranging up to 25 years, exceeds £A3 million, 138 loans being to Australians (£A3,074,000) and 131 to natives (£A113,000). These loans have been used especially to finance new cocoa plantings both by European and indigenous planters. No new applications were considered after 1962 and, except for further disbursements of loans already made, the scheme has come to an end.

In the indigenous sector, credit facilities have been even more limited. The day-to-day needs of most native planters have been met from village gardens. With land available, tree crops could be planted without limiting food production. Bank lending to individuals has been negligible partly because of the indigene's lack of understanding of banking practice and partly because of the lack of acceptable security with no recorded individual land titles. However, as already noted, loans were made to indigenous planters under the Ex-Servicemen's Credit Scheme, all on the security of the leases granted under the Land Ordinance. Another source of credit has been the Native Loans Fund, established in 1955: most lending has been to indigenes granted land under various settlement schemes for the establishment of tree crops. The rate of lending quickened after a slow start, and by mid-1963, 372 loans totaling £A291,620 had been approved. However, very little of the increase in indigenous production has come from settlement schemes. Again in 1955, a scheme was started by which the Administration could guarantee loans made by commercial banks to indigenes for approved purposes. Though valuable, this scheme has been very restricted in scope: more than 80 percent of the £A282,000 guaranteed by the Administrator has been lent to Native Local Government Councils in the Gazelle Peninsula to finance cocoa fermentaries. Thus, most of the increase in production by indigenes for the market has come about without the assistance of development credits.

Government Spending

While the growth of the export sector has been an important stimulus to the expansion of the money economy since World War II, the major impetus has been the rise in government expenditures. Expenditures of the Administration amounted to £A2.3 million in 1946/47. By 1962/63, expenditures had increased 13 times, to almost £A30 million. In addition, direct expenditures in the Territory by departments of the Commonwealth Government amounted to £A4.9 million and expenditures by the Local Government Councils to almost £A350,000. Thus, total public expenditures in that year exceeded £A35 million. By comparison, export earnings in 1962/63 were little more than £A16 million, while the Gross Domestic Product (GDP) in the money economy was estimated at £A55 million. The rate of growth of Administration expenditures—about 14 percent annually since 1950—was about 40 percent higher than the rate of growth of domestic exports and 25 percent above the growth of GDP in the money economy.

In 1963/64, budgeted expenditures of the Administration again increased sharply (by 25 percent, to £A37.5 million), and direct expenditures by the Commonwealth Government in the Territory and by the Local Government Councils will undoubtedly exceed previous levels.

A direct effect of the growth in spending has been a sharp rise in employment and income. Employees of the Administration increased from 1,400 in 1950 to more than 6,000 in 1963. Until recent years, there were no indigenes qualified to fill the middle-range and higher posts in the Administration, although by mid-1963 there were 125 in permanent and temporary higher level posts. The increase in employment has, therefore, been preponderantly of expatriates. The numbers of indigenes employed by the Administration as laborers, in minor positions and in the police force, though large absolutely, have increased rather slowly from about 16,500 in 1954 to less than 19,000 in 1963.

In the first decade after World War II, the Government re-established the Administration and extended its control throughout the Territory. It also re-established and expanded public health services. From the mid-1950s the emphasis on health programs has continued, and increasing attention has been given to expanding the school system and developing economic services, notably agriculture and communications. Between 1956 and 1963, the staff of the Health Department increased almost threefold, to more than 1,000. The numbers employed in the Departments of Agriculture and Posts and Telegraphs increased by two and one-half and four times to reach 425 and 350, respectively, in 1963, while Education Department personnel increased more than seven times to about 1,370.

The pattern of spending has, of course, reflected these trends. Expenditures on health exceeded or approached one-fifth of Administration expenditures in many of the post-war years, but the proportion has recently declined. Spending on education sharply increased to almost 14 percent of Administration expenditures in 1962/63, while spending on agriculture and forestry, and posts and telegraphs increased to almost 6 percent and 4 percent, respectively. If spending by the Commonwealth departments and the native local government councils is also taken into account, health and education services each absorbed almost 12 percent of total public expenditures in 1962/63, while 6 percent went to agriculture and forestry, about 11 percent to transport and almost 5 percent to communications. Services such as housing, water supplies and electricity, provided largely by the Administration, absorbed about 11 percent of total expenditures. Spending on administrative services and law and order has absorbed a high proportion (almost 28 percent) of the total.

Public Investment. Investment expenditures have accounted for a high proportion of total public spending—just over 30 percent in the past five years. Much of this investment, however, has been in assets which do not produce an immediate increase in the economy's productive capacity. In common with other employers, the Administration has had to provide housing for most of its personnel, and staff housing has absorbed almost a quarter of all public investments over the quinquennium. Other buildings—schools, hospitals, offices, etc.—have taken a further large share; in 1962/63, other buildings absorbed an additional 26 percent of investment expenditures. Spending on basic services such as electric power, water supplies, telecommunications, roads, harbors and aerodromes has absorbed about 30 percent of all investment expenditures over the five-year period.

Despite substantial expenditures on investment, the country does not have a well-developed infrastructure. Electric power capacity is small— only 21.5 megawatts—and of this, half is located at only two centers, Port Moresby and Bulolo. There are no railways and there is no national road network, but only a series of disconnected road systems. Port capacity is inadequate in three of the Territory's four major ports and there are serious deficiencies in coastal shipping services.

Nevertheless, having regard to the pattern of development, the infrastructure is not grossly inadequate. Economic development has been highly localized. Most plantations have been located in quite well defined but widely separated pockets of development, many in coastal areas, readily accessible to the sea and to ports served by overseas ships. Mining and manufacturing is even more concentrated in just a few centers. The bulk of export traffic has moved to the ports by road or coastal shipping. The condition of the roads of major importance, such as those in the Gazelle Peninsula, along the east coast of New Ireland, between Lae and Bulolo, along the coast north of Madang and in the area of Port Moresby, is fair to good. Air services between the highlands and the coast are generally adequate, and having regard to the small quantities of traffic involved, provided a reasonably economical means of transporting coffee for export. With very small urban concentrations and only the beginnings of manufacturing industry, there has been no demand for large quantities of electric power. Moreover, such deficiencies in the infrastructure as there are have not prevented a rapid growth of output and exports. However, there is in general little reserve capacity, and much greater investments will be needed in the future to support a satisfactory growth of output.

The Costs of Government. The costs of government have been high in relation to the scale of the economy, largely because of the rapid expansion of government services. Other factors have, however, been important. One of these has been the difficulty of access to the outer islands and to the mountainous interior of the country, and the high costs of transport of men and material by air. Another has been the dependence on imports for a high proportion of foodstuffs and equipment in the absence of local sources of supply. Still another has been the adoption of standards for new facilities, such as housing, schools and hospitals, which in some cases have been related more closely to the standards of an advanced society than of one in the very early stages of economic development.

Probably the most important factor, however, has been the necessity to employ expatriates in government in the absence of qualified indigenes. The salaries and conditions of service of expatriate staff have had to be such as to attract people from Australia, where the standard of living is one of the highest in the world. In addition to salaries which are comparable with Australian levels, generous leave allowances, fares to and from Australia, grants for education, and transport subsidies have had to be provided, as well as standards of housing and other amenities approximately comparable with those in Australia. In urban centers the Administration has laid out townships with spacious lots, paved roads, electricity, water, sanitation and other amenities, most of the costs of which have been borne by the Administration and which have been used largely by government employees, who constitute one-third of the non-indigenous work force.

The total costs for salary and other expenses of employing expatriates in government are disguised because the charges for housing and other services are generally nominal or much below cost, but it is certain that these charges add considerably to the salaries paid. Where indigenes with the appropriate qualifications are available, large savings are possible, but there are as yet very few trained or qualified indigenes. To achieve economies in government, therefore, probably the most important step is to accelerate the education of the indigenes to fill adequately the middle-range and higher positions in the Administration.

Government Revenues

More than two-thirds of government expenditures have been financed by grants from the Commonwealth of Australia. In 1962/63, the grant to the Administration of £A20 million and the direct expenditures by Commonwealth departments resulted in almost £A25 million or 71 percent of total public expenditures (of £A35 million) being met by the Commonwealth Government. In 1963/64, the Commonwealth grant to the Administration was increased to more than £A25 million. Though income in the money economy has grown, largely as a result of greater government spending, and revenue raised by the Administration has increased, the proportion of Administration receipts raised in the Territory has not increased over the past ten years, and the absolute gap between expenditures and local revenues has steadily widened. The Territory has become increasingly dependent on external aid, which on a per capita basis is now exceeded only in Israel and Jordan among countries with populations of comparable or greater size.

Of the £A9 million of local revenues of the Administration in 1962/63, customs duties contributed just over 30 percent, direct taxes on companies and individuals another 30 percent, and the balance came from a variety of sources including excise and stamp duties, license fees, royalties and rents and the sale of goods and services.

Tax rates have been low. To provide incentives for expatriates to work and invest in the Territory the effective rates of direct taxation have been about half the Australian levels or less. To keep costs-of-living down, imported articles consumed in quantity have been admitted free or at low rates of duty. Even articles which could be classed as semi-luxuries or luxuries are taxed at rates lower than those applicable in Australia. Thus, the weight of taxation on the non-indigenous community is relatively light. The tax burden on the indigenes is also light. Export duties were abolished in 1959 and an income tax substituted. Partly because the proceeds of sale of export crops are often shared, under the prevailing system of communal ownership, among several producers, very few indigenes pay income tax, their incomes being generally below the taxable minimum. Their contribution to indirect tax proceeds is also small. In 1962/63, the indigenes probably contributed in direct and indirect taxation no more than £A540,000, or less than 10 percent of tax revenue raised by the Administration. In addition, they paid taxes to Native

Local Government Councils amounting to about £A260,000. Even allowing for a further £A75,000 or so paid by indigenes as non-tax revenue,
their contribution from current revenue to the financing of total public
expenditure in 1962/63 will have amounted to less than 3 percent. This
compares with estimated incomes of indigenes engaged in the cash
economy totaling £A16 million, or about 30 percent of the gross product
of the monetary sector.

Besides the revenues raised in the Territory, the Administration obtained relatively small sums through public borrowings. This began in
1960/61, when about £A552,000 was raised; during the next two years,
total borrowings were almost £A1.4 million and the target for 1963/64
was £A1.7 million, equal to about 4.5 percent of estimated Administration
expenditures in that year.

The Domestic Market

The rise in exports and in government spending has brought a rapid
growth in market demand. This has stimulated the expansion of commerce and manufacturing to serve the local market and the construction
industry. Agricultural production marketed locally has been small. It has
consisted primarily of subsistence crops, of which a very small part of the
output has been sold in the market.

Apart from simple copra driers on plantations, manufacturing before
World War II was limited to small sawmills and a few plants producing
soft drinks, bakery goods and desiccated coconut. With the growth of the
local market in the past decade, new industries have been established. A
brewery was opened in 1952 and this was followed by plants producing
twist tobacco, furniture, paints, concrete products and cigarettes. The
output of sawn timber, soft drinks and bakery products has also substantially increased, and engineering repair and maintenance work has
expanded rapidly. The Administration has assisted new industries by
reducing duties on imported materials and equipment and by giving
tariff protection in certain cases. Manufacturing is still hampered by a
small and highly fragmented local market, despite the growth of the past
decade, but the expansion of output since 1956, when statistics were first
collected, has been impressive. If manufactures produced for export
(principally plywood and coconut oil) are excluded, the growth of industrial production has been of the order of 20 percent a year, and manufacturing (including the export industries) probably now contributes
about 10 percent of GDP in the money economy.

As in agriculture, this growth has been achieved despite little provision
of development credit. Only in the case of the plywood plant was capital

provided by government for new industry. Private capital has come principally from Australia, but also from Canada and Malaysia. Part of the finance for expansion has come from retained profits. Bank lending to industry has been very small; loans outstanding were only £A141,000 at June 30, 1963.

Limited statistics on the output of the construction industry have been collected for recent years. These figures, together with data on public expenditures on construction and employment trends in the industry, indicate that output has risen quite sharply in the past two years. This growth has been achieved despite limited numbers of indigenes qualified for skilled and semi-skilled work in the industry and despite the difficulty of attracting skilled workers from Australia. Notwithstanding the rapid growth of output, limitations of local contractual capacity have slowed to some extent the implementation of government projects, and the relatively small size of most projects in the Territory has meant that large contractors have rarely been attracted from overseas.

Payments Abroad for Goods and Services

While the rise in market demand has given some stimulus to local production, the pattern of demand is such that the great bulk of supplies continues to be imported. More than three-fifths of personal incomes in the money economy are earned by the non-indigenous community whose average incomes are high, since they are related to standards in Australia. Their demand is spread over a wide range of relatively high-quality products of which few could be manufactured economically in the Territory. Furthermore, large sums are spent abroad on foreign travel as expatriates go to Australia on leave, and on the support of dependents in Australia, particularly children in school. Payments abroad of interest and dividends are also substantial. As a result, total foreign payments for goods and services are very high in relation to the output of the money economy. In 1962/63, imports (including freight and insurance but excluding re-exports) were valued at £A29 million, and total foreign payments for goods and services amounted to £A34 million, equal to more than 60 percent of the GDP.

Imports. Surprisingly, in a predominantly agricultural country, food imports are large, amounting to a quarter of the total. About half the food imports consist of high-quality and processed foods consumed by the small non-indigenous population, such as fresh and frozen meat, dairy products, and fresh and canned fruits and vegetables. The remainder consists of a few commodities imported in large quantities for consumption chiefly by the native people, such as canned meat (£A1 million), canned fish (£A600,000), rice (£A1.4 million) and sugar (£A400,000). Total meat imports are of the order of £A1.8 million, reflecting the very small development of livestock production despite areas well suited to cattle raising. As fishing techniques have changed little since the arrival of the European, local supplies that enter the market economy are scanty, and imports—chiefly from Japan—are large.

Other consumer goods account for a further one-third of total imports. Most of this consists of high-quality goods consumed by the non-indigenous population but a substantial part of the imports of clothing and textiles, which comprise 10 percent of total imports, is consumed by the indigenes. Imports of clothing especially have risen rapidly in recent years, at a rate about four times faster than the growth of the non-indigenous population. Here consumption by the indigenes must have risen appreciably.

With little manufacturing in the Territory, two-thirds of imports are manufactured goods, and imports of materials for industry are still very small. Reflecting the high rate of investment, almost a third of all imports are capital goods, and of these machinery and transport equipment make up one-third.

Income and Employment

The most comprehensive data on the growth of the economy are provided by the national income estimates. Estimates for the money economy have been made for a number of years, the earliest being 1950. As the basic data, particularly in the earlier years, was scanty, these estimates must be considered only as approximations. They show a growth of domestic product, measured in current prices, and excluding non-marketed production, of from £A15 million in 1950/51 to £A55 million in 1962/63, an average rate of growth of 11 percent a year. The information on price changes is very limited. Such data as are available, such as a cost-of-living index for Port Moresby for the period 1948 to 1957 and an index of import prices for the period 1949 to 1962, suggest that prices may have risen by about 50 percent since 1950. On this basis, the growth of domestic expenditure in real terms would have been of the order of 7 to 8 percent annually over the past 12 years.

With the expansion of the Administration and of activity in the private sector, there has been a fast rise in non-indigenous employment to about 15,000 in 1962/63 (estimated to have risen by 50 percent since 1954). This increase largely reflects the flow of technical, managerial and administrative personnel from Australia. Following the strong demand for skilled personnel in Australia, wages and salaries of this group have risen considerably in recent years. Indigenes have entered employment at a much slower rate (an increase of about 14 percent to approximately 80,000 since 1954) and their wages have risen more slowly, since these are not influenced by trends in the Australian labor market. On the other hand, the rapid expansion in production of cash crops by the indigenes has brought a fivefold increase in income from this source since 1950/51, a growth rate much above that in the non-indigenous sector. Over-all, indigenous incomes have grown slightly faster than non-indigenous incomes since 1950/51 and now represent about 30 percent of the gross product of the monetary sector.

As the indigenes are normally qualified only for unskilled or semi-skilled work, their average earnings, related to local conditions and not affected by the competitive Australian labor market, are generally much below those of expatriates. In 1962/63, the average income of indigenous employees (including income paid in kind but excluding such benefits as free medical services and fares to and from the place of employment which are paid for by the employer) was estimated at £A160, while the average income of non-indigenous workers was £A1,800. The limited size of the cash economy is illustrated by the fact that, if income paid in kind is excluded, the average cash income for indigenous employees was much less, being approximately £A70. From the sale of cash crops, the average income was about £A15, assuming approximately a quarter of a million native producers of cash crops. These averages, however, mask wide differences. Many plantation workers receive a cash wage of less than £A20 a year, while several hundred skilled indigenes in business and government earn well over £A500 a year. Among producers of cash crops, differences are almost as striking. Many sell a little copra from which they earn just a few pounds. Others, such as the Tolai in the Gazelle Peninsula, who have had commercial contacts with Europeans for almost a century, have developed extensive coconut and cocoa plantations which yield annual returns to producers estimated to average £A100 to £A120.

The majority of the native people have no cash income and depend for their livelihood on the production of the subsistence economy. The subsistence economy has been known to be large, but it is only very recently that data became available on which an estimate of subsistence output could be based. These data are still incomplete, and the estimate is recognized as being only an approximation.

Subsistence agriculture in 1961/62 was estimated to have yielded some 2.7 million tons of produce valued at about £A57 million at imputed market prices. Animal products (pigs and poultry) produced for consumption were estimated at a further £A5 million. Fish and other marine products, game and produce gathered from the forests were valued at about £A7 million, so that the total value of food products consumed in the subsistence economy was estimated at almost £A70 million.

In addition, subsistence workers provided free labor for community projects such as village works, and road and airfield construction and maintenance, to which a monetary value was imputed on the basis of the estimated number of days worked. A monetary value was imputed also for investment in the expansion of village gardens, in canoe-building and in the replacement and maintenance of tools insofar as these were not bought from the monetary sector. Finally, an assessment was made of the value of maintenance and construction work on subsistence sector-housing.

The total value of output in the subsistence sector was estimated at £A90 million in 1961/62 and slightly more than this in 1962/63. If the income accruing to the indigenes in the money economy is added, total indigenous incomes in 1962/63 amounted to £A107 million or about £A50 per capita. This figure can be considered only a very rough approximation. In relation to living standards in other countries at a roughly comparable stage of development, this figure appears high.[6] Nevertheless, the people of the Territory are clearly better off than great numbers elsewhere. There is no shortage of food, the climate is benign and needs for clothing and shelter can in most cases easily be met. No estimates of production in the subsistence sector have been made for earlier years, so that it is not possible to derive a rate of growth of per capita income.

With the fast growth of income in the money economy, personal consumption expenditures have also risen rapidly (by 11 percent annually at current prices) and current expenditures of Missions and public authorities slightly faster since 1950/51. A high rate of investment has been maintained over the period. In the past three years, domestic investment has equaled 23 percent of gross domestic expenditures in the money economy. In the later 1950s, private investment was substantially in excess of public investment largely because of heavy expenditures on oil exploration. In more recent years, private investment has declined to less than 10 percent of domestic expenditures, a decline due in part to political uncertainties. At the same time, public investment has sharply increased to more than 13 percent of domestic expenditures. As already noted, a large part of public investment has been in assets which do not add immediately to the country's productive capacity, but such evidence

[6] The magnitude of subsistence income reflects in part the valuation of output at imputed market prices. An alternative valuation at imputed "on farm" prices would give a substantially lower figure. On the latter basis, the value of subsistence output would perhaps be of the order of £A55 million, and total indigenous per capita income about £A35 in 1962/63.

as there is suggests that much private investment has been highly productive. It has already brought a rapid rise in output and income, and the full returns from this investment have not yet been realized.

There are few data on the financing of private investment. Foreign capital has been invested in plantations and new industrial ventures, and as mentioned above in oil exploration. However, probably the greater part of private investment has been financed from reinvested profits. Many private ventures have been highly profitable, and private savings have been high, high enough to finance substantial investments in the Territory and permit a sizable outflow of capital. From the limited data available it appears the capital outflow in recent years has been of the order of £A3 to £A5 million a year. Compared with private investments estimated at £A5 to £A6 million annually in the past three years, the outflow of capital has been of major proportions. It has been attributed partly to a decline in confidence among investors stemming from uncertainties about the political future of the country. More recently the investment climate has improved. Apart from the modest amounts raised so far through public borrowing, investments by the Administration have been financed entirely from grants provided by the Commonwealth Government, since in all years current expenditures by the Administration have been far in excess of internal current revenues. Some investments took place directly by departments of the Commonwealth Government and small amounts were invested by native local government councils. Estimates of income and expenditure are shown in Table 1.

TABLE 1: Estimates of Income and Expenditure 1950/51, 1960/61–1962/63

(£A million)

	1950/51	1960/61	1961/62	1962/63
INCOME				
MONETARY SECTOR				
Indigenous Incomes [a]				
Wages and Salaries	3.7	12.0	13.0	12.9
Incomes from Unincorporated Enterprise	0.7	2.6	2.6	3.0
Non-indigenous Incomes				
Wages and Salaries	5.2	16.0	19.7	23.6
Income from Unincorporated Enterprise	3.8	3.7	4.3	4.5
Company Incomes	—	6.5	6.3	7.5
Income from Property	1.0	0.8	0.8	0.8
GDP at Factor Cost	14.4	41.6	46.7	52.3
Indirect Taxes less Subsidies	0.7	2.4	2.8	3.1
GDP at Market Prices	15.1	44.0	49.5	55.4
SUBSISTENCE SECTOR				
Subsistence Output [b]	66.1	87.8	90.2	91.3
EXPENDITURE				
MONETARY SECTOR				
Personal Consumption	9.6	29.6	33.1	34.3
Current Expenditures of:				
Missions	0.5	1.9	2.1	2.4
Public Authorities	4.6	15.2	17.8	19.6
Gross Domestic Investment:				
Private	2.8	7.1	5.9	6.4
Public Authorities	2.4	7.9	8.3	10.6
Total Domestic Expenditures	19.9	61.7	67.2	73.3
Exports of Goods & Services	7.4	14.3	14.3	16.4
Less Imports of Goods & Services	−12.2	−32.0	−32.0	−34.3
Gross Domestic Product	15.1	44.0	49.5	55.4
SUBSISTENCE SECTOR				
Consumption [b]	52.0	69.5	71.6	72.5
Private Investment	3.5	4.1	4.2	4.2
Community Investment	10.6	14.2	14.4	14.6
Total Expenditure	66.1	87.8	90.2	91.3

[a] Not including rental value of owner-occupied houses of indigenes employed as wage earners, estimated at roughly £A0.2 million in all years.

[b] Including subsistence output of wage earners and their dependents, as follows:

	1950/51	1960/61	1961/62	1962/63
Indigenous	5.3	7.2	7.3	7.2
Non-indigenous	—	0.6	0.7	0.8
	5.3	7.8	8.0	8.0

SOURCES: The Social Accounts of the New Guinea Market Economy for 1949/50 and 1950/51 by Prof. T. W. Swan; Department of Territories: National Income Estimates for 1960/61–1962/63. Subsistence sector estimates made by Mr. E. K. Fisk of the Australian National University, based partly on data derived from the "Survey of Indigenous Agriculture 1961–1962" published by the Bureau of Statistics, Territory of Papua and New Guinea.

CHAPTER 2 *A PROGRAM FOR ECONOMIC DEVELOPMENT*

BASIC OBJECTIVES

In its request to the Bank, the Commonwealth Government of Australia asked that the Mission make recommendations to assist it in planning a development program for the Territory of Papua and New Guinea designed to stimulate economic growth and raise the standard of living of the people. The Commonwealth Government stressed that its major aim is to help the inhabitants of the Territory to become self-governing as soon as possible and to ensure that when this aim is reached the Territory will, to the greatest extent feasible, be able to stand on its own feet economically. The task, therefore, is to marshal the human and material resources available to the Territory through a development program which will continue the process of development toward the economic objective of the Commonwealth Government. To this end, the Mission has prepared a program for economic development focused in particular on the next five years 1964/65–1968/69. In agriculture and livestock, the projections cover ten years since a number of the crops take years to mature.

If the Territory were left to its own means there would not be the technical skills, the management or the finance to develop the economy at any reasonable pace. Continued financial support from the Commonwealth Government will be necessary if economic progress is to be made. In fact, if progress toward the goal of economic viability is to be as rapid as possible, it will be necessary that financial support be increased over and above that now being made available by Australia. With increasing support in the amounts projected later in this chapter, the Mission is convinced that the natural resources of the Territory are such that substantial economic growth is possible in the next five to ten years. The Mission also believes that with education and training the indigene can be motivated and is capable of taking an expanding role in the economy and in government. But the molding of the indigene and the resources into a modern economy will not be an easy task. It will take great effort. It will be expensive. It will take time.

While substantial economic growth is possible over the next five to ten years, economic viability in any meaningful sense cannot be achieved

31

within several decades. The physical and human resources have not been developed to the point where economic viability is yet in sight. The program projected for the next five years can only set the pattern that development should take.

The Mission has assumed that the Commonwealth Government will be prepared to increase its financial assistance to the Territory. The availability of finance has not, therefore, been regarded as the prime limitation on the scale of the program which the Mission has formulated. The prime limitation has been the availability of skilled manpower which will have to come mainly from Australia. Given this limitation, the program formulated by the Mission provides for development at as rapid a rate as is possible of achievement by an aggressive Administration following sound policies.

The Mission believes that major emphasis in the development program should be given to the stimulation of production and the advancement of the indigenous people. Only by these means can the real income of the native people be raised, the tax base broadened, the disproportionate gap between government expenditures and revenues raised in the Territory narrowed and the widening deficit in the balance of payments—now met by grants from the Government of Australia—reduced.

Expansion of Production

Given the limitations of the Territory market, economic progress means in the first instance expanding production for export, and the best prospects for export growth lie in the fields of agriculture and forestry. These are the only major resources about which enough is known to permit a rapid development in the next several years, though an additional increase in exports would be possible were oil to be discovered in large quantity. Current data indicate only a limited potential for mining. Manufacturing is mainly dependent on the internal market. Tourism offers a more immediate possibility and should be promoted.

The physical resources for a major expansion in the production of agricultural, livestock and forest products exist in more than adequate supply. There are at least 6 million acres of usable land area for crop production, of which only about 1 million acres are used at present. Of the 80 to 90 million acres of forest, at least 25 million acres have a commercial potential. Some 10 million acres of virtually unused natural grassland are available for livestock production, providing the opportunity for reducing imports of meat and, in the long run, substantial meat exports.

The export potential for agricultural products is based primarily upon copra, coffee, cocoa and rubber. The Mission believes that, with the exception of coffee, the prospects in international markets for these commodities fully justify a continued expansion of their production. There are substantial prospects for the increased production of coffee, but here the Administration will have to be guided by market conditions from time to time. Marketing channels are well developed. Suitable soils in amount and quality exist for expansion, together with the necessary technical knowledge. European planters are experienced in these commodities. An increasing number of native planters are gaining experience. In addition, two new crops, tea and pyrethrum, and several others of lesser importance present real possibilities for development. Thus, the guidelines for agricultural development are well defined.

On the forestry side, a small export industry already supplements local needs. The forest resources exist for a major expansion and the market outlook is promising.

In manufacturing, there are no known natural resources to provide the basis for large-scale export industries. The potential for expansion will depend primarily upon the speed and magnitude of the increase in incomes from agricultural, livestock and forestry development, and it is to these that priority must, therefore, be given.

In formulating its recommendations for development, the Mission has drawn up planting programs for agricultural crops and programs to develop livestock and forestry which, although ambitious, are capable of attainment. In the indigenous sector, we have projected as fast an expansion as the expected availability of the staff needed to direct and guide the program will permit. In the European sector projections are based primarily on the further development of lands already held by Europeans where, with encouragement and support, substantial additional development is possible. The program does not provide for large new areas to be taken over for European development. Nevertheless, the Mission considers it essential for the successful execution of the program that additional land be made available to Europeans. Settlement of Europeans on a limited scale on new plantations will be necessary for the cattle and tea programs to be started, for purposes of demonstration in new areas where commercial agricultural development has not yet started on any significant scale, and for expansion in European production on a reasonable scale.

If executed, the recommended programs could result in an increase in export earnings from the main agricultural commodities to approximately £A23 million annually in five years, £A34 million in ten years and £A50 million annually at full development of the plantings made during the next ten years. A substantial margin for continuing expansion would remain. In addition, the Mission estimates that earnings from forest products could be stepped up to almost £A7 million annually in five years. These earnings, totaling £A30 million annually by 1968/69, would represent a doubling of the existing export production of agricultural and forest products.

The projected rise in export earnings would be a major contributing factor to further growth of the economy. Later in this chapter, we give a projection of the Administration budget for the next five years for some categories of expenditures based on rather minimum assumptions. Nevertheless, it implies an average rate of growth of public expenditures during this period of about 10 percent annually. On the basis of the projections of exports and public expenditures combined, it should be possible to realize a rate of economic growth during the next five years of the same order of magnitude as that obtained during the past decade when, as mentioned in Chapter 1, domestic expenditures in real terms probably grew by about 7 to 8 percent annually.

Advancement of the Indigene

It is appropriate that Australia should substantially concentrate its efforts on the advancement of the native people. This advancement will come through the native taking a much greater part in expanding production and by accelerating his training and education. The agricultural and livestock programs provide for the native farmers to take a major part in increasing production. Training and education will come both from practical experience and in-service training, as well as from formal education. The most urgent need is the expansion of secondary, technical and higher education. Primary education, which has advanced rapidly with large numbers of students in the first standards, should concentrate on making the full primary course available in existing schools rather than on broadening the primary base by establishing new schools. Secondary and technical training should proceed at the fastest rate which the output of primary students will permit.

To achieve the production targets of the development program, secondary-level training should concentrate on the development of individuals who can contribute usefully to the agricultural, livestock and forestry programs, to other sectors of the economy, and to administration and the public service generally. The teaching program should be closely oriented to these ends, particularly in the short term.

The primary responsibility for providing educational opportunities must rest with the Administration in cooperation with the missions. Nevertheless, the private European employer can and should also contribute. In-service training has started. Much more is needed. The Mission is convinced that such training, if properly conceived, can bring substantial benefits both to employer and employee.

THREE PRINCIPLES

While the Mission is convinced that substantial progress can be made over the next five to ten years in expanding production and in advancing the indigenous people, it is also convinced that much of the benefit of this effort could be lost unless policies appropriate to conditions in the Territory are followed. In particular, the Mission believes that there are three broad principles or policies, the adoption of which will have a major impact on the success of the development program. Their significance is wider than this, however. In the longer term, the application of these policies can largely determine the speed of advance and the ability of the Territory to achieve financial viability. They relate to the concentration of effort, the selection of standards suitable to the Territory, and the need to foster greater responsibilities among the people.

Concentration of Effort

To obtain the maximum benefit from the development effort, expenditures and manpower should be concentrated in areas and on activities where the prospective return is highest. For example, the physical characteristics—the great mountain ranges, deep gorges, rivers and swamps—are serious barriers to development of parts of the Territory. On the other hand, there are large areas of good land which are relatively accessible and where development is relatively easy. These are the areas to which priority should be given, having regard to the fact that their development will fully tax the manpower and other resources likely to be available to the Territory in the next five to ten years. The Mission, on economic grounds, strongly recommends against an across-the-board policy which distributes scarce manpower and finance throughout the Territory without due regard to the benefits to be derived in comparison with those realizable elsewhere. The Mission recognizes that there are political factors which may have to be taken into consideration.

The Mission has proposed a program whereby the skilled manpower of the Department of Agriculture, as an example, would be concentrated on agricultural and livestock programs in areas with greatest promise in human and physical resources. In turn the resources to be devoted to the expansion of basic infrastructures should be concentrated in areas and on services where the potential returns are greatest. In transport, priority should be given to the development of the roads, coastal shipping services and ports required to handle the projected expansion of agricultural, forestry and livestock production. Once the economy has grown, the question of the allocation of resources to develop the more difficult areas can be considered.

In over-all government spending also, priorities should be established. An increase in spending on agriculture, forestry, transport and education will require a curb on the growth of other expenditures. For example, spending on curative health programs should grow more slowly than in the past. There is need for restraint in expanding general administrative services, which have absorbed a high proportion of total Administration expenditures in recent years.

Standards

The standards of Administration services and facilities should be related to Territory conditions, if the maximum numbers of people are to benefit from the money spent on the program. Moreover, in the longer term it is vital that Territory standards, applying also to wage and salary levels, should be adopted if financial viability is to be achieved.

The Mission has noted that so far the over-all cost of administration has been high because it has been necessary to employ Europeans and pay salaries geared to Australian levels. Also, the Mission has been impressed with the new hospitals, court buildings and houses and some of the other facilities that have been planned and constructed generally to European standards. The development of curative health services, and in particular the ratio of hospital beds to population, has been more in line with those found in some countries of Europe than with those found in the less developed countries. Considering the state of development and the wide dispersal of population, the projection of primary education throughout the Territory also is more in keeping with the standards of highly developed countries. It is quite unlikely, even on the most optimistic estimates, that continued development along these lines can even in the long term be supported by the resources of the Territory itself.

The Mission recognizes that salary levels for expatriates in the Administration, as well as in business, have to be geared to Australian levels in order to secure the skilled personnel required. However, this should not set the pattern for the future. Salary levels in the public service should be set at levels in line with living standards and costs in the Territory. For the expatriate an additional allowance will be necessary. Also the standards of schools, hospitals and housing, and the level of services provided should, wherever possible, be related to Territory conditions.

The gradual conversion of the public service to one largely staffed by indigenes, the adoption of simpler design standards for buildings and the maximum use of materials of local origin in construction would permit substantial savings in the costs of government and would contribute toward the eventual goal of economic and financial viability.

Fostering Responsibility

The approach of the Administration in the past, as exemplified by policies affecting the indigenous people including the Administration's own employees and, to a lesser extent, the private European sector, has been largely one of benevolent paternalism. Such an approach under the conditions existing in the Territory in earlier years was quite understandable. As a modern economy emerges, however, and as increasing numbers of the indigenous people acquire education and a greater understanding of the modern world, a shift in emphasis toward policies giving greater responsibilities to the people is essential and, indeed, inevitable.

Notable progress in this direction has already been made. The setting up of Native Local Government Councils with quite a wide range of powers and responsibilities was an important step. The granting by the Administration of additional powers to the councils is a further advance. The Mission believes that still greater responsibilities should be given to the councils, particularly in education, health and feeder road construction.

The Mission believes that in urban government also, the time has come when at least in the larger centers urban governments should be set up with responsibility for administering and, to the extent feasible, financing the more important public services. The Mission's views on this are given in Annex I of this report.

In the more strictly economic sphere, many services have been provided by the Administration free or at charges greatly below costs. Housing for public servants, water supplies, sanitation and sewerage services in urban areas, telephone and telegraph services, and health and education facilities have been provided at no charge to users or at more or less subeconomic rates. The Mission believes it is important that a tradition of providing economic services at subsidized rates should not become established. Such a tradition, if maintained, could impose serious financial burdens on the Administration in the future and impede the development of public services. The Mission considers that the charges for urban water and sewerage services, electricity and telephone and telegraph services, should be such as to make the systems generally self-supporting, and that the rents of houses owned by the Administration should be raised to economic levels. Such an increase in charges will have to be compensated by salary adjustments for public servants, but net savings in the costs of government and a more economic allocation of resources can be secured as a result.

In measures affecting the indigenous people, the Mission endorses the gradual shift to payment of a full cash wage rather than the payment of a wage largely in kind. In respect to health and education services, the Mission believes that the indigenous people should contribute to the costs either individually or communally by providing the land for building and maintaining rural primary schools, teachers' houses, medical aid posts and rural health centers. A system of payment, either in cash or in kind, for drugs and medical services should also be introduced. By these means economics in government can be secured and, perhaps of even greater importance, an appreciation by the people of the costs and responsibilities which are a necessary part of self-government can be fostered.

CONDITIONS FOR IMPLEMENTATION

The mobilization of the key resources needed to successfully implement a development program will also require action on a number of fronts, both by the Commonwealth Government and by the Administration.

Land Tenure

The social institution which affects the organization of production most profoundly is land tenure. The indigenes own 97 percent of the land. About 1 percent is under the control of Europeans, either as freehold land or as leasehold from the Administration. The balance of 2 percent is owned and continues to be held by the Administration.

With few exceptions, native land is owned communally, but individuals can establish use rights for hunting, food gathering and gardening. Inheritance of use rights is complex. This tenure pattern, evolved by custom, and protected originally by tribal war and now by orderly administration, may have fitted traditional subsistence production but it does not meet the requirements of an emerging commercial agriculture. The native commercial farmer needs the assurance of rights to lands upon which perennial crops can be grown and cattle grazed without undue risk of conflicting claims arising under the traditional tenure system.

Recognizing the importance of the problem, the Administration has worked toward the concept of individual recorded titles. At the request of a native claimant, the Administration will investigate the ownership, survey the land and record rights accorded by custom. This procedure has proved so difficult and time consuming, and progress has been so slow, that a new approach must be found.

There is a growing volume of evidence that the indigenes are making progress in arranging with their villages and clans for the continuing use of land upon which perennial tree crops can be planted. The Mission suggests that a reasonable approach to the land tenure problem would be to place greater responsibility on the native people, including the Local Government Councils, to work out their own solutions adapted to varying circumstances. This approach would not make possible the recording of an individual title but at the same time would be no real disadvantage provided that comparable flexibility in approach could be achieved in regard to security for credits extended for assisting production by the indigenes.

The Mission also recommends continuation of the policy of acquiring of land by the Administration from indigenous owners and of leasing this land to Europeans where needed for execution of the agricultural, forestry, livestock, industry and other programs. Also in selected areas the Europeans should be able to lease land directly from native owners on terms approved by the Administration. Such leases should contain clauses for payment of compensation for improvements and the term should be limited to 30 to 35 years. Lands leased to Europeans should be located where there is no serious land pressure and native interests should be fully protected.

Attention should be given to revising the terms under which the Administration leases Crown land. Future leases might be limited to 30 to 35 years, and should carry improvement clauses with provision for payment for improvements upon termination. The Administration should also enforce development clauses to ensure that usable land under European control is brought into production.

Where the Administration, in the execution of its responsibilities for good government, needs to acquire land, it should not hesitate to do so through legal procedures in the event the owners are reluctant to sell or lease to the Administration. There have been a series of cases where worthwhile development has been seriously hampered or even prevented by the unwillingness of native owners to sell small areas of land and the Administration has in turn been reluctant to exercise its responsibility to acquire the land through legal proceedings.

The Role of the European

The mobilization of unskilled indigenous labor for development should not be difficult; the manpower potential is large and there is evidence that many more workers could be recruited for wage employment than are now at work. The mobilization of capital and managerial, administrative, professional and technical skills will be much more difficult. For a considerable number of years to come the European will have to supply them on a gradually decreasing scale. Educating and training the indigene to fill the higher positions in a modern economy cannot be accomplished in just a few years. The continuing participation by the European, both in the private sector and in the Administration, is vital for the objectives of the advancement of the indigenes and economic development to be realized.

The European agriculturist has demonstrated what cash crops can be grown. He has developed processing techniques. He has developed export markets and marketing procedures. He has employed the indigene and motivated him to grow cash crops. There are very real advantages in having European planters associated with native workers and farmers to provide basic training and to demonstrate modern techniques and the ways of a modern economy. In addition the Europeans can make a major contribution to increasing production in the Territory. It is for these reasons that the Mission has, in its agricultural program, allowed for a substantial contribution from the European sector. At the same time it has paid special attention to the rapid expansion of production by native planters.

The comparative need for the European in other sectors of the economy is even greater. Though some technical and clerical training is being given, and a few indigenes have advanced to sub-professional levels, there is no native graduate from a university, and no native industrialist or professional man. In commerce, industry, banking and the professions, the European must continue to supply his skills and capital if further development is to be achieved.

For the European to make the contribution envisaged by the Mission, special efforts must be made to encourage those already in the Territory to stay and to attract others to come. The confidence of the European has been shaken by political developments in countries in the surrounding area, and by uncertainty about the political future of the Territory and about his own role in it. As already noted, the lack of confidence has been a factor in the outflow of capital.

The role of the Commonwealth Government of Australia, first in guaranteeing national security and secondly in providing continued large-scale financial help to the Territory, is essential in establishing confidence and in stimulating continued European cooperation and participation.

An attractive economic climate for the European investor in the Territory is also essential. This is particularly important as he has alternative opportunities in Australia, the principal source of personnel and capital. An attractive economic climate will be helped by the Administration formulating and following a clearly defined development policy and program. The Administration should use its tax policy to attract private capital and management. The light burden of the income tax is justified and should be continued. New industries which can contribute materially to development should be attracted by tax concessions. Tariff policies should be used selectively to promote investment in new industries. Credit, discussed later in this chapter, must be provided in adequate quantity and on reasonable terms. In the Territory, as elsewhere, profitability is the factor having the greatest influence on investment. On the evidence available, the Mission believes that, with appropriate incentive policies, the profitability of well-conceived enterprises is likely to be attractive to the private investor.[1]

Staffing

Equally important is the role of the European in government. With few exceptions the indigene has not yet reached the level of education and training to fill professional or technical positions. To train and educate the indigene and at the same time direct and guide development will require a substantial addition to the staff of the Administration. This applies particularly to the Departments of Agriculture, Stock and Fisheries, Forests and Education. For example, to direct the substantial expansion of cash crops and livestock and to carry out other functions such as research and training, the Department of Agriculture will need to hire an estimated 400 professional and technical staff over the next five years, an average of about 80 per year. The secondary school program, just getting under way, will require more than 500 teachers over the same period for Administration schools and in addition the mission schools will need about the same number.

The principal source of additional staff must be Australia, though recruitment from New Zealand, Europe and other places should not be

[1] The Mission believes that the adoption and implementation of its recommendations will go a long way toward stimulating confidence. If lack of confidence continues to be a problem there may be need for an investment insurance or guarantee scheme. The Mission notes that the Australian Government is studying the possibility of introducing a scheme to ensure Australian investments in overseas countries, including Papua and New Guinea, against non-commercial risks.

overlooked. The Mission has made some attempt to assess the capacity of Australia to supply the necessary personnel. The Department of Agriculture in the Territory would need somewhat less than one-quarter of the likely annual output of both degree and diploma-level graduates in agriculture in Australia if this were the only source to be drawn upon. However, two additional sources, new science graduates and individuals already qualified, can be expected to assist in filling the needs.

There are some 27,000 secondary school teachers and 12,000 vocational teachers in Australia in addition to the annual output of newly qualified teachers. The Mission believes that this pool is large enough to supply the Administration's needs if appropriate policies are followed.

In the Mission's view, the problem of recruitment in most categories is less one of availability than it is of conditions of employment. A powerful incentive is needed in addition to those of attractive salary and leave conditions. The Commonwealth Government can provide such an incentive if it is prepared to work out ways and means of ensuring that service in the Territory will count in all respects as service in Australia. The Mission suggests that the Commonwealth Government, as a matter of national policy, devise arrangements whereby appropriate organizations in the Federal and State governments would second staff for Territory service without loss of status and opportunity in Australia. Interchangeability of staff should be the underlying principle in any such arrangements.

To supplement the Administration's permanent staff, short-term appointees may also make a useful contribution. This is especially so as it becomes increasingly difficult to offer expatriates long-term careers in the Administration. The Mission believes that in some professional fields short-term contracts would prove to be attractive, and that other skills could also be acquired on this basis. Service in the Territory has novelty and adventure. Given the opportunity, many young Australians might be willing to work there for short periods before committing themselves to careers at home. The Mission suggests that the Commonwealth Government should consider tapping this source of skills by establishing a service on the lines of the British Voluntary Service Overseas Scheme and the United States Peace Corps.

Response of the Indigene

The rate of development will be closely related to the response of the indigene; as he seeks to improve his physical well-being the pace of development will quicken. However, improvement in the well-being of the people in a primitive society means change, and change disturbs customs and the way of life. The tendency of the indigene has been to cling to the past, to traditions, to special beliefs and to oppose the unknown. As a result many doubts have been raised as to the willingness and ability of the indigene to adopt new ideas and to make the necessary effort to expand output and improve his well-being.

Nevertheless, the process of change has started. The Mission has noted that increasing numbers of indigenes are taking part in the cash economy. There is evidence to show that, given the necessary stimulus and guidance, the indigene does respond to income earning opportunities. The output of coffee, copra and cocoa marketed by indigenes has increased with great rapidity in the past eight years. New plantings, not yet in production have been made at an accelerating pace. This performance by a people not hitherto involved in a cash economy has been such as to encourage the Mission to believe that its projections in respect to indigenous participation in the agricultural program, although ambitious, are not unrealistic.

The indigene's role in other sectors of the economy—industry, commerce, the professions and administration—has been limited by the very few who have completed the necessary educational requirements or have acquired experience to make it possible for them to take part. However, the indigene has responded to opportunities for employment in the Administration, in the building and other trades which require skills as well as in the operation of stores and cooperatives. His role can be expanded by providing further educational and training opportunities.

The indigene has responded to schooling opportunities. The numbers in primary schools have increased dramatically since World War II. The indications are that the indigene will take advantage of more advanced education and training as facilities and opportunities are provided.

While substantial progress has been made in bringing the native people forward, the Mission is convinced that the motivation of large numbers to take part in a modern economy is as difficult a task as any that faces the Administration. It will not be adequate for only a few to take part; many must do so. A major effort by the Administration in expanding education and extension services will be needed to bring this about, and the Mission has allowed for these in its program. It is realistic that the private European, with a stake in the future of the Territory, should also make a real effort in this direction.

Development Credit

In the execution of the development program, credit is of fundamental importance to both the indigenous and the European sector. The Mission considers that credit in adequate amounts and on suitable terms cannot be provided by the existing banks and other credit organizations.[2]

The trading banks have played and must continue to play an important part in financing working capital, but their policies and procedures have restricted their role in providing long-term development credit. Savings banks in the Territory lend only for housing and to the Administration. Nevertheless, the Mission believes that the trading banks should be able to take an increasing part, along with the Territory Development Finance Company (mentioned below), in financing sound development.

The Commonwealth Development Bank does not have either a separate office or staff in the Territory but operates through branches of the Commonwealth Trading Bank. The policies applied in the Territory are those established for development lending in Australia and in practice cover only a rather narrow margin of risk in addition to that assumed by the trading banks.

To provide development capital on terms and conditions meeting the specific requirements of the Territory and in the amounts needed, a new institution is required. The Mission therefore recommends the establishment of a Territory Development Finance Company especially for the Territory. It should be organized as a separate entity with authority and resources to develop its own policies to fit the conditions of the Territory. The finance company will have high overhead costs at least in the early years and can hardly be profitable enough to attract private investors without a large subsidy. It is assumed, therefore, that the bulk of the capital needs will have to be provided by the Commonwealth Government either directly or through the Administration and that the finance company will be a government institution.

The Mission estimates that some £A20 million will be required over the next five years to finance additional plantings of tree crops, livestock development, forest exploitation, transport services, new manufacturing establishments and tourist facilities. For purposes of planning, the Mission recommends that £A15 million of this capital be subscribed by the Commonwealth Government. Chapter 8 outlines in greater detail the Mission's recommendations for a Territory Development Finance Company.

Planning for Economic Development

As indicated throughout this report, the task of development undertaken in the Territory is expensive. Therefore, the resources available

[2] These institutions and their operations in the Territory are described in Chapter 8.

locally, together with those provided by Australia, both human and physical, should be used most effectively. Planning can contribute to this end. We would suggest that Australia should not afford the luxury of proceeding with development without effective planning.

The Mission has in this report outlined a program for economic development. We would emphasize that much more detailed planning will be required by the Administration to prepare and implement a development program which will bring the best returns.

The Mission recommends that the planning organization in the Administration be strengthened. The nucleus for a planning group already exists in the form of the Central Policy and Planning Committee. Membership of this committee should be expanded to include the heads of four or five of the departments responsible for major programs. Also, a small but adequately qualified Planning Staff, under the direction of a senior and experienced economic adviser should be recruited to serve as the secretariat of the committee. Under the direction of the committee, this planning staff should be responsible for assessing the availability of financial and physical resources, coordinating and stimulating the development activities of departments and agencies, evaluating projects and programs prepared by departments within the over-all plan, and reviewing and evaluating progress with the object of recommending appropriate action and change.

The basic responsibility for initiatives and programs should rest with the individual departments and agencies directly concerned with formulating and executing development projects and programs. It is essential, therefore, that the planning staff work closely with the technical staff of the departments and agencies both at the center and in the 15 administrative districts throughout the Territory. The Mission wishes to stress the contribution officers of the districts can make to the planning process.

Economic planning should cover both the long and short term. An annual plan, as the basis for the annual budget, and a plan covering a longer period, of about five years, should be prepared. The plans should be published both as an indication of government intent and as a guide to the private sector.

The planning staff should be intimately associated with the preparation of the Administration's budget. In form and presentation the budget documents are at present adapted almost exclusively to administrative purposes. Changes are needed to make them more useful for planning purposes. The Mission would also stress the need for improvements in the flow of statistical information in relation to planning. Details of the Mission's recommendations on these points and on planning generally are contained in Annex II.

Administrative Organization

The Mission considers that some reorganization of the administrative structure is needed to enable the development program to be implemented effectively. Several of the departments of the Administration, as currently set up, are not well adapted to the execution of a program of the type proposed. Moreover, administration is excessively centralized.

To a very large degree, departmental organization has grown out of the regulatory and supervisory functions of the Administration which so far have been of prime importance. The stage has now been reached where departments must assume more direct responsibility for the implementation of development activities. To this end, they should be strengthened by the addition of suitable staff and reorganized to cope with the specific tasks ahead. The Mission has made specific recommendations in this regard for the major departments concerned. Particular attention is directed to the recommendations in the parts of the report dealing with agriculture, livestock, forestry, transport, education, health and housing.

The Territory is still in the early stages of development. Communications are frequently poor. The staff in several districts are quite isolated. These factors, coupled with the concentration of decision-making in the headquarters staff at Port Moresby, frequently hamper effective administration in the districts. It is important that district staff be given authority to make decisions and implement programs and projects which have the general approval of the Administration. The district staff have a firsthand and direct knowledge of local potentials and of the problems to be faced in the districts. They eventually have the responsibility for implementing the Administration's policies and programs. The Mission believes that the morale, interest and productivity of the district staff would improve materially if they were given greater opportunity to use their initiative and skills. Such delegation of authority will require, in some districts, a strengthening of the staff.

SECTOR RECOMMENDATIONS

The following summary is intended to provide a brief account of the major recommendations made by the Mission in the subsequent chapters dealing with the sectors of the economy. For an understanding of the basis for and reasoning underlying these recommendations it will be necessary to refer to the full text without which the Mission's proposals cannot be fully understood or used as a guide in formulating policies and programs. The period considered is 1964/65–1968/69 except for the agricultural and livestock programs which cover a ten-year period.

Agriculture, Livestock, Forestry and Fisheries

The program involves essentially an acceleration of the development of the major forms of production that have characterized this sector of the economy. In addition, several new developments are proposed. The program aims to move the indigene away from purely subsistence agriculture into the production of commercial crops, largely on a small-holder basis, at as fast a rate as the availability of the staff needed to direct and guide the program will permit. It proposes to make the maximum practical use of European producers to aid the Territory toward a more viable economy. To this end, production programs are spelled out by major crops for both indigenous and non-indigenous farmers and operators. These production programs are not hard and fast, but are guides which are capable of being exceeded under a vigorous Administration. The planting program is projected for ten years because a high proportion of the types of commodity concerned involves perennial crops (or livestock), which take up to ten years to mature.

The programs for coconuts, cocoa, rubber and the new crop, tea, are summarized in Table 1. The percentage increases expected from the indigenous sector for coconuts and cocoa are larger than from the European. The Mission has not been able to recommend any planned increase in coffee production because of the terms of the International Coffee Agreement to which Australia is a signatory, but estimates at least a doubling of coffee production from existing plantings. Increased exports of coffee to Australia are not subject to restriction. Attention is drawn to the possibilities of pyrethrum, peanuts, African oil palm and bananas, and specific recommendations for testing and development have been made.

TABLE 1: Ten-Year Planting Program, 1964/65–1973/74

(acres)

Crops	Indigenous		Non-indigenous		Total Plantings by 1973/74
	Plantings Mid-1962	Planting Program	Plantings Mid-1962	Planting Program	
Coconuts	253,000	240,000	261,000	120,000	874,000
Cocoa	20,000	70,000	98,000	75,000	263,000
Rubber	—	12,000	31,000	75,000	118,000
Tea	—	8,000	—	8,000	16,000
Total	273,000	330,000	390,000	278,000	1,271,000

The livestock program provides for the establishment of a beef cattle industry at a rate which would bring a tenfold increase in cattle herds to a total of 300,000 head in ten years, of which native operators would have 150,000 to 200,000 head. Also, a commencement of dairying in the Highlands is proposed.

Forest products are considered capable of being stepped up from approximately 80 million log super feet cut in 1962/63 to a level of at least 300 million log super feet annually in five years. This rate of output could be easily maintained thereafter, and in fact, increased without depletion of forest resources. Large-scale enterprise will be needed for the logging and processing of timber.

In the light of existing data, the Mission is not optimistic about the contribution fisheries can make to development. Nevertheless, there is good reason to continue technical assistance aimed at increasing the production of subsistence marine fish. Research work on fisheries, particularly in the coastal waters of the New Guinea mainland and islands, with primary emphasis on the development of commercial fishing potentials, is recommended.

The European, with his knowledge of production techniques, and given suitable incentives, should be able to achieve his share of the planting program without great difficulty. Achievement by the indigene of his share will require a major expansion of extension work and large-scale training. Agricultural research, designed to capitalize on existing knowledge of tropical agriculture, should be expanded.

Provision is made for a substantial expansion of agricultural education. The more than 2,000 sub-diploma intermediaries required by the Departments of Agriculture and Forests should be recruited from the comprehensive secondary school system and given subsequent in-post training. The Vudal Agriculture College should be expanded and a similar institution started in the highlands, with educational programs encompassing training in forestry as well as agriculture. Selected students should be sent abroad for training at the university level.

To implement the development program, there will be need to recruit in the next five to six years from outside the Territory more than 450 professional personnel for the Departments of Agriculture and Forests.

The Department of Agriculture should be strengthened by organizing three well-balanced technical units, namely, Research Planning and Evaluation, Animal Industry, and Development and Marketing, each under an Assistant Director of the Department. Internal reorganization within these divisions will be needed.

In view of the difficulties and high costs of land settlement, this development method should be limited to trials on a small block basis until the results indicate a justification for large-scale settlement as a method of future development.

A total of £A9 million in credit for the first five years, and another £A9 million for the second five-year phase will be needed.

Secondary Industry, Handicrafts, Tourism, Mining and Power

The Mission considers that the greatest contribution the Administration can make to the expansion of *secondary industry* will come from the formulation of policies conducive to investments and from providing information to investors. Potential investors as a rule have little knowledge about the resources and investment opportunities in the Territory. The Department of Trade and Industry should be strengthened to enable it to make studies of new manufacturing possibilities and to collect basic information of interest to potential investors. As already discussed in the section on Conditions for Implementation, the Administration should continue to provide incentives by suitable tax concessions and tariff policies. Land needed for industrial development should be acquired and made available to private industry. The Government of Australia can also make a major contribution by allowing liberal entry of Territory products into the Australian market. Credit for new and expanding industries, to be provided by the Territory Development Finance Company, has been estimated at £A3 to £A3.5 million over the next five years.

The Department of Trade and Industry should also be strengthened to make possible an expansion in the number of cooperative societies and supporting associations, as well as assist in the improvement of their efficiency. Greater use should be made of local building materials not only to reduce imports but to encourage investment in processing facilities and to stimulate local employment. *Handicrafts* have a larger potential than presently being realized and handicraft production and marketing should be encouraged.

Tourism can be greatly expanded and should be promoted. Probably the most important single step to this end would be the re-introduction of the international air service to provide direct connections with the Far East and Europe and North America through the Philippines. The necessary cost-benefit study for the expansion of the Port Moresby or Lae Airport should be made a part of the transportation program. Improved accommodations and tourist facilities are required and credit should be made available through the Territory Development Finance Company. Credit requirements have been tentatively estimated at £A0.4 million.

The outlook for large-scale *mining* development is not encouraging. Gold mining provides a source of cash income to small operators and individuals, and the Mission endorses the Administration's policy of technical assistance to indigenous gold producers. Although oil exploration results have so far been disappointing, the geology of western Papua justifies further exploration, and the Mission endorses the policy of the Commonwealth Government in applying to the Territory its subsidy for oil exploration. Substantial natural gas resources have been found, but prospects for commercial exploitation in the foreseeable future are not encouraging. The geological branch of the Department of Lands, Surveys and Mines, which has a wide range of responsibilities, should be strengthened.

To meet the rapidly growing demand for electric *power*, new capacity should be built during the next five years. The Mission endorses the program of the Electricity Commission to install new capacity at Rouna to supply Port Moresby and to build the first stage of a power plant on the upper Ramu River to supply the highlands, Lae and Madang. A review should be made of the present rate structure for electricity to ensure that rates are more closely related to the cost of providing electricity to consumers.

Transport and Communications

The major *transport* deficiencies at present are in overseas port facilities, particularly at Rabaul, Lae and Madang and in coastal shipping services. First priority should be given to the improvement of these major ports and a long-range development plan for all overseas ports should be prepared as soon as possible. No new overseas ports should be developed during the next five years with the exception of completing the port at Kieta, possibly the wharf at Wewak and to meet the specific needs of large-scale forest exploitation.

A comprehensive program to reorganize and modernize coastal shipping should be prepared. The coastal fleet should be expanded and re-equipped, and in addition, there is need for the introduction of economic regulation, training of personnel (especially indigenes) and the construction of small wharves, jetties and necessary access roads.

At present, no special organization exists for the management and operation of ports and the Mission supports the Administration's proposal to establish a Harbors Board with authority for port management and control. Overseas shipping rates by water are high and an effort should be made to reduce them by changes in the present system of subsidy and in promoting tariff changes or possible rate concessions.

The trunk road from Lae to Goroka, now under construction, should be completed to provide an all-weather road from the highlands to the coast. In addition, road construction should concentrate on opening up new agricultural and forest areas. New feeder roads to link with trunk roads, air-strips and coastal anchorages should have priority. A Road Division should be organized within the Department of Public Works with responsibility to carry out the road program and the Commonwealth Department of Works asked to assume responsibility to staff this division.

For many years to come, parts of the Territory will continue to depend mainly on air transport, and in passenger transport, air services will continue to take first place. To achieve more economical operations air traffic should be concentrated at fewer airports, larger planes used, small strips (made obsolete by good road connections) closed and the duplication of traffic-handling establishments and routes (at least on low-traffic-density routes) eliminated.

Small aircraft can make an important contribution to transportation. The position of the light aircraft operators should be reviewed, the independent carriers given more expansion opportunities, and the introduction of new aircraft should be encouraged. An effort should be made to achieve better coordination between the aviation authority, the airlines, the Administration and the air transport users.

It is important that problems in respect to road and air transport, ports and coastal and overseas shipping be considered as a whole. To ensure this, a Department of Transport should be established with responsibilities for regulating, economic planning and promotion of better transport services. The department should not be involved in operations, technical or engineering planning, or design.

Credit will be needed by the operators to modernize the coastal shipping fleet. Credit will also be needed for road transport (trucks and terminal and maintenance facilities), harbor storage facilities and air transport. The Territory Development Finance Company should provide the credit estimated at somewhat more than £A7 million over the next five years.

The licensing policy for private, limited purpose *communication* networks should be reviewed to establish criteria for licensing such networks, to establish priorities and to determine fees. Public carriers (airlines, licensed coastal vessel operators and long-distance truck operators) should be given priority in the allocation of frequencies. Charges for telephone and telegraph services should be adequate to make the operations generally self-supporting, at least in the major centers.

Education

The highest priority in education should be given to the expansion of secondary and technical education. If, however, the numbers in secondary schools are to increase rapidly, the numbers of children completing primary education must also rise. The first priority in primary education should, therefore, be the consolidation of the schools already started by adding to them year by year the necessary higher standards until all students who have entered at the preparatory level have the opportunity of pursuing a full primary course. Beyond that, additional enrollments should be limited. Preparatory places provided in Administration schools should complement, not compete with, those in mission schools and increases in primary enrollment in Administration schools due to transfers from mission schools should be limited. For the majority of pupils, the completion of the primary course should become the normal terminal point. With only a modest increase during the next five years in preparatory enrollment in Administration schools and none in approved mission schools there would be, nevertheless, by 1969 an increase of about 100,000 over the level of 150,000 in primary schools in 1963. About 60 to 65 percent of all primary school-age children will then be enrolled, assuming a number of children of primary school age by 1969 of 400,000. For secondary and technical education, every effort should be made to increase the enrollment from the level of 4,600 in 1963 by more than 20,000 by 1968/69.

The Mission believes that combining the academic and technical streams into comprehensive secondary schools would better meet the requirements of the Territory. At least the first three years of secondary education, whether academic, agricultural, industrial or commercial, should be given in comprehensive secondary schools. This would avoid rigid selection at too early an age, bring together students following different courses of study and make possible operating economies.

A program of adult education closely oriented to village development should be initiated on an experimental basis. Once a satisfactory formula has been found, expansion should follow.

The Mission believes that it is no longer necessary to recruit expatriate teachers for primary schools. Primary school teachers should hereafter come from the indigenous population. Educational qualification for new primary school teachers should be gradually raised. There are adequate teacher colleges and a sufficient supply of potential candidates to provide the numbers of primary teachers required. The great bulk of secondary school teachers will have to be expatriates. Approximately 1,000 additional teachers will be needed over the five-year period for Administration and mission schools.

Mission schools should continue to play an important role in the educational effort and the financial support given by the Administration should be substantially increased.

Local communities should be primarily responsible for providing the land, and constructing and maintaining school buildings and teacher houses for primary schools. The Administration should be responsible for secondary school buildings, including the necessary housing.

There is a great need for research into the problems of educating the indigene. A research and production unit to deal with curricula, textbooks, and teaching material and aids should be established in the Department of Education.

The Mission supports in principle the establishment of a network of radio stations capable of giving better coverage of the Territory. Radio has a real potential for adult and school educational purposes. The potential for television should be studied.

Health, Housing, Water Supply and Sewerage

Health. The Mission endorses the Department of Public Health's intention to expand the programs of preventive medicine and health education. Health centers should be organized throughout the Territory with the local communities providing the land and buildings and the Local Government Councils taking responsibility for a growing share of the operating costs. Aid posts should be continued and new ones established only when there can be adequate supervision. Local Government Councils should take a greater responsibility for aid posts. A small home economics unit should be organized to develop a program aimed at helping infant and welfare nurses and health centers' staff working with village women.

Only relatively minor improvements should be made in the curative health facilities over the next five years. Greater attention should be given to the use of the existing facilities and to training of the indigene. The Mission endorses the Administration's policy of training indigenes as assistant medical officers as well as the other training programs of the Department of Public Health for medical assistants, nurses and aid post orderlies. Appropriate facilities should be provided.

The Mission endorses the policy of financial and other assistance to the missions for hospitals, aid posts and training programs when essential to complement the public health activities of the Administration.

The Mission believes that it is important to the development of a society responsive to the demands of a modern economy that the native people as well as the Europeans should pay in cash or in kind a reasonable charge for the services and the drugs received at hospitals and other medical facilities operated both by the Administration and by the missions.

Housing. The main responsibility of the Administration in this field over the next five years will be to provide housing for its staff, particularly expatriate staff. The availability of housing is an essential prerequisite for obtaining the additional staff needed to carry out the development program.

So far, the Administration has leased houses to its staff at sub-economic rentals. The Mission recommends that over the longer term employees, both European and native, should be encouraged to find their own housing. This change can come only gradually, but the charging of economic rents, compensated by salary increases, would remove a major obstacle to its occurring. The Administration should introduce economic rents, and encourage its personnel to acquire their own houses by making available credit under its present housing loans scheme.

The standards and costs of staff housing should be related to the gradual change in the composition of the public service to one mainly staffed by indigenes. Costs could be reduced by the greater use of local materials, especially in the more remote areas. Greater use should be made of local materials both to save costs and to stimulate the development of local skills and local employment.

The Administration will have to assume greater responsibilities for housing indigenes in urban areas. The Mission commends the approach of "self-help" housing as the only one likely to provide adequate accommodation without imposing excessive costs on the Administration.

The magnitude and complexity of housing needs are such that a single housing authority responsible for the housing of Administration staff and for urban housing programs would provide the most economical organization. The Mission recommends the organization of such an authority.

The Mission recommends that the prices charged for *water*, *sewerage* and *sanitation* services should be brought up to economic levels. As higher charges may have an effect on demand for these services, the Administration should review projected capital expenditures for projects to provide such services.

BUDGETARY IMPLICATIONS OF THE PROGRAM

Administration

The programs recommended by the Mission will require increasing expenditures by the Administration in the years to follow. A rise should also be anticipated for categories of expenditures, not covered directly by the Mission's recommendations, reflecting increasing costs of an expanding administration.

To assess the budgetary implications of the program recommendations against the background of the public finance picture as a whole, the Mission made a projection of the budget of the Administration for the five-year period 1964/65–1968/69. The projection was based on the requirements of the program and not on available financial resources. The grants to the Administration by the Commonwealth Government of Australia are on an annual basis. It was not possible for the Commonwealth Government to estimate for the Mission the magnitude of funds it might make available over the next five years.

Expenditures by the Administration are currently financed to the extent of about two-thirds by the annual grant of the Commonwealth Government of Australia. The expenditures have been growing since 1958/59 on average by more than 15 percent annually.

Total average annual expenditures resulting from the projection, together with the implications for the pattern of Administration expenditures by broad functional categories, are shown in Table 2; the details of the projection and the underlying assumptions are discussed in Annex III.

The Mission's projection leads to the result that on average £A50.2 million would be needed annually by the Administration during the next five years. This is about one-third more than budgeted expenditures during 1963/64 and more than twice the average yearly expenditures during the five-year period 1958/59 to 1962/63. The projection is based on the assumption of a modest rise (about 5 percent) for expenditures not following directly from its program.

The budget picture as projected implies an increase in the share of expenditures for the *Commodity Producing Sectors* (agriculture, stock and fisheries, forestry, lands, surveys and mines, trade and industry and the proposed Territory Development Finance Company) from an average of about 9.5 percent during most recent years to almost double this level during the next five years. The rise is explained mainly by the budgetary provision made for the Territory Development Finance Company (6 percent), its funds to be used largely for credit in this category as well as some for lending to transport. In addition, the budgetary share of agriculture and forestry combined is expected to be about 9 percent, up from about 6 percent.

Economic Overheads (including transport, electric power, posts and telegraphs) are expected to require about the same share of expenditures as in the past five years (16 percent), with an increase in emphasis on investments in the transport sector (up from about 7 percent to about 9 percent).[3]

---

[3] The apparent fall in the share of electric power is not real; it is explained by the exclusion of some expenditures now financed directly by the Electricity Commission (see Table 2, footnote a).

TABLE 2: Territory Administration Expenditures and Revenues

	1964/65– 1968/69 Annual Average (£A million)	1964/65– 1968/69	1963/64	1958/59– 1962/63
		Percent of Total		
EXPENDITURES				
Commodity Producing Sectors				
Agriculture, Stock and Fisheries	3.10	6.2	4.4	4.4
Forestry	1.55	3.1	1.1	1.6
Lands, Surveys and Mines	1.05	2.1	2.5	2.1
Trade and Industry	0.80	1.6	1.7	1.4
Territory Development Finance Company	3.00	6.0	—	—
	9.50	18.9	9.7	9.5
Economic Overheads				
Roads and Bridges	3.40	6.8	5.4	5.9
Ports	0.50	1.0	0.6	0.4
Coastal Shipping	0.15	0.3 .	—	—
Aerodromes	0.30	0.6	0.4	0.5
Electric Power	1.85 [a]	3.7 [a]	2.4 [a]	4.6
Posts and Telegraphs	1.75	3.5	3.7	4.1
	7.95	15.8	12.5	15.5
Social Services				
Education	7.50	15.0	15.7	11.2
Health	5.40	10.8	11.9	15.2
Housing	2.15	4.3	5.3	7.3
Water Supply and Sewerage	0.80	1.6	1.9	1.8
	15.85	31.6	34.8	35.5
General Administration, Law *and Order*				
Law, Order and Public Safety			6.5	8.6
Legislature			0.1	0.1
General Administrative Services			29.0	24.4
	16.90	33.7	35.6	33.1
Various Public Works			4.7	5.1
Miscellaneous			2.7	1.3
Total Expenditures	50.20	100.0	100.0	100.0
Annual Average Expenditures		£A50.2 mil.	£A37.5 mil.	£A22.9 mil.
REVENUES				
Internal Revenue	13.8	27.5	28.1	31.7
Public Borrowing	36.4	72.5	4.5	1.7
Commonwealth Grant			67.4	66.6
Total Revenues	50.2	100.0	100.0	100.0
Annual Average Revenues		£A50.2 mil.	£A37.5 mil.	£A22.9 mil.

Notes: Expenditures for Vocabulary Stores in 1964/65 to 1968/69 have in part been allocated to individual items, whereas for previous years they are all included in General Administrative Services.

[a] Exclusive of maintenance expenditures of £A0.4 to £A0.5 million annually, now financed directly by the Electricity Commission.

SOURCES: For 1958/59 to 1963/64, computed from Department of Territories—Economic and Functional Classification of Public Authorities Finances; for 1964/65–1968/69, Annex III.

For *Social Services* (education, health, housing, water supply and sewerage) the share is about 32 percent, 3 to 4 percent lower than in the past. The share of education would be considerably higher (some 15 percent against 11 percent during 1958/59 to 1962/63) and that of health substantially lower (somewhat less than 11 percent against about 15 percent during 1958/59 to 1962/63).

Finally, the share of expenditures for *General Administration, Law and Order* (together with expenditures for various public works and miscellaneous purposes) would be about 34 percent of the total. This sector includes some expenditures which for lack of detailed information could not be allocated to other sectors.

Although we have not tried to project all categories of public expenditures for each of the next five years separately, it follows from our sector programs that expenditures may be expected to rise in particular during the beginning of the period, at least if delays in implementation can be avoided. During the first year of the program, 1964/65, expenditures would rise especially due to the allocation to the Territory Development Finance Company of £A3 million and an increase in spending on transport by about £A2.5 million over the level budgeted for 1963/64. Another year of substantially rising expenditures would be 1968/69, when on the basis of present plans expenditures by the Electricity Commission alone would rise by about £A2.5 million, due mainly to the Upper Ramu Scheme. In the other years of the program, the increase in expenditures is expected to be by comparison smaller. A special financial arrangement might be considered for the government contribution to the Territory Development Finance Company, in order to bring out its special nature and to limit the amounts of the annual grants proper.

Projected expenditures have been assumed to be financed from internal revenues (taxation and other current revenues) to the extent of 27.5 percent. This target implies a rise by somewhat more than 10 percent annually over the 1963/64 estimate for internal revenue, a rate of growth which might well exceed somewhat that for the Gross Domestic Product. The Mission believes that the Administration should aim, as a minimum, at a revenue effort of this order of magnitude to limit the dependence on the Commonwealth grant. The Mission also believes that if a determined revenue effort is made, this target should be possible of attainment. In Chapter 8, the Mission discusses in more detail the various possibilities for raising additional current revenue.

If the Administration were to succeed in financing 27.5 percent of its total expenditures from internal revenue, this would still mean a lower percentage than that obtained in the past.[4] It would be desirable to finance a larger percentage of the Territory budget from internal revenue. Possibilities for raising more revenue are limited, however, by the desirability to keep the tax burden for Europeans at an attractive level for incentive reasons and by the slow impact of increased government spending on the levels of output and income of the economy at large. The returns from proposed public expenditures to support the recommended programs in agriculture and forestry will be forthcoming largely after the end of the five-year period. The basis for raising more revenue during the next five years from production in the private sector will, therefore, be mainly rising production from increased plantings in the past.

On the basis of the assumptions made, an average of £A36.4 million would have to be raised annually from the Commonwealth grant plus public borrowing. This corresponds to an average rise over the next five years for the two items combined of somewhat more than £A3 million annually.

The size of the anticipated budget deficit to be covered by sources other than internal current revenues accentuates the need for careful spending policies. As indicated before, expenditures for most items not covered directly by the Mission's program have been assumed to rise by no more than 5 percent annually, which is much lower than growth rates of the past. In order not to increase the dependence of the Territory on outside assistance more than the circumstances demand, the Administration should limit expenditures with a low developmental impact to those that are strictly essential. In this context, attention should also be concentrated on possibilities of increasing efficiency. The size of the budget deficit also accentuates the need for economy in construction and for the adoption of simple construction standards, advocated by the Mission throughout the report.

Public borrowing is only a recent phenomenon in the Territory. It was started in 1960/61 and so far a total of almost £A3.7 million has been raised, of which £A1.7 million in 1963/64. Public borrowing is justifiable if the proceeds are used to finance expenditures which strengthen the productive, and consequently the revenue potential of the economy. Under Territory conditions, the Mission considers as most suitable to loan

---

[4] According to the budget estimates for 1963/64 about 27.3 percent of expenditures will be covered by internal revenue if a correction is made for expected tax rebates (no such correction has been made in Table 2). The assumed percentage for the next five years is, therefore, at about the same level as that for 1963/64. Also, the 1963/64 budget figure for internal revenue was raised by roughly £A1 million due to a change in accounting procedures. Allowing for this, the fall in the percentages for 1963/64 and the next five years in comparison to the percentage for 1958/59–1963/64 in fact becomes somewhat larger than that indicated by Table 2.

financing revenue-producing projects which can be expected to earn enough to cover the service of the loan. The projected capital expenditures of the Electricity Commission (in the calculation assumed to be financed through loans by the Administration to the Commission) and possibly some of the future investments in ports by the Harbors Board, once established, would appear to meet this criterion. Beyond that the Mission would caution against the contracting of substantial amounts of public debt by the Administration. Since the internal revenue base is so small, the debt service burden would soon equal a sizable proportion of this revenue and in fact make the Administration increasingly dependent on Australian grants for the payment of debt service.

The Mission wants to emphasize that its projection is unavoidably based on somewhat arbitrary assumptions, particularly for those categories of expenditures which it was not in a position to examine in detail. Also, as already stated, for some groups of expenditures projected increases are based on rather minimum assumptions. For these reasons the projection as a whole is primarily illustrative and does not purport to be a firm recommendation on total expenditures. The Commonwealth Government of Australia and the Administration may have good reasons to deviate from the assumptions in a number of instances. The Mission's main concerns have been that priority should be given to those expenditures that will directly strengthen the productive potential of the Territory and advance the indigene and that the amounts spent on other items be kept moderate, or be reduced if possible, in order to limit the increasing dependence on the Australian grant.

Local Government Councils

The Mission's recommendations will result not only in increased expenditures by the Administration, but also by Local Government Councils.

It is recommended that Local Government Councils, where practicable, and local communities be made responsible for the construction and maintenance of primary schools and ancillary buildings, and proposed that they share, on the basis of their financial capacity, in the costs of aid posts, rural health centers, local roads, improvement of local water supplies and possibly sanitation projects. With regard to rural health centers and local water supplies, a cost-sharing system has already been introduced. The Mission also emphasizes the desirability of organizing urban governments with responsibility to administer the urban centers.

The Mission has not tried to project the budgetary expenditures of Local Government Councils since it did not have an adequate basis for doing so. The Mission recognizes that, particularly in those rural areas which have not made progress in production of export crops, the taxable capacity is limited. Subsidies by the Administration may be required in such areas to defray the expenditures of local councils for the purposes mentioned. Although the Mission has not made specific allowance for this in its budget projections for the Administration, it does not believe that this will alter its projections substantially; first, because some of the activities mentioned are now paid for by the Administration and second, since in view of its recommendations for standards of construction for schools and other buildings, additional expenditures may be expected to be only modest.

Commonwealth Government of Australia

Australia, in addition to making available the annual grant to the Administration, spends fairly substantial sums in the Territory which are not channeled through the budget of the Territory, but appear in the budget of the Commonwealth. During 1962/63, expenditures were somewhat less than £A5 million, the most important single item being civil aviation with one-third of the total.

From an economic point of view there is no justification for considering Territory and Commonwealth expenditures apart. In drawing up a development plan, all public expenditures, to the extent possible, should be considered, including those of the Commonwealth Government and Local Government Councils.

Although the Mission has not been in a position to include direct Commonwealth government expenditures in the Territory in its budget projection, they should be expected to remain a rather important factor in the public finance picture of the Territory.

CONCLUDING REMARKS

To reach the stage when the Territory will be able to stand on its own feet economically will require external assistance both in substantial amounts and over an extended period of time. The level of this assistance is very large in relation to the domestic financial resources of the economy and on a per capita basis. Even with economic progress the gap between public expenditures and public revenues and consequently the dependence on outside support can be expected to increase. This is not unique, in comparison with many other countries at an early stage of development, but the size of the task is especially formidable in the case of the Territory.

It places a heavy responsibility on Australia, itself a country of less than 12 million people, from where most of the required external resources, human, physical and financial, inevitably will have to come. The Commonwealth Government of Australia is to be commended for its increasing efforts to develop the Territory. However, development is still at an early stage and the program recommended by the Mission can only be realized if the Government of Australia will support it on the full scale required.

The weak financial structure of the Territory makes it in principle desirable to concentrate on investment projects with returns which would be forthcoming quickly. Given, however, the pattern of agricultural production, possibilities in this regard are very limited. Gestation periods of tree crops are long and returns consequently delayed, although ultimate returns on the basis of present experience are attractive and sometimes high. Although data are lacking, capital output ratios should in many instances be high, due to lack of economies of scale (small and widely dispersed population) and, particularly in the case of transport investments, the geographical characteristics of the country. These factors increase the cost of developing the Territory economically.

The ultimate aim of economic development should be to bring the Territory to a stage of economic viability with self-sustaining economic growth. The country would then have reached a tolerable standard of living without the further need of substantial financial assistance from outside; in addition, it would be able to finance a rate of investment almost entirely from its own savings large enough to allow some further rise in income per capita. The Mission is unable to forecast how long it would take the Territory to reach this stage in view of the many variables and unknowns involved, not the least being the rate at which the indigenous population itself can be stimulated to improve its material well-being. By any reckoning and even on the basis of the most favorable assumptions, however, the development phase will take several decades.

In the process, the budgetary deficit and more generally the gap between investment and saving in the economy to be bridged by external assistance will rise, before a turning point will be reached. The attainment of this point is primarily dependent on magnifying the productive capacity of the economy, which will have to provide the source for generating larger amounts of savings. In addition, the present gap between financial requirements and resources will have to be narrowed down in particular by economies in government administration. To this end, the progressive replacement of expatriate staff by trained indigenes is all important. Moreover, it is vital that the temptation be resisted to build government services up to a standard which the country will never be able to afford.

Although the Mission has not attempted to make a forecast of the budgetary deficit beyond the next five years, the magnitude of the problem can easily be demonstrated on the basis of the projection of the ultimate increase in export proceeds from the planting programs for major crops recommended for the next ten years. This increase, including the effect of some fall in production by old trees, is estimated by the Mission at about £A27 million from 1968/69 through the early 1980s, when all new trees would be fully bearing. Even if it were possible to collect one-quarter of the increment in export proceeds through taxation, this would still produce no more than about £A6.8 million. This is less than 20 percent of the projected average annual deficit to be covered by the Commonwealth grant plus domestic borrowing during the next five years.

The rate of population growth will also be an important factor. At present, this rate is only a little above 2 percent but it could well rise substantially and there are indications that this is happening in some areas where living conditions have improved. The higher this rate, the larger the amounts of investment (and financial assistance) that will be needed to bring about the same rise in living standards.

CHAPTER 3 *AGRICULTURE, LIVESTOCK, FORESTRY AND FISHERIES*

RESOURCES AND SCOPE FOR DEVELOPMENT

Like many underdeveloped countries, the economy of the Territory rests almost completely on agriculture. Internally, the economy is a subsistence one based on agriculture, livestock, forestry and fisheries. Externally these industries earn nearly all of the export income, engage more than half the people employed in the monetary sector and nearly all the self-employed. They offer good scope for development.

As a background to an appraisal of the potentials of the primary industries, it is necessary to examine more closely than was done briefly in Chapter 1 those special aspects of topography, climate and soils, which separately or together control the land use of the Territory.

Topography

Both the mainland and the major islands are dominated by massive mountains. The central cordillera of the mainland, which forms a complete divide between north and south, is not a single chain but a complex system of ranges separated by broad upland valleys. These valleys, with altitudes of 5,000 to 10,000 feet, form the so-called New Guinea Highlands. The foothill zones have become deeply dissected by river systems to yield an intensely rugged juvenile topography. Volcanic areas of the mainland, which are limited to relatively small zones, likewise have resulted in difficult formations. New Britain, New Ireland and Bougainville are characterized by extensive mountains with upland valleys, much less extensive however than those of the mainland. The main consequence of the rough, broken topography is to make a very large proportion of the land virtually unusable for agriculture and forestry for reasons of contour alone.

In addition to limitations imposed by the terrain, extensive swamps cover large areas. On the southwest littoral of the mainland, the great delta plain of the Daru coast is one of the most extensive swamps of the world. There also are large swamps in the northwest littoral. From the mountains of the hinterland, the river systems carry heavy loads of alluvium with which they are building their deltas. Most of the rivers have extensive mangrove and nipa palm swamps at their mouths. In addition, the Sepik and Ramu rivers in particular flow through extensive riverine swamps of sago, bamboo and forest for hundreds of miles.

Quite apart from the obvious direct effects of the terrain on land use, it must be emphasized that the very great problems of access and isolation resulting from the rugged topography impose special limitations to the agricultural development of much of the Territory.

Climate

Along with topography, climate is a major determining factor in land use. The Territory lies wholly within the tropics and experiences a typical monsoonal climate. The northwest monsoon season extends from December to March, and the southeast monsoon from May to October. Since both these winds pass over vast expanses of ocean prior to reaching the Territory, they arrive heavily laden with moisture. Average annual rainfall is high, ranging from 80 to 100 inches for most districts. Many areas receive more than 200 inches. A few, like Port Moresby, lie in a rain shadow and record anamolous figures of 40 inches or less.

Although in some areas the distribution of rain (200 to 260 days) is remarkably uniform throughout the year, this is not typical for most of the Territory. Except in the Moresby area, the great mountain ranges of both the mainland and the larger islands lie across the track of the rain-bearing winds, so that most places have a definite seasonal distribution, receiving the greater percentage in one or the other of the two main wind seasons. The topography thus has a profound conditioning effect on local climates (see map on facing page).

Temperatures are not extreme for a tropical climate. For most lowland, coastal and island areas, the daily mean temperature is about 81 degrees fahrenheit. Seasonal variations are generally small, rarely exceeding 5 degrees. The mean maximum in the lowlands is about 90 degrees and the minimum about 70 degrees. The diurnal range is 10–15 degrees in the lowlands. In the highlands, temperature varies greatly with altitude. At the 6,000 feet level, the mean temperature is about 61 degrees, with day temperatures rising to 90 degrees and night figures falling to 40 to 60 degrees. Seasonal changes again are very small. In all zones, temperature varies mainly with altitude; among geographical areas changes are slight and unimportant.

Lowland humidity is uniformly high at about 80 percent, with very little seasonal variation. Fluctuations are much greater in the highlands. Even when this zone is enveloped with clouds for days or weeks at a time, conditions are not oppressive, being associated with low temperatures.

RAINFALL

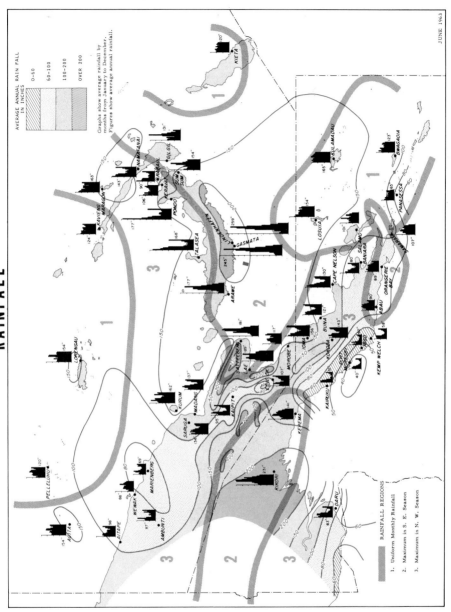

AVERAGE ANNUAL RAIN FALL
IN INCHES

0–60
60–100
100–200
OVER 200

Graphs show average rainfall by
months from January to December.
Figures show average annual rainfall.

RAINFALL REGIONS

Uniform Monthly Rainfall
1. Uniform Monthly Rainfall
2. Maximum in S. E. Season
3. Maximum in N. W. Season

JUNE 1963

Although wet/dry seasons exist in many zones, this term is relative since even in the so-called dry season, precipitation ranges from 2 to 4 inches per month. The variable weather of the temperate zones of the world is not evident, even in the highlands. The climate is thus well adapted to the production of crops characteristic of wet tropics. The same conditions impose limitations to forms of animal production unsuited to the combination of high temperature and high humidity. The highlands provide a bracing and vigorous environment for humans. The lowlands and islands provide a tropical climate to which the non-indigene can become acclimatized.

Soils

Extensive and accurate information on soils is not available. Modern soil surveys have been made only over a few selected areas. From these studies, from the observation and experience of local professional and commercial agriculturists, and from the long established pattern of land use of the native population, sufficient is known to permit a few important generalizations.

The luxuriant rain forest which covers most of the Territory gives a misleading impression of widespread highly fertile soils. In fact, most of the soils are of low fertility. Continuous heavy rainfall causes constant leaching of nutrients of soils under the forest. When this cover is removed for cultivation, the small accumulation of fertility is quickly used up. Many of the inland soils are shallow, heavily leached and relatively infertile.

There are notable exceptions. The broad lowland valleys of the Markham and Ramu carry deep alluvial loams of high fertility. Similarly, many areas exist in the highland valley systems where alluvial clay soils, or soils of volcanic origin can be very productive. Limestone is also an important parent material of soils in the highlands. In deep valleys or on the slopes below limestone escarpments, there are concentrations of fertile brown loams, constantly renewed by wash from the rock formations above. Volcanic soils of the Eastern and Western Highlands have been derived from Pleistocene ash and basalts. Examples of both types are to be found throughout the Mt. Hagen, Goroka, Chimbu and Aiyura areas. Rich red soils of more recent volcanic origin also occur on the Sogeri tableland and in the Popondetta and Kokoda valleys.

Soils of the coastal regions, both mainland and island, are of varying fertility. They range from shallow, relatively infertile complexes formed from decomposed coral, to deep alluvial and volcanic ash soils of recent origin. It is the latter two types that offer the greatest possibilities for agricultural development. The alluvial soils tend to be of varying quality. They are widespread throughout the coastal plains and the broad river valleys. They exist not only on valley floors but are frequently well developed on adjoining slopes. The volcanic types also vary in fertility, the richest tending to be those of more recent origin. Volcanic soils readily become degraded by leaching as they mature. Extensive areas of very highly fertile volcanic types occur on northern New Britain, on Bougainville and on the southern part of New Ireland. Not all volcanic soils of recent origin are fertile however. A notable example is on the Buin plains of Bougainville which pose special difficulties to cropping.

The greatest soil fertility problem is that of leaching. All soils leach badly under heavy rainfall. This has already been responsible for considerable degrading of the alluvial soils of the extensive Sepik and Daru plains. Erosion, stimulated by pour-use methods on unfavorable slopes, is also responsible for soil loss in some districts.

From this general background, it might be inferred that the defects of topography, climate and soils are so serious as to condemn the Territory as an agricultural country. This would be wrong. The extensive areas of reasonable topography and suitability of the climate for wet-tropic agriculture, together with the good fertility of many soils, make it possible to advance the Territory along the road of economic prosperity through development of agriculture.

Land Resources

Total land resources are estimated at about 117 million acres. The mainland contributes about 85 percent, the remainder coming mostly from New Britain, New Ireland and Bougainville, the three largest of the 600-odd islands making up the rest of the Territory. A breakup of this area into broad-use categories, as summarized in Table 1, shows that crop land accounts for over 1 percent of the total, grassland 11 to 12 percent, forested land 70 percent and unclassified the remaining 17 to 18 percent.

The large area in grassland is virtually not used at all, and only about 1 million acres of forest lands are at present owned and controlled by the Administration. Thus, about 2 percent of the total land is currently in use for agriculture and forestry.

Land capability studies based on aerial photography, mapping and soil surveys have not yet been made on a sufficient scale to define accurately the potential for increased primary production. For this reason, all figures of development potential cited by the Mission with respect to specific forms of production have been estimated on a conservative basis.

TABLE 1: Land Resources by Use, 1961/62

(thousand acres)

Use or Type of Vegetation	Papua	New Guinea	Total	Percent
Crop Land Cultivated	406	832	1,238	1.1
Estimated Grassland Area	7,006	6,508	13,514	11.5
Estimated Forested Area	42,000	40,000	82,000	69.8
Unclassified Area	8,532	12,178	20,710	17.6
Total Land Area	57,944	59,518	117,462	100.0

SOURCES: Production Bulletin No. 4, 1962; Department of Agriculture, Stock and Fisheries, Annual Reports, Papua and New Guinea, 1961/62.

In respect to agriculture, the available information suggests that it is not unreasonable to assume that at least 5 percent of the 117 million acres, or about 6 million acres, have a good potential for crop production. Exploitation to this level would achieve a fivefold increase in land use independent of any gains through increasing efficiency of existing methods.

On the grassland side it is estimated that about 10 million acres could be used for animal production. Some of this could go to agriculture if and when required for this purpose. The balance of existing native pastures are likely to be permanently unusable due to swamps or are of such low potential value as to be hardly worth development in the foreseeable future. An example of the latter is the dry Savannah areas. The output from grassland, like that from agriculture, involves an additional long-term potential through improved pasture types and more efficient methods of utilization.

Forests are one of the great unused resources. Variously estimated to cover about three-quarters of the land resources of the Territory, about 60 million acres are of doubtful commercial use because of precipitous contour or the swampy nature of the land. The remaining 20–30 million acres on slopes of less than 30 degrees have a large commercial potential.[1] There are some 2.5 million acres which are presently available to the Administration, or which could be obtained, for commercial use.

Combining these estimates, the potential land-use figure becomes about 19 million acres or 16 percent of the total land area, against 2 million acres or 2 percent in use at present. These estimates do not, of course, include the additional large areas of forest lands described above. On these figures the Territory must be regarded as a relatively underdeveloped country in terms of primary production.

[1] The estimates mentioned here are those of the Department of Forests (see in this report under Forestry); they are somewhat higher than those given in the sources underlying Table 1.

AGRICULTURE

Subsistence Agriculture

It is very important to appreciate that the peoples of the Territory are not short of food. There is no shortage of usable land. The few instances of relatively high population density (the Chimbu area of the highlands, the Gazelle Peninsula of New Britain, and the Maprik area of the Sepik) are not due to lack of land; rather, tribal areas became established as a consequence of war and these areas became frozen as a result of native land tenure customs and the relative inflexibility of official land-tenure policies.

The over-all adequacy of land is obvious from the low population density of 11 persons per square mile, and from the very small proportion of good land currently used. On average, subsistence farming each year uses less than 0.2 acres per person. At least fifteen times this figure is readily available.

Starchy root crops, of which the sweet potato is by far the most important, provide the main staples. Taro, yams and cassava are also used extensively. The banana is a key crop. The groundnut is a recent introduction of increasing importance. Leafy vegetables and legumes of the bean type, maize and sugar cane make a substantial contribution to diets. All these are the products of gardening—the main form of subsistence agriculture. Gardening is supplemented in all areas by foraging, hunting and fishing. A wide variety of edible nuts and fruits are gathered from wild or planted trees. Of these, the coconut, breadfruit, mountain pandanus and betel nut are important. Wild sago, nipa palm and lowland pandanus also provide large amounts of food. Although no large game animals exist (except for a few imported deer), the some 100 species of mammals, nearly all small marsupials, are hunted for food. Snakes and lizards which are plentiful are also eaten. Insects, both larval and adult, provide seasonal variety in the diet. Fishing is more important to coastal and riverine peoples who have access to a wide variety of edible types from the 1,400 species that occur in reef and adjacent waters. Inland peoples are more restricted in fishing opportunities.

In addition to game and fish, about half a million head of domesticated pigs and a similar number of poultry are consumed annually. Unfortunately, the pig is a major cultural element so that much of the pig meat is eaten at large sing-sings or ceremonial feasts and then mainly by adults. Poultry are prized more for their plumage for ceremonial dress than for eggs or meat. In consequence, neither the pig nor the hen makes an effective contribution to the daily protein intake.

There is no quantitative lack of food. The increasing needs of any family group are readily met by additional gardening effort. Qualitatively, there need be no lack of animal protein amongst lowland peoples, though the neglect of the fish potential is noticeable. Most groups are not seagoing, so that fishing is confined largely to waters very close to land. Amongst inland groups and highland peoples, protein shortages occur both in absolute and qualitative terms. This is specially the case in respect to nursing mothers and to children, post-weaning and on through adolescence. The difficulty is easy to meet, particularly in view of the large areas of unused pasture land suited to animal production, the potentials of fish foods, and the ease of growing peanuts and other useful vegetable sources of high quality protein.[2]

Food production methods, as distinct from crop types, in the different regions have many points of similarity. The basic system of agriculture is that of bush or grass fallow. Land is cleared and cultivated for one year or more and then allowed to revert to a natural vegetative cover. The period in crop depends partly on yields as affected by falling soil fertility, increasing incidence of weeds, plant disease and pests, and partly by land availability. The substantial dependence on sweet potato as a major crop forces rapid shifts to new areas. The system involves a major clearing effort each time a new garden is established. It is generally conservational in its effects, in that it tends to minimize physical and chemical degradation of soils. The native farmer is neither a true peasant tied to the continuous cultivation of a limited area, nor a true nomadic cultivator involved in shifting agriculture over wide areas so characteristic of many parts of the tropic world. Rather he is a farmer who practices a regular movement of cultivation within a clearly defined area.

Cultivation methods are primitive and similar everywhere. The stone axe and the digging stick were the traditional implements. The former has been largely replaced by steel knives and axes, while the latter is giving way slowly to the straight-handled steel spade and hoe. These innovations have lessened the work load but do not appear to have led to any significant increase in production per unit area or in total cultivation. Family needs basically control the extent of operations. Only a small proportion of production is used in barter or other forms of trade.

Gardening procedures are closely interwoven with social structures and culture patterns. Thus, there is a distinct sexual division of work, sometimes enforced by taboos particularly in more primitive areas. The clearing of land and its preliminary preparation is the responsibility of men. Planting, cultivation, tending, weeding and harvesting is the task of

[2] The Mission's recommendation on problems of diet is given in Chapter 7 under Health.

women. There are a few exceptions to this. Fertility cults which ascribe sexual characteristics to plants are responsible for one. Dry cultivation plants like the yam may be considered as male, and wet cultivation plants like the taro as female. In some areas where the yam is important, its production is the sole responsibility of men, who frequently compete to obtain the largest tuber by procedures involving intensive sub-surface cultivation and feeding.

Most root crops cannot be stored but must be consumed when ready or when lifted. The yam is the major exception. It is stored in special huts or spirit houses. The necessity for immediate consumption at maturity of most foods is an additional factor limiting cropping mainly to subsistence needs.

Although production methods have evolved in an exceedingly primitive society, without aid from agricultural science, the native farmers have developed a sound basic knowledge of the requirements of their crops. They are aware of the different fertility needs of these, and their consequent suitability to soil and climate. They are equally conscious of their varying cultivation requirements. The first has determined the type grown in the different regions. The second has been responsible for typical cultivation procedures for key crops. Depending primarily on roots and tubers, on gathering of fruit and sago palm, most people are still below the cereal-growing stage in their evolutionary development.

Thus, the sweet potato is the major crop of the cooler upland areas. In its cultivation, the whole of the topsoil is broken up and scooped into planting hills or mounds. Bananas have become the important lowland crop of areas with suitable rainfall. Plantation production has not commonly developed, the banana being incorporated into the garden or planted in small groves. Taro is the staple crop of the lowland rain forest areas of moderate fertility. Cultivation is minimal, ground being burned after clearing, and the taro tamped into shallow cylindrical holes with the bulk of the surface soil left undisturbed. Yams are most common on the well-drained soils of high mineral fertility, particularly those of volcanic origin. Soils are deeply worked prior to planting and during the growth period. Much attention is devoted to keeping the soil round the base of the vine as loose as possible to encourage tuber development. Cassava, as a salt tolerant plant, is characteristic of estuarine areas though by no means confined to these. It is planted in well-cultivated soils, often at the end of the first year's cropping as an insurance against periods of food shortage. These examples are indicative of the stage reached in agricultural knowledge and application (see Table 2).

Clearly defined natural regions are associated with differing types of subsistence and commercial agriculture. Very broadly, the Territory

TABLE 2: Crop Yields

(tons per acre)

	Lowlands and Islands[a]	Highlands[a]	Typical Tropical Countries
	Average	Average	Range
Bananas	10.1	10.1	5–15
Taro (Col)	4.4	3.5	2–5
Taro (Xen)	14.2	8.2	—
Sugar Cane	25.5	25.5	20–45
Yams	8.4	6.8	3–6
Cassava	27.0	7.4	4–15
Maize	1.9	1.5	1–1½
Sweet Potatoes	5.1	6.2	2–6

[a] The yields appear to be high and should not be considered as applicable to all areas.

SOURCES: Department of Agriculture, Stock and Fisheries; G. Wrigley, Tropical Agriculture, Batsford Ltd., London, 1961.

consists of three distinct geographic regions; the lowlands, the islands and the highlands. Each of these have their characteristic topography soils, climate, vegetative cover and peoples. It will be necessary to make frequent reference to them. More fundamentally, however, the Territory is divisible into five ecological zones, some of which are common to both lowlands and islands. These are: (1) coastal lowlands, (2) lowland swamps, (3) lowland grassland, savannah or savannah woodlands, (4) lowland rain forest and (5) the highlands. These ecological zones are of special significance to subsistence agriculture. In addition they determine the location and character of the various forms of commercial agriculture.

Coastal Lowlands. These are for the most part narrow non-swampy strips. The soils of this zone have been derived mostly from coral. They are sandy and of low fertility. Admixture with material of volcanic origin has improved them in some instances. They lie mostly along the beaches or the immediate neighborhood thereof. The coconut, banana and breadfruit are the important crops.

Coconuts play a dominant role and much of the natural vegetation has been replaced by coconut palms. Gardens grow some cassava and sweet potato with a little taro on wetter sites. Garden cultivation methods follow the bush-fallow system. Traditionally, cultivation of the coastal lowlands is allied with the use of inland gardens to supplement the more limited coastal potential. This dual form of farming has dwindled under the advent of westernization with some inland food production tending to be replaced by imported goods purchased for cash obtained from the sale of coconuts. This is specially true of several islands, particularly New Ireland.

The enervating climate and general ease of securing sufficient subsistence food for the family unit makes for a relatively unprogressive community. There is little incentive to devote special energy toward increasing the efficiency of agriculture in such congenial surroundings.

Lowland Swamps. The tidal and saline swamps provide considerable foraged food from stands of mangrove and nipa palms. Large bi-valve (mud oyster) and crab are specially valuable as subsistence foods. The fresh water swamps, which vary in their usefulness with the amount of seasonal flooding, are characterized by stands of sago palm. These cover very extensive areas of the Sepik, the lower Ramu, the mouth of the Fly on the Daru coast, and the Purari delta of Papua. The sago palm grows particularly well. Stems yield an average of 300 lbs. of crude starch when harvested just before flowering. Good stands permit the harvesting of 20 to 25 stems per acre per annum. In addition to thinning of natural stands to increase yields, native farmers recognize definite varieties or strains, and plant selected suckers or seedlings near their villages. Flowering is sometimes prevented to increase yields. Figures of up to 900 lbs. of crude starch per stem have been recorded from naturally sterile palms.

Though the sago palm has largely gone out of use for human food in other tropical countries, the large areas involved in the Territory where alternative agricultural possibilities are very limited, makes it the basic staple for the peoples of the lowland swamps, particularly in the Sepik.

As an adjunct to sago, gardening is practiced on river levees and any available cultivable land. These average less than 0.1 acres per person. Taro is the most important root grown, but wherever possible, sweet potato, yams and cassava are also cultivated. Sugar cane, bananas, paw-paws, coconuts and breadfruit play only a limited role. Some vegetables, notably amaranthus and chillies, are also produced.

In the riverine parts of the region, crocodile meat, fish and wild fowl supply acceptable additions to the diet and are bartered for special foods from more fortunately located peoples. The sago palm borer, which is found in almost every palm harvested, lends protein and flavor to an otherwise monotonous base diet.

Despite the extraordinarily difficult terrain, the wet, humid and generally enervating climate, the people tend to be larger and better developed than in most other regions. Records from a patrol of an area of the upper Sepik provide an example of the variety of plant food used by the people contacted.[3]

---

[3] The list comprises sago, taro, yams, banana, mami, sweet potato, peanuts, coconuts, cassava, breadfruit, beans, tomatoes, tulip, cabbages, pumpkins, ferns, amaranthus, bamboo shoots as well as many others not identified. Records of food of animal origin exhibited a similar variety, with crocodile making a major contribution.

Lowland Grassland, Savannah and Savannah Woodlands.
These are the undulating coastal plains, extending to the foothills of the
mountain ranges in the drier regions. The extensive grassland areas of the
lowland plains and plateaus of the Markham and Ramu are believed to
have evolved (in most cases) under the influence of forest removal for
cultivation and subsequent burning of regrowth by peoples in bygone
ages. Continued burning, to facilitate the hunting of small game and as a
defense against attack, has prevented reversion to forest even in areas
where the rainfall is high. The main species of pasture plants are kunai
grass and kangaroo grass, the former being the most widespread except
on the drier areas where the latter is more important. On wet sites,
Ischaemum, and in some localities Saccharums, occur extensively, often
associated with scattered Phragmites.

Within the grassland zone, the dry belts centered around Port Moresby
and between the Fly River and the border are more correctly designated
as savannah, with eucalypts as the tree dominants, or savannah woodlands, with melaleucas most numerous. Within each type and throughout
all the grassland areas, heavier tree growth, with some deciduous species,
occurs in gullies and river valleys. The Savannah country is virtually
unused.

All these relatively dry environments have necessitated the evolution of
special gardening techniques. Cultivation has to be more specialized than
on easier soil types and in wetter climates. Use is made of the contour for
water conservation. Thus, along the hillsides, rectangular beds are built
for cassava, yams and sweet potato by digging and overturning large
clods. This method is allied with banana cultivation on moist alluvia of
the scattered valleys. These are planted along with root crops. The lower
rainfall and consequent reduced leaching tends to permit the same areas
to be cultivated for longer periods than are typical for wetter zones. Thus,
on the better alluvia, gardens may be used three to five years before
shifting.

One special aspect of the grassland zone needs emphasis. Throughout,
regular burning of the grass cover is typical. This has proved harmful on
steeply sloping areas, being associated with sheet and gully erosion, and
the normal consequences thereof. However, this repeated burning has
not caused any marked soil degradation or loss on gentle slopes and level
grounds at low altitudes. Recovery of the grass cover is very rapid following the first rains, and sufficiently strong thereafter to prevent normal
erosion effects.

The zone as a whole is relatively unused, supporting a very low population density in relation to its proportion of cultivable land. Apart from
the greater difficulties of food production much of it has become unused

partly because of the high incidence of malaria, and partly because lowland plains have offered less natural protection from tribal enemies than have lands of more difficult access.

Lowland Rain Forest. This zone includes most of the non-swamp land from the coastal strip to the 3,000-feet altitude level. In parts, it extends right to the coast. The forest is floristically rich and luxuriant, with many affinities botanically to the Indo-Malayan region. It is three-tree layered, with the canopy at 120 feet or more with occasional emergent trees, a second layer at 75 feet and the third stratum at 20 to 30 feet. Beneath these are the shrub and ground layers.[4] This description emphasizes the almost fantastically difficult problem of hand clearing with the primitive equipment used. In preparation for gardening, the small trees are felled with axes and knives, and with the cut undergrowth, are piled and burnt around the larger trees, thus killing these gradually. Decay of dead trees thereafter is extremely rapid.

Gardens are scattered throughout the region on the forest-fallow pattern. The region exhibits a patchwork of garden plots, of regrowth, of secondary forest and of virgin forest. The regrowth consists of small quick growing softwoods such as figs, acacia and macaranga. In some places bamboo breaks develop.

Food production, apart from the heavy labor of clearing, is relatively easy throughout the zone. At one time, taro was the chief staple, but this has given way to the banana, sweet potato and cassava. The banana in particular now tends to be the major staple. Taro cuttings are planted in individual holes dug with the digging stick on the burnt surface. They develop under shade which diminishes as the tall trees die and collapse. Legumes and sweet potatoes are interplanted. The garden is allowed to revert to forest after one year's use, although bananas and paw-paws may continue to yield for a further period. Reversion is rapid, and normally the land is left from 10 to 15 years before the process is repeated. The average area cultivated is about 0.3 acres per person.

In localities where there is greater pressure on land the fallow period is shortened. In these circumstances new gardens can involve the removal of regrowth and secondary bush. When this is continued over several cycles, grass takes over. Under these conditions the forest edges retreat and grasslands of the type already described come into being.

Foraging for a wide variety of fruits, nuts and other edible plant material is a major part of subsistence agriculture in this zone. The forests yield limited numbers of game, both birds and animals. Altogether, the lowland forest zone supports a high proportion of the population.

[4] Robbins, R. G., Australian Territories Vol. 1, No. 6, 1960.

The Highlands. This zone is characterized by two different forest types, the montane rain forest and the montane cloud forest. The tropical rain forest of the lowlands gives way to the montane type at about the 3,000-foot level. Vines disappear, tree ferns replace palms and the forest structure is simplified to a two-tier strata. The complex includes oak, beech, pine and mixed forests of podocarp pines and broad leaf trees. At the lower altitudes, oak type forests predominate; at the higher, beech types take over. Above 9,000 feet a dramatic change occurs. All tropical features disappear in the true mist-shrouded montane cloud forest. Ecologically, this type shows close affinities to both warm and cool temperate rain forests of Australia and New Zealand. A single-tree layer with a compact canopy at 30 feet is made up of gnarled and crooked trees, festooned with a thick mantle of dripping mosses and liverworts. These also spread over the floor to form a thick spongy carpet. The atmosphere is damp, and the forest has a drab appearance brightened only by rhododendrons and orchids. Here is a silent haunt of the New Guinea birds of paradise.

Agriculture is confined to the montane rain forest zone. This is not all tree covered. A great deal of the lower forests have long since been cleared from the valley floors and easier mountain slopes up to the limits of native farming at about 8,500 feet. Large areas (at least 2 million acres) have been given over to grassland. Much of this involves dense stands of the tall sword grass and pit-pit. In the drier parts, short grass species have invaded the zone from the adjacent Markham and Ramu valleys. Small natural phragmitites, swamps and sedge bogs occur where drainage is impeded.[5]

Special mention must be made of the three-quarters of a million people who live in this unusual environment. They account for about 40 percent of the total population. In the Western Highlands contact with Europeans dates back only 30 years. Even now, some may not have made contact. A primitive, Stone Age folk, virtually cut off by precipitous mountains from the rest of mankind, they have developed an unusually efficient type of subsistence farming.

The people live in small villages. Each village has land-use rights to well-defined surrounding areas. Gardens are operated by families or individuals. Sweet potato is the dietary staple, accounting for about 90 percent by weight and more in calories of the adult diet. The remainder comes mainly from taro, green vegetables and maize. Sugar cane is also grown, mainly for chewing. Pork is consumed at organized sing-sings. These festive occasions are peculiar to the highland people. Extending

[5] Robbins, R. G., Proceedings of the Symposium on Humid Tropical Vegetation, Tjiawi, Unesco, Dec. 1958.

often over many days and in some cases involving many clan groups, they may result in the slaughter of 90 percent of the pig population so that years elapse before the number of pigs is again sufficient to allow another sing-sing.

The system of agriculture followed is best described as long-fallow cultivation. The extremely mountainous terrain, the scarcity of level land, and the generally higher population pressure has led to methods which are distinctly conservational in character. Gardens are cultivated for three to six and even ten years, before they are returned to long fallow for periods ranging from five to twenty years. Garden plots may enjoy short-fallow periods of a few months to two to three years, during which they are untended and grass cover becomes re-established. Many gardens are cultivated in this way four or five times before being abandoned to long fallow. The length of the cycle in each case is governed by crop yields and the incidence of disease and insect pests. Cycle length also varies with population pressure. Thus in the Chimbu area, the period under cultivation probably equals the period under fallow.

Crop rotation as distinct from land rotation plays a minor role. Restoration of fertility under fallow is aided by the planting of casuarina trees before abandonment. These add both nitrogen and humus, as well as providing useful timber for fencing, building and firewood. While the foregoing describes the general cultivation pattern, much variation exists from place to place.

Gardening methods likewise can be generally described. Land use begins with the clearing of forest, brush or grass. Burning of unwanted materials follows. Enclosure is the next essential step since all gardens must be protected from the depredations of pigs which are ubiquitous and commonly roam free. Protection is accomplished by building stake fences, often of casuarina wood obtained from the area to be enclosed. In some districts post and rail fences replace stakes.

Two main cultivation techniques are used. In the Western and Southern highlands, grass and other herbaceous material removed from the area is collected, and the whole of the surface cultivated to a depth of a few inches. The dead, partially composted herbage is then placed on the garden plots and covered with earth obtained from shallow drainage ditches dug between the heaps. The heaps or mounds are then planted. In areas where drainage and soil conservation are both problems, as in the Chimbu, drains 1 foot wide and 6–30 inches deep are dug down and across the slope at intervals of about 10 feet. The soil and subsoil from these drains is then thrown upon the intervening land to form raised garden beds.

In addition to the ubiquitous sweet potato, a wide variety of crops is planted. Maize is one of the first sown, usually on the perimeters of beds. It is harvested in three months. Sweet potatoes mature in four to eight months at lower altitudes but may take as long as 12 to 18 months in higher regions. Yields are high and can exceed 10 tons and even 15 tons per acre. A few tubers are harvested at a time so that bearing continues over several months. Taro and yams are used on suitable soils. Green vegetables of amaranthus, solanum and hibiscus types are commonly found, along with imported types such as cucumbers, squash, cabbage, onions, leeks, peas, beans, tomatoes and even potatoes. Sugar cane and bananas are of major importance below 7,000 feet. Bananas are planted in garden plots, usually one per plot. Groundnuts are of increasing importance and often have a whole garden plot assigned to them.

Since there are no distinct seasons in the highlands, planting of any crop occurs almost at any time. This is a key factor in ensuring a regular supply of food. Along with the variety of crops grown, it is also responsible for the picture presented by the average garden—a patchwork of neat plots of mixed crops at all stages of growth, and a particularly complete ground cover. Portions may even be in grass fallow. When the garden is abandoned, pigs are allowed to forage amongst remaining tubers and other edible material. Bananas and sugar cane are harvested for a time after abandonment.

In addition to gardening, tree crops are significant in highland subsistence farming. The most important species is the nut-bearing mountain pandanus. This grows wild at from 6,000 to 11,000 feet to supply a useful source of nuts supplementary to those obtained from cultivated groves. Groves are mainly about 6,000 feet. They are maintained by farmers living at lower levels. Highland breadfruit is widely eaten.

Apart from the domesticated pig and fowl there is a scarcity of animals, a fact that could account in part for the earlier prevalence of cannibalism. Hunting, in contrast with its importance in lower zones, is of minor importance here.

Improvement of Subsistence Agriculture. Two major weaknesses in subsistence agriculture need correction. In the first place, land-use methods must move very much further in the direction of soil conservation, fertility maintenance and efficiency. Secondly, production must be directed toward qualitative improvements in the diets as well as to meeting quantitative deficiencies that sometimes occur.

In respect to the first, it is true that the methods used today are conservational rather than destructive in character. It is equally true that they could be even more so. At present they avoid much of the harm of many other forms of shifting agriculture. However, into the concept and practice of rotation of land must be introduced the concept and practice of rotation of crops. The simple technique of the past and present will not suffice as population builds up and over-all food needs increase. It will suffice still less as more and more land is diverted from true subsistence farming to commercial farming based on perennial tree crops. It may be argued that the change needed is a long-term one, unimportant in the short run. This would be unrealistic. Any fundamental change in traditional farming patterns always takes a very long time to accomplish even in advanced and relatively enlightened societies. The 30-year gestation period of hybrid corn in the United States is a classical example of the time lag in agriculture. The time needed for basic changes is likely to be even greater in a primitive community. The time to begin the change is now.

With respect to the second requirement, qualitative deficiencies in the diet, particularly in the case of young age groups and of pregnant and nursing mothers, do exist in some areas. For better over-all health, growth and work ability, the excessive starchiness and bulkiness of the normal diets, the low level of protein intake, and the lack of high quality protein of animal and vegetable origin should be modified. Though famines are unknown, crop failures result in local food shortages from time to time. Improved methods and types of production could ensure against both these weaknesses.

Just how the two groups of problems are best approached is a matter for applied research. A great deal of experimentation is necessary to find just how to use the considerable bulk of information that has accrued from research in other tropical countries. Applied research is also essential to develop any new techniques necessary under the particular environments involved. Both approaches must be oriented to the unique cultures of the people concerned, in the handling of whom, no guidelines exist save those already evolved in the exceedingly short period of contact with the non-indigenous population.

On the straight technical side there are many guidelines. A good deal of effort must go into studying the problem of suitable crop rotations. The role of the legume needs special attention, both for use in rotation and during the fallow period. Manuring practices, possibly including that of composting, need close examination and evaluation. Contour farming methods superior to the present crude approaches need development. The role of tree crops, particularly leguminous trees, in conserving soil and improving fertility cannot be neglected.

The farm animal, as a factor in a balanced agriculture aiming both at full utilization and conservation of resources, must be introduced. The use of the ruminant is basic to better methods of land use. Likewise, the role of the pig and the hen, with respect to their potential contributions both as food and as aids to fertility maintenance and increase, cannot be ignored. All these innovations involve "on-the-spot" testing and research.

Fish can play a major role in improving diets. Methods of achieving a greater availability of this food should be devised both for coastal and inland peoples (see section on Fisheries).

The introduction of new crops needs great expansion not only to test the value and place of species not presently grown, but to take advantage of the possible superiority of strains and varieties of existing types which have been improved by selection elsewhere and not yet tried in the Territory. This work must focus on root crops of higher protein content, on fruits and nuts, as well as the whole gamut of cereals and legumes which, because of their storability, could make a substantial contribution to the food production picture.

Concurrently with research into new and improved forms of production, the problem of storage, preserving and use must be tackled. Existing crops, with the exception of yams, are highly perishable. Methods of improving the storability of existing major staples should be developed as a prerequisite to marketing. Improved storability could indeed be the key for a gradual transition from subsistence gardening to more market-oriented commercial farming. This field will become of increasing importance as subsistence farmers move into commercial farming involving both barter and cash sales.

Research alone will not accomplish the objectives; the key to application is extension, which must be oriented toward as rapid an introduction of improved methods as possible. Already astonishing progress has been made by the extension personnel of the Territory, particularly in view of the short period of contact and the special problems created by the character and customs of the people and the difficult terrain. Despite the wide range of difficulties that have to be surmounted, sufficient has been done to indicate that much greater progress can be achieved. The particular needs of extension both in the context of subsistence farming as well as in other aspects of the agricultural economy will be presented later. At this stage, it is important to stress that further advance in the efficiency of subsistence farming will be small and slow unless geared to an efficient, development-oriented extension service.

In this orientation, the special role of the women, who are responsible not only for most of the day-to-day farming operations but also for decision-making on key agronomic issues, cannot be ignored. Women, too, need to be taught to prepare and cook and use new and strange crops such as peanuts, soya beans and pigeon peas for these to become acceptable. Indeed, ways and means of getting improved methods through to the "Meri" is a prerequisite to lifting subsistence farming to higher levels of efficiency.[6]

Furthermore, any improvement program in subsistence agriculture would be unrealistic if it did not take into account the overriding importance of a motivating force of considerable strength. It is unlikely that any significant changes in the pattern of land use will follow mere exhortations on the score of improved conservation and crop yields. This is likely to be true even if based on adequate demonstration of the superiority of new methods. Equally, persuasive efforts to increase efficiency through new and better crops must fail if based solely on the score of improved nutrition. Much stronger incentives are needed, and the obvious approach is through the cash economy.

It is recommended that improvements in the purely subsistence sector of agriculture continue through the introduction of suitable crop rotations and by the introduction and testing of new and improved types of crop; through development of more intensive applied research; through expansion of the extension service; and through the concurrent advancement of the indigenous farmer into the field of commercial agriculture.

Commercial Agriculture

Commercial agriculture in the Territory takes two main forms—the plantation production of perennial crops for export and the production of dual-purpose crops, surpluses of which can be sold or bartered. Until recent years, plantation production was almost entirely in the hands of European operators but indigenous farmers now play an increasing part. The production of dual-purpose crops is almost entirely confined to native farmers.

True plantation agriculture began shortly before the turn of the century with the establishment of coconut plantations in coastal regions by a few adventurous white settlers, traders and companies on both mainland and islands. Rubber plantations came next, and then some cocoa and coffee. The planting of Arabica coffee by European farmers followed the opening of the highlands for agricultural development after World War II.

Commercial agriculture has had two major setbacks. The first was during the economic recession of the 1930s which reduced the price of copra to unprofitable levels. The second was during World War II when international trade was disrupted, a large proportion of experienced plantation operators killed, plantations were abandoned and trees and equipment seriously damaged. After the war, rehabilitation was rapid

[6] See the Mission's recommended program for Adult Education in Chapter 6.

under the stimulus of post-war prices and war damage compensation from the Australian Government.

The extent of current operations of the non-indigenous sector can be gauged from the following table showing the number of holdings, area (whether freehold or leased from the Administration) and land use.

These data, contained in Tables 3 and 4, highlight several points. Of the agricultural products, all of the rubber, about 75 percent of the copra, 75 percent of the cocoa and about 60 percent of the coffee is produced by European farmers. Yet the holdings of these operators number only 1,181 and the total land area under their control is just over 1 million acres— less than 1 percent of the total land area, and only about 5 percent of the land estimated capable of economic development.

Some holdings are farmed by the Administration. Many holdings are too small to make economic units and are combined in operation. The

TABLE 3: Non-indigenous Agricultural Holdings, 1962 (year ended March 31)

	No. of Holdings	Land Tenure (thousand acres)			Land Use (thousand acres)	
		Freehold	Leasehold	Total	Cropped	Unused
Lowlands	535	98	445	543	138	405
Islands	463	310	125	435	214	221
Highlands	183	—	53	53	10	43
Total	1,181	408	623	1,031	362	669

SOURCE: Production Bulletin No. 4, Bureau of Statistics.

TABLE 4: Non-indigenous Production, 1961/62 (year ended March 31)

Crop	Number of Holdings	Area[a] (thousand acres)	Production (tons)
Coconuts[b]	667	261	83,500
Cocoa[b]	427	98	7,000
Rubber	57	31	4,500
Coffee	236	9	2,000
Peanuts	58	6	2,300

[a] Including immature trees.

[b] Holdings with interplanted coconuts and cocoa have been included twice (under both coconuts and cocoa); figures are therefore not comparable with those in Table 3.

SOURCE: Production Bulletin No. 4, Bureau of Statistics.

available statistics give the number of owners, lessees and share farmers as only 325. However, a further 718 Europeans, Asians or people of mixed race are engaged in farm work as managers, foremen or workers. About 40,000 indigenous laborers are employed by European farmers.

The tenure of this land is of special interest. Only about 40 percent is freehold, the balance being leased from the Administration. Of the freehold land, 75 percent is located in the islands, 25 percent on the mainland. Europeans own no land in the highlands, all farms being leased from the Administration. Most of the freehold land was purchased prior to World War I. It is a firm policy that only the Administration can purchase (alienate) land from native owners.

The land-use picture is equally instructive (see Tables 3 and 4). Only 35 percent of the land under European control has been used for cropping. Even allowing that much may not be suited to economic production, it is obvious that a substantial margin exists for further development within existing European holdings.

Except as laborers on plantations, the indigenes contributed little to commercial farm production prior to World War II. Up to this time their participation in cash crop farming was haphazard and largely ineffective. They were disinterested in producing crops for any other purpose than immediate food needs or as barter for articles such as cooking equipment, baskets, spears, etc. There had been some attempts to persuade them to plant tree crops, notably coconuts, and to make copra for sale from surplus nuts. For a time compulsion was used. The main commercial aspect of native farming before the war was a limited sale of root and garden produce to the Administration and to planters.

Since the war and particularly since 1956, the change has been phenomenal. Continued association with the cash economy, helped considerably by contact with the military forces of several countries during the war, resulted in a willingness on the part of many indigenes to use their time and energy in turning coconuts to copra, in planting new areas, and in trying new crops. The war also aided by opening up the interior. With peace, the Administration engaged in a progressive policy of encouragement of native farming for cash. By 1956, much experience had accumulated from the performance of mission stations, plantations and the experiment stations. Concurrently, considerable progress was made in building up an efficient agricultural extension service and in developing an understanding of how to assist the native people.

A very good example was set from 1951 onward by the success of the Tolai people of the Gazelle Peninsula. This group rapidly became involved in commercial farming based on coconuts and cocoa, as well as garden crops and pig-rearing.

By 1962, native participation in commercial production reached impressive levels. They held nearly 50 percent of the area in coconuts and produced about 25 percent of the copra production. They controlled 60 percent of the land in coffee and produced over 40 percent of the coffee output. They farmed 17 percent of the cocoa areas and produced somewhat less than 25 percent of all cocoa (see Tables 5, 8 and 10).

Dual-purpose crops also came into use to an increasing degree. Native farmers grew some 3,000 tons of peanuts of which 261 tons were sold in 1962. Rice provided 342 tons for sale. Some 3,000 tons of garden crops, mostly roots, were sold. The quantity bartered is unknown.

Description of production systems and of programs for increased production are most conveniently handled on a commodity basis. Thus, attention will be directed first to the five main export crops (coconuts, cocoa, coffee, rubber, peanuts and passion fruit), and then to potential crops such as tea, pyrethrum, oil palm, bananas and others. In all cases, the Mission has attempted to be as precise as possible in its recommended program, believing that it is more meaningful to state tentative figures, which can be changed in the light of experience, than it is to rest on the safe ground of generalities.

Coconuts. The first coconut plantations were established in the Gazelle Peninsula, when it was under German control. The German administration encouraged copra production, as did Australia, in its zone. By the end of World War I, there were 130,000 acres of palms from which there was an export of approximately 23,000 tons of copra. Copra has dominated the export scene since that time, except for the ten years between 1930 and 1940, when low prices and a large gold output relegated copra to a secondary position. Though once again losing ground in relative importance due to the advent of new crops, it still earns about two and one-half times as much as cocoa, the next most important commodity. The acreage and volume of production (which are still increasing) and the main areas concerned are shown in Table 5. However, unless the rate of planting is further increased, production will decrease as more palms become non-productive from age.

The total acreage stands at over 500,000 and total output at about 112,000 tons.[7] Production comes from four main districts—New Britain, New Ireland, Bougainville and Madang on the mainland. These account for 68 percent of the coconut area and 82 percent of production. This high share is due to the high proportion of mature palms and the high yields in the specially favorable environments concerned.

The acreage of palms under indigenous control is stated to be almost as great as that on plantations. Copra output, however, is significantly

[7] Including oil in a copra equivalent.

TABLE 5: Coconut Acreage and Copra Production, 1961/62[a]

District	Mature and Immature Acreage (thousand acres)			Production (thousand tons)		
	Non-indigenous	Indigenous	Total	Non-indigenous	Indigenous	Total
Central	17.1	14.5	31.6	5.3	1.0	6.3
Gulf	1.6	28.1	29.7	.6	1.3	1.9
Milne Bay	15.3	30.0	45.3	2.9	3.3	6.2
Northern	[b]	2.8	2.8[b]	[b]	.1	.1[b]
Western	[b]	4.2	4.2[b]	[b]	.1	.1[b]
Bougainville	30.8	20.8	51.6	13.3	3.1	16.4
Madang	35.2	16.2	51.4	11.0	1.5	12.5
Manus	11.5	6.0	17.5	2.7	.5	3.2
Morobe	4.9	8.5	13.4	[b]	.5	.5[b]
New Britain	81.2	75.3	156.5	26.8	10.8	37.6
New Ireland	59.7	28.6	88.3	19.6	6.2	25.8
Sepik	2.5	17.6	20.1	[b]	.5	.5[b]
Acreage or Production not Accounted for	1.5		1.5	1.3		1.3
Total for Territory	261.3	252.6	513.9	83.5	28.9	112.4
Percent Immature	16.5	42.6	29.3			

[a] For non-indigenous sector year ended March 31; for indigenous sector year ended June 30.
[b] Figures incomplete or not available.

SOURCES: Production Bulletin No. 4, Bureau of Statistics; Annual Extension Report 1961/62 of Department of Agriculture, Stock and Fisheries.

lower than on plantations as only the surplus, after subsistence, is available for sale, excess nuts are not always harvested and copra tends to be made only intermittently when cash is needed. Incentives are inadequate to maintain regular harvesting schedules. Transport difficulties from some coastal plantings are great. It is estimated that an additional 10,000 tons of copra a year could be derived from existing native stands in their present condition.[8] Also, a much higher proportion of the native-owned trees, as compared to plantation trees, are still immature, the figure being approximately 44 percent as against 17 percent. Production efficiency is also a factor. Surveys indicate that half of the native acreage has been planted haphazardly so that palms are not properly spaced for maximum yields. And at least 10 percent are so crowded, due to germination of nuts where they fall, that they do not bear at all.[8]

[8] Department of Agriculture, Stock and Fisheries.

There have been several specific deterrents to plantation growth. Initially, low prices of the 1930s—when copra fell to £A5 per ton—put an end to the previous high planting rate. Profitable prices since World War II have not been reflected in increased output. Planters have regarded coconuts as a wasting asset, so that replanting activities have left much to be desired. This is evident from the age distribution of existing plantation palms. About 13 percent planted before 1900 are now senescent or senile; 21 percent dating from 1900 to 1914 have passed their prime; only 53 percent established between 1915 to 1950 are in their prime; while 13 percent planted since 1950 are juvenile or just beginning to bear.[9] Finally, the stresses of World War II, political uncertainties of post-war years, credit problems and the long period of gestation have discouraged investment in this crop.

Production Methods. The coconut palm is easy to grow. Selected nuts are sprouted in nurseries. Young palms are set out on cleared land at 50 to 70 per acre. Until the palms rise well above the ground cover, hand weeding is necessary. Thereafter they require little attention especially when leguminous ground-cover crops are established and cattle used to control their growth.

Diseases are few and losses from this cause negligible. Insect pests, notably the Rhinoceros beetle and the Black Palm weevil are troublesome in some districts and control measures are often necessary during the establishing phase. Scapanes species is also important.

Little labor is required on established plantations, one man handling 10 to 15 acres. Copra is sun or artificially dried. Palms begin to bear in the seventh year, attain maximum yield at ten years, and begin to decline at 50 to 60 years. Economic life extends beyond this point under very favorable conditions as on Bougainville where palms planted over 70 years ago are still the heaviest yielding and most profitable in the Territory.

The yield of copra per acre on plantations averages 7 cwts. There is considerable variation with districts. Thus the plantations of Manus and Milne Bay yield less than 5 cwts., New Ireland 7.8 cwts., New Britain 8.2 cwts., and Bougainville 10.2 cwts. per acre. Individual estates have recorded outputs of over 1 ton per acre. At £A60 per ton, gross cash return averages about £A20 per acre. Of recent years, considerable areas of coconuts have been underplanted with cocoa. On suitable soil types, this additional tree crop does very well, under the shade of the palms, to yield an additional gross cash return of £A50 to £A70 per acre.

Background to Development. Consideration of the role of coconuts in the future, particularly from the viewpoint of increased output, must take

[9] Coconut Products Ltd.—private communication.

cognizance of several interacting factors, some favorable, others unfavorable.

As the first unfavorable factor relative to other important alternatives, copra production is an extensive form of land use. Yields and gross returns are low and not particularly attractive except in large acreages. Almost alone amongst the major crops of the world, coconuts have not benefited from any major technological advances. Compared with other crops few gains have been recorded from selection or breeding for higher yields, use of fertilizers, or from mechanizing either production or processing. The crop involves a long time lag between investment and full return so that investment is not attractive except on a long-term basis. On the marketing side, copra suffers seriously from competition of edible oils, such as soya bean, which have benefited from technological improvements so that they are being produced with increasing efficiency at lower costs. Thus output of soya bean oil increased about 250 percent in the last 20 years, while coconut oil expanded less than 30 percent.

Serious as these weaknesses are, full attention should be paid to the advantages of coconut production. Establishment costs are low, requiring relatively little labor and cash. Maintenance costs are negligible once the plantation is in full production. Harvesting requires little labor. Both establishment and production lend themselves to contractual arrangements, the former on the basis of the number of viable trees at a specified age, and the latter on that of tons of copra harvested, so that even supervision needs can be small. The crop requires little technical knowledge. It is one that is well understood by the indigenous population which attributes special wisdom to the tall palm and its fruit: a nut will never fall and hurt a human because "it has eyes to see." The nut represents both food and "cash in the bank." Coconuts too do not necessarily involve monoculture. Costs of establishment and maintenance can be reduced, and returns per area unit expanded, by using the palm as a shade tree or a companion crop. On the marketing side, coconut oil has many strengths. It is used for a very wide range of products and is interchangeable with other edible oils. Both qualities make it unlikely that it will be subject to quantitative marketing restrictions which threaten or restrain the expansion of other export crops. Major copra producing countries—the Philippines, Indonesia, Ceylon and India—are faced with much more intensive pressures on land use than is the Territory. Price-wise, examination of the several market variables suggests that the long-term outlook for copra is good, though a gradual fall below the average price of recent years can be expected. A corresponding fall is also likely for competitive oils and fats since world supplies of these are likely to increase somewhat faster than demand. Within this picture, Territory copra should be able

TABLE 6: Coconut Development Program

(acres)

| Year | Indigenous Sector | | Non-indigenous Sector | | Total |
	"Normal"	Additional	"Normal"	Additional	
1964/65	15,000	4,000	5,000	6,000	30,000
1965/66	15,000	6,000	5,000	9,000	35,000
1966/67	15,000	10,000	5,000	10,000	40,000
1967/68	15,000	10,000	5,000	10,000	40,000
1968/69	15,000	10,000	5,000	10,000	40,000
1969/70	15,000	10,000	5,000	5,000	35,000
1970/71	15,000	10,000	5,000	5,000	35,000
1971/72	15,000	10,000	5,000	5,000	35,000
1972/73	15,000	10,000	5,000	5,000	35,000
1973/74	15,000	10,000	5,000	5,000	35,000
Total	150,000	90,000	50,000	70,000[a]	360,000

[a] Includes 20,000 acres in new estates interplanted with cocoa.

to maintain a strong competitive position. In addition, the existence of the Copra Board's price stabilization fund of £A3.8 million provides a special insurance against extreme price decline.

Planting of coconuts will not depend only upon the relative investment potentials and price outlooks. In many of the coastal areas and on many of the lowland rain forest soils, the coconut is the obvious crop of choice in many instances and the only choice in others.[10] People of these zones will be better off with a modest income from copra than without any income at all.

Development Program. From discussions with the Administration, it is apparent that a development-oriented policy for expanding coconut plantings has not received very much attention. The Department of Agriculture estimates that European plantings have ranged between 3,500 acres and 8,000 acres, with an average of 5,000 acres annually over the last eight years. During the same period, indigenous plantings are estimated to have ranged from 3,000 acres to 18,000 acres annually and are likely to level out at an annual rate of 15,000 acres. Both situations have eventuated without any special policy other than advice and encouragement to indigenous farmers.

These figures (listed as "normal" in Table 6) have become the base of what might be termed the Administration's program for the years ahead. It is necessary to stress that normal plantings on plantations are merely replantings, barely sufficient to maintain the present size of this sector. Similarly, normal plantings for the indigenes merely involve continuation of what is estimated to be the present rate of planting.

[10] African oil palm would provide an alternative (subject to further testing).

Taking all factors into consideration the Mission believes that it is neither desirable nor necessary to remain content with the present rate of plantings, and that a definite set of objectives together with ways and means of insuring these, are important to the expansion of the coconut industry. It is clear that land and labor are available, but to bring about a substantial expansion the Administration will need to prepare a plan of action including adoption of policies to encourage and provide incentives to plant, gear the extension program to the size and quality needed to get the job done, and provide credit or see that it is available on terms needed to meet the requirements of the program.

In order to clarify the inputs or needs for an expanded program, the Mission has projected planting objectives that encompass both the so-called normal planting activities and additional plantings to substantially increase production of copra. A ten-year planting program to this end is set out in Table 6. Ten years is a long-term view but in coconuts, which take ten years to come into mature production, a long view is necessary. Action taken in the first years sets the base for and determines the pace or rate of plantings thereafter. It is important that, as experience is obtained, annual adjustments, upward and downward, should be made in the program. It should also be stressed that in setting out a precise program for this, as well as for other crops, the Mission does so believing that the suggested rate of plantings is reasonable of attainment but the program could be larger or smaller, depending on the emphasis, effort and funds given it by the Administration.

The targets envisage the continuation of normal planting plus additional planting that would rise from 10,000 acres in 1964/65 to 20,000 acres in 1966/67 and thereafter; from 1969/70 onward the level of additional planting would be 15,000 acres. After ten years, total new plantings under the program would amount to 360,000 acres—equal to approximately 70 percent of the now existing acreage. However, 75,000 acres would represent replanting requirements of which 25,000 would be in the indigenous and 50,000 in the non-indigenous sector.

The target must be regarded not merely in terms of more acres of coconuts.[11] It envisages maximum association between coconut and cocoa as a means of maximizing returns, and in providing a better distribution of labor costs, income and investment risk. As much as possible of both normal and additional plantings should involve this concept. To the extent of 20,000 acres, the copra program is intimately bound to the cocoa program which follows later.

[11] See also the Cattle Section for a discussion of the potential for cattle on coconut plantations.

Plantings by Non-indigenous Farmers. The total new planting target for plantations amounts to 120,000 acres, of which 50,000 acres represent replanting needs and the balance additional acreage, which is phased to occur at a less rapid rate in the second five years. Several factors of key importance will determine whether these levels are reached. Some of these, such as land tenure organization and services, are common to all development programs for agriculture and as such are handled separately in this report. Others are specific. The first involves land. Much under-developed land is already in the hands of the Europeans and the Administration (see Table 7). While some of this may not be particularly suitable for coconuts the first requirement is to survey available land resources so as to delineate areas that can be used. Only on the basis of such knowledge can planning be effective and the necessary steps taken to stimulate development. Since the total number of properties involved is small this is not a big task.

The second specific factor is the "stand-still" attitude of planters. Considering the barrier to development that this represents, there should be a careful re-appraisal of all leasehold agreements with a view to ensuring that land use and management is in accordance with development clauses. If necessary and possible, these clauses should be strengthened. New leases should contain clauses which will stimulate planting. Every effort must also be made to ensure that owners of freehold land develop their holdings up to the production potentials.

Some real incentive, however, will be needed to encourage additional plantings. Even the anticipated normal schedule of replantings is unlikely to be obtained without this. The most effective incentive is likely to be

TABLE 7: Land Potential for Cocoa and/or Coconut Development

(acres)

District	Freehold & Leasehold	Indigenous Owned	Crown Land	Total
Bougainville	20,000	150,000	—	170,000
Northern[a]	25,000	135,000	66,000	226,000
New Britain	30,000	360,000	—	390,000
New Ireland[a]	25,000	20,000	—	45,000
Total[b]	100,000	665,000	66,000	831,000

[a] Some of this is better suited to rubber.
[b] Other districts, i.e., Manus, Morobe, Central and Sepik have land reserves suitable mainly for coconut; Madang District has land suitable for cocoa and coconut development.

SOURCE: Department of Agriculture, Stock and Fisheries.

credit. The amount needed will not be great. Estimates have been based on £A5 per acre for replanting or planting without clearing, and £A15 per acre for new plantings involving clearing. The average need is assumed to be £A10 per acre. It is also assumed that 50 percent of the replantings and all the additional plantings may require credit of this magnitude. In addition, a total of £A16 per acre will be needed for maintenance over a four-year establishment period. Calculated in this way, the planters' total credit needs for 120,000 acres could amount to £A2.5 million over the ten years, of which £A1.5 million would be needed for plantings during the first five years.

Planting by Indigenous Farmers. The total of new plantings for the indigenous sector is set at 240,000 acres, of which 25,000 acres more or less would be required to maintain existing acreage. Of the total plantings 150,000 acres represent normal plantings and 90,000 acres are additional. This planting falls into four main categories. It may be haphazard individual effort; it may be on a more organized basis involving village concentrations; it may be part of a definite settlement program; or it may be through plantation production by entrepreneurs.

Planting by individuals is likely to continue without a special program but it should be encouraged. The potential contribution of individual effort to the over-all program could be important, but the Administration, through well-directed extension, should make every effort to minimize its haphazard character insofar as this involves poor planting practices, the use of unsuitable soils and irregular harvests.

The second method, based on village concentrations, presents the greatest short-term potential in a true development sense. It envisages the planting of economically viable family units of at least 10 to 15 acres in suitable village locations. Clearing and planting could be effected without hiring labor. Continued living by the families in established homes obviates the need for housing provision, subsistence and cash allowances. Credit, however, would be needed to cover the cash cost of establishment and maintenance for the non-bearing years. Sample budgets[12] indicate that a 15-acre unit becomes economically viable seven to eight years after commencement, debt free in 11 to 13 years and provides a net cash income of £A200 to £A300 per annum thereafter. Where cocoa is interplanted the surplus is considerably greater than this.

The contribution of the third method, through land settlement, will depend upon the extent to which the settlement approach to development is adopted. If the Mission's recommendation that this approach be confined to a small-scale trial basis is accepted, it is unlikely to contribute large acreages to the coconut program in the next five years. Assuming,

[12] Department of Agriculture, Stock and Fisheries.

however, that smallholder cocoa/coconut units are involved in whatever is done in settlement, eight-acre holdings of this type will involve a total credit provision of about £A750 each.[13] This is about six times the amount needed for 15 acres of coconuts under the village concentration system. The difference arises from the need to provide housing materials, subsistence and cash allowances because of the transfer of people to completely new areas. In estimating credit needs for this coconut program, however, the same credit allowance is provided as for village concentration units since the special costs of settlement are fairly chargeable against settlement as a method and not against copra development *per se*.

The possibility of establishing indigenous-owned plantations recognizes the existence of a few individuals with the necessary background, capacity and interest to develop small coconut plantations as entrepreneurs. It is likely that the number of these will increase. Their main need will be credit, and this would be required at the same level and on terms similar to those applicable to European planters. Provision must be made for this.

In calculating credit needs of the indigenous sector, it is assumed that half the normal plantings and all the additional plantings will need the stimulus of credit. These plantings are estimated at about 165,000 acres. Taking the "village concentration unit" as a base, establishment and other capital costs[14] will require £A6 per acre, and maintenance costs[15] over the non-bearing years £A2.3 per acre or a total of £A8.3 per acre. Some provision, however, must be made for additional credit to those willing and able to speed up operations by hiring labor in clearing, planting and weeding. By making an over-all credit allowance of £A10 per acre all needs should be covered. On this basis, the amount totals £A1.65 million. An additional £A350,000 should cater for entrepreneurs making a total credit requirement of the native sector of £A2 million. Taking an over-all view and bearing in mind the many unknowns involved, a total capital injection of about £A4.5 million should suffice for both the European and the native farmers.

Implementation should result in increased production of copra from new plantings of 38,000 tons in the year the program is completed. Thereafter, output will increase as palms mature (in a further ten years) to an annual additional output of 128,000 tons, worth £A7.7 million annually in increased export revenue.[16] Returns are based on the conservative price of £A60 per ton.

[13] Department of Agriculture, Stock and Fisheries.

[14] Drier, tools, seed nuts and pest control.

[15] Tools, insecticides.

[16] The quantities mentioned in this paragraph are not strictly comparable with those given in Table 30 on page 172, since the latter also reflect the output of old trees.

The question of adequate staffing to attain the targets has been left until last because of the intimate association of coconuts and cocoa, the next commodity to be dealt with. Provision has been made in staff projections for an additional 26 field officers and 100 intermediaries for the coconut program alone. To a large degree their efforts will complement those of the field staff of 80 plus 600 intermediaries allocated to the cocoa program. With an extension force of this magnitude, a program of the size outlined should be attainable.

Cocoa. This crop was introduced by the German administration shortly after 1900. Although present-day cocoa production is small, amounting to less than 1 percent of world output in 1961/62, the commodity has moved to second place as a source of export revenue. Exports reached the 1,000-ton mark in 1954/55. Since then annual growth has been fast; in 1961/62, 10,000 tons were produced and in 1962/63 exports exceeded 14,000 tons.

The island of New Britain contributes more than half of the output. While new plantings have been made in all districts and are spreading to areas not previously used for the crop, the rate of new planting has been greatest in the Northern District and in New Ireland. The expansion trend is reflected in the fact that in 1961/62 the mature acreage was matched by an equal acreage of immature cocoa. The ground work has thus been laid for a considerable expansion in output irrespective of further plantings.

European growers operate on between 400 and 450 holdings, with approximately 98,000 acres of planted cocoa. The crop has taken on well with indigenes, over 5,000 of whom have planted 20,000 acres.

Production Methods. The soils and climate where cocoa is recommended suit the crop admirably from the viewpoint of both yield and quality of product. The main planting material has been derived from the Trinitario complex. Mature stands of sole-planted cocoa yield an average of about 800 lbs. of dried beans per acre. As much as 2,000 lbs. per acre are obtained on some estates on Bougainville.

Cocoa is grown as a sole crop or is planted under coconuts. The latter method accounts for about 75 percent of European plantings. The standard practice under the sole-planting system is to clear and burn the forest cover and plant Leucaena glauca to provide shade for cocoa seedlings, which are underplanted about six months later. The shade is reduced as the cocoa trees mature, until about 50 percent of sunlight strikes the crop. An important variation of this method involves a partial clearing of the forest, the simultaneous planting of Leucaena and cocoa seedlings, and the subsequent killing of the remaining natural trees as the Leucaena takes over shading responsibility. This allows earlier establish-

TABLE 8: Cocoa Acreage and Production, 1961/62[a]

District	Acres (Mature and Immature)			Tons of Dry Beans		
	Non-indigenous	Indigenous	Total	Non-indigenous	Indigenous	Total
Central	1,378	31	1,409	39	[b]	39
Milne Bay	[b]	34	34[b]	[b]	[b]	[b]
Northern	6,335	2,024	8,359	79	20	99
Bougainville	13,090	2,079	15,169	1,655	99	1,754
Madang	13,194	964	14,158	1,046	21	1,067
Morobe	2,746	769	3,515	176	6	182
New Britain	49,875	13,394	63,269	3,686	1,943	5,629
New Ireland	9,674	540	10,214	260	70	330
Acreage or Production not Accounted for	1,621	147	1,768	31	2	33
Total for Territory	97,913	19,982	117,895	6,972	2,161	9,133

[a] For non-indigenous sector year ended March 31; for indigenous sector year ended June 30.
[b] Figures incomplete or not available.
SOURCES: Production Bulletin No. 4, Bureau of Statistics; Annual Extension Report 1961/62 of Department of Agriculture, Stock and Fisheries.
NOTE: Small acreages are also grown in the Gulf, Manus and Sepik districts.

ment of the cocoa, and less disturbance of the natural biological balance. A further modification is to combine complete removal of shade with the use of artificial fertilizers as a method of obtaining very high yields from mature stands. This technique, however, is still in the testing stage.

In the combination of copra and cocoa production, the Territory has led the world. Cocoa seedlings are underplanted in the coconut plantations to take advantage of the ideal shade conditions provided by the high canopy of the palms. Most underplanting has occurred on old coconut plantations, where the process is often speeded up by the sowing of tropical kudzu as a cover crop to improve the soil nitrogen status. The two crops may also be combined in new coconut plantations, the cocoa seedlings being underplanted about three years after the palms. Apart from the obvious cash advantages of a two-crop economy, these systems confer mutual operational advantages. Coconuts are easier to gather, labor utilization is better spread, and the problem of weed control of both crops is lessened.

Cocoa trees begin to bear in the third year and reach maturity by the eighth. They have an estimated life of 40 years under favored conditions and on poorer soils with lower rainfall a more realistic estimate is 25 to

30 years. Territory cocoa is remarkably free from serious disease hazards. Witch's broom, swollen shoot and cushion gall, which often decimate or seriously damage plantations in other cocoa producing countries, do not occur. Die-back[17] and black-pod disease exist but are under adequate control. Insect pests can be troublesome. Weevils are the most important. Longicorn beetles and capsids also cause damage.

The Department of Agriculture has established an excellent research center at Keravat where the work on selection, breeding, agronomy, vegetative propagation and fermentation has been of a very high standard. The Department has considerable experience in developing cocoa production amongst indigenes, its operations in the Tolai area of the Gazelle Peninsula being quite outstanding. These have set the pattern for large-scale development of the industry by the native sector. It has provided invaluable guidance to European operators. The Department also exercises a major measure of control and direction of the industry through the registration of all growers and inspection of produce for export.

Background to Development. Market potentials are of key importance in determining the scope for increased cocoa production. It is unfortunate that this commodity, for which the country is so well adapted, tends to be in over supply. World production is well over the 1 million ton mark,[18] a figure that has prompted efforts recently to secure international agreement on production and marketing controls.[19] Though no action resulted, there is a possibility that an agreement restrictive to Territory development could eventuate. If the rise in world consumption would be about 4 percent per annum in the next decade and the increase in world production would be kept within this limit, implying a reduction of the rate of increase of production from the 5 percent rate over the last ten years, world output in 1970 could still reach 1.6 million tons. This estimate illustrates the magnitude of the problem. While it is not unreasonable to expect that a commodity agreement would permit the Territory, as a relative newcomer in the field, to obtain some share of the increased output, there could be a definite limit to the extent of her participation in world trade.

Of some importance is the favorable position of the Territory in respect to world "flavor" cocoa production.[20] Alone, among 17 countries producing this type, the Territory has been increasing its output significantly. Since the 1930s the share of world demand for flavor cocoa has ranged

[17] Since the Mission completed its field work, reports of extensive outbreaks of die-back in the Gazelle Peninsula have been received.

[18] Figures quoted here and in the next paragraph are in metric tons.

[19] International Cocoa Conference, Geneva, November 1963.

[20] The proposal at the Geneva Conference was to exclude "flavor" cocoa from control.

between 7 and 10 percent of that for all cocoa. Projecting flavor cocoa's share at 8.5 percent of all cocoa, the world flavor consumption by 1970 could be 135,000 tons against a present level of about 85,000 tons. In the event that production from other countries continues to stagnate or, at the best, to increase only slightly, the potential market available to the Territory could lie between 45,000 tons and 60,000 tons of flavor cocoa annually.[21]

To what extent the Territory can succeed in becoming a major supplier of flavor cocoa depends on three main factors: first, the genetic make-up of the cocoa tree population which is being closely watched by competent staff; second, the standards observed in harvesting, handling and processing which at present leave a lot to be desired; and third, market developments which point in the direction of less emphasis on the traditional use of flavor cocoa for special purposes versus increasing demand for high-quality base cocoa.

Rather than concentrating all efforts on producing a high proportion of flavor cocoa, the Territory would be well advised to study the experience of leading base cocoa producers. Processing in these countries is carried out in individual smallholder units with close supervision of final grading and inspection. Decentralized processing has the advantage of minimizing the time lapse between the breaking of the cocoa pod and the beginning of the fermentation process. Cocoa users attribute uniformity and quality of Accra cocoa mainly to the strict inspection of all exports. Accra cocoa, though classified as base cocoa, now commands prices comparable with or better than those of much flavor cocoa. Market prospects for uniform high-quality base cocoa are good. The Territory should pay greater attention to quality control on that portion of the harvest that must be sold as base cocoa. It should also develop more aggressive marketing arrangements to make the Territory product better known and appreciated in the United States—the largest cocoa user.

Territory cocoa enjoys no preferential treatment in Australia as do coffee and rubber. Australian purchases account for only about one-third of production, the ratio having fallen off in recent years. In the event of price falls, it would be as well for the Territory also to popularize its product in Australia and, if deemed useful, seek some measure of preferential treatment.

Insofar as land reserves for additional cocoa are concerned, there is still scope for underplanting existing coconut plantations. The extent of this is more limited than it was, the most suitable soils having been so used already. Underplanting has accounted for most of the European acreage so far, 80 percent of mature and 65 percent of immature cocoa

[21] Estimates IBRD, Economic Department, 1964.

being grown this way. Even at these levels, however, cocoa has been underplanted on less than 30 percent of the total European land used for copra production.

A second source is land at present unused which is suited to cocoa and/or coconut production, as summarized in Table 7. From the data in this table, it is clear that far more potential cocoa land exists than could possibly be handled in the foreseeable future. At the same time, much of the most suitable areas are located in the more sparsely inhabited parts of Bougainville, New Britain and the Northern District. Exploitation of much of this would involve resettlement by transfer of population which would be a most expensive exercise.

Cocoa planting has been proceeding at a rapid rate for many years. Thus for the seven years to 1962, European planters averaged 10,500 acres a year of new plantings, while indigenous growers established 1,400 acres annually. The rate of plantings by Europeans fell from a peak of over 12,000 acres in 1961/62 to about 9,800 acres in 1962/63.

Development Program. Although these background considerations pose many uncertainties and indicate the need for caution in devising a development policy for cocoa, the potential gains of a strong positive program are so great that they warrant a very high priority for this commodity in planning. Increased production at the levels set out in Table 9 could, in due course, result in an export income from this crop as great as the present total export revenue.

The planting acreages and rates in Table 9 are advanced as attainable targets in a physical sense. They should be reviewed from time to time in

TABLE 9: Cocoa Planting Program

(acres)

Year	Indigenous		Non-indigenous	
	"Normal"	Additional	"Normal"	Additional
1964/65	1,500	1,500	2,000	7,000
1965/66	1,500	2,500	2,000	7,000
1966/67	1,500	3,500	2,000	7,000
1967/68	1,500	4,500	2,000	7,000
1968/69	1,500	5,500	2,000	7,000
1969/70	1,500	6,500	2,000	4,000
1970/71	1,500	7,500	2,000	4,000
1971/72	1,500	8,000	2,000	4,000
1972/73	1,500	8,000	2,000	4,000
1973/74	1,500	8,000	2,000	4,000
Total	15,000	55,500	20,000	55,000

the light of market developments and other factors. They call for a continuation of the current normal rate of native planting, along with a graded additional planting program for this sector rising from 1,500 acres per annum in the first year to a maximum rate of 8,000 acres by the eighth year. They also assume that Europeans will maintain an annual planting rate of 2,000 acres without special aid, plus an additional rate of 7,000 acres for the first years and 4,000 acres annually for the last five years.

A graded rate is advisable for plantings by indigenous farmers because of the organizational and other problems involved in motivating the large number of farmers required. A high rate in the first five years for the European sector is desirable so as to take full advantage of the high potential of this group as quickly as possible. Ultimately, total annual indigenous plantings under the program would reach a level about double that of the European sector.

Planting Program for European Farmers. The contribution of the European planters is relatively modest. In no year is it greater than 9,000 acres, a figure more than 3,000 acres below that achieved in 1961/62 and 1,500 acres below the seven-year planting average up to that time. This sector is tending to slow down its rate of growth. The impetus given to the industry by the Ex-Servicemen's Credit Scheme has come to an end. There is evidence that some individuals have actually exceeded the acreages they can conveniently handle during the immature stage with existing resources. There have also been indications of lack of confidence in the future of the Territory as an investment risk.

Under these circumstances, the Mission emphasizes the need to create greater confidence to stimulate continued growth. Adequate credit assistance on reasonable terms would help materially as would the making available of additional land both for existing planters where necessary and for new planters where this is desirable. New planters could be of great help in opening up the sparsely populated, high-quality cocoa areas of Bougainville and New Britain. A limited, well-planned location of two to four new European estates annually over the first five years could provide a most valuable stimulus and demonstration to indigenes. Indigenes from outside the area could be employed, gain experience with cocoa and those that wished to do so could be encouraged and assisted to settle in the area and grow cocoa. Relatives of these persons could be encouraged to join them, providing a source of labor for the indigene and the European as well as starting a development sequence. New estates of this type should be provided in every area where settlement type experiments are located. Under proper planning and supervision this could be a cheaper way than by government-sponsored, large-scale settlement.

Accordingly, the non-indigenous planting program calls for three types of effort: continuation of normal planting at a modest annual rate of 2,000 acres; additional interplanting with coconuts at an annual rate of 2,000 acres; additional sole planting at a rate of 4,000 acres annually for five years and 1,000 acres thereafter; and finally new coconut/cocoa planting at the rate of 1,000 acres annually.

On a credit basis, and in this respect the experience of the Ex-Servicemen's Credit Scheme provides useful guidelines, it is suggested that credit for interplanted cocoa would involve £A60 per acre; sole-planted cocoa, £A70 per acre; and new plantations combining coconuts and cocoa, £A120 per acre. Except in the last case, allowances cover establishment and maintenance costs only. It is assumed that existing growers could provide the finance for extra processing and handling facilities out of income. On these estimates, the total credit need amounts to £A4.15 million, of which £A2.6 million would be required in the first five years.

Additional technical staff requirements for this sector do not create any problem. A hard core of experienced cocoa producers now exists. These are not only capable of doing what is expected of them but could be a material help to the Administration in assisting in the training of indigenous field officers, smallholders and entrepreneurs. This aid should be sought.

Planting Program for Indigenous Farmers. The normal plantings are likely to be made over scattered areas and are unlikely to need any greater extension effort than has been applied in recent years. They should not need the stimulus of special credit.

The additional acreages, however, present special problems. The great majority of these should be organized as smallholdings on a village concentration basis. To facilitate extension work, smallholdings should have a target of at least five acres. If central fermentaries are to be used, these holdings should be reasonably adjacent in blocks. Fermentaries organized along the pattern developed in the Tolai cocoa area, but modified to permit each smallholder to have a financial interest in the processing side, would require blocks of 50 to 100 acres.[22]

Smallholdings of this type would require finance for tools, planting material, disease control and a share of the processing capital. Subsistence and housing needs and the labor cost of land-clearing would not require aid. It is estimated by the Department of Agriculture that the establishment costs would be met by the provision of approximately £A10 per acre while cash maintenance needs would require a further £A12 per acre. Thus a five-acre unit would need credit provision totaling £A110

[22] The Administration should investigate further the relative merit of central fermentaries as against small units on the Ghana pattern.

spread over five years. From the viewpoint of viability, sample budgets prepared on a basis of very conservative yields and prices indicate that the accumulated debt should be repayable in nine years and that thereafter, smallholders could enjoy a net cash surplus of at least £A200 per annum. If all the additional target acreage of 55,500 is derived from smallholder development along these lines, a total credit provision of £A1.22 million would meet the situation for the ten years of the program. Of this, only £A0.39 million would be drawn on over the first five years.

Some credit provision, however, should be made for the possibility of assisting selected entrepreneurs to operate larger-scale, fully commercial units. The Mission is strongly of the opinion that this type of indigenous operation should be very much encouraged. Credit incentive would need to be £A70 per acre, the same as allowed for the European planter. On the assumption that 10 percent of the target acreage might be obtained in this way, the more or less 7,000 acres involved would require an additional credit provision of £A0.34 million[23] for the ten years, making an over-all credit need of £A1.56 million.

These three main lines of attack—scattered units, village smallholders and large-scale entrepreneurs—could be supplemented by planned settlement to the extent that this approach is used by the Administration. Even if confined to a small-scale trial basis during the period in question, the contribution of several thousand settlement units, each with eight to ten acres of cocoa in the several potential settlement zones, could be of considerable assistance in reaching the target acreage. In this event, reliance on the village smallholder method would be reduced to some degree.

Lest it be assumed that these recommendations make the task sound too easy, it is relevant to stress the point that no development of any consequence in any segment of the primary industry is likely to occur unless the overriding problems of motivation, land tenure and technological services are solved. The first two, common to all crops, are dealt with later. The technical staffing requirement for a cocoa program of the scale advanced is by no means small, and could well be the major limiting factor.

Cocoa is more demanding of extension services than is copra or rubber. It is more difficult to grow, to keep free from disease and to process to a high-quality standard. Indigenous participants will need both training and supervision quite apart from initial motivation in respect of which extension officers must also play a vital role. The department has a large staff operating in the cocoa areas. On the assumption that 20 existing officers could concentrate on a cocoa program and that each extension

[23] At £A48 per acre (£A70 minus £A22).

officer might be expected to initiate 20 smallholder units annually, 60 technicians would have to be recruited over the first six years to handle the task. In fact, final determination of annual and total target acreage has been derived largely from these relationships. Apart from additional qualified extension personnel, the cocoa force of 80 would need to be backed by at least 600 native field assistants. These would have to be trained during the course of the work. Staff needs of this order have been provided for in recommendations covering the Department of Agriculture.

If the total program is achieved, production from existing and new plantings should total 38,000 tons valued at £A8 million at current prices by 1968/69, and reach 55,000 tons valued at £A11.6 million at the end of the program term in 1973/74. Even this understates the potential contribution since, at this stage, 30,000 to 35,000 acres will not be bearing and a like area will not have reached mature production. Together, these should add a further £A6 million to the export income in due course. The program as outlined thus aims at a cocoa industry with an export potential of £A17.6 million annually.[24]

Coffee. This crop was also introduced under German administration, but until organized commercial production began about 1950, coffee was grown mainly on mission stations and experimental areas. The opening up of the highlands for production for export, by the granting of a small number of leases to Europeans for coffee planting, and the concurrent encouragement of indigenous farmers to grow coffee, provided the basis for very rapid development. Exports increased from 33 tons in 1950 to 3,500 tons in 1961/62 and 4,800 tons in 1962/63, lifting the crop to third place as an export revenue earner. Distribution of acreage and production is shown in Table 10.

Three districts dominate the scene—the Eastern Highlands, the Western Highlands and Morobe. Commercial planting began at Goroka in the Western Highlands. This was followed a little later by plantings in the uplands of Morobe around Wau. Extension to the Western Highlands occurred in 1953. In the ten years to 1962, planting moved at an accelerated pace, averaging annually 38,000 trees in Morobe, 170,000 in the Eastern Highlands and 224,000 in the Western Highlands. The rate has slowed down materially since Australia became a party to the International Coffee Agreement (ICA).

European coffee estates number 236. By 1962, these had between 9,000 acres and 10,000 acres planted and a production of nearly 2,000 tons. Altogether, European operators accounted for about 40 percent of the acreage and 57 percent of the output.

[24] All prices at £A210 per ton.

TABLE 10: Coffee Acreage and Production, 1961/62[a]

District[b]	Acres (Mature and Immature)			Production (Tons)		
	Non-indigenous	Indigenous	Total	Non-indigenous	Indigenous	Total
Central	529	141	670	11	6	17
Milne Bay	32	566	598	c	21	21
Northern	79	843	922	c	26	26
Southern	c	60	60	c	3	3
Bougainville	c	136	136	c	2	2
Eastern Highlands	3,738	6,860	10,598	943	905	1,848
Madang	76	208	284	1	4	5
Morobe	1,282	3,862	5,144	218	365	583
New Ireland	c	108	108	c	c	c
Sepik	c	286	286	c	3	3
Western Highlands	3,480	1,773	5,253	809	150	959
Acreage or Production not Accounted for	153	74	227	3	c	3
Total for Territory	9,369	14,917	24,286	1,985	1,485	3,470

[a] For non-indigenous sector year ended March 31; for indigenous sector year ended June 30.

[b] The following districts are not listed because they have either less than 100 acres in coffee trees or less than 2 tons of coffee bean production: Gulf, Western, Manus, New Britain.

c Figures incomplete or not available.

SOURCES: Production Bulletin No. 4, Bureau of Statistics; Annual Extension Report 1961/62 of Department of Agriculture, Stock and Fisheries.

Coffee production by indigenes is one of the top success stories of the Territory. The Administration has been remarkably successful in stimulating native interest in the crop, in distributing planting material, in providing training for growing, harvesting and processing and in supervising the new industry. From an active beginning about 1954, plantings by indigenes soon exceeded those of Europeans in the three main districts, so that by 1961/62 over 60 percent of all coffee acreage and about 43 percent of the output was under indigenous control. On the assumption that in most cases native coffee units are one-quarter of an acre (and the average is probably less than this), a large number of native families obtained a cash income from coffee production after only eight years of planned extension effort. This has been a phenomenal development considering the short time these people have had contact with the outside world, and to whom commercial farming was a completely novel concept. The success of the program augurs well for the future economic development of natural resources of the highlands by indigenes.

Production Aspects. About 90 percent of the coffee is of the Arabica type. It is grown mainly at altitudes between 3,000 and 6,500 feet. A little native production extends to higher levels. Almost all the planting material has been derived from seed introduced in 1947 by the Highlands Experiment Station at Aiyura. Robusta type coffee is grown in coastal districts.

Mature Arabica yields an average of about 900 lbs. per acre of dried beans on coffee estates. Individual properties report yields exceeding a ton. Quality is of a high standard. New Guinea coffee has commanded prices that have been remarkably stable and have averaged well over £A400 per ton in each of the past five years.

Most of the estate coffee has developed on good quality grassland soils, mainly because of the lower costs of establishment on this type relative to forest land and its ready availability. In contrast, native farmers have tended to use land under forest cover. In the former case, shade trees, both temporary (Crotalaria) and permanent (Casuarina, Albizzia and Leucaena) are used. Management methods present no unusual features. Pruning methods have not yet been stabilized, all the major systems being under trial. Weeding and mulching are the major work problems during the establishment phase. Estates use native male labor. Even the native farmers regard the crop as a "male" one. Only a few estates use female labor for picking. European estates make some use of artificial fertilizers. They are all operated by their owners or by European managers.

The crop is free from serious diseases and insect pests. Rust has not appeared. Brown eye spot causes some loss in weakened or debilitated plants and in plants where there is inadequate shade. The stem girdler weevil is the worst insect pest.

Although there are exceptions, processing systems fall into two well-defined patterns. Native farmers process to the parchment stage, and sell to estates possessing finishing equipment, to central processing plants operated as commercial enterprises, or to the Administration (in remote areas). European coffee estates tend to be equipped to carry out the whole process to the dried and graded bean stage. The Department of Agriculture inspects produce at point of export. Most of the harvest occurs over the May-July period.

Background to Development. Marketing problems impose very real limitations to any program of expansion. No specific export quota has been applied under the ICA, and exports to Australia (as the Trustee country) are exempt from quota. However, under the present agreement, which expires in 1968, the Territory's exports to member countries, other than Australia, will become subject to control once they exceed 100,000 bags or approximately 6,000 tons.

The total export in 1962/63 was 4,800 tons, of which 2,800 tons went to Australia and 2,000 tons to other countries. To accommodate anticipated rising production in the years to come, in addition to increased exports to other countries exports to Australia will have to be stepped up, or markets will have to be found in non-quota countries[25] to the extent that Australia and other member countries together will fail to absorb total output.

Australia has taken steps to encourage greater use of New Guinea coffee. It implemented tariff arrangements in 1963/64 so that Australian manufacturers qualify for a rebate of 2d per lb. on all coffee imported from other sources providing they use 25 percent New Guinea coffee, and a rebate of 5d per lb. if their use of the Territory product reaches the 30 percent level. Unfortunately, New Guinea coffee for Australian manufacturers has tended to be expensive relative to cheaper grades of Arabica and Robusta coffee. A large quantity of instant coffee is also imported. In 1963, about 25 percent of the total coffee imported by Australia (10,600 tons[26]) came from the Territory.

Australia could well increase coffee consumption. Present annual levels amount to little more than 2.5 lbs. per capita. Large numbers of coffee-drinking European peoples have immigrated to Australia since World War II, and an increase in consumption of half a pound per head would increase imports by about 2,500 tons annually. Normal population growth is expected to increase imports a further 2,000 to 3,000 tons in the next five years.

The Territory should be able to dispose of its expected crop until the time the ICA expires if an active campaign is organized to further popularize New Guinea coffee in Australia, and if an active selling campaign is organized to exploit the potential markets in non-quota countries.

Of fundamental importance, however, are satisfactory arrangements under the ICA after 1968 to take care of expected production. The Territory has cooperated in taking steps to reduce further organized expansion of the industry. No new coffee estates can be established. Plantings are restricted to existing leasehold areas. Indigenous plantings too are not being encouraged, the distribution of planting material having been limited. Despite these precautions, it is anticipated that the total

[25] Japan, Korea and Thailand are obvious possibilities.

[26] Excluding about 350 tons "instant" coffee, equivalent to about 1,000 tons of raw coffee beans.

yield in ten years (1973/74) may exceed 20,000 tons.[27] Even this output, however, is less than 1 percent of world coffee exports. As a late arrival on the scene, and as an emerging country to which coffee is a key crop, the Territory has a good case for sufficient provision to enable her to handle her expected output. There are only limited alternatives for production of commercial crops and coffee of high quality which can be produced at relatively low cost, is needed for development.[28]

Against this background, the Mission recognized the limitations imposed by the ICA at this stage, and accordingly confined its attention to present policies and methods rather than to expansion.

European Estates. Most coffee estates are economically viable or will be as plantings mature. Growing practices are fair to good. Owners or managers are improvement conscious. Processing and marketing are effectively organized as borne out by the large proportion of the product that is sold at premium prices. Aside from regular improvements which can be expected from normal progress in technology, there appears to be a need for close examination of the economics of providing complete processing units on each estate. Although many of the units are makeshift, it is likely that over-capitalization has already occurred in this direction, particularly where the area of bearing coffee is under 100 acres. Units of at least 100 acres are probably minimal to justify the large capital outlay involved in modern equipment.

Some attempts to overcome this weakness have been made. Progressive planters have organized large processing units on a corporate or cooperative basis with other planters and/or native growers. This approach should be encouraged as a way of making more efficient use of capital, and particularly as an effective way of developing a partnership with indigenous producers. It is essential for the future welfare of the Territory that indigenous people become not only competent in production and processing but also familiar with the economic and technical aspects of processing and marketing upon which a high-quality, high-price, viable industry depends. Such development would help to produce native entrepreneurs, and farm and business leaders. It could improve the social and economic status of such people. Every effort should be made to develop and consolidate this emerging partnership by policy measures and the provision of adequate credit.

Two further weaknesses noted are characteristic of almost all coffee

[27] Contributing £A8 million annually at £A400 per ton. To obtain this price the present high quality of coffee will have to be maintained.

[28] In addition to Arabica coffee, the predominant crop, substantial potential exists for growing Robusta coffee. The Mission did not pursue this matter because of the present limitations resulting from the ICA.

estates. First, production on the estates is almost entirely limited to coffee. Second, supervision of unskilled indigenous labor is vested exclusively in European owner/managers, who rarely delegate responsibility to native assistant managers or foremen or attempt to train any such personnel.

With the coffee future currently prescribed and large land areas unused on most estates (about 75 percent), supplementary activities should be developed to reduce vulnerability due to a single-crop enterprise. Cattle production and tea offer good possibilities. These are fully dealt with in other sections. Any such diversification of activities, however, would have to be linked with a change of policy on the management side by training indigenes to assume greater responsibilities. The Administration could help in this by instituting an apprentice and training scheme which would involve planter participation, initially at the training level and later at the employment stage. In their own, as well as the country's interest, the more efficient planters could make a valuable contribution in this way.

Finally, and with special reference to the preceding discussion of the marketing problem, planters should be encouraged to further strengthen and develop existing marketing organizations. The desirability of a levy on production to finance research and market development might be explored.

Indigenous Sector. Coffee represents the highland people's major source of cash crop income and the organization of this activity merits special attention. Of major importance is the need for consolidation. A large proportion of the native acreage under coffee occurs in tiny scattered units which are not only sub-economic in structure, but are also costly and difficult to aid through extension and supervision. Product quality is also handicapped through excessive dispersal of effort. This pattern of development was probably unavoidable in view of the nature of the original problem. Development had to be tackled on an individual basis and land-tenure difficulties by no means helped to avoid scatter.

The Mission has no simple formula for, or unique approach to, the solution of this inherent structural weakness. It believes, however, that the key probably lies in the evolution of a positive land-use/tenure policy which is development and production oriented. Solutions will probably have to vary with each local setting. Essentially, the rights to land use of family units for perennial tree crop production must, in some way, become accepted by the native people as necessary to their advancement.

Within this basic problem, the Administration should continue its efforts to increase the efficiency of indigenous growers. It should also aid growers to develop central processing units with the basic objectives of improving quality of the product and increasing their cash return. Despite the difficult world trade outlook for most coffees, quality coffee of the type that can so easily be grown in the highlands should always be salable.

It is recommended that market promotion of coffee be expanded in Australia and in non-quota countries; that a quota, sufficient to absorb the foreseeable production for the ten-year period, be sought when ICA re-examines the existing basic quotas, and that the claims of the Territory be strongly pressed. The development of cooperative or corporate central processing embracing both sectors should be strongly encouraged, and credit should be used as a weapon to this end. There should be increased participation by indigenes in management and supervision within the industry, with the objective of developing an enduring and profitable partnership of all concerned.

Rubber. Para rubber was planted in Papua in 1903. Exports were recorded first in 1918, but did not reach the 1,000-ton mark until 1935. Apart from temporary setbacks during World War II, and in early post-war years, production has increased steadily since that time. It now approaches 5,000 tons annually. If planting were to continue at current rates, production should reach the 10,000-ton mark in the next ten years. This volume is very small relative to world production of which the Territory's share at present is about 0.2 percent. It is small, too, in contrast to that of neighboring countries, Malaysia and Indonesia, which at present have an annual output of about 850,000 and 650,000 tons, respectively. The distribution of acreage and production is shown in Table 11.

Plantations close to Port Moresby account for about 75 percent of both area and output. The remainder is produced in the three adjacent districts. The number of plantations is only 57, an increase of only six in the last ten years. All are commercial enterprises, owned and operated by

TABLE 11: Rubber Acreage and Production by District, 1961/62
(year ended March 31)

| District | Acres | | | Production |
	Immature	Mature	Total	Tons
Central	6,401	16,701	23,101	3,465
Gulf	667	1,935	2,602	311
Milne Bay	81	646	727	152
Northern	1,216	3,603	4,819	601
Total	8,365	22,885	31,249	4,559 [a]

[a] Including 30 tons from Bougainville.

SOURCES: Production Bulletin No. 4, Bureau of Statistics; Annual Extension Report 1961/62 of Department of Agriculture, Stock and Fisheries.

Europeans. The indigene has not yet participated in rubber production to any extent, the total output from native tappings from a former government plantation amounting to only 24 tons in 1962.

Production Methods. Methods are similar to those developed in Indonesia and Malaysia. Early plantings were not of high-yielding rubber, however, and growers were rather slow to appreciate the potentials of high-yielding clones. Accordingly, yields from old stands are rather low, averaging less than 400 lbs. per acre. Improved stocks were introduced from Malaysia in 1955, and since then only material of this type has been planted or used for rejuvenating old stands. In Malaysia high-yielding clones produce over 1,000 lbs. per acre at about ten years after planting. Initial results of plantings in Papua indicate potential yields of this magnitude. The yield increases from 200 lbs. in the fifth year to this level. Individual stands in Malaysia have yielded as much as 2,000 lbs. per acre.

Product quality is high. At one time, quality and grading control was poor, but this has improved in recent years in consequence of expert advice from Malaysia.[29] At present, the proportion of No. 1 ribbed smoked sheet (RSS) is actually higher than demanded by the Australian trade which handles the entire output.

Plantations are all managed by Europeans employing indigenous labor for establishment, tapping and processing. Male labor gangs are recruited on a two-year-term basis, so that frequent training and constant supervision is necessary. One man handles about four acres of rubber on the alternate daily tapping system.

Background to Development. Any plan to increase rubber production must consider market prospects. In this respect, the commodity is subject to favorable and unfavorable influences, the precise significance of which is difficult to assess.

Natural rubber is subject to severe competition from synthetic rubber. The latter accounted for more than half the world consumption in 1962.[30] In the United States, which uses 45 percent of total world production, the ratio in favor of synthetics was even higher at 73 percent. The development of improved synthetics which equal or excel the essential properties of natural rubber could shift these ratios still further in favor of synthetics. From this viewpoint, the outlook for rubber is not bright, though increasing world consumption of total rubber products is likely to increase the absolute amounts of natural rubber required.

The world output of natural rubber is expected to grow at a rate of 2.8 percent annually from 1960 to 1965 and at 3.2 percent annually over

[29] Mann, C. E. T., Papua and New Guinea Agricultural Gazette, Volume 8, Nos. 2 and 3, 1953/54.

[30] IBRD, Economic Department.

the subsequent five years.[31] The production trend of synthetics is less predictable. This applies also to the demand for natural rubber from the Soviet bloc countries. In general, most forecasts predict an over supply of natural rubber during the remaining years of the present decade. A resulting price decline of rubber should slow down the rate of substitution and lead to a more balanced supply/demand situation by 1970. The new price level then established for the natural product could be about 20 percent below current rates. This would mean a price of about 1/9d per lb. f.o.b. Port Moresby.[32]

These unfavorable trends in world market prospects are counter-balanced by the factor of trade assistance by Australia to the Territory. Australia pursues a positive policy in favor of Papuan rubber planters, by providing both a guaranteed market and price support. The whole of the present output is absorbed at prices involving a price support of 1d per lb. This support would increase under the existing agreement to a maximum of 3d per lb., should world prices fall as low as 1/6d per lb.

Australia should consume about 100,000 tons of rubber annually by 1970, of which at least 40,000 tons is likely to be the natural product. In these circumstances, it is not unreasonable to assume that Australia could absorb at least 20,000 tons of rubber annually from the Territory by 1970. The program recommended is designed to accommodate this limit around the middle of the 1970s.

Other factors must also be evaluated when considering increased production. Clonal seed rubber does not come into tapping until four and one-half to five years and reaches full bearing ten years after planting; bud-grafted rubber is ready for early tapping at five and one-half to six years and full-bearing 10 to 12 years after planting. Bud-grafting requires more exacting techniques including tapping which makes it less suitable for indigenous producers at their present stage of development than for the estates. In Papua, about 98 percent of the estates have planted clonal seeds apparently because the Administration subsidizes the cost of importing the seeds. However, in Malaysia bud-grafted rubber tends to yield 300 to 500 lbs. per acre above clonal seed rubber. As the new plantings in Papua mature, the Department of Agriculture can make yield comparisons between the two methods. If clonal seed rubber in Papua does not produce as high a yield as bud-grafted rubber, a shift should be made to bud-grafted rubber. The additional yield can be a decisive factor in making Papuan rubber competitive, justifying the Mission's yield projections of 1,000 lb./acre for non-indigenous estates (800 lb./acre for

[31] IBRD, Economic Department.

[32] Later we have made the assumption that after 1970 the price might fall by another 10 percent.

the indigenous sector). The time lag between planting and full returns, particularly in bud-grafted rubber, is, of course, a serious bar to investment unless stable conditions are assured for the investor. However, once in production, satisfactory returns are realized. Assuming an average yield of 1,000 lbs. dry rubber, the gross return per acre at current prices exceeds £A100. Production costs on the existing rubber estates producing 800 lbs. per acre are of the order of 1/2d to 1/4d per lb., indicating that rubber can be produced competitively for sale in the world market.

Unlike coconuts, rubber is not an easy crop to handle. Tapping is a skilled task which, if not properly carried out, can result in damage to the tapping panel or even death of the trees. Regular systematic tapping is also essential to maintaining high yields. Processing also is not foolproof. Thus constant supervision of unskilled labor is necessary at all stages of production and processing. For these reasons, rubber is not well suited to indigenes at their present stage of development. At the same time, there is no real bar to participation in rubber production by selected indigenes. The degree of selection, the efficiency of training and the amount of extension supervision would be the main factors determining success. The difficulties are very real and at the early stages of the program only modest participation in rubber planting by the indigenes should be anticipated. There is no shortage of land for a large expansion of rubber planting. This is clear from the following estimates. These exclude areas usable for cocoa production (see Table 12).

The planting of an additional 100,000 acres of rubber—three times the present acreage—would absorb only one-eighth of the land potentially available. In fact, the land reserves of the Central District alone could accommodate more than twice this level of new plantings.

TABLE 12: Areas with Potential for Rubber Development

(acres)

District	Freehold and Leasehold	Native-owned	Crown	Total Area
Morobe	112,000	25,000	—	137,000
Northern	25,000	50,000	66,000[a]	141,000
New Ireland	25,000	50,000	—	75,000
Gulf	—	100,000	—	100,000
Central	50,000	75,000	100,000	225,000
Sepik	—	250,000	—	250,000
Total	212,000	550,000	166,000	928,000

[a] Probably an over-estimate; includes some land suitable for cocoa.

SOURCE: Department of Agriculture, Stock and Fisheries.

Labor also seems unlikely to be a limiting factor. Women have not yet been employed in the Territory for tapping, whereas in Malaysia, many women tappers are employed. An additional area of 100,000 acres of rubber could employ a labor force of 25,000. While there is no doubt as to the adequacy of supply of labor, there is room for improvement in the use of plantation workers. Greater reliance on resident workers, together with the employment of female tappers from resident families, could result in improved labor efficiency, greater income for workers and lower costs.

Despite the many pros and cons, and the undoubted difficulties and problems, the potential gains are so great that a vigorous development policy for rubber is justified. This should involve both non-indigenous and indigenous planters.

Development Program. From discussions with the Department of Agriculture and with leading rubber planters, the planting rate set out in Table 13 is considered capable of attainment with appropriate effort and organization.

It will be noted that the greatest burden will lie upon the non-indigenous planters, for whom the program sets a target of 75,000 acres of new rubber by 1973/74. Over the past four years, planters have been establishing 1,500 acres annually, so that the target envisaged means an average 6,000 acres per annum more than could be expected to occur without special measures.

The target for indigenes, while relatively modest during the first five-year phase, is more ambitious thereafter, and amounts to a total of 12,000 acres. The general argument is that if the rate of 400 to 1,000 acres is attained during the earlier period, the stage will be set for the higher rate of 1,000 to 2,000 acres annually during the later years.

TABLE 13: Planting Program for Rubber

(acres)

Year	Indigenous	Non-indigenous	Total
1964/65	400	1,500	1,900
1965/66	500	3,500	4,000
1966/67	600	5,500	6,100
1967/68	800	7,500	8,300
1968/69	1,000	9,500	10,500
1969/70	1,200	9,500	10,700
1970/71	1,500	9,500	11,000
1971/72	2,000	9,500	11,500
1972/73	2,000	9,500	11,500
1973/74	2,000	9,500	11,500
Total	12,000	75,000	87,000

An important factor, together with experienced planters, for a successful development along these lines will be credit. This is a fundamental need of the European sector, not merely because of the incentive which a realistic credit scheme would provide, but because of its contribution to generating confidence in the future. It would be unrealistic to expect such large increases in the annual planting rate without a special stimulus of this type.

On the indigenous side, it is also considered that credit could provide a strong motivating force. It would provide a powerful lever to extension workers in securing the necessary interest of native villagers in planting minimum acreages in units, consolidated in contiguous development blocks, and in organizing group processing and marketing. It would be essential for the emergence of entrepreneurs.

Large-scale Estate Plantings. The program should be capable of execution largely by existing planters. At the most, only a small number of new plantations would be needed. Existing planters possess the requisite technological and managerial experience, so that there will be little call on the limited extension reserves of the Administration. Planters are capable of growing most of their own planting material so that here again they would be largely independent of official nurseries. They can recruit and train the labor force.

Financially, too, the stage is set for economic expansion from established bases. Accommodation for management and labor, processing factories and transport facilities already exist. Expansion of these basic needs out of income could occur gradually as new areas of rubber come into production. Credit would be needed only for establishment of new plantings and their maintenance over the unproductive period.

The major function of the Administration would be to provide appropriate incentives. In addition to the basic need for credit on favorable terms, it will be necessary for the Administration to continue its existing seed subsidy program and its testing and multiplication of superior planting material. It would need to ensure that any additional land required by planters is made available to them, and should provide land from its existing resources for any new plantations necessary. In addition, it would have to obtain assurances from the Australian Government of the maintenance of its present favorable trade policy in respect to Papuan rubber.

The seed requirements for the plantation sector will be substantial. On the assumption that 300 seedlings are needed per acre to provide 180 trees per acre, and that approximately 40 percent of the planting material would be supplied by Administration seed gardens, approximately 13.5 million seeds would need to be imported involving a total seed subsidy at £A3,000 per 100,000 seeds or £A400,000. Of this, about £A150,000 would be needed in the first five years, according to projections of the Administration. The Mission would urge, however, a shift toward bud-grafting if the clonal seed rubber coming into production shortly does not give a yield equal to that of bud-grafted rubber. For the estate sector, bud-grafting should replace the use of clonal seeds on two-thirds to three-fourths of the new plantings.

In calculating probable credit needs it has been assumed that half of the expected normal plantings of 1,500 acres annually, are not likely to need special credit provision, leaving only 67,500 acres to be assisted. It is also assumed that the stimulus would be adequate if credit be available for establishment and maintenance costs only. The cost of planting material, felling and clearing forest, lining, holing, planting, and initial weeding is assessed at £A35 per acre. In addition, maintenance until the end of the fifth year at an annual cost of £A10 per acre requires a further £A40 per acre. The total credit amounts to £A5.1 million of which £A1.8 million would be loaned in the first five years. It is possible that the larger, well-established plantations may not need as much aid as this.

Indigenous Production. If rubber-growing is profitable on estates with the high costs of European management and hired labor, there is no reason why smallholders should not participate in areas where soil, climate, and market location are suitable. Land opportunity costs are low particularly in areas where no other crop competes for land use. Labor opportunity costs are likewise low. Indigenous populations elsewhere have been trained successfully to handle rubber. Thus in Malaysia in 1963 over 300,000 tons of rubber came from native smallholder units of less than 100 acres. In Sarawak and Thailand rubber production has developed largely on native smallholder units.

In the Territory there appear to be three major limitations; access to land of suitable tenure, absence of technological experience of indigenes in suitable rubber areas, and lack of motivation. The land-tenure problem, common to all new permanent-type crops is discussed elsewhere in this report. The second arises from the preference of planters for labor imported from the highlands rather than from coastal areas where experienced workers could later practice what they had learned. Training is vital to any indigenous program. The position is similar in respect to motivation. The program must have a built-in capacity to stimulate interest in this new crop.

The program recommended has been devised by the Department of Agriculture. It is designed to take full advantage of the experience of the department in research, propagation and extension to date. Essentially it is to encourage the development of smallholder units of five to six acres, on a village concentration basis. To make supervision, processing and marketing feasible, the aim would be for contiguous, minimum size blocks of 50 to 100 acres. To avoid undue spread of the services of limited numbers of extension officers and other crucial resources over a large area, the program would be concentrated around pilot villages in selected areas of the Central, Northern and Sepik districts.

Indigenes wishing to participate would be given a course of training at the Administration school at Mageri and a new training center to be established at Kapagere. The aid of planters in training indigenes would be sought, trainees spending a specified period on estates. Adequate training of this type would be a prerequisite to credit provision.

All planting material would be supplied at cost by the Department of Agriculture. The existing nursery service would be expanded by the establishment of two new gardens in the Northern and Sepik districts to supplement the operations of the present organization at Bisianumu.

Family labor would be used for establishment and maintenance, and housing and subsistence would, in view of location, not have to be provided. Processing would be carried out by participants on a cooperative basis. Credit would be needed for the cash costs of establishment and maintenance and of processing equipment, estimated to amount to about £A90[33] per six-acre smallholding. The total credit needs for the ten-year target of 12,000 acres amount, on the basis of six-acre units, to £A180,000 of which £A49,000 would be used in the first five years.

Budget projections indicate that six-acre smallholders of this type could repay all loans by the ninth year after planting, and at conservative yield estimates of 800 lbs. and 1/6d per lb., would provide an annual cash return of £A300 to £A360 thereafter.

A relatively large addition to the extension staff of the Department of Agriculture will be needed. This is estimated at 20 extension officers and six project managers over the ten-year period.

Implementation of the whole program is estimated to yield an extra 8,000 tons per annum by the end of the ten years. Assuming a price, after 1970, of about £A177 per ton (30 percent below the 1962/63 price) the return would show an extra £A1.4 million annually. These figures underestimate the ultimate contribution of the program to the export income since half the trees at this stage will not be bearing. When in full production, after another five years, the extra yield should be of the order of 30,000 tons annually, worth £A5.3 million. With existing capacity, the total export at that time should be about 42,000 tons, or almost nine times its present level, and be worth £A7.4 million annually thereafter.

[33] Seedlings £A8, tools and equipment £A6, tapping equipment £A47, share of processing equipment £A25, contingencies £A4.

Peanuts. This crop was introduced to the highlands primarily to provide a source of high-quality protein, particularly for children and nursing mothers; development was sponsored jointly by the Department of Agriculture and the Department of Public Health. Annual production of indigenous gardeners is estimated at about 3,000 tons of shelled nuts of which only about 10 percent is available for sale or exchange. Production by European growers was organized in the Markham Valley after the war. In 1962, about 6,000 acres yielded 2,300 tons of shelled nuts for export. Production is geared to the edible nut trade so that export potentials are limited. Most of the output goes to Australia.

Viewed as a cash crop, peanuts are not well suited to the climate and soils except for the drier parts of the Markham Valley. Even here, large-scale production is limited through the lack of suitable rotational crops with which to combine it. Some success, however, has been achieved by using peanuts during the establishment phase of coconuts. As a subsistence crop in the highlands, the growing of peanuts can be considered successful and should be encouraged.

The crop is relatively disease free, the only serious source of trouble being from moulds (the incidence of which appears to be enhanced by the high proportion of immature nuts frequently harvested). Uneven ripening is characteristic, and harvesting has to be done when the earliest nuts start to germinate so that a percentage of the nuts are immature and fit only for processing.

Because of these problems, the crop received special attention from the Plant Industry Division of the Department of Agriculture from 1951 onward. Variety, spacing, fertilizer and planting time trials were laid down. The earlier introductions, Virginia Bunch and White Spanish, remained the most successful and are still the main varieties grown, the latter being most used in the Markham Valley. Yields are not high, being of the order of one-half to one-third ton of shelled nuts per acre on European estates. Yields in indigenous gardens are believed to be of the same order but reliable data are lacking.

Lack of market opportunities, of suitable land and of profitable rotational crops to use in combination with peanuts, appear likely to restrict further export development by Europeans, who indeed are more likely to reduce output than to increase it. Such a decline could be arrested if growers would combine cattle-raising with their operations. The sowing down of cropped land to improved pastures and its use under grass by cattle for six to ten years could increase the nut yield as well as provide a lucrative supplementary source of income. The peanut growers of the Markham Valley should be the target of special efforts in the drive to build a larger cattle industry.

Poor returns as a cash crop seem likely to restrict indigenous production substantially to subsistence needs. This does not mean that further production increases will not be recorded. Many groups still do not grow the crop. Much education is needed to stimulate greatest consumption by age groups who would especially benefit from consumption of peanuts. Both departments concerned should maintain their efforts to secure wider recognition of its virtues.

Passion Fruit. This vine was introduced to the highlands after the war. It grows well and fruits prolifically without much care or management. It is ideal for smallholder garden production, and has provided a small cash income to growers since the early 1950s, when a factory for the extraction of pulp was erected at Goroka. This is supplied by indigenes. The extracted pulp is air-freighted to the coast, frozen and shipped to the Australian market. The development of markets for passion fruit pulp is limited by competition from other fruit juices and synthetic flavors which are significantly cheaper. To assist in retaining and expanding the market in Australia, the Government has granted duty-free admission for 45,000 gallons of Territory passion fruit pulp annually. Exports at about 425,000 lbs. annually earn an income of approximately £A80,000.

Since passion fruit is valued as a flavoring for soft drinks, ice cream, fruit salad and other desserts, and since both the American and European areas present potentials for such products, there is a good case for initiating food technology research on the product to render it less bulky and perishable. A successful outcome of such studies would justify the exploration of new markets. Production could be stepped up to almost any multiple of the present output.

Tea. The possibilities of tea-growing in the highlands have been appreciated for some time. In fact, Australian agriculturists began test plantings at Aiyura when this station was opened up in 1936, only three years after the Upper Highlands were first penetrated. Initial experience was promising, and on specialist advice from India, the Administration established an experimental plantation at Garaina in the Morobe District in 1947. The selection of this isolated site, linked only by air with other centers, was unfortunate and has been at least partly responsible for the relatively slow progress made.[34] It was not until 1962 that a small prefabricated factory was completed for factory-scale processing trials of tea from some 300 acres of Assam tea that had been planted earlier.

The experimental work done has shown that quite good yields of 800 to 1,000 lbs. per acre are obtainable. The product processed and sold so far has graded better than plain tea. Recent sales on the London market have been made at 4/-d and over per lb. Local women have proved

[34] Chosen primarily to permit testing of mechanical harvesting.

capable tea pickers and the work is popular with them. Agronomic techniques suited to the Territory have been developed, and seed gardens established which could immediately provide seeds to plant 1,000 acres annually. The seed gardens could be increased without difficulty. The Department of Agriculture estimates that there are at least 100,000 acres of land suited to the crop in highland areas. The stage thus appears to be set for a take-off into commercial production.

Background to Development. The world tea market exhibits reasonably favorable aspects for entry of the Territory. The market is dominated by India and Ceylon, but East African countries are now replacing older producers such as Indonesia and China. The expansion of tea consumption is occurring not so much in traditional tea-drinking areas as in new markets in the lower income areas and in producing countries themselves. Price projections anticipate some pressure in a downward direction of the order of 10 to 15 percent, affecting mostly the poorer quality grades.

The Australian market offers a special opportunity for the Territory. As a tea importer, consuming nearly 30,000 tons annually, Australia could readily handle all the output which could possibly come from the Territory for many years, particularly since the type and grade grown meets Australian taste requirements.

It is important, however, to stress that action is a matter of urgency. The growth of tea is slow, bearing commencing at four years and reaching a maximum in eight to ten years. In the event of production/price relationships deteriorating, the Territory, as a slow starter, could face serious marketing problems if an international commodity agreement on tea-marketing was to come into existence which related exports only to previous performance.

Tea production in the highlands is also of special importance in view of the restrictions on coffee, the only important cash crop in the highlands. Tea would make possible the economic advantage of diversification and also have the political advantage of providing opportunities for indigenes not now participating in the cash economy and from which pressures to do so are bound to come.

Development of a tea industry involves one special feature which so far has not confronted the Administration and which makes it essential to invoke the aid of commercial organizations. Copra, coffee, and cocoa are all crops which involve two-stage processing, of which only the first, which is relatively simple to operate and cheap to install, must be carried out in the producing country. Tea, in contrast, involves one-stage processing of a green leaf product which must be handled to the final stage within a few hours of harvesting. Tea factories are expensive; a unit to handle the product of 1,000 to 1,200 acres, producing about 1 million lbs. of tea annually, costs about £A150,000. Management for quality production must be experienced and of a high standard. Location in relation to producing areas and road access to reduce transport costs are vital to economic operation. It is most unlikely that adequate factory provision and operation could be effected without enlisting the direct participation of experienced tea companies. Such participation would bring concurrent marketing benefits which could be very important in establishing the New Guinea product. There is evidence that commercial interests with substantial capital resources and expertise are ready and willing to participate directly in tea production and processing in the Territory.

In the tea-producing countries, there is experience on how to organize tea development. The successful approaches fall into three broad groups: estate development where production, processing and marketing is the responsibility of tea companies; nucleus estates, where a tea company grows a sufficient area to justify its basic investment in processing and marketing, but relies on a considerable proportion of smallholder tea from closely adjacent units to make the whole operation economically viable to all participants; and smallholder production to supply all the green leaf for cooperative or corporate-owned processing factories. Nucleus estates are in operation or under trial in several countries and smallholder production is now under way in Kenya. As yet, however, there is much less experience available of these systems than of commercial estate production.

In the particular environment of the highlands and from the recent experience in establishing a tea industry in Kenya, the nucleus estate method offers the greatest promise. The crop is quite unknown to highland farmers so that it would be unrealistic at this stage to organize on the basis of smallholders only. Social/political issues make sole dependence on estate development unwise. On the other hand, it is unrealistic to expect large-scale interest of tea companies with the necessary expertise and marketing contacts to invest the large amounts of capital needed, unless such nucleus estates are so organized that they could operate independently of smallholder participation if necessary. Therefore, each nucleus estate should have access to sufficient land (1,000 to 1,200 acres) suitable for tea to permit it to attain economic independence should the indigenes fail to enter the production field. Initially, such estates should be encouraged to plant 500 to 700 acres of tea at least; smallholders with at least one acre each should be enlisted to grow 500 to 700 acres per nucleus estate.

Once nucleus estates, at two or three per year, have been established, other or modified approaches could be tried. The important point is to begin immediately to attract outside interest in proposals along these lines. It is likely that a source of readily available credit would provide a considerable stimulus. Such credit, up to 50 percent of factory and establishment costs of nucleus units, could aid in attracting the necessary outside capital. Advances, at least in respect to planting material, may be necessary for smallholders. This would require credit provision of about £A100,000 for each estate, and a further £A20,000 for the associated smallholders.[35] Ten units would require a total of £A1.2 million over five years.

Two thousand acres of tea a year, particularly under company direction, should be possible of attainment. The Administration would need to step up its nursery program, to institute training of indigenes, to continue its research operations and to assist in road development. The companies coming in could aid with research in view of their overseas contacts, but it is highly desirable that experimental facilities be provided in the highlands, the area it will have to serve. The Garaina experimental plantation should be retained only as long as necessary to produce planting material.

If during the next five years ten nucleus estates were to be established, each with a capacity of 1 million lbs. of tea annually, this would, at a price of 4/-d per lb., ultimately generate export proceeds of £A2 million.

Pyrethrum. In attempts to find a cash crop for the Upper Highlands, the Administration began experiments with pyrethrum, introduced from Kenya, in 1938. Plants flowered in 1939 and 1940 but all material was lost during the war. Further introductions from Switzerland and Japan in 1952 proved unsatisfactory. Viable seed was obtained in 1956 from Japan, France and the Congo (then the Belgian Congo) and in 1957 from Kenya. These provided the base material for breeding and selection studies which have resulted in the development of stocks with a high pyrethrum content, suited to local conditions.

A large number of test gardens in the highlands have demonstrated the suitability of soils and climate for the crop at altitudes above 6,000 feet. It has been found that by selection of location and of time of transplanting, the harvest period can be widely spread over the year, so that continuous factory operation in processing should not be difficult. The crop is singularly free from pests and disease, the only trouble recorded being from root rot on poorly drained sites. The yield of dried flowers per acre has ranged from averages of 500 lbs. at 5,000 feet to 800 lbs. at 8,000 feet. Drying of flowers has been unreliable at high altitudes due to cloud and rain. More work is needed to develop cheap heat dryers suited to

[35] Credit would not be needed by smallholders should seed be provided free by the Administration; a loan approach, however, has many advantages over free distribution.

indigenous smallholder production. Ample planting material now exists so that the stage is set for entry into commercial production.

The main justification for the Territory attempting to break into the pyrethrum trade is the dearth of suitable cash crops for high altitude native farmers. Coffee can no longer be extended with confidence and like tea is not really suited to the higher elevations where pyrethrum grows. Some cash crop is desirable for the people living in these areas.

From this background, it is not unexpected that Administration thinking is in terms of large numbers of smallholders each initially with one-tenth of an acre of pyrethrum. Plans have been laid to plant 600 acres on this pattern by 1964 and 1,000 acres by the following year. Assuming an average yield of 600 lbs. per acre, this plan would involve the motivation of some 10,000 individual smallholders to obtain a minimum target output of only 300 tons. Since the cash return from one-tenth of an acre at 1/6d per lb. would be under £A5 a year, it is questionable whether such large numbers could be persuaded to grow the crop for such unimpressive rewards. It is even more doubtful whether the very great effort and expenditure necessary in extension work to achieve a target production of pyrethrum worth only £A50,000 a year would be worthwhile. It is thus imperative to increase the unit size of gardens up to a one-acre mark.

Further to the question of garden size attention must be drawn to the fact that pyrethrum production in countries with successful performance records has been organized in large rather than miniature smallholder units. Thus Kenya, which produces over 10,000 tons annually and accounts for over two-thirds of world output, derives only 25 percent of this from smallholdings. Even these are organized or are being organized to provide 2.5 acres per unit. Tanganyika and Ecuador, which are also large producers, show similar production patterns. Consideration must be given to developing the industry in the Territory on reasonable sized plots. One acre of pyrethrum could return from £A40 to £A50 gross annually to the grower.

Marketwise, the crop is subject to considerable uncertainty. The principal producing country, Kenya, has been forced to restrict production by 50 percent during the last two years, her previous virtual monopoly having been successfully challenged by Tanganyika and Ecuador. World consumption has shown no significant expansion trend, the product having had to face increasing competition from alternative synthetic insecticides with superior lasting effects. Recent unfavorable reactions to some of the best alternatives as DDT and dieldrin, on grounds of residual toxicity to humans of foodstuffs with which they have been in contact, has changed this situation somewhat. This could be a temporary phase, however, since modern high-powered chemical industries are unlikely to be content to lose their market. New, improved insecticides currently coming off the production line could well step up competition to serious levels once more. Pyrethrum is unsurpassed in its quick knockdown effect on insects. On the other hand, its non-residual character is a great weakness, since many users prefer materials which do not require repeated costly applications to be effective.

In view of the many marketing uncertainties, the Mission is of the opinion that the Administration would be justified in pressing on with commercial development of the crop only if firm arrangements can be made with a reliable commercial company with not only the necessary expertise in processing but with established market outlets. A sufficient base production to justify the investment in factory and market arrangements would be the best guarantee of a permanent outlet for indigenous smallholder production.

The Mission recommends that research and training in pyrethrum production should be continued, that plans for smallholder pyrethrum gardens should be directed toward units of at least one acre and that arrangements be made with a reliable company to handle processing and marketing on a commercial scale.

Other Crops. A number of other crops with export potential, or which could ease the burden of imports, should be investigated or further studied by the Department of Agriculture. *African oil palm* should grow well in many lowland coastal regions. Selected planting material has already been introduced for testing. This work should be continued. However, lack of relevant research and of experience in commercial production leads to the conclusion that commercial growing of African oil palm is not likely to materialize within the near future. Therefore, the Mission suggests that the Administration consider encouraging private capital to engage in pioneering development and be prepared to provide positive incentives. Two or three plantations should be started in sparsely populated areas of New Britain or Bougainville. Capitalizing on their experience and contacts in other parts of the world, these companies could transfer planting material, technology, and development capital to the Territory. An arrangement similar to that which the Mission has proposed for nucleus tea estates could accelerate commercial oil palm development.

Rice is another crop which cannot be ignored. Small quantities of rice are grown mainly on non-irrigated land of the Sepik and Gulf districts. Attempts to step up research and commercial rice-growing have so far met with disappointing response. In spite of this record, a re-appraisal of rice-growing and its priority in the development program is now in order.

At present, over 20,000 tons of brown rice are imported at an annual cost of £A1.25 million. Being less perishable and bulky, easier to trade and to prepare than root-crop staples, rice is gaining popularity among plantation workers and urban people. As incomes rise and as more people enter the market economy, the demand for rice will increase. Higher importation and a further drain on the cash resources of the Territory could be avoided by stepping up local production or by controlling the importation of rice.

The outlook for increased local supply hinges on three main factors: technology affecting yield; market price; and acceptance of rice-growing as a farm activity and as a source of farm income.

Rice technology is undergoing rapid changes. Superior varieties and more efficient production methods for tropical rice growing are being developed. The International Rice Research Institute located in the Philippines will play an important part in this development. The Territory should establish a working relationship with the Institute and take advantage of its research and experience. A breakthrough in rice technology alone is not likely to result in the desired production increase. Of equal importance is the assurance of an attractive price level, coupled with an effective government purchase and marketing program.

A third factor, which reportedly has had an adverse effect on local rice production, is the reluctance of indigenes in coastal lowlands to engage in rice cultivation. Admittedly, this type of farming is more demanding of labor, capital input and management than the accustomed ways of subsistence gardening. While rice may never assume the dominant place it has in other tropical countries, there is reason to believe that improved production methods, coupled with attractive prices and a well-planned extension program, should make rice-growing acceptable to progressive smallholders in suitable areas. Limited scope of other crop alternatives, particularly in the Gulf and Sepik districts, makes the pursuit of this objective even more important.

Bananas are another potentially significant crop. This crop has not received much if any attention either for subsistence or commercial production. Long a popular and important crop in garden food production, the Mission gained the impression that much higher yields could be obtained by greater attention to selection of better varieties and improved cultural techniques. Of much greater importance is the extent to which production for export could be developed. Japan is currently importing bananas from Formosa and Ecuador. Imports have risen rapidly in recent years especially from Ecuador, but have yet to reach the 1934–38 level. Import values are still small, amounting to £A5.5 million in 1962. Transport to Japan would be much shorter, easier, and less costly from the Territory than from Ecuador. It is suggested that attention be given to exploring the potential of the Japanese market and to developing quality banana production for such a trade by indigenes. The Territory is suited to banana production. The Mission believes, however, that this could be accomplished only through operators experienced in organization of production and harvesting on plantations and smallholdings, local transport, handling, shipping and marketing.

Sugar cane production should not be neglected in future work. As one of the countries of origin of this plant, commercial growing in New Guinea should be feasible. At present, sugar cane grows wild and is used for chewing by the indigenes. Sugar consumption of the order of 8,000 tons annually imported from Australia, is at too low a level to justify commercial sugar production at this stage. When consumption approaches 20,000 tons annually, the position could be reviewed in view of the exchange-saving potential.[36] Testing of suitable planting material, investigating yield and harvesting problems should be stepped up.

Tobacco production is also of some interest in view of the recent establishment of cigarette manufacturing. Experimental work on the possibilities of supplying at least part of the needs of this factory should be initiated preferably in cooperation with the tobacco company concerned. Similarly, experimental work with Burley tobacco, mainly for twist, should be continued.

LIVESTOCK

Organization of Industry

Animal production plays a minor role in the agricultural economy yet the country is suited to livestock and particularly to ruminants. Limited development of specialized cattle ranching, dairy farming, pig and poultry farming by Europeans has occurred. The indigenes do maintain a substantial pig population under primitive systems of husbandry, not as a recognizable part of agricultural production, but for prestige and cultural reasons. Thus, pig meat contributes little to the regular diet of the people.

There are vast areas of natural grassland at present completely unused. Large parts of these are unsuited to crop production at their present state of fertility, so that ruminants and particularly cattle provide the best approach to their use. In addition, there are large areas within established patterns of agriculture into which the animal could be introduced. There are also extensive areas of forest land which could be converted to grassland.

[36] Even at this level processing of unrefined sugar only would be justified.

Climatically there is no serious bar to the use of grazing animals. Over the greater part of the Territory, grass growth is virtually continuous. Droughts either do not occur or are of relatively minor and local significance. There is no winter nutritional stress anywhere. The only problem is that of heat stress which results in the lowlands being unsuited to high performance of cattle breeds (Bos taurus) from temperate zones. Experience within the country has demonstrated that an infusion of Zebu blood (Bos indicus) permits cattle to produce well in this zone.

The country is notably free from serious animal disease. Since all farm livestock except pigs have had to be imported, it has been possible to exclude the major scourges of the livestock world. The existing cattle population is freer from disease than that of any other country. The same situation applies to other classes of exotic livestock. Even the native pig is remarkably free from major diseases.

Finally, the present production of meat animals, excluding pigs, to which special factors apply, is sufficient to supply only one-third of a pound of edible meat per person per annum. The Territory is short of animal protein.

The Livestock Population. The cattle population was estimated on June 1, 1963, at approximately 30,000 head of which somewhat less than one-third were cows of breeding age (see Table 14). The majority of these were beef-type animals, the dairy-type numbering approximately 1,150.

TABLE 14: Cattle Population by Districts

District	1962	1963
Central	4,600	5,070
Gulf	120	130
Milne Bay	570	890
Northern	1,000	1,240
Southern Highlands	60	70
Western Highlands	2,120	2,250
Bougainville	120	100
Eastern Highlands	1,860	2,290
Madang	2,340	3,480
Morobe	8,680	10,610
New Britain	1,400	1,000
New Ireland	640	760
Sepik	600	850
Western	100	100
Manus	170	170
Total	24,380	29,010

SOURCE: Department of Agriculture, Stock and Fisheries—Animal Industry Division.

Cattle were first imported in the last decade of the nineteenth century. Importations proceeded intermittently until World War II, by which time the total population approximated 20,000 head. During the war, herds were slaughtered for food by the armies involved and only a few individual animals survived in isolated pockets.

Cattle importations prior to World War II were made to supply milk and meat to plantation personnel, and to provide work animals. They were grazed mainly under coconut palms where they had the additional function of keeping down undergrowth and making the collection of coconuts easier. There does not appear to have been any attempt to interest native farmers in cattle production during this phase except by Lutheran missions at Madang, Finschhafen and Boana (near Lae). No specialized cattle farming was developed by Europeans, except for a few herds of dairy cows established to supply milk to the urban population of Port Moresby and Lae.

Since World War II, specialized cattle ranches have been established under European control on properties leased from the Administration; restocking of a few plantations has occurred to a limited degree; religious missions have developed herds in most centers; and a beginning has been made with the distribution of cattle to indigenous farmers by the Administration.

Post-war importations of cattle were mainly of Shorthorn (beef) and Jersey (dairy) breeds. These were obtained from Australia, to which the Territory is limited as a source of supply, as required by disease control ordinances. With the development of Zebu cross cattle in Queensland and the Northern Territory, the more recent importations have been animals with a small percentage of Zebu blood, mainly Brahman, Santa Getrudis and Droughtmaster. Bulls of these breeds, both imported and bred in the Territory from the purebred Brahman stud under Administration control at Bisianumu, have already made a substantial impact on the local herds so that the majority of commercial cattle now carry at least a small percentage of Zebu blood.

A few European farmers have taken up pig production. Their piggeries are located mainly in the vicinity of towns. The total number of animals kept is about 5,000 head. They have been derived from imported Berkshire stock.

Pigs, kept by nearly all indigenous communities, are believed to number about 1 million head. They are of unknown origin and probably arrived with the migration of peoples from the north. They are small, multicolored and unimproved. Grading-up toward the European-type pig is occurring. On their own initiative indigenes have sought and obtained boars of the Berkshire breed from Europeans. This stimulated the Administration to establish pig-breeding centers at both its highland and lowland stations to provide pigs for distribution to indigenes for grading-up purposes. The impact of these developments is noticeable in many areas, though it is equally obvious that the process has still a long way to go.

Estimates based on a sample of 100 villages suggest that indigenes own about three-quarters of a million head of poultry. These also probably originated in Asia. They are unimproved, small and of unknown productivity, and are used mainly for meat and feathers. Grading-up to improved types with imported stock from Australia is just beginning. The Administration set up recently a poultry-breeding center to provide birds for distribution to indigenous farmers. It plans a more extensive program in this direction.

Ten commercial poultry units are operated by European producers located mostly in the vicinity of Port Moresby and Lae. Most religious missions carry some poultry. All stock are imported from Australia as day-old chicks.

Horses number about 1,500. These are mostly owned by Europeans or the Administration and are located on cattle ranches.

Sheep are now virtually non-existent. There are a few head on individual European and mission farms. Early German settlers and Lutheran missions attempted to establish Asiatic breeds prior to World War II with little success. A large-scale and expensive attempt by an Australian philanthropist to introduce Romney Marsh sheep to the highlands in recent years failed. Heavy intestinal parasitism was a major problem. These experiences have brought the species into disrepute, so that it is generally considered that the Territory is unsuited to sheep. Sheep are not generally adapted to the wet humid tropics. High temperatures and humidity, together with but small seasonal variations in the night/day ratio, adversely affect the reproductive efficiency of the species. It is questionable, however, whether sheep should be written off. Adapted breeds, adequate precautions against introduction of internal parasites with imported stock, together with specially prepared and managed pastures, could well succeed in many locations, as has been the case in the highlands of Kenya which have many climatic affinities with the Territory highlands.

A few goats exist in small isolated herds. They survive with difficulty. In general, they are not sought after by indigenes because of their destructive effect upon subsistence gardens and tree crops. For this reason they are not actively encouraged by the Administration. Taking all circumstances into consideration, this seems a reasonable attitude.

Production Systems. A brief description of the husbandry systems in use with the different types of stock is necessary as a background to a discussion of potentialities.

Lowland Cattle Ranching. True cattle ranching is in its infancy, having developed within the last ten years. It is practiced on five pastoral leases mainly in the Markham and Ramu valley systems, and on lowland hill lands near Bulolo. Little more than 100,000 acres are involved. All properties carry only a fraction of the potential stock. Carrying capacity without pasture improvement is 1.4 to 6 acres.

All cattle ranches aim at both breeding and fattening.[37] Steer progeny are grown to carcass weights of 450 to 550 lbs. at two to two and one-half years of age. Crossbreeding with Zebu type sires is practiced but no well-defined pattern has evolved. Operators are still largely at the trial and error stage. All have the same objective of evolving combinations of temperate and tropical breeds, adapted to their conditions. Animals with about 50 percent tropical blood appear most efficient. Progress is restricted by the lack of sufficient well-bred bulls of Brahman, Santa Getrudis, Africander and Droughtmaster breeds. On the whole, reproductive efficiency is reasonable. Calving percentages range from 40 percent with straight European breed females to 80 percent and better with crossbreeds. Calving proceeds throughout the year. Mortality is relatively low, averaging less than 5 percent.

General management follows traditional methods of Australian cattle stations. Main features are minimal subdivision to control cattle of different age, sex and degree of relationship, the provision of water points and well-designed cattle yards, together with frequent handling to control parasites. Only limited attempts have been made to improve native pastures. Cattle are grazed on young re-growth from burned native swards. Controlled burning of appropriate areas provides a succession of suitable feed. The main species of native pasture plants are kunai, kangaroo, saccharums and rottboellia.

Highland Cattle Ranching. Despite the existence of extensive areas of unused native grassland in upland valleys of the Western and Eastern highlands, only limited areas have been acquired by the Administration for pastoral development. The largest unit at Baiyer River is run by the Administration. Europeans have leased several smaller pastoral runs.

The temperate-like climate permits European breeds to perform with reasonable efficiency. Accordingly, Shorthorn and Aberdeen Angus beef cattle predominate. Calving percentages are good. Calves branded from

---

[37] Cattle leases in the upper Markham and lower Ramu valleys were expected to breed store cattle for subsequent fattening on "ground-nut" farms in the lower Markham. This has not eventuated, ranchers preferring to market at finished weights.

Shorthorns at Baiyer River average better than 75 percent of cows mated. Carcasses of 600 lbs. at two to two and one-half years are commonly produced.

Despite the adaptability of European breeds, there is some indication that even under these more favorable conditions, a small percentage of tropical blood is an advantage. Crossing with Africander and Santa Getrudis is developing.

Management methods and grazing techniques are on the lowland pattern, but more attention is paid to introduced species of grasses and legumes with marked improvement in carrying capacity. In particular, elephant grass and guinea grass and the leguminous vines (Centrosemas and Puerarias) have more than doubled the stocking rate. Excellent swards of paspalum and molasses grass with Centrosemas have been established in the Mt. Hagen area after orthodox seed-bed preparation. On these, one beast per acre is carried. All properties could carry many more cattle on existing native swards without pasture improvement.

Dairy Cattle Farming. This is on a very small scale. Europeans have established herds of 40 to 100 cows in the vicinity of the larger towns to provide fresh milk to the urban population. Mission stations also carry a few milking cows. They do not produce for sale.

Jerseys are used in the lowland and coastal areas, and Illawarra Shorthorns in the highlands. Although both are well adapted to the respective climates insofar as breeding and growth rate are concerned, milk yields are very low, ranging from zero gallons to 400 gallons of milk per lactation. This could reflect the combined effect of heat stress and low-quality food on the efficiency of milk production, or be a consequence of poor breeding. There has been no conscious selection of dairy cattle on a performance basis, except on Administration stations during the past three to four years. Most dairy stock have been bred from a few imported animals which were probably not of superior quality in the first place. Quality sires have not been regularly imported. These points, together with individual performances of 600 gallons and over per lactation by Administration-owned Jerseys in the very difficult environment of Port Moresby, suggest that inherent poor quality of the dairy cattle is a major factor contributing toward the general low level of production.

A high proportion of existing dairy herds are milked by machine. Milk sellers meet sales resistance with produce from herds hand milked by native labor. Consumers claim to be suspicious of such milk on grounds of sanitation.

Most commercial dairy herds graze on pastures improved with introduced species. Grain feeding is too costly. Production on native pastures is extremely difficult. These can be maintained in a palatable nutritious state only by burning. This technique, while admirably adapted to extensive beef cattle ranching, is unsuited to small-scale intensive grassland dairy farming.

Plantation Cattle. In the pre-war days, plantation stock were entirely subservient to copra production and did not make for a viable cattle industry. Since the war, several factors have operated against continuation of this system. War resulted in the slaughter of most of the stock. The remaining animals became highly inbred and lost vigor. Most plantations date from the turn of the century, so that replanting of coconuts has been necessary. Large areas have been temporarily removed from grazing due to risk of stock damaging young palms. The underplanting of coconuts with cocoa has taken most plantations suited to this high-yielding crop out of cattle grazing. Finally, planters are wary of cattle, as normally managed, because of their tendency to reduce nut yields by compacting the soil around palms.

Many properties exist, particularly in New Ireland, which are unsuited to cocoa and which could return to cattle production once coconut replantings are sufficiently far advanced. There are others where it is unlikely that all the suitable land will be underplanted with cocoa because of supervision and labor problems which restrict cocoa acreages to units of manageable size. In such cases, cattle might be reintroduced without complicating supervisory management.

Coconut plantations provide an ideal environment for cattle. Plantings of legume species have become firmly established as cover crops. These, in conjunction with the native paspalum, are admirably adapted to the plantation environment and provide high-quality nutritious cattle fodder. The shade from the plantation palms and the frequency of air movement under the canopy considerably reduces heat-stress. Stocking rates of one beast per acre are found where management is good and rotational grazing obviates soil compaction. Reproduction and growth rates can be comparable with the good temperate zone standards.

Cattle farming on rubber plantations has made a useful beginning in the Sogeri and Kokoda areas. At Sogeri, land not ideal for rubber has been sown to pasture. Extraordinarily high stocking rates of two beasts per acre and growth rates of 450 to 500 lbs. carcass weight in 14 to 18 months with straight-bred European-type cattle (Aberdeen Angus) are being obtained at Kokoda. The cattle of all ages there would hold their own in terms of quality and weight-for-age with grass-fed animals anywhere. This performance is remarkable for wet humid tropics and a British breed. It could be due in part to the helpful influence of regular cold night temperatures in association with heavy wet fogs.

Native Cattle Farming. Native cattle projects are a new venture and an attempt to introduce cattle to native farmers. They are operated on a group or village basis. Under the scheme, individuals showing interest in cattle are selected for six to twelve months' training on one of the Administration's cattle stations. During this time, village associates fence and plant a small selected area of five to eight acres with improved species (usually elephant grass) and erect an approved cattle shed and handling yard. On completion of training, a herd of five in-calf heifers are purchased from the Administration at a price in line with the local commercial value. The scheme provides loan finance for fencing, shed and yard.

During the day, the cattle are herded on communally owned grassland adjoining the enclosed area of improved pasture to which they are confined only at night. Although theoretically unsound, since cattle are mainly night grazers in tropical countries, the method works well at existing stocking rates because the enclosed pastures generally have adequate grass for night feedings. It could break down as herd size increases unless accompanied by a corresponding increase of the area enclosed.[38]

The projects are closely supervised by officers of the Animal Industry Division[39] which also loans the services of a perambulating bull. Each project has a target size of 30 head of stock. Economically, each should be viable and capable of returning a net cash income of £A200 per annum to operators from the fifth year onward. It is obviously too early to be certain of the value of the native cattle project approach, but it is one giving great promise of success. This view is supported by the performance in the Boana area of native cattle owners who farm between 300 to 400 head built up from three to four head which survived the war. These are grazed on localized patches of pasture on old garden enclosures in high rugged bush country.

Pig Farming. Pig production by the indigenes is extremely primitive. Two methods can be recognized. Under the first, the pig is allowed to fend for itself by rooting in forest and grassland. The second involves housing to the extent that pigs share the same dwelling as their owners and a limited amount of hand feeding and suckling by humans occurs. Ownership is defined by ear, hoof or tail marks. Castration is practised, but sufficient boars are left for matings which are indiscriminate—sows seeking their mates in the forests.

Observation suggests that the level of efficiency is very low. Only two to four pigs are reared per litter. Sows breed at a very early age and small size. Permanent stunting is evident. Growth rate is very slow. The fact

---

[38] Enclosing cattle at night in this way is in part responsible for the low-level performance of cattle in many tropical countries, i.e., India and Fiji.

[39] Department of Agriculture, Stock and Fisheries.

that large-scale native celebrations, or sing-sings, at which extensive slaughtering of pigs takes place for ritual purposes, occur only at intervals of some years (seven years in many clans) is an indirect measure of the time taken to build up sufficient numbers of animals of adequate size.

Essentially, the pig is a direct competitor with humans for similar types of food. For this basic reason, it is unlikely that any marked improvement in efficiency or any major increase in pig numbers can be expected, unless indigenes produce food crops in excess of family requirements. Such development is least feasible in the three highly populated areas of the highlands and the Sepik.[40] Even in the remainder of the Territory it is unlikely unless pressures make pig production a worthwhile speciality of some farmers of the group. This has occurred near Rabaul, where native producers supply pig meat to the town. Apart from these considerations, the dominant importance of the pig, not as an economic form of animal production, but as an integral part of the cultural system, severely limits the contribution it could otherwise make.

Pig production methods of Europeans follow orthodox patterns, with housing modified to suit the environment. Feeding is based on imported grains. Local production of grains has been tried but abandoned because of low yields and harvesting problems due to varying ripening rates.[41] Dependence on imported goods results in high costs. Profitability is dependent upon high prices obtainable mainly from the indigenous population for pigs purchased largely for social reasons. Efficiency of management on European farms varies widely from very poor to very good. There appear to be few operators in the medium and top range. This is probably a consequence of pig production being merely a side line to a major enterprise, completely different in character.

Poultry Farming. The indigenes run poultry mainly as scavengers and with comparable efficiency. Only a few individuals have been persuaded to enclose and to manage on a controlled basis. The introduction of improved strains of birds is likely to extend this. However, the general absence of grain farming makes it unlikely that any extensive development of poultry production will eventuate.

European producers operate either on a battery or deep litter system. The former is eminently suited to the environment and to the most efficient use of expensive imported foods. Foods are usually fully processed preparations. On the whole management is good. Most operations appear to be profitable, due mainly to the high price of imported eggs and poultry meat. Further development along these lines can be expected as the urban population increases.

[40] Chimbu, Wabag and Maprik.
[41] The Administration grows some sorghum at Baiyer River.

Animal Health. Cattle face virtually no major health hazard. They are practically free from tuberculosis (0.043 percent) and contagious abortion (0.18 percent). Rinderpest, foot-and-mouth disease, contagious pleuro-pneumonia and haemorrhagic septicaemia have been excluded. Cattle tick, the incidence of which has been largely a legacy from lack of control during World War II, has been cleared from all districts except for small pockets in isolated areas of little potential. The only difficult problems are those associated with screw-fly strike and internal parasites. Screw-fly, which is ubiquitous, is a problem at altitudes below 5,000 feet. Regular four- to six-week prophylactic treatment of all cattle and their inspection at least every two days is necessary. Newborn calves have to be protected immediately against navel strike. Under these conditions, the existence of screw-fly is a blessing in disguise. It makes the frequent handling of cattle unavoidable. This makes them extremely quiet, a valuable attribute in a country where lack of control could result in many cattle going "bush," and essential if a native population, which has never had contact with such a large species, is to learn to handle cattle without fear. The internal parasites present are those characteristic of temperate zones, and so far have proved of minor importance. They could assume greater significance as stocking rates increase.

Diseases among imported pigs are likewise of little practical significance provided the stock are kept indoors on concrete. Free range animals become infested with internal parasites, particularly kidney worm. Indigenous pigs all suffer from this parasite along with a large number of other internal worms. Anthrax occurs in native pigs in some areas from which pig movement is restricted to confine its incidence.

Poultry are also free from serious diseases. Infectious Laryngo Tracheitis, which is widespread in Australia whence all new stock are derived, and Newcastle disease have been kept out. Coccidia and other common parasites are present but do not present serious problems.

Marketing of Livestock Products. There is no well-defined organization for marketing livestock or livestock products. Live cattle are sold to ranchers and native producers. Fat steers are killed mainly on farm killing-floors for immediate plantation consumption or for sale to meat traders. Approximately 1,600 head were killed for meat during 1961/62— equivalent to 18 percent of the total fresh, chilled and frozen meat consumed in the country. The kill for 1962/63 is estimated at about 2,000 head. Prices for cattle average 2/-d to 2/3d per lb. dressed weight, making a 600 lb. carcass worth £A60 to £A65.

There is no recognizable trading in pig meat by natives except in the Rabaul area. There is some barter of live animals especially for bride prices and festivals for which gifts are often made. European producers sell most of their output direct to indigenes. Some are slaughtered at pork weights (50 to 70 lb. carcass) for meat traders. Prices average £A7 per head for weaner pigs at eight to nine weeks of age and 4/6d per lb. carcass weight for porkers. There is no production of bacon. Pigs slaughtered by European producers in 1961/62 totaled 2,700 head. The local kill amounted to 45 percent of the total trade in chilled and frozen pork.

Eggs are traded to retailers in the towns, prices averaging 6/4d per dozen. Broilers sell at 5/-d per lb. On slaughter, laying hens return their capital cost as chickens plus rearing costs selling at 15/-d each. Production meets about 60 percent of total needs.[42]

Administration of the Animal Industry. Administration of the animal industry is the responsibility of the Animal Industry Division of the Department of Agriculture. This division maintains quarantine control of imports of livestock and of meat. It supervises all stock movements. It provides a free veterinary service to stock owners and administers disease and pest control programs. It inspects meat intended for sale for human consumption. It is responsible for animal-husbandry advisory work and for breeding and multiplying livestock for distribution, primarily to indigenous farmers. It also conducts experiments on pasture improvement and animal production methods.

Eight livestock stations are maintained. Those at Bisianumu and Moitaka are mainly concerned with multiplication of Zebu cross animals based on the Brahman and Aberdeen Angus. The stations at Erap and Baiyer River are mainly multiplying centers for the lowlands and highlands, respectively, with Africander and Brahman cross Shorthorn at Erap and Shorthorn Africander cross Shorthorn and Red Poll at Baiyer River. Herds of Jersey are maintained at Moitaka and Kurakakaul. The latter, along with the stations at Goroka and Erap, also multiplies Berkshire pigs for distribution. A small Shorthorn dairy herd is maintained at Goroka. The stations at Kila Kila and Lae are primarily laboratory and quarantine centers.

The division is ably led, the key staff keen and efficient, with the operation in general soundly based. It has done first-class work in securing and maintaining a healthy animal population. In addition to its normal duties, the division engages in training indigenous farmers to handle cattle and pigs, both to stimulate indigenous production and to provide field staff for its work.

Beef Production

A large cattle industry capable of contributing significantly to the economy could be established. There are 12.5 to 13.5 million acres of

[42] Europeans produced 800,000 dozen eggs and 14,000 head of poultry in 1962.

TABLE 15: Grasslands (estimated)

District	Millions of Acres	Estimated Stocking Rate
Western	4.04[a]	1:15–20
Sepik	1.65	1:10–20
Central	1.56	1:6
Madang	1.15	1:6–8
Eastern Highlands	0.91	1:4
Morobe	0.90	1:4
Milne Bay	0.90	1:6
Western and Southern Highlands	0.83	1:4
Northern	0.60	1:6
Total	12.54	

[a] Mostly Eucalypt Savannah.

SOURCE: Department of Agriculture, Stock and Fisheries.

native grasslands, of which less than 150,000 acres have been earmarked for grazing. Deducting the 4 million acres of Savannah grassland of the Western District on the score of inaccessibility, 8.5 to 9.5 million acres could be used for cattle-raising.

This estimate does not include the area of pasture under coconut palms, the area existing or which could be developed within the land used by the indigenes for subsistence farming (land in fallow), and the area of uncleared forest land suited to pasture establishment. On a conservative basis these three sources could add a further 2.5 million acres to the potential.[43]

The area of native grassland needed to maintain a cattle beast ranges from 2 to 20 acres. Using a mean figure of about 6 acres, the 11 to 12 million acres of available or potential grassland could support a national herd of nearly 2 million head of mixed ages. Improvement of native swards with sown grasses and legumes increases the stocking rate by three to four times. Taking the lower figure, the improvement of 25 percent of the available grassland lifts the cattle potential to 3 million head. Improvement of 50 percent of the area raises it to 4 million head.

During the three years from 1960 to 1962, the Territory imported approximately 8 million pounds of canned meat, mostly beef, and 2.3 million pounds of chilled or frozen beef and beef products annually. These have cost approximately £A1.8 million annually (£A1 million for canned meat and £A0.8 million for fresh meat). While it is unreasonable to expect complete replacement of canned meat by fresh under tropical conditions, considerable savings in canned meat could be made from a

[43] Estimate supplied by the Department of Agriculture, Stock and Fisheries.

local cattle industry. All the imported chilled and frozen beef could be replaced by the local product, while the present low level of meat consumption could be markedly increased.

To date, official policy in respect to cattle production has been cautious. The Administration has been necessarily occupied with the development of cash crops because of their export potential and because they provided a rapid way of introducing indigenes to a cash economy by methods not too far divorced from their experience. The almost complete lack of contact between the indigene and large farm animals, and consequent doubts as to his willingness to accept and ability to handle cattle stock, appear to have dominated official thinking. Caution also resulted from the need to test the suitability of climate and pastures for cattle-raising. This has inevitably taken many years.

At the same time the Administration's policy has been purposeful. It has set up testing and multiplying cattle stations; it has imported potentially suitable breeds; it has established an admirable health and advisory service; it has aided the establishment of a small number of strategically located cattle ranches; and it has made a beginning with the introduction of cattle into native farming.

The time has arrived, however, for a radical change in emphasis. The development of cattle production should now become a major rather than minor activity. Apart from the contribution a cattle industry could make to the national economy, such an industry provides the only large-scale means by which the indigenous people can make effective use of the millions of acres of natural grassland.

In particular, the Administration should change its present attitude to land acquisition so that the few additional large blocks required are obtained to permit accelerated growth of cattle numbers. In addition to providing funds for its own operations, it should develop the mechanism for the equally important credit facilities to both indigenous and non-indigenous operators. It should take steps to develop essential marketing facilities so that meat products can be processed and distributed. It should improve road transport so as to facilitate movement of livestock and products. It should establish trade policies necessary to ensure adequate replacement of meat imports by the local product.

A target, in terms of size and time, is essential to the planned development of any new industry. The size of any operation and the period of time involved, together, largely determine the quantity and character of the necessary inputs of land, labor, capital and administrative machinery. Such a target must be realistic. It must be related to ultimate potentials. It must take cognizance of the immediate availability of basic resources. In a livestock project, it must recognize the biological limitations to growth of any animal population. It must be in line with market demand and potentials. It must conform to the requirements for economic viability of the enterprise.

The Mission has considered all these factors and believes that a reasonable target over the next ten years would be a national herd of 300,000 head. This is a tenfold increase over the present herd. On an estimated take-off of 15 percent, it would provide an annual kill of 45,000 carcasses. The present total consumption of beef and beef products is estimated to be equivalent to about 35,000 carcasses.[44] An expanded local output of 45,000 head should be easily absorbed by partial replacement of current imports, and by increased consumption likely to result from the expanding economy, the changing dietary habits of the people and the expected increase in population.

Although this target is relatively modest, it is a much more extensive operation than anything attempted or visualized so far.[45] It is capable of achievement with adequate organization. In particular, it depends upon a planned and rapid increase in the size of the breeding herd. The breeding herd in 1962 numbered 8,000 head. Applying standard population increase procedures and basic assumptions[46] applicable in the Territory, it has been calculated that the target herd number of 300,000 head of mixed age and sex could be achieved in ten years by the immediate addition of 15,000 breeding cows. Spreading the acquisition over a three-year period, a total of approximately 18,000 breeders would be necessary. Importation at the rate of 6,000 animals per annum should be within the capacity of Australia to supply, is within the capacity of the quarantine service to handle, and is a reasonable number in terms of location and management.

Breeding Herds. Expansion depends basically upon solution of the many problems associated with the multiplication of livestock. The key unit is the breeding herd, the management of which is all important to the achievement of the ultimate objective. The issues involve more than the mere mechanics of stock multiplication. The animals must be adapted to the environment. They must conform to reasonable standards of production efficiency. They must be under efficient managerial control.

Cattle of guaranteed adaptability are unlikely to be obtainable. It will be very difficult to purchase sufficient female stock with the necessary

[44] Local kill 1,600; imported frozen 6,700; imported canned 27,000.

[45] The current five-year plan of the Administration has a target of 50,000 head of cattle with 2,500 in native hands.

[46] Effective calving rate 80 percent; annual mortality 5 percent; normal sex ratio 50 percent; annual take-off during build-up period 10 percent; and heifer culling during build-up period 10 percent.

minimal proportion of Zebu from Australia. Controlled grading-up in the Territory to the standard required will be necessary. Under these circumstances, the target is unlikely to be reached unless sufficient key breeding herds are located in large groups. This necessitates European control so that the skills of established and experienced cattlemen are made use of, the full benefit of expensive selected sires obtained and advantage taken of the potentials of artificial breeding.

It would be a serious mistake to locate imported cattle in small groups under indigenous management. Cattle take at least a year to acclimatize. The process is slower and more difficult the greater the proportion of European blood. Calving percentage is low from new stock. The difficulties of grading-up to necessary standards are immeasurably greater with herds of five to ten cows than with herds of several hundred. Direct tie-in of indigenous farmers to the initial breeding-up phase of industry establishment would involve serious disappointments and jeopardize the whole project.

The alternative is to give the responsibility during the formative stage to the Administration and to European ranchers. As the most easily organized source of stock for the native farmer, the Administration should continue its present cattle multiplying operations, should bring its existing cattle stations up to full carrying capacity and should increase the number of these in districts where they are needed most. The present breeding herd of 1,850 head on Administration stations at Moitaka, Bisianumu, Erap, Baiyer River and Kurakakaul should be increased by 2,000 head. New stations should be established to carry a further 2,000 breeders. Suitable locations would be Musa, Dobadura, Kabuna, Goroka and Urimo. This would give approximately 6,000 head of breeding cows under Administration control.

The majority of existing cattle ranches are understocked. Specialized ranches and properties with cattle on a fairly large scale could increase their total breeding herds from the present level of 6,000 head by 9,000 head. In addition, the many cattle owners of small to medium-sized herds in association with coffee, coconuts, rubber and mixed farming, now carrying approximately 1,250 breeders, could add at least a further 1,000 cows to these.

The foregoing proposals leave a deficit of approximately 4,000 breeding cows (Table 16) to provide the required 18,000 additional cows. These would have to be accommodated by leasing land already owned by the Administration or by obtaining additional land for lease to experienced Australian cattlemen. These new leases should be concentrated in the Markham, Ramu, Watut and Wau/Bulolo areas to have ready access to Lae abattoirs. Blocks with a potential of at least 10,000 breeders are

TABLE 16: Key breeding Herds (three-year period)

Operators	Present Cows	Projected Cows
Administration	1,750	3,750
Administration (new)	—	2,000
Private Ranches	6,000	15,000
Private Ranches (new)	—	4,000
Mixed Farmers	1,250	2,250
Total	9,000	27,000

readily available. This zone has the advantage of large areas of unused land the acquisition of which, in the ultimate interest of the people, should present a minimum of political difficulties while easy access to the main market point would generate the necessary confidence of investors. Ideally, any new lands acquired should be leased for short terms (33 years) with compensation for value of improvements in the event of non-renewal or take over at any stage by a future government. There are reasons to believe that sufficient Australian cattlemen could be persuaded to invest in cattle ranching in the Territory under such circumstances. Only two or three additional operators would be needed.

Stimulation of private enterprise to participate in the program would necessitate continuation of the freight subsidy on imports until the required number of females and males (since bulls also will be needed) have been obtained. Under a well-planned organization the current maximum freight subsidy of £A35 per head, which has tended to become the actual subsidy, is likely to be greater than needed. The operation is sufficiently large to make the charter of a special cattle boat, at substantially lower rates, a more economic proposition than the present system of importing in small lots. Two additions to the present subsidy conditions are desirable. First, the assistance should be limited to cattle breeds and crosses likely to be adapted to the property for which they are intended. Failure to recognize this could lead to wastage of subsidy funds. Second, the subsidy must be offered to all existing as well as new ranchers if their full cooperation is to be assured.

Participation by Indigenes. Extensive participation by indigenous farmers is not only a major objective but is vital to the attainment of the program. Four years after commencement, the nucleus breeding herds of the Administration and private ranchers will have been built up to approximately 30,000 head of breeding cows through direct import and natural increase. At this level, the properties concerned will be at full capacity (without extensive pasture improvement) insofar as breeding stock are concerned. Thereafter, their requirements will be limited to normal replacements available from home-bred female stock (about 15 to 20 percent of the breeding herd) leaving the balance available for distribution to native farmers.

From this stage onward, both existing and newly established Native Cattle Projects can be supplied with breeding cows as well as or in lieu of steers. By the tenth year native operators should be farming 150,000 to 200,000 head of cattle, of which 50,000 would be breeders. At this stage, too, the Administration and ranching properties would be carrying 100,000 to 150,000 head of cattle of mixed age and sex.

The whole program will break down unless sufficient participation by indigenes is obtained. In this phase of the operation, the native cattle projects approach must be pressed ahead with vigor. The present scheme needs modification to fit the program. Female breeding stock will not be available for distribution to the indigenous farmers in large numbers for approximately five years. Indeed, the present system of providing indigenes with female cattle from Administration ranches is militating against the most efficient development of the industry and restricts the build-up of key breeding or multiplying herds.

There is a conflict of interest here. However, there would be direct aid, rather than conflict, if the native cattle projects concentrate on the use of steer cattle instead of breeders for the first four to five years. There are many advantages in such a change. Indigenes, unused to cattle, could be trained more easily with steers than with cows whose managerial requirements are more exacting. Association of cattle with a cash economy from the outset would reduce the risk of cattle developing a prestige value based on numbers as a major motivating force. Fat steers could be sold annually for cash, assisting materially in stimulating meat consumption by the indigene, and setting the stage for a sound economic local cattle industry. There would be the additional practical gains of a more rapid build-up of breeding herds on all key multiplying farms by sale of steers as yearlings to indigenes and a marked economy in the bull requirement during this formatory phase. In addition, the full quality gains possible from artificial insemination could be realized.

Since participation by the indigenes is likely to depend very largely on the native cattle project approach, 5,000 to 7,000 projects, each with 20 to 30 head of stock, must be in operation by the end of the ten-year term. This will involve an extensive training program.

Marketing. The program calls for a thirtyfold increase in the supply of locally produced beef over a ten-year period. Supplies would rise to a level which would permit complete replacement of imported chilled and frozen beef, partial replacement of imported canned meats and some

TABLE 17: Current Beef Consumption and Projected Supply

Type of Meat	Current Consumption	Supply in Five Years	Supply in Ten Years
Carcass Equivalent 500 lbs.			
Local Kill [a]	1,600	15,000	45,000
Imported Fresh [a]	6,700	—	—
Imported Canned [b]	27,000	27,000	16,000
Total	35,300	42,000	61,000
Per Capita (in lbs.) [c]			
Fresh	1.5	2.3	6.1
Canned	4.0	3.5	1.8
Total	5.5	5.8	7.9

[a] Assuming that a 500 lb. carcass yields 350 lbs. of fresh, chilled or frozen edible meat.
[b] Assuming that a 500 lb. carcass yields 300 lbs. of canned meat.
[c] Assuming a rate of population growth of somewhat more than 2 percent a year.

increase in per capita consumption. Relevant projections are shown in Table 17.

All producers must be assured of a continuing profitable market for local beef if investment in and development of the industry is to occur. The special problems of marketing in the Territory require close study and planned action. The basic marketing problem is that of adjustment of imports to local production and consumption trends. For this purpose, the mechanism of quantitative control of imports is the easiest approach. The data in Table 17 suggest that it should not be difficult to make the necessary adjustments. During the first five years, a small per capita increase of about one-quarter of a pound of meat per annum would absorb all the increased local output without any reduction of canned meat imports. During the second five-year phase the problem increases in magnitude, although the physical difficulties should be much less since the marketing channels for disposal of fresh meat should have been developed by this time. During this phase some replacement of canned meat may become necessary. The projections assume a 40 percent cut in this item with a further increase in total per capita meat consumption of about 2 lbs. per annum.

The most controversial aspect here relates to canned meat supply. It may be argued that such a large reduction is unrealistic in a tropical climate where it is difficult to keep fresh meat. Apart from the fact that no such reduction would be necessary if per capita meat consumption doubled in the ten years—and this is by no means improbable considering the small amount of consumption involved and the force of economic and social changes likely to be generated—examination of the canned meat trade suggests that a substantial cut could be made. Calculations, based on the minimum legal meat ration of indigenes in paid employment, indicate that about 80 percent of canned meat imports are probably consumed by indigenes in employment. The evidence suggests that about 45 percent of these are located in two main areas—the Gazelle Peninsula and the Port Moresby area. A large proportion of the remainder is concentrated in Madang and in the Morobe District (Lae, Wau and Bulolo). More than half the total paid-labor force is thus concentrated in relatively small geographic areas to which the organization of fresh meat supplies is not difficult. Furthermore, the trend toward cash wages could conceivably increase the demand for fresh over canned meat. It does not seem unrealistic, therefore, to plan for a decrease of up to 40 percent in imported canned meat.

The question of price is also important. At present, fresh meat is competitive with imported chilled and frozen, and at this price is profitable to producers. Cheaper cuts are competitive with canned meats. Under these circumstances no special price-control policies should be necessary. In the long run, producers may have to face a lower price, especially when production reaches the export level. By that time, however, the industry should be firmly established and capable of operating profitably at lower price levels.

It should be noted in passing that the scale of the project is too small to warrant serious consideration of local meat-canning. Such a project could become a viable proposition, after the ten-year development phase, should cattle herds continue to expand. It would have to be in a position to export since at least 50,000 head of cattle would have to be processed annually to make canning economic, and at this level, output could be well in excess of local consumption. In these circumstances, however, it might be more profitable to export carcass meat, pre-cut and frozen, to nearby countries within which the demand for meat could well expand sufficiently to make such a trade possible.

Essential to the economic viability of the program is the development of marketing services for handling locally produced meat. These are quite inadequate at present. Farm killing floors could not handle the projected output. Meat traders have restricted freezer space for holding and handling fresh carcass meat although the nucleus equipment exists in that now used for handling imported pre-cut frozen joints. There are inadequate cutting-up facilities and none for processing by-products and off-cuts.[47] Roads in cattle districts are poor and not well suited either to

[47] Mince, sausages, corned beef, tallow, dripping, hides, etc.

walking or trucking cattle. They do not exist in several important cattle zones. Shipping facilities between Territory ports are inadequate especially in respect to freezer space.

The first requirement is that of slaughterhouses. The Administration is proceeding with the erection of an abattoir at Lae, with a capacity to slaughter 300 head daily (chilling only 90 per week). Since this will serve the zone of largest immediate potential, the project is soundly conceived. Several subsidiary units are a matter of urgency. Slaughter floors are needed at Port Moresby, Goroka, Mt. Hagen and Rabaul (mostly for pigs) even to use existing production. These need be neither large nor costly.

Assured of a regular supply of fresh meat, it should not be difficult to persuade meat traders to provide the necessary extra wholesale, processing and retail-handling facilities. The Administration should work to this end. As an additional aid, native markets serving indigenous consumers should be encouraged and equipped to retail fresh meat.

On the transport side, the slaughterhouse at Lae will not be able to operate at anything like capacity without extension of the present main road in the Markham Valley to the top of the Ramu Valley to tap cattle from the large grassland areas located there. The presently planned extension of the Lae-Eastern Highland road via Kainantu to Goroka would provide a vital cattle link. Further road improvements, in the Waghi-Baiyer River valleys with extension to the Jimmi River valley, serving slaughter facilities at Mt. Hagen and eventually linking the Western Highlands with Madang, would open up cattle country to markets. Sea transport similarly must receive close attention. Arrangements will have to be made to ensure that shipping companies are organized to handle local meats between Territory ports. Adequate freezer space must be allowed for in planning the re-equipment program for coastal shipping.

Organization, Research and Health Control. It is important that the organizational responsibility for developing the field side of cattle development be vested in one organization. The Animal Industry Division of the Department of Agriculture provides an appropriate control body. Officers of this division would have the front line responsibility but would require full cooperation of the officers of the Extension Division in implementing the program with native farmers.

While adequately staffed to fulfill its present rather small-scale activities it would require both augmentation and reorganization to play the role suggested. In particular, more officers capable of covering the husbandry side (breeding, feeding and management) would be needed. These need not be veterinarians. For preference, they should be diplomates or graduates in agricultural science who have specialized in animal husbandry. The Mission's general views on recruitment and staffing apply to this problem. Provision for an appropriate staff has been made in the Mission's recommendations for expansion of the personnel establishment of the department.

Provision must also be made for animal research. This is visualized as a responsibility of the research section of the department. Though not a limiting factor at present, the absence of organized research in the animal production field could become a serious handicap as the industry expands. Indeed, full exploitation of the potential will be impossible without much more investigational work than has been possible so far. A beginning should be made immediately. Research is needed in the fields of pasture improvement for cattle, in cattle management on native and improved pastures, on crossbreeding levels in relation to location and performance, on factors affecting reproductive efficiency, on the control of internal parasites, on screw-fly control, on the role of toxic plants and on the general role of animal health and animal management in the local scene.

Of special significance is the future official policy on animal health control. Present ordinances are closely tied to Australian standards. Veterinary authorities in Australia regard the Territory as a first line of defense against the introduction of exotic diseases to Australia from the North. In consequence, they oppose strongly any relaxation or deviation from present high standards. This policy has three main effects. It restricts the Territory to Australia as a source of livestock; it prescribes a slaughter policy to eradicate any exotic disease that may reach the Territory; it prohibits the importation even of cattle semen for breed improvement from countries other than Australia.

The first would handicap the program severely should it result in inflated cattle prices for the 18,000 head of imported cattle needed. Australia itself is short of Zebu-type cattle, and if the authorities insist on maintaining the embargo, Australia should meet any extra cost incurred. The second could destroy even the present embryonic industry almost overnight. For example, introduction of foot-and-mouth disease to West Irian (via Indonesia) is a new and imminent risk. If so introduced, it could not be kept out of the Territory, to which it would be brought by pigs and wildlife. A slaughter policy would exterminate existing cattle herds and would not eradicate the disease which must continue unchecked in the forest pigs. Further cattle imports in such circumstances would be futile. Under these conditions, maintenance of a slaughter policy is unrealistic and could deny a cattle industry to the Territory. It should be abandoned in favor of vaccination. This is a proven, practical technique for controlling the disease to economic levels. Insofar as semen imports are concerned, the embargo is also a severe and unjustified handicap. Grading-up of existing and introduced cattle stocks with high-quality, Zebu-type breeds is an essential part of the program. The Zebu cattle of Australia are few in number and provide a relatively narrow genetic base from which to build. This base should be widened as it can be, both easily and cheaply, by importing suitable material from other sources, particularly the United States.[48]

Dairy Production

Most of the existing pasture is located in tropical lowlands although extensive areas and a large potential for increased acreage exists in the highlands. Tropical grasslands are not well adapted to milk production. Quality of feed, while good enough for growth and fattening of cattle, is usually too low to support worthwhile milk yields. Even introduced, improved pastures tend to have nutritional weaknesses in the tropics. Available species are limited and subject to rapid time changes in nutritional value. In particular, the protein status is usually too low, and a really satisfactory tropical pasture legume to correct this situation has yet to be found. Independent of the nutritional side, high-level milk production imposes a severe physiological stress on the cow, the significance of which increases markedly with high temperatures and humidity. The combination of these two sets of factors—nutritional and physiological— makes commercial milk production a hazardous enterprise in any tropical environment.

As a result of these forces, the chances of developing a substantial dairy industry to produce milk and milk products in the lowlands are poor. Dairying is likely to be limited to its present size and function in producing fresh milk for the European urban population. In these circumstances no special program of expansion is justifiable. Assistance can be limited to guiding existing producers toward greater efficiency particularly in the area of better stock quality.

The indigenous population, now largely without milk, could well use this foodstuff, particularly for children, and this need could be catered for by imports of cheap milk powders which have long been in excess supply in the dairy export world.

This is not the situation in the highlands. Here, pastures of milk-producing quality can be developed. Here, climate approaches that of the temperate region. Neither climate nor nutritional stress are limiting factors. In terms of the physical background and resources, dairy farming

[48] The Mission appreciates that these recommendations could have implications for trade with Australia.

based on grassland is possible. A fair comparison can be made with the highlands of Kenya, where similar circumstances have permitted the growth of a substantial dairy industry, which caters for a large internal market and contributes to export income. Though developed originally by European farmers on orthodox lines, the Kenya industry now incorporates a large and growing number of African smallholders, each with two to seven cows.

A case exists, therefore, for recommending that the native cattle project located in the highlands be supplied with cattle of reasonable milk potential. The dual purpose breeds—Australian Illawarra, Shorthorn and the Red Poll—have demonstrated their suitability to this environment. Using these breeds, native farmers should be introduced to dairying. With adequate safeguards, increased milk production could be of great value to human health, particularly that of children. In addition, the butter and cheese now imported by the Territory—500 tons annually—could be produced in the highlands. The Administration should plan a small manufacturing unit for the area with a capacity of at least 500 tons of butter. It would require a supply pool of approximately 12,000 to 15,000 cows. Its timing should be geared to the local build-up of herds and the educational status of the people.

To encourage native dairy farming, it is desirable that responsibility for dairy (milking shed) inspection and control be vested in the Animal Industry Division. In view of the advisory aspects involved, it is unsound that this should be a function of the Department of Public Health which cannot be expected to be either knowledgeable or interested in farm production. The Animal Industry Division, however, must cooperate with the Department of Public Health in maintaining adequate health standards at production, marketing and processing points.

Pig Production

Although there are many serious limitations to any marked expansion of pig production, these should not prevent attempts being made to change the existing pattern of production and to increase output. Many subsistence level communities of other countries have improved living standards through more enlightened pig production methods.

The limitation of feed supplies could be met if the Mission's recommendation for stepping up the output from subsistence gardens were implemented. Much of the extra food produced could be cashed, through the pig, by specially trained native farmers. Feeding in enclosures built of cheap native materials, but with concrete floors rather than under free range conditions, could have a profound effect on production efficiency—

not only through controlled feeding but through the reduction in the parasitic burden relative to free range stock. The Animal Industry Division should not dismiss these possibilities as impractical. Indeed a concentrated effort to test the approach on an experimental basis should be a matter of high priority in the extension program of the future. The pattern established by the Tolai people near Rabaul could be used.

On the breeding side, the work of the Animal Industry Division in providing indigenes with cheap improved stock is commendable. However, the survey designed to follow up the fate of pigs so disposed of could well indicate the desirability of modifications. For example, the present policy of distributing purebred European stock might need to be changed to one of using more vigorous selected crossbred animals derived from controlled breeding of native sows and European boars. There is some evidence that many of the highly bred animals currently distributed fail to survive the primitive conditions to which they are exposed.

Insofar as European pig farming is concerned, the evidence suggests that present methods based on importation of all food are of questionable profitability. Recently, several producers have gone out of business. Unless larger supplies of locally produced feeding stuffs can be organized, this form of enterprise is likely to decrease rather than increase.

Poultry Production

There is limited scope for increased production of eggs and poultry meat at present. Limitations of food supply and husbandry methods exist of a magnitude and nature comparable with those limiting pig production.

While the priority of a well-balanced poultry program is relatively low, a start should be made with more progressive native units as demonstration points, from which more enlightened and efficient production could spread. The policy of distributing European breeds to indigenes is to be commended. In common with the pig stock distribution scheme, however, it suffers from the defect of being a unilateral approach which could be more successful if combined with efforts to step up the level of husbandry.

European production and marketing is well organized and operated. Complete dependence upon imported feeding stuffs necessitates high local prices, which nevertheless are competitive with imported poultry products. So long as these can be supported, production is likely to continue in its present form. Production costs might be lowered through the production of local grains, but such development is likely to be a long time ahead. This section of the industry needs no special attention but could benefit from a trained poultry expert. Most of the poultry operators are amateurs who have come to the industry from other walks of life. They frequently strike problems of disease, feeding and husbandry, experiencing losses avoidable with expert recognition and advice.

Controlled poultry production by indigenes should be encouraged. This approach should be combined with a program of distribution of improved stock. A poultry expert should be added to the strength of the Animal Industry Division.

Need for Finance

Insofar as pigs and poultry are concerned, the proposals are modest, involving mainly a change in emphasis. The cost is within the capacity of the normal budget of the Department of Agriculture to absorb. In contrast, considerable capital injection will be necessary for the beef production program. The needs of the Administration and private sectors, for the first five-year phase, are summarized in Table 18. Finance for the second five-year phase will be limited to the needs of the participating indigenes.

On these figures, the total capital requirement will be £A1.88 million, of which £A0.79 million will be needed by the Administration, £A0.57

TABLE 18: Capital Requirements of Cattle Program, 1964/65–1968/69[a]

(£A thousand)

	1964/65	1965/66	1966/67	1967/68	1968/69	Total Five Years
Administration						
Cattle	30	45	45	5	5	130
Freight	25	38	38	—	—	101
Land Purchase	15	15	—	—	—	30
Station Development	50	50	50	—	—	150
Slaughter Floors	10	10	10	—	—	30
Freight Subsidy	100	125	125	—	—	350
Sub-total	230	283	268	5	5	791
Private Sector (European)						
Cattle	120	150	150	—	—	420
Station Development	50	50	50	—	—	150
Native Sector						
Cattle	25	25	38	50	63	201
Station Development	40	40	60	80	100	320
Total	465	548	566	135	168	1,882

[a] Cattle at £A30 per head; transport £A25 per head; land £A1 per acre; station development in the private sector £A10 to £A12 per breeding cow; slaughter floors £A10,000 each; initial cattle per native project £A125 and development per native project £A200. Prices as at 1963.

million by the European private sector and £A0.52 million by the native private sector. The Administration's requirements include the freight subsidy on cattle imported by the private sector amounting to £A350,000 and land purchase for new cattle stations both Administration and private of £A30,000.

Annual recurrent costs are summarized in Table 19, spread over a five-year recruitment period. Transport and incidentals reflect the normal ratio to salaries and other costs which has existed in recent years. The data cover only the expenditures for additional staff requirements. They do not include the already existing current expenditures of the Animal Industry Division.

TABLE 19: Recurrent Expenditures of Livestock Program, 1964/65–1968/69

(additional expenditures; £A thousand)

	1964/65	1965/66	1966/67	1967/68	1968/69
Salaries	13	32	46	60	70
Wages	10	20	30	35	40
Transport and Incidentals	7	18	24	30	35
Total	30	70	100	125	145

Special credit facilities will have to be created to finance the program. Credit up to 50 percent of the needs of the private sector is desirable as an incentive to investment. Credit for existing ranchers and farmers should be organized so that new stock can form the basis of collateral without reference to other farming activities. Stock mortgages of this type are common in Australian finance and should present no serious difficulty in organization. New ventures could be handled on a complete investment basis so as to cover land development as well as stock. About £A0.3 million will be needed on a 50 percent basis by the non-indigenous sector during the three-year build-up period.

It is difficult to estimate the credit needs of indigenes participating in the program. There is much evidence that reserves of capital exist in some quantity and, taking this factor into consideration, the financial provision should anticipate a need for up to two-thirds of the investment. This would amount to two-thirds of £A0.52 million or about £A0.35 million during the first five years. Credit requirements during the second five years of the ten-year period, using the same ratio, work out at £A0.95 million, giving a total for ten years of about £A1.3 million.[49]

[49] For 6,000 projects (1,600 during the first five years and 4,400 during the second five years).

FORESTRY

Forests which clothe about three-quarters of the Territory are one of its major assets. Variously estimated to cover 80 to 90 million acres, about 60 million acres are in swamps or on slopes so precipitous as to make them of questionable commercial value, at least at this stage of development. The remaining 20 to 30 million acres have forests with an industrial potential of considerable magnitude.

Though most of the forests are untouched, a small but useful timber industry has developed which supplies almost all the local timber needs and has an exportable surplus. During 1961/62 and 1962/63, the output of logs, sawn timber, plywood and other forest products was valued at £A2.6 million in each year, half of which was exported. The industry employed 450 Europeans and about 3,000 indigenes, paying wages valued at about £A1.2 million per annum.

A preliminary survey of forest resources was made by a professional Australian forester as far back as 1908, but it was not until 1922 that the first commercial sawmill began operations at Port Romilly. A small Forest Service was established in 1938. Until 1942 two small units formed the whole of the milling industry in Papua. In New Guinea, nine small mills were set up before the war, largely under the stimulus of low copra prices and the need to supplement plantation incomes. Only local requirements were supplied except for a small export of New Guinea walnut to the United States. Export began in 1937/38 with 3 million super feet of logs to Australia. By the outbreak of war, exports had risen to 7.5 million super feet.

During the war years, extraction was undertaken by the armed forces and over 80 million super feet of sawn timber and a large quantity of round timbers were harvested for military use. At their peak, military sawmilling operations were producing at the rate of 40 million super feet a year. The military established a unit to survey the forest resources with an instruction to maintain records suitable for handing over to a civilian forestry unit in due course. This survey group, using air photo interpretation, mapped the major vegetative types of the north coast of New Guinea, and the islands of Manus, Bougainville and New Britain. Some 1,500 botanical specimens were collected and used as a basis for the herbarium at Lae, which now contains more than 54,000 specimens. After the war, the present Department of Forests was formed, some of its personnel being recruited from the disbanded army survey team. The department continued the survey work started by the military. The areas covered by the military, supplemented by subsequent activities of the land research and regional survey teams of the CSIRO as well as the Department of Forests are shown on the map facing page 156.

Organization of Industry

Forest Classification. The classification of forest areas, as currently delineated, is set out in Table 20.

TABLE 20: Classification of Forest Areas, June 30, 1963

(thousand acres)

	Papua	New Guinea	Total
Reservations			
Territory Forests	47	25	72
Timber Reserves	22	—	22
Other Administration Land			
Purchased for Forestry Purposes	—	89	89
Timber Rights Purchased	108	877	985
Land under Permits and Licenses	177	9	186
Total	354	1,000	1,354
Native-owned (approximate)	39,500	49,000	88,500
Estimated Grand Total	40,000	50,000	90,000

SOURCE: Department of Forests.

Territory forests refer to land permanently dedicated to forestry purposes. Timber reserves refer to Administration or Crown land over which timber concessions can be granted with control of harvesting activities. Land purchased for forestry purposes is self-explanatory. Timber rights purchased cover the purchase by the Administration of the right to remove timber from a specified area over a stipulated period of five to forty years. In the latter case, the landowners may retain rights to harvest some classes of forest produce, to hunt and cultivate on land not carrying merchantable timber. Land under permits and licenses comprises land over which timber rights only have been purchased to permit controlled exploitation of areas where land alienation was not possible.

In addition to control of these natural forest areas, the Department of Forests has established small plantations of hoop and klinki pine at Bulolo/Wau and of teak at Keravat and Brown River. The total plantings in 1963 covered about 10,000 acres. All plantings are at the immature stage.

Milling Activities. Nearly all the forest land owned and controlled by the Administration, which now totals about 1.3 million acres, is on lowland or foothill country and in areas where population is relatively scarce. Some idea of the main locations currently being utilized and their

TABLE 21: Indicators of Forest Utilization, June 30, 1963

| | | Area Sawmills | | Capacity |
	Permits and Licenses	Area (thousand acres)	No. Established	(thousand super ft. logs per day)
Central	36	193	15	73.1
Western	1	65	2	3.5
Gulf	3	31	4	23.5
Southern Highlands	—	—	3 [a]	5.1
Northern	3	9	2	9.0
Milne Bay	2	37	5	24.0
Morobe	12	117	6	97.0
Western Highlands	4	4	12	28.0
Eastern Highlands	3	3	7	31.5
Madang	1	0.1	3	4.5
Sepik	2	11	9	32.5
New Britain	18	222	11	55.2
Bougainville	2	16	3	6.5
New Ireland	1	0.4	—	—
Total	88	708	82	393.4

[a] Public Works Department.

SOURCE: Department of Forests.

relative importance can be obtained from Table 21, which summarizes the number of permits and licenses granted by the Administration, the areas covered by these, the number of sawmills established and their capacity.

The New Britain, Morobe and Central districts are by far the most important, together accounting for 75 percent of the timber permits and acreage with 39 percent of the mills and 57 percent of the daily cutting capacity. These data also indicate that most of the individual operations are so small that they are not properly considered as commercial units.

This is even more clear from an examination of individual data of the 55 private sawmills; there are only five with a log capacity per day in excess of 15,000 super feet, eight fall in the range of 10,000 to 15,000 super feet per day, ten range from 5,000 to 10,000 super feet, and 32 can handle only up to 5,000 super feet their average capacity being only 2,000 super feet per day. Of the remaining 27 mills, five are run by the Department of Public Works, three by the Department of Agriculture, each with a small daily capacity of about 1,500 super feet, and 19 by religious missions each with an average of 4,000 super feet daily.

On the permit side, only one is for a forest block in excess of 100,000 acres; one covers between 50,000 and 100,000 acres; five apply to blocks ranging from 20,000 to 50,000; 17 control between 10,000 and 20,000 acres; while 64 give access to areas of less than 10,000 acres each. Of the latter, 27 permits and licenses are for areas of under 1,600 acres.

Apart from sawmilling, the Commonwealth-New Guinea Timbers Ltd. operates a plywood factory at Bulolo with a log capacity of 20,000 super feet per day. This began operating in 1954 under joint ownership of the Australian Government (a 50 percent plus interest) and Canadian and Australian private interests.

Type of Timber. The lowland forests are extremely varied in their composition and are typical of tropical rain forests. The lower montane forests may be dominantly beech or oak, except for a few localized stands of pine species of which klinki and hoop are the most important. By and large, however, a very wide range of timber species exist in most lowland and hill rain-forest areas. The Department of Forests lists 163 marketable species whose timber qualities have been assessed by standard techniques.[50] Of these, 30 fall into the durable class and are suited for use in the ground or for unprotected exterior use in buildings; 32 are resistant to lyctus borer; 70 have a density rating in excess of 40 lbs. per cubic foot; 33 have a strength rating high enough to make them suitable for heavy construction; 19 are suitable for veneers; 27 have special values for furniture; and a large percentage are suitable for most house-building purposes though some require protective treatment.

Until ten years ago, the bulk of the export trade was supplied with five hardwood timbers: taun, kamarere, kwila, erima and walnut; and two softwoods, klinki and hoop pine. The two latter were used for most of the plywood export for which they are ideally suited. New Guinea walnut commands high prices for its special suitability for high-quality furniture and has been exported in large quantities. Today, as a result of trade promotion by the Department of Forests, based on increasing knowledge from testing of unfamiliar species, over 40 hardwoods and an increasing variety of softwoods enter the export trade.

This great variety of timber types in any one forest is well illustrated by the specifications of the "Tonolei Timber Area"[51] of approximately 100,000 acres, estimated to contain 500,000,000 super feet of merchantable timber. Tenders for this block were called in 1963. Yield is estimated to range from 2,000 to over 50,000 super feet per acre. Wide variability is shown not only in the number of timber species concerned but also in the contribution of each to total yield. A summary of this situation is shown in Table 22.

[50] Properties and Uses of Papua and New Guinea Timber Samples, Department of Forests, September 1962.

[51] Australian Timber Journal, Vol. 29, August 7, 1963.

TABLE 22: Timber Variability, Tonolei Timber Area, New Britain

Name	Super Feet[a] (million)	Percentage of Stand
White Beech	4.9	1.0
N. G. Rosewood	1.1	0.2
Amoura	1.1	0.2
Taun	87.0	17.2
Calophyllum	60.8	12.0
Vitex	28.5	5.6
Satinash	7.3	1.5
Yellow Hardwood	6.1	1.2
Miscellaneous	1.0	0.2
Brown Terminalia	144.9	28.6
Red Silkwood	43.0	8.5
Erima	26.8	5.3
Terminalia	17.9	3.5
Dysoxylum	5.2	1.1
Grey Canarium	4.1	0.8
Miscellaneous	4.6	0.9
Celtis	9.9	2.0
Cheesewood	7.5	1.5
White Silkwood	6.2	1.2
Cryptocarya	2.8	0.6
Albizzia	2.4	0.5
Miscellaneous	32.5	6.4
Grand Total	505.6	100.0

[a] Net merchantable volumes over 7 feet g.b.h. (girth).

Quite obviously this variability in a commercial forest creates special problems both in harvesting and marketing. Many of the species are not yet well known to foreign buyers. The quantities of each are frequently so small that marketing tends to be effected in "mixed" parcels. While suited perhaps to makers of particle board, this technique is not relished by general buyers, particularly when they have only limited knowledge of the species concerned.

The handicap of variability is offset to a considerable degree by the large size and straight boles of many of the major species contributing to yield. Thus, Brown Terminalia provides merchantable boles over 150 feet with a girth above buttress of 15 feet; Taun and Calophyllum have boles up to 120 feet and up to 14 feet diameter and can achieve stocking rates on the better stands of 80,000 super feet per acre; Vitex commonly grows to merchantable boles of 60 feet with a girth of 15 feet; Red Silkwood often exceeds boles of 90 feet with 12 feet girth; Erima, which is a very

TABLE 23: Timber Production, Local and Export Trade, 1961/62–1962/63

Type	1961/62		1962/63	
	Quantity (thousand ft.)	Value (£A)	Quantity (thousand ft.)	Value (£A)
Local Trade				
Sawn (su. ft.)	17,000	1,200,000	15,000	1,050,000
Plywood (sq. ft. ³⁄₁₆-inch basis)	6,000	210,000	5,800	200,000
Total		1,410,000		1,250,000
Export Trade				
Logs (su. ft.)	1,980	49,000	14,766	319,000
Sawn (conifers; su. ft.)	1,585	119,000	3,095	235,000
Sawn (nonconifers; su. ft.)	1,152	72,000	651	51,000
Plywood (sq. ft. ³⁄₁₆-inch basis)	26,358	935,000	17,161	697,000
Veneer Sheets (sq. ft. ¹⁄₁₆-inch basis)	5,052	32,000	5,594	36,000
Total		1,207,000		1,338,000
Grand Total		2,617,000		2,588,000

SOURCES: For local trade: Department of Forests estimates; for export trade: Overseas Trade Bulletins, Territory of Papua and New Guinea.

large riverine species common throughout the Territory, reach 200 feet in height with a girth above spurs of 20 feet.

Present Production. The size and scope of the existing timber industry is summarized in Table 23.

Total log cut was approximately 80 million super feet in each year. Sawn timber yield was about 40 percent of log super feet. Cutting for local production accounted for approximately half the trade in the two years concerned. The greater part of this came from sawn timber. On the export side some major fluctuations are apparent. Export of logs increased about sevenfold over the two years, the bulk of the increase being taken by Japan. Similarly, sawn timber exports doubled in the case of conifers but fell nearly 50 percent in the non-conifer types. This was a reflection of the increased export in the log form which tended to be largely the non-conifer type. Plywood exports fell in the second year due mainly to marketing difficulties in Australia to which the bulk of this product was sent.

Log prices vary considerably with species and quality. Top quality walnut returns up to £A15 per 100 super feet on wharf. The average saw log commands about £A2 per 100 super feet for good-quality, well-known species at the wharf. Sawn timber returns from £A6 to £A9 per 100 super feet depending on locality, species and quality. The highest prices are obtained for furniture timber.

Administration. Responsibility for administration of the forest industry is vested in the Department of Forests, organized with four main divisions: Management, Botany, Silviculture, and Utilization and Marketing. The department is responsible for forest protection, control, afforestation, research and forest resources. It is just getting into its stride and warrants strong support from the Administration.

The staff employed in 1962/63 amounted to 37 professional officers, 64 sub-professional officers and technicians, and 37 administrative assistants and clerks. These were approximately half the established positions in each category, a situation which has been maintained since 1951/52. In addition, the department employs about 1,000 indigenous workers of various types.

The Territory is short of trained foresters with university training. To obtain professionals the department offers cadetships leading to university degrees in forestry from Australia. Four such cadetships are offered each year. To date, absence of indigenous applicants, with the necessary university entrance qualifications, has limited cadetships to Australian recruits.

At the sub-professional level, a new forestry school was established at Bulolo in 1963. Designed to cater for indigenous students, this school has a theoretical teaching capacity of 40 students a year for two-year courses leading to employment as technical assistants or forest rangers. At present, however, living accommodation restricts the total intake to ten per annum or a total of twenty. Even this, however, has not been fully used, the entry in 1963 being only three indigenous full-time students. Lower grades of sub-professional staff are now also trained at the Bulolo School. These students are of a lower educational standard than for the two-year courses. They are given six-month courses leading to employment as forest field workers. This type of training commenced in 1962 at three regional centers, but is now consolidated at Bulolo. The Mission considers that, in accordance with its views in respect to support staff for agriculture (to be discussed later), the comprehensive secondary schools system, reinforced by in-post training, should be drawn on for this level of forestry staff. Only in this way can Bulolo be developed as a sub-professional training center of any significance.

The Mission has grave doubts whether the program for training in forestry, as planned, is adequate to produce either the quality or the number of professional and sub-professional staff needed by the Department of Forests. The forests are potentially a large earner of income but to develop a prospering forest industry fully qualified professionals are required to meet the needs of an expanding Department of Forests and the additional demands of what should be a rapidly growing forest industry.

For the time being the professional staff can only come from the outside, and no stone should be left unturned to obtain the quality and number of professionals needed by the department. As indicated throughout this report, the Commonwealth Government, as a matter of national policy, should see that qualified professionals are made available to the Territory.

The education program should begin to lay the basis for well-trained professionals and sub-professionals. The training in forestry should be the equivalent of that which is to be given in the diploma course in agriculture at Vudal, and the agricultural college to be located in the highlands as recommended by the Mission. To make maximum use of the faculty and the facilities, and to make possible a stronger teaching staff, it is suggested that the forestry and agricultural schools for the highlands be merged. Forestry and agricultural officers will be working together in arriving at future land-use arrangements, and if training of forestry officers is inferior to that of their opposite numbers in agriculture, the programs and public support for the former will suffer. The graduates of the diploma course would have at least quasi-professional standing and have capabilities for further development and training. The best of the diploma course graduates might, after field experience, be selected for further training in Australia or elsewhere.

Background to Development

Potentialities. From the general survey work already done (see map facing page 156) much is known of the general extent and character of timber resources. At the same time, vast areas have yet to be examined in detail by field reconnaissance, and other extensive blocks remain to be surveyed. Based on existing information, the Department of Forests estimates that nearly 1 million acres of forest having timber of a high market potential are presently available or can shortly be made available for commercial use. In addition, there are 1.5 million acres of easily accessible timber stands of comparable value which could be obtained for logging or milling. These two groups are estimated to contain marketable timber totaling 7,000 million super feet. At an average log return of £A2 per 100 super feet in the log, they have a potential value of approximately £A140 million. The areas and quantities are listed in Table 24.

TABLE 24: Estimated Timber Resources, 1963

Location	Area (thousand acres)	Volume (million super feet)
Presently Available[a]		
Bulolo/Wau	50	500
Lae Area	100	300
Hoskins	100	400
Port Moresby Area	100	200
Rabaul Area	100	100
Tonolei	100	500
Gogol	130	300
Miscellaneous	300	500
Totals (rounded)	1,000	2,800
Easily Accessible		
Kulu/Dagi	80	300
N. Coast New Britain	500	1,200
S. Coast New Britain	100	500
Sagarai	100	300
Northern Districts	100	500
Vanimo	200	500
Sogeram/Ramu	400	1,000
Totals (rounded)	1,500	4,300

[a] Either owned or leased by Administration or Administration negotiating purchase or lease.

SOURCE: Department of Forests.

The Department of Forests points out that the estimated area of forest land on slopes of less than 30 degrees is more than ten times the areas listed, or more than 25 million acres. Volume estimates are based on current utilization limits which restrict operations to a few species and a minimum girth of 7 feet. They assume a low average yield of 2,000 super feet of log per acre. This figure is conservative.[52] It is greatly exceeded in practice over much of the forest land already in use and could be further increased by improved per-acre utilization under good management.

It is further argued by the department that a reasonable Mean Annual Increment (MAI) for rain forest is 400 super feet per acre; this appears conservative. Even if 50 percent of the blocks listed in Table 24 are eventually taken from permanent forest for conversion to agricultural use, the remaining blocks could sustain an annual cut of 500 million super feet indefinitely. This is more than six times the existing log output. On the

[52] Tonolei is advertised at 5,000 super feet with part running to 50,000 super feet per acre.

FOREST RESOURCES SURVEYS

JUNE 1963

Areas investigated from air photos

Areas investigated by field parties

CSIRO Land Resources Regional Survey

0   25   50   75   100   125   150   175   200
MILES

assumption that these estimates are reasonably based, it is obvious that the timber production potential is sufficiently great to warrant an aggressive policy of commercial development.

Markets. A key factor in determining the extent to which these resources can be made use of is the marketing prospect. In the past, the Territory has looked primarily to Australia. Since Australia imports annually 1 million super feet in logs and sawn timber from the Philippines and Malaysia of a type similar to that available in the Territory, this market should be vigorously explored.

A great scope also lies in the East Asian market, particularly Japan. A comprehensive survey of timber production trends and market prospects in the Asia-Pacific region by FAO and ECAFE in 1961 lends strong support to this probability (see Table 25). New Guinea is included as part of Insular Southeast Asia in these projections. Japan constitutes the greater part of the East Asia complex where the greatest deficit is predicted. Japan is interested primarily in the import of timber in log form, to the production of which Territory producers are already accustomed. This market survey assumes that the trends have even greater significance since the requirements relative to supply are likely to further increase after 1975, so that the need for increasing supplies in the long term is far greater than indicated by the anticipated deficits of that year. It should be noted that the Territory has already been taking advantage of this situation by exploring the Japanese market.

TABLE 25: Comparison of Forecast of Supply and Demand of Industrial Wood in the Asia-Pacific Region

(in million m^3(r) ^{a})

	1960			1975		
	Supply	Consump-tion	Surplus(+) Deficit(−)	Supply	Require-ments	Surplus(+) Deficit (−)
Continental Southeast Asia	8.9	9.0	−0.1	20.0	16.4	+3.6
Insular Southeast Asia	13.3	11.3	+2.0	30.0	20.6	+9.4
South Asia	7.6	8.5	−0.9	9.0	19.4	−10.4
East Asia	42.9	43.0	−0.1	60.0	79.7	−19.7
Oceania	12.8	15.0	−2.2	20.8	25.3	−4.5
Total	85.5	86.8	−1.3	139.8	161.4	−21.6

^{a} m^3(r) = cubic meter of roundwood.

SOURCE: Timber Trends and Prospects in the Asia-Pacific Region, a study prepared jointly by the Secretariats of the FAO of the United Nations and the United Nations Economic Commission for Asia and the Far East, Geneva, 1961, p. 87.

In addition to the external market, the potentials of the local market are not inconsiderable. Although the program of the Mission for the various sectors of the economy calls for a slow-down in the construction of hospitals, the demand for industrial timber for local European type housing needs, secondary schools and other purposes is likely to be considerable over the next few years. In addition, a well-organized local timber trade could reduce markedly the present import of building materials such as fibro-cement, replaceable in many instances by timber, and of pre-fabricated timber buildings and assembled building panels. These three items cost £A350,000 in 1962/63. Also, with the natural growth of the local population and a rising standard of housing, local timber needs (including those for fuel requirements) may be expected to grow rapidly.

Organization. The most serious problem, to be solved before a development program of any significant size is feasible, is how to attract experienced logging and milling interests of adequate size, financial backing and market contacts. Commercial harvesting of the timber resources for the export market is best handled by private enterprise. Because of the nature of the task of extraction of such large trees in difficult terrain, heavy large-scale equipment is necessary. World timber prices are strongly competitive. There is, therefore, the need for low-cost production which again emphasizes the desirability of large-scale units. The prime necessity for better grading of the wide variety of timbers concerned requires a level of managerial and marketing skill more likely to be available to large-scale operators. It has already been pointed out that the existing industry is comprised largely of very small operators, the majority of whom cannot be regarded as meeting these basic requirements. Important as these small units have been and still are in meeting local needs, a soundly based forestry industry will require greater experience, organization and finance than most of them can command. There is, therefore, need for the attraction of operators who can meet the requirements of handling a sizable operation.

Basic to the attraction of large-scale interests is the need to acquire any new timber rights necessary. These must be in large enough blocks to warrant considerable capital investment by large-scale loggers. The Administration must be ready and willing to implement its powers and to acquire the necessary forest blocks at a rate sufficient to keep pace with any development plan decided upon. The Mission has noted that indigenous landowners tend to be unwilling to sell forest land, but are more willing to dispose of timber rights for varying periods. This approach is realistic and should be fully exploited. Some of the timber rights agreements made along these lines, however, so limit the number and size of species that can be cut, that the Department of Forests feels that desirable natural regenerative work tends to be precluded. This defect should be avoided in future negotiations with indigenes. While the immediate need is for harvesting of a small part of the existing reserves of timber, the forests should be regarded nationally as an improving rather than a wasting asset. Accordingly, the Administration should work out a policy and plan for implementation which will ensure at least minimal productivity and potential.

An exception to this approach involves the conversion of land of high agricultural potential to farming purposes. Much of this type of land exists. Here, complete harvesting of the forest cover is rational. In terms of acquisition, however, this will probably necessitate either land purchase or 30- to 35-year lease of land by the Administration rather than lease involving only the right to cut timber.

In order to encourage the necessary capital investment by private enterprise, the normal contract terms of the Administration may require revision. It is the practice to call for public tenders for forestry permits. The conditions of the tenders stipulate not only proof of capital resources and provision of the necessary logging equipment and/or mills within a stipulated period of time, but also have placed the responsibility for the provision of access roads, bridges and wharves on the successful tenderer. This has permitted, indeed necessitated, royalty payments being set rather low, on average at about 5/-d per 100 super feet. From discussions with forestry authorities, it appears that the method has one disadvantage which could be very serious. It is argued that the capital responsibility for roads, bridges and wharves, where needed, so increases the element of risk because of the investment costs involved, that very few substantial operators are prepared to engage in logging or milling in the Territory. The element of political and economic uncertainty associated with the Territory investment climate of recent years contributes to this reluctance. An alternative approach would be for the Administration to provide the necessary infrastructure from its own resources and increase royalty charges to meet the cost. This method, while perhaps more justified in the case of forest blocks intended for permanent agriculture where roads and bridges must be determined by agricultural use as well as forest harvest, has the disadvantage of high costs. Commercial forest interests responsible for both construction and maintenance are likely to operate more cheaply. It is also a method that increases the stress on administrative and organizational resources. In consequence, the Mission would suggest an approach by which the roads, bridges, etc., would be constructed by the operator to specifications prepared by the Administration, and the costs taken into consideration in the contract.

The Administration might further increase the attractiveness of proposals to interest efficient operators by offering the use of some of its special technical skills during the initial period. Within the Administration there is considerable and in some cases almost unique specialized experience in identification, machining, seasoning, etc., of unfamiliar woods and in labor-training, as well as knowledge of climate and road construction. While any interested operator would have or would speedily obtain some competence in such matters, the Administration should consider a package offer which would include availability of such special skills. As part of a package, the Administration might design and cost the logging road system in order that the cost of roads and timber be clearly separated.

It is most desirable that the Department of Forests develop a rational system of granting concessions that will attract efficient operators. To this end, the Department of Forests could well benefit from the employment of a competent consultant (not identified with any potential concessionaire), to assess the feasibility of commercial operation in several possible concession areas and the reasonableness of proposed rates of royalty payment, including estimates of the cost of establishing access (roads, bridges, wharves, etc.), transportation from stump to processing point, and manufacturing to the degree necessary for the world market.

In addition, the proposed Development Finance Company should be in a position to advance credit to large timber operators up to more or less 50 percent of the total investment costs. This would spread the investment risk and provide an incentive of real worth. In any case, the finance company should be prepared to consider credit for part of the cost of equipment and mills which are likely to be substantial in any large-scale program.

Development Program

The Department of Forests prepared a five-year program of development for 1962/63–1966/67. This, however, was extremely modest when viewed in the light of making effective use of a large existing asset. It envisaged increasing cutting to a total of 120 million super feet of logs per annum by 1966/67 representing only a 50 percent lift over the actual output of 1961/62.

At the same time, the program was well balanced involving not only utilization at a higher rate, but covering extension of previous reforestation activities, provision for new forest stations, provision for extension and improvement in training of both Europeans and indigenous forestry personnel, completion of reconnaissance and assessment of economically merchantable forest areas, continued collection of botanical material and reinforcement of forestry research.

The Department of Forests, when the Mission was in the Territory, revised the projections to 180 million super feet by 1968/69 from a base of 80 million super feet in 1962/63. The Mission believes that even this rate of development is modest in view of the department's own estimate of the immediate potentials as illustrated in Table 24. While the Mission is fully conscious of the many problems involved in a substantially larger program, it is also conscious of the very great contribution which the timber resources could make to an economy, the rate of growth of which should be accelerated as rapidly as soundly conceived arrangements can be made.

Accordingly, the Mission recommends that the targets summarized in Table 26 should be set by the Administration and that active organization should proceed to realize them.

TABLE 26: Timber Production Targets by Volume, 1964/65–1968/69

(million)

	1964/65	1965/66	1966/67	1967/68	1968/69
Total Logs (su. ft.)	110	150	200	250	300
Export Logs (su. ft.)	45	75	115	155	200
Sawn Timber (su. ft.)	23	25	28	30	34
Plywood (sq. ft. ³⁄₁₆-inch basis)[a]	25	25	25	25	25
Veneer Sheets (¹⁄₁₆-inch basis)	5	25	50	60	70

[a] Could be increased under more favorable arrangements with Australia.

It will be noted that this program envisages an increase in log output to the level of 300 million super feet in five years, commencing 1964/65. This output will be divided between export logs, sawn timber, plywood and veneers as indicated. The ratios are substantially in line with those adopted by the Department of Forests in its projections insofar as sawn timber, plywood and veneers are concerned, with the greater part of the increased output taking the form of export logs. In terms of feasibility, it will be noted that the suggested output is well within the capacity of the available or readily accessible forest areas to produce. The department estimates these as capable of yielding at least 500 million super feet per annum of log in perpetuity, or more than twice the recommended rate until faster utilization will take place.

The Mission suggests that the increased output be in the form of export logs only as the most realistic first approach to obtaining outside investment. Milling should be developed as soon as possible. Export log operations will make the least demands on capital investments and on the scarce local labor skills and at this stage may be an advantage. But such operations provide less employment, are subject to greater fluctuations of markets, tend toward a more temporary exploitative type of operation, and moreover, unless particular care is taken, usually entail lower standards of utilization since only the more valuable logs are shipped. Milling and processing operations, on the other hand, obviously give greater employment, bring greater income and contribute more to development. Desirably, a two-stage contract system should be adopted, starting with the export of logs but providing for the subsequent installation of mills and the expansion of operations.

Whatever the degree of processing of logs cut, realization of the production targets advocated by the Mission need not result in a lasting loss of productive assets to the country. Cutting of trees on land with a high agricultural potential, thus making this land directly suitable to agricultural development, is a necessary prerequisite to this development, whereas, in cases where cutting on permanent forest land is involved, no lasting loss of forest need occur provided the Administration takes the right measures to safeguard re-growth.

Clearly, however, the point previously made about the need to enlist the cooperation of large-scale enterprise must be re-emphasized as a prerequisite to such a program. It is difficult to conceive that nearly a fourfold increase in harvest rate could possibly be handled in any other way. Half a dozen large-scale enterprises could easily do so. To this end, the Administration would be well advised to reconsider its normal method of operating through tenders in favor of direct negotiation with some of the better known international timber companies. Their expertise in operation, along with their experience and contacts in marketing, could well pay handsome dividends from the viewpoint of achieving a worthwhile export timber industry. In the search for such cooperation, the possibility of obtaining direct participation by commercial interests, in the area likely to provide the greatest market, should not be overlooked. This could have the added advantage of insuring that log output of the level so readily available would, in fact, be marketed without difficulty.

Infrastructure Requirements. The additional roads, bridges and wharves which would be necessary to handle the additional timber areas based on the Department of Forests' estimates, total £A4.2 million. Of this, wharves total £A700,000, bridges £A500,000 and roads approximately £A3 million. Serious consideration should be given to methods of financing these. The capital cost appears high but this is not so when it is appreciated that it could be largely recouped in 15 years (should the Administration accept responsibility[53]), by an increase in the royalty charge of the additional logs to be cut from the present average rate of 5/-d per 100 super feet to 7/-d per 100 super feet. On this basis, additional royalties would amount to about £A1.22 million over the first five years and a further £A4.4 million in the next ten years, assuming the same cutting rate—a total of £A5.62 million.

Staff. Obviously the Department of Forests will need to increase its staff to handle an expanded program of these dimensions. Since the type of staff required is for a strictly commercial activity, this does not necessitate a *pro rata* increase in existing departmental staffing or of its projections for the smaller program recommended by it. These programs cover a great number of activities of a different type and while they should be continued at their present level, the bulk of additional staff requirements should be geared specifically to rapid and early utilization of the extra forestry areas for which the main requirement will be production supervision. Justification for extension of further afforestation and other expanded activities will be far more easily made when a large-scale forestry industry is a reality.

Staffing projections for the revised five-year program of the Department of Forests called for a 60 percent increase in existing staff made up of 25 professional officers, 48 technicians and 15 clerks. This would provide a total establishment of 226 as against the present level (1962/63) of 138.[54] On the assumption that each additional 20 to 30 million super feet of timber per annum requires one additional technical officer, the above estimate is increased by ten technical staff.[55] In view of the particular character of the recommended program, some revision as to numbers and types in each category will be necessary.

Value of Production. Table 27 projects the annual value of production under the program. On this basis, output should rise to a level of over £A8 million per annum in five years.

[53] As indicated earlier, the Mission favors an approach whereby the operators would be made responsible for the infrastructure, the expenditures being considered in relation to other conditions spelled out in the contract. In order to ease the burden on the contractor, the Administration may find it necessary to reimburse the contractor for such costs. On this assumption the estimated costs are included in projected Administration expenditures. However, if the contractor were to finance the costs, the Administration's expenditures on infrastructure would be smaller, revenue from royalty would be smaller, and the need for funds for the Development Finance Company (assuming that it would finance part of the cost of the infrastructure) would be larger.

[54] A further 200 to 300 indigenous support staff would also be needed.

[55] This assumes that no additional appraisal staff will be required for this volume.

TABLE 27: Timber Production Targets by Values, 1964/65–1968/69 [a]

(£A million)

	1964/65	1965/66	1966/67	1967/68	1968/69
Local Trade					
Sawn Timber	1.12	1.19	1.26	1.30	1.33
Plywood	0.20	0.20	0.20	0.20	0.20
Total	1.32	1.39	1.46	1.50	1.53
Export Trade					
Logs	0.90	1.50	2.30	3.10	4.00
Sawn Timber	0.49	0.56	0.70	0.80	1.05
Plywood	0.70	0.70	0.70	0.70	0.70
Veneer	0.03	0.30	0.60	0.80	0.90
Total	2.12	3.06	4.30	5.40	6.65
Grand Total	3.44	4.45	5.76	6.90	8.18

[a] Logs at £A2 per 100 su. ft.; sawn timber at £A7 per 100 su. ft.; plywood and veneers at current values. Veneers from 1965/66 onward at about double the price of earlier years due to assumed processing of higher quality timber.

This value would be increased by three and a half times per unit volume for timber exported as sawn timber rather than as logs.

Participation by Indigenes. Of necessity, development of the timber resources at this stage is primarily the responsibility of expatriates insofar as capital provision, management and expertise are concerned. This does not mean that indigenous people will not benefit directly from or will not be involved in the operation. The industry would provide work at cash wages for at least 12,000 and provide at £A4 a week a wage return of about £A2.4 million a year. Fulfillment of the training program of the Department of Forests would also provide continued employment at various levels for a large labor, support and technical staff. The indigenous population as a whole would also benefit by the over-all strengthening of the economy and by the contribution to government income from royalties and tax payments. Native landowners concerned would benefit directly through sale of timber rights.

Proposed Expenditures. Public expenditures during the next five years for forestry development consist of capital and recurrent expenditures. Estimated capital expenditures have been summarized in Table 28.

Expenditures on roads, bridges and wharves required to open up the additional timber areas have already been mentioned. For purposes of planning, the whole amount of £A4.2 million has been considered as a charge to the Administration budget, although expenditures for the

TABLE 28: Projected Capital Expenditures for Forestry Development

(£A thousand)

	1964/65–1968/69	
	Total	Annual Average
Roads, Bridges and Wharves	4,200	840
Purchase of Timber Rights and Forest Land	500	100
Buildings and Forest Station Development	350	70
Plant, Machinery and Equipment	175	35
Total	5,225	1,045

Administration might be smaller.[56] The amounts projected for purchase of timber rights and forest land, buildings and forest station development and plant, machinery and equipment are global estimates, in part based on indications provided by the department. The estimate for purchase of timber rights and forest land might well have to be increased considerably if there is to be rapid progress in the acquisition of land for permanent forestry.

Current expenditures are those for the Department of Forests and for Vocabulary Stores. The Mission believes that the amounts given in Table 29 should be about adequate to accommodate requirements under the recommended program, including additional staffing needs, discussed earlier.

TABLE 29: Current Expenditures on Forestry

(£A thousand)

	1963/64	1964/65–1968/69	
	(Budget)	Total	Annual Average
Department of Forests[a]	419	2,700	540
Vocabulary Stores	61	350	70
Total	480	3,050	610

[a] No correction has been made for some small items included in the budget of the department which are of a capital rather than a recurrent nature.

FISHERIES

Fisheries now play a very minor role in the economy, both cash and subsistence, though in coastal areas most indigenes do some fishing and the few people living on the shores of Lake Murray and the Murik Lakes

[56] See p. 163, fn. 53.

(west of the Sepik River mouth) depend very largely on fish for subsistence. In the highlands, with few local species of fish in natural waterways, production is very low. The Fisheries Division has estimated that fish production as a whole is about 10,000 tons a year or an average of 10 lbs. per person. Only 20 percent, or about 2,000 tons, is estimated to be traded, either for barter or for cash.

Substantial quantities of canned fish are imported from Japan and consumed by the indigenous population. Fish imports have risen sharply in recent years from about 1,500 tons in 1956/57 to about 5,000 tons in 1962/63, and the value has risen over the period from £A242,000 to about £A600,000. The landed cost of imported canned fish is about 1/-d for a 15-ounce can. The cost of fresh fish in the markets of the larger coastal towns is much higher, ranging from about 2/-d to 4/-d a pound.

Spear fishing remains the traditional mode of fishing for the indigenes, but at appropriate places there is reef fishing by hand line, in-shore and off-shore netting, beach seining and shallow-water trapping.

The greatest development of commercial fishing is found along the Papuan coast. Perhaps a hundred or more native craft, mostly of the catamaran type, have been motorized, with loans from the Native Loan Fund. The use of ice, which can extend the range of craft as well as delay spoilage, has been encouraged by the Fisheries Division. The Federation of Native Associations has a vessel, mainly for the transport of copra along the Papuan coast, which is fitted with a freezing compartment of three tons capacity. This vessel operates between Samarai in the east and Beara in the west, drawing fish supplies from freezers established at three points along the coast. The expansion of production to supply the Port Moresby market is still hampered, however, by deficiencies in the marketing arrangements and freezer capacity there.

Native fishermen also supply small quantities of fresh fish to the other major coastal towns and a few fishing vessels, owned and operated by non-indigenes, deliver their catch to these centers—Rabaul, Lae and Madang—making use of whatever spare freezer space is available. As in Port Moresby, the local markets are very small, prices tend to be high and the scale of operations very restricted.

Marine Resources

Some 1,450 species of fish have been identified in Territory waters, but fishing tests indicate that the bulk of fishery resources is composed of 20 or so species such as tuna, Spanish mackerel, sweetlips, trevally and barramundi. The most important species for indigenous fishing are mackerel tuna, runner and malabur.

Recent coastal surveys have concentrated on the waters of southern and eastern Papua. The principal surveys have been carried out by small-mesh trawl nets and in-shore netting, and although some highly productive areas have been discovered the variations in catch have been large. In trawling, no commercial fishing ground producing large fish has been discovered. There is evidence of a great stock of small fish of less than four ounces each. In some areas the catch of prawns has been promising. In the Yule Island area, the in-shore crayfish run, investigated over the last several seasons, is believed good enough to support a small local industry.

An extensive survey of trolling grounds east of Samarai carried out over a period of two years, demonstrated fairly conclusively that some excellent fishing grounds exist in this area, based on troll fish—Spanish mackerel, trevally and dog-toothed tuna.

In-shore tuna schools have been surveyed for size and composition along the New Guinea coast and schools of fish extending over ten miles have been sighted on recent surveys out of Lae. The greatest concentration probably exists to the west of New Ireland.

Barramundi has been recorded along most of the Papuan coast and is abundant in the rivers and estuaries on the Gulf of Papua, particularly in the Fly River system up to and in Lake Murray. During the spawning seasons these fish move down to the river mouth and into coastal waters. It is during this period, which extends from mid-November to late March, that the quality is suitable for export markets; however, quantities sufficient for commercial catches are possible the year round.

Reefs off the east coast of Bougainville are similar to but much smaller than those of the Louisiade Archipelago, and produce the same species of fish. Good line-fishing reefs lie north of the Gazelle Peninsula, and the south coast of New Britain is considered excellent for small-scale seining.

Fresh Water Fisheries

There are many areas of fresh water ranging from near sea-level to the Mt. Wilhelm Lakes at an altitude of over 11,000 feet. Limited surveys of fresh water systems have indicated generally a very sparse fish population, but there is a high potential productivity in estuarine and lowland rivers. Lake Murray, which connects with the Fly River, is probably one of the richest fishing grounds in the Territory.

The main achievement to date in fresh water fisheries has been the introduction of weed-eating species to lowland waters. Along the south coast of Papua there are now extensive areas stocked with tilapia and considerable numbers are taken during the southeast monsoon when fresh winds hinder coastal fishing. These fish average about three-fourths of a pound and are of good flavor. It is estimated that about half of the fish marketed in Port Moresby during the southeast monsoon period are tilapia. Other species introduced into lowland waters include the snakeskin gouramy and the giant gouramy.

Experimental pond culture has been carried out by the Fisheries Division at Dobel and Aiyura in the highlands, and Singapore carp have been grown to about 10 pounds in 12 months, primarily on a ration of sweet potatoes. Spawning has been observed after two and a half years. Several species of carp have been introduced into ponds and dams on plantations; growth is reported to be satisfactory but no information is available on spawning. There seems no reason to doubt that pond production is technically feasible. The Fisheries Division estimates that about 10 lbs. of sweet potatoes and 1 lb. of peanuts is sufficient to produce 1 lb. of fish.

A Program for Fisheries Development

There are serious obstacles to the better utilization of the fish resources. Subsistence fishing techniques are generally primitive and productivity is low. Commercial fishing has been seriously hampered by poor marketing organization, inadequate preservation and processing facilities and transport difficulties. These problems have kept fresh fish in relatively short supply, even in the larger coastal towns. Prices have been high and the market very restricted.

With regard to inland markets, the primary obstacle to the greater utilization of local fish resources has been the absence of a suitable technique of preservation. No large-scale processing of fish is as yet undertaken either by canning, drying, smoking or by producing fish meal. The indigenes have few means of preserving fresh or frozen fish. Hence the chances of developing a large-scale market for fresh fish in the interior are small, unless the production of fresh-water fish can be greatly expanded.

Research has not produced conclusive results about the types of fish which might be most suitably introduced to highland waters. Pond fish culture has not been readily accepted by the native people. Economical pond culture depends largely on the availability of cheap fish food. Suitable sources of fish foods may be developed but the difficulties of organizing extensive pond fish culture among the indigenes on the basis of feeding with sweet potatoes and peanuts appear to the Mission formidable. The Mission believes, therefore, that at least in the short term, the bulk of fish supplies to the highland population will have to come from marine fisheries.

There is little doubt that the productivity of subsistence marine fisheries can be increased by the continued provision of technical assistance and the introduction of improved equipment and techniques. This technical assistance should be given through the extension service of the Department of Agriculture, Stock and Fisheries. In conjunction with the work of the extension service, financial assistance to native fishermen should be provided, where appropriate, by the proposed Development Bank. There is a need for the Administration to assist in the organization of supplies of equipment (particularly nets), of processing, of refrigeration and marketing.

In relation to commercial marine fishing, the best prospect appears to be the exploitation of the barramundi fisheries in the Gulf of Papua. The Fisheries Division has estimated that three small boats equipped with iceboxes and operating out of Daru, within a radius of 60 miles, could catch, between October and April, some 120,000 lbs. of barramundi and 100,000 lbs. of other species of fish. The local market, principally in Port Moresby, could probably absorb about 150,000 lbs. of the catch, provided that more adequate cold storage capacity could be made available and marketing facilities improved. Trial shipments of barramundi have been made to the Melbourne market where good prices were obtained (4/-d per lb.) but whether the Melbourne, Sydney and Brisbane markets could absorb sufficient quantities to ensure success is unknown. Nor is it certain at present that fish in adequate quantity are available. In any event, for exports to Australia to be profitable, they would have to reach several hundred thousand pounds of fish.

The work of proving the extent of the barramundi fisheries should continue, and a detailed study should be made of the scale required for a successful commercial fishing venture. This study should include a study of markets. Commercial fishing companies have been exploiting barramundi fisheries along the Queensland coast for many years, and their expert knowledge should, if possible, be drawn upon.

Relatively little is known about the fish resources of the New Guinea coast and of the Bismarck Archipelago. There seems to be sufficient evidence, however, that supplies of fresh fish to the major coastal towns could be increased if technical improvements were made in fishing operations, if freezer capacity at the ports were increased, and marketing arrangements improved. Here, as is the case for Port Moresby, the local markets for fresh fish are small, and modern large-scale fishing operations would not be justified on the basis of supplying the local markets. Efforts should be aimed at increasing the quantity and regularity of supplies to meet local requirements and to reducing market prices.

Besides increasing supplies of fresh fish to coastal areas, the other major need is to develop an economical source of processed fish to supply the demand of the inland areas, which is now met from imports. In addition to the possibility of fish ponds, fish could be canned. However, the Mission cannot recommend the establishment of a local cannery and the development of a deep-sea fishing fleet without adequate evidence that the price of the product would be competitive with the price of the imported article. The cash incomes of the indigenous people are so low that, except insofar as canned fish is bought by employers of labor as part of the statutory ration, any significant price increase might well reduce the demand substantially.

The possibilities of establishing successful deep-sea fisheries, using indigenous labor, do not seem good. While the coastal people have traditionally fished in coastal waters, there is no tradition among them of deep-sea fishing. The Japanese have developed high expertise in deep-sea fishing, especially for tuna, and there seems little chance that a local enterprise could compete successfully with Japanese fleets in costs of operation.

The Mission understands that interest has been shown by foreign companies in establishing a canning plant in the Territory. If detailed studies show that a canning plant to supply the domestic market would be economic, in the sense that it could successfully compete with imports without heavy protection, the Administration should give encouragement to the plant. To achieve an economic scale of operations, part of the production might have to be exported. If there is the potential for a profitable canning plant, the Mission would urge the Commonwealth Government to give sympathetic consideration to allowing products from the cannery free entry to the Australian market.

Other forms of fish processing such as drying and smoking should also be expanded and the Administration should continue to provide technical assistance to the coastal people in developing these techniques.

In addition to investigating the possibilities of commercial exploitation of the marine resources of the Territory, the Mission recommends that further research into fishery resources should be undertaken, particularly along the coasts of New Guinea and of the Bismarck Archipelago. As indicated above, the Mission does not envisage that deep-sea fishing undertakings will be developed in the next several years, and it believes, therefore, that research should be confined primarily to coastal waters. It believes also that the research effort should be oriented not to a systematic study of marine life, but rather to acquiring information which would enable commercial fishing ventures to be developed. Besides the development work on marine fisheries, the Mission recommends that research into fresh water fisheries should continue as should the work of introducting new species of fresh water fish into inland waters.

Organization and Staffing

The Mission believes that the present size of the Fisheries Division of the Department of Agriculture, Stock and Fisheries does not warrant its continuation as a separate division of the department. While recognizing that excellent investigational work has been done by the division in the past, the Mission suggests that greater emphasis should be given in future to extension work and to the development of commercial fishing potentials. As indicated above, further research work will be required. The Mission believes that an appropriate organization would be for the research functions of the Fisheries Division to be organized as a special section of the proposed Research Division recommended for the department. The Mission also recommends that a group should be established, within the proposed Extension and Marketing Division of the department, to be concerned specifically with fish extension work and market development. The Mission also recommends that the advice of the Fisheries Division of the FAO should be sought in establishing this group and in recommending the nature and scope of its activities.

The present staff of the Fisheries Division consists of only six professional and sub-professional officers, compared with an establishment of twelve. The Mission would suggest that the fishery biologists, at present employed, should work with the Fishery Research Section of the proposed Research Division. Additional research officers will be required, together with supporting staff, but the Mission cannot be precise about the numbers required. The research officers should act as advisers to the fisheries extension service and, for inland fisheries, the agricultural extension officers should, where possible, act as fisheries extension officers also. For marine fisheries, the Mission believes that specialized fishery extension officers will be required.

PROGRAM IMPLICATIONS

Contribution of Programs to Balance of Payments

The programs outlined in the previous pages of the report for cash crops, livestock and forestry, if successfully implemented, will together provide a major contribution to the balance of payments.

Major Crops. The volume and value of production of the major crops to be expected are summarized in Table 30. The estimates were derived from the target acreages set, and from conservative yields and prices. By way of comparison, export prices actually received for the four major agricultural commodities during the last five years are given in Table 31.

TABLE 30: Projection of Volume and Value of Major Commodities

Commodity	Base Year 1962/63	1968/69	1973/74	To Full Bearing[a]
	Volume (tons)			
Copra	109,000	141,000	176,000	243,000
Cocoa	14,100	38,000	55,000	84,000
Rubber	4,700	8,000	18,000	42,000
Coffee	4,800	12,000	20,000	20,000
Tea	—	—	1,125	4,500
	Value (£A million)			
Copra at £A60/ton	7.4	8.4	10.5	14.6
Cocoa at £A210/ton	2.9	8.0	11.6	17.6
Rubber at £A197/ton	1.2	1.6	3.2[b]	7.4[b]
Coffee at £A400/ton	2.0	4,8	8.0	8.0
Tea at £A450/ton	—	—	0.5	2.0
Total	13.5[c]	22.8	33.8	49.6

[a] All crops planted up to 1973/74 will reach full bearing age by 1982/83.
[b] Based on the assumption of a further price decline (below the £A197 level) of about 10 percent to £A177.
[c] Actual export value, based on prices given in Table 31.

TABLE 31: Price Levels of Major Commodities

(£A per ton f.o.b.)

Year	Copra[a]	Cocoa	Coffee	Rubber[b]
1958/59	93	350	471	261
1959/60	99	284	481	341
1960/61	72	228	482	295
1961/62	61	198	453	258
1962/63	68	211	415	246

[a] Including oil in a copra equivalent.
[b] Including scrap.

SOURCE: Bureau of Statistics.

Beef. The increase in output of beef foreseen under the livestock program would, at current prices,[57] be worth about £A0.7 million by 1968/69 and £A2.2 million by 1973/74.[58] As discussed earlier, it is anticipated that the enlarged supply of beef would be used largely to accomodate a rise in domestic consumption due to population increase and some increase in per capita consumption; in addition, some substitution for present imports of canned meat should be possible, which substitution might at present prices be valued at about £A0.4 million by 1973/74.

Timber. The export of timber might, under the program recommended by the Mission, be expected to rise from about £A1.3 million in 1962/63 to £A6.7 million by 1968/69, which amount at the then existing cutting rate would rise further if it were found possible to export, at that time or later, an increasing share of production as sawn timber rather than as logs.

Prerequisites to Development

Frequent reference has been made to problems common to all the individual programs in the field of primary industry. These have to be solved for any worthwhile progress to be made. They lie in the areas of land tenure, agricultural extension, education and research, credit, land settlement, marketing and organization. Each is of such significance to economic development as to warrant separate treatment.

Land Tenure. The social institution affecting most profoundly the organization of agricultural production is land tenure.[59] The grave limitations to agricultural development imposed by existing land-tenure systems have been highlighted sufficiently in the foregoing account of farming. The nature of the problems, however, has been but sketchily referred to.

Tenure ailments which have their origin in land shortage do not occur in the Territory. Excessive fragmentation, concentration on share tenancy, high rentals and indebtedness to landlords so common in some countries of Asia and the Middle East are noticeable by their absence. The key feature from which most developmental limitations spring is that the concept of individual ownership as recognized in the western world does not exist. Land for the most part belongs to the group or clan.

[57] Of about 10 lbs. carcass = £A1.

[58] This does not allow for the substantial increase in the value of the unslaughtered herd, due to both increase in numbers and fattening.

[59] While the agreed terms of reference of the Mission did not mention tenure, it was the informal understanding with the Government of Australia that it was not the responsibility of the Mission to propose a formula for solution of the land-tenure problem. However, it was agreed that the Mission would make such suggestions as it considered appropriate for the Australian Government's consideration in seeking solutions for the many problems involved.

There is no uniform pattern of native land-use rights. Rights to land differ from clan to clan, village to village, area to area. There is often a distinction between group rights and individual rights. While ownership is vested in the community, individuals may establish limited use rights by occupancy, clearing and cultivation. In the main, open grassland and forest is claimed by the group and is available to all members; individual use rights apply mainly to arable land. Inheritance of use rights is likewise complex. In some communities this is patrilineal, in some matrilineal, and in others land-use rights are derived through membership of the family.

Group rights to land prior to the Administration were maintained by use, custom and war. In the highlands, for example, war was a frequent method of land acquisition as well as consolidation. A significant outcome of land adjustment by warfare was the lack of development of level and often more productive valley land. Such lands were poor fighting ground, both in attack or defense, and it became unused in favor of the less productive slopes and ridges. As the result of the efforts of the Administration to establish law and order and the introduction of the concept of peaceful co-existence, war was outlawed. The ownership patterns existing at the time of first contact with the European were sanctioned by the controlling authorities as legal. It is significant that in this situation no solution has been found, as a substitute for warfare, to land rights.

This general pattern was perhaps satisfactory so long as hunting, food-gathering and subsistence gardening were, as they still are for most of the population, the main forms of land use. It does not fit the introduction of tree and other cash crops of a perennial nature. Land-use rights for subsistence agriculture may not give rights to plant and harvest the fruits of permanent tree crops. Conflicting claims to the fruits of the trees may arise during the life of the planter and after his death. The tenure system is quite unsuited to the rapidly emerging commercial farming scene which needs the assurance of permanent use rights by individuals to specific areas of larger size than needed for subsistence gardens.

This general picture applies to the bulk of the land. Only a small fraction has been alienated. Europeans have freehold title over 565,000 acres or 0.5 percent of the land. In addition, the Administration has purchased from indigenous owners 2.768 million acres or 2.4 percent of the land, of which about 700,000 acres have been leased to Europeans for farming purposes. The balance is held as reserves or for public purposes. Thus, over 97 percent of the land remains under direct native control, subject to native tenure systems.

The guiding principle behind Australian administration, under its own and under United Nations trusteeship, has been to safeguard land resources in the interests of the Territory and its people. Its mandate has been stated as an obligation to safeguard all land for the time when it will be needed by the indigenous population.

On the other hand, Australia has undertaken to develop the Territory, aiming at a viable developing economy as a foundation for political self-determination and self-government. The implication on land-tenure policies is clear. If the policy to develop a viable economy is to succeed, a way must be found to remove the tenure obstacles to more efficient land use.

Land may be taken out of custom by acquisition by the Administration. In addition, the Administration in 1952 established a Native Lands Commission to inquire into and to record rights to land accorded by native custom. Progress was slow because of the complexity and variety of customs and the language and other difficulties of inquiry. In 1963, the Native Lands Commission was merged with a Land Titles Commission. A proposal was before the Legislative Council in June 1963 for an ordinance which would permit conversion of land held under custom into land with individual registered title free from the limitations of customary use rights and inheritance. The proposal provides for a voluntary system requiring complete inquiry about customary rights and agreement of all of the holders of customary rights.

The experience of the Native Lands Commission indicates that progress in the application of this legislation will almost certainly be slow, relative to the need for expanding indigenous agricultural production. Individual ownership is desirable but if Administration assistance to natives for the planting of cash crops or for cattle raising is to be limited to natives with lands for which the Administration has determined ownership, made surveys and recorded title, little progress can be expected in implementing the Mission's recommendations for agricultural development.

In seeking a solution, it must be kept in mind that land customs are firmly embedded in the social structure and at this stage an arrangement which would attempt to short-cut the laborious process of inquiry and the need for full agreement in taking the land out of custom into a tenure arrangement suited to cash production could well fail by non-acceptance by the people.

There is, however, a growing volume of evidence that the native people are making progress in arranging with their villages and clans for the continuing use of land upon which they can plant tree crops. The coffee production in the highlands and cocoa planting in the lowlands by indigenes are examples of this. The Administration could well take a more flexible approach to the problem of land tenure and not only assist the natives who want an individual title to obtain that objective, but encourage native groups to work out their own solution to obtaining individual ownership or control of the land within native customs. The local government councils could make a useful contribution to this difficult problem. This, of course, would not make possible the recording of title under standard European procedures and in accordance with existing policy. It would require comparable flexibility on the part of the credit organization designed to assist and stimulate native production. In this approach there could be much more delegation of responsibility from central to district and to sub-district staff and much more active collaboration with local groups and leaders.

It is also highly important that there should be acceptance of the view that arrangements must be made for Europeans both to continue to operate existing holdings and to obtain additional lands at present held by natives. Review of existing leases on Crown land should be made, not with the objective of early termination but for the purpose of increasing the efficiency of land use on a continuing basis for the benefit of the Territory as a whole. Further leases might be limited to 30 to 35 years and carry improvement clauses with provision for payment for improvements upon termination and a right of renewal unless land is required for production by natives. [60] With respect to obtaining additional lands from natives, the present practice of the Administration buying land from the natives for lease both to Europeans and to natives should be continued. The natives, however, are reportedly increasingly unwilling to sell their lands. The Mission, therefore, suggests that the Administration consider a policy and procedure whereby it leases from native groups and sub-leases to European or native farmers. Also it would appear that natives, in some areas, would be prepared to lease, not sell, land to Europeans and particularly Europeans they know. The Mission suggests that Europeans should be able to lease directly from native owners on terms approved by the Administration, the leases containing clauses for payment of compensation for improvements and the term limited to 30 to 35 years.

It was noted by the Mission that the Administration has been reluctant to exercise the right of eminent domain where natives have been unwilling to sell land. Wherever land is required by the Administration to carry out the functions of responsible government, it should not hesitate to take the land by judicial proceedings, paying a fair compensation to native owners. The establishment of a new farm-training center for indigenes in the Eastern Highlands on a most unsuitable site far distant from the existing substantial nucleus of the Goroka livestock,

[60] Section 55 of the Land Ordinance 1962 provides for the payment for improvements in the event of non-renewal on the expiration of a lease.

pig and dairy unit closely adjacent to the town and alongside many thousands of acres of unused land is an example of a decision foreign to the concept of responsible government. The decision was based on expediency. It incurs unwarranted costs on a continuing basis for facilities that can never be efficient. Several other such cases were noted.

The Mission gained the impression that there were large areas of waste land, or land not being used by anyone and that some of these lands would at sometime be needed for development. The Mission suggests that the Administration take action to declare such land Crown land, before serious claim is made by others. The land could be used for the common good of the Territory, in effect, for the benefit of all of the people.

The Mission wishes to emphasize the urgent need for the Administration to review its present land tenure policies and procedures with the basic objective of accelerated economic development and suggests that it should be prepared to adopt varied and alternative approaches in accordance with the social and economic needs of each environment. It should gear both extension and credit services to its land tenure policies.

Extension Services. Modern agriculture is dependent upon the backing of well-organized competent extension services. True at any time for any country, this is of special significance to one just emerging from a primitive state to make a place for itself in a competitive world. It is vital to the attainment of all the export commodity targets which the Mission has recommended. As such, it must have the highest priority next to that of land tenure in administrative thinking and action.

Paramount to the achievement of production targets is the educational aspect of the process. Extension education prepares rural people for making rational adjustments and choices in an ever-changing technological and economic environment. Economic development results from the improvement of physical as well as human resource productivity.

There can be few environments where the conditions facing the agricultural extension worker are more difficult and challenging. The land and its people are unique. The social and physical obstacles are many. Despite this, the Territory has already built the nucleus of a high-powered extension service. In the few years since the war, and starting with a handful of men whose first task was the rehabilitation of war-ravaged areas, the service has reached out to cover the Territory with a team of about 200 professional and sub-professional officers supported by appropriate specialist groups and a large number of indigenous intermediaries.[61] This service has the clearly defined objectives of raising the level

[61] Clerical and supporting staff, mainly indigenous, numbered about 3,000 in the Department of Agriculture in 1962.

of subsistence farming, of increasing the standard of living, of bringing about the optimum use of resources, and of contributing to economic advancement by technical training and by stimulating changes in interest and outlook. Its major target is the welfare of the indigenous population, its assistance to the European sector being incidental and designed to aid achievement of the main objectives.

Marked progress has been made, evidence of which is to be found throughout the foregoing account of the status of agriculture and live-stock production. In view of the formidable task which lies ahead, however, it is necessary that a re-appraisal be made of the extension needs of the Territory and the organization required. The Mission holds the view that from now on, objectives should be more development oriented than has been the case so far. This does not mean that the aims that have motivated the service should be abandoned. Rather does it imply that their attainment be sought mainly through the achievement of specific production targets which are essential if the Territory is to build a viable economy of a reasonable standard. To this end, some changes in attitude and approach are necessary.

Basic to these is a re-appraisal of the policy which currently aims at providing a complete extension coverage without reference to local resource potentials. Complete, even coverage of an entire population and area may be desirable in some countries for political and social reasons. It is not a realistic policy for the Territory. Technical man-power is in very short supply. It will be found most difficult to recruit the technical force essential to an expanded agricultural program of the dimensions envisaged. The Territory cannot afford to dissipate this resource on a widely scattered basis. Extension officers should be con-centrated in areas with promising combinations of developmental re-sources, both physical and human, with proper attention to accessibility and markets. Parts of the Territory have such poor resource combinations, or are so inaccessible to services and markets that it is folly to attempt uniform agricultural coverage. Obviously the Mission lacks the detailed knowledge of local conditions necessary to make a critical assessment of locations chosen for extension stations and extension centers. It notes, however, that an additional 100 centers are planned during the next few years. Even though the location of some of these may have to be determined by the need to make administrative contact with new groups of people, sufficient scope exists for deciding new locations with direct reference to the specific needs of the individual development programs. As an example, it will be noted that the Mission has made no recommenda-tions for program development for the Western District and would con-sider further dispersal of extension effort in this area unnecessary. Indeed, a strong case can be made for withdrawing the existing agricultural personnel for service where they could be more useful. In contrast, more men are needed to handle programs in the Sepik. Essentially the issue is one of priority and timing. Ultimately, complete effective coverage and further extension of the type of activity that has dominated action so far may be desirable and even necessary, but this should not be attempted until major progress has been made in stepping up the production of export crops to the levels indicated as feasible. In view of the shortage of technical manpower, it is wasteful to contemplate any other approach.

In addition to greater concentration of effort in selected areas of high potential, re-appraisal of the existing policy, which has confined direct extension effort to men, is overdue. The Mission appreciates the great difficulties of making effective educational contact with the indigenous women but is impressed with the fact that a large proportion, not only of the actual work but also of decision-making in agriculture, is entirely in the hands of women. In these circumstances, ways and means have to be found of attracting their interest and cooperation. Their role in subsistence farming, in utilizing farm products, in harvesting crops, in improving the levels of home life and in developing new values is so crucial that the extension service cannot afford to bypass them. Women, both European and indigenous, should be recruited to the extension service as the best way of achieving a break-through. A trial should also be made of wives accompanying husbands to farmer-training courses.[62]

Farmer-training has to be expanded to cover a much larger number. The need for more than 5,000 native cattle projects alone highlights this. A very great effort and a special organization is necessary to cope with the tens of thousands of better farmers which the program calls for. Currently, farmer-training is conducted not only at district extension stations but at minor extension centers and resident locations of agricultural officers as well. Its operation depends too much on the personal interest of officers with other duties and responsibilities. More effective progress would be made by strengthening considerably the training staff of the Extension Division by appointment of specialist teams, by locating these at district centers and by formalizing training to a greater degree. It is desirable that courses should be organized on fixed time schedules to avoid the continuous uncontrolled comings and goings of trainees and permit the planning and implementation of courses with more meaningful content. Re-appraisal of selection methods is also necessary if the wastage during training is to be reduced below its present high level, estimated to be around 25 percent in some centers. Gearing

---

[62] For a related discussion, see the Mission's recommended program for Adult Education (Chapter 6).

of selection to individuals who are to participate in programs to plant coconuts, cocoa, etc., and are likely to need credit should eliminate much of the current wastage.

Finally, extension work in the future should accept responsibility for appraisal of individual farming operations and proposals for credit purposes. This responsibility would provide the extension officer with a new and powerful weapon for making effective contacts. Close liaison with the proposed Territory Development Finance Company (see Chapter 8) will be necessary. This arrangement does not envisage extension personnel becoming involved in debt collection, but rather that they should be the technical arm of the credit organization.

Agricultural Education. An educational program geared to the needs of the primary industries is yet another prerequisite affecting development. On a longer-term basis, education in technical agriculture will play a major determining part in the full exploitation of natural resources.

Three levels of training must be catered for. First, it is essential that the level of competence of indigenous farmers be raised. From this group will come the farmers and entrepreneurs who will be needed in ever increasing numbers. Training of farmers is the responsibility of the Agricultural Extension Service, as already discussed. Second, it is also vital that large numbers of indigenes be trained to provide the technical and administrative intermediary staff of the organizations, public and private, involved in agricultural development. Third, indigenes must be trained for professional and sub-professional careers in these same organizations.

Organized technical agricultural education barely exists at present. Only one agricultural school—at Popondetta—designed to operate at the sub-diploma (certificate) level is functioning. Two others are planned. The recently established Popondetta School, controlled by the Department of Agriculture, has classrooms, laboratory and dormitory facilities for two classes of a two-year course, each of 30 students. It is operating at only half capacity with students whose basic educational qualifications (Form 2) are so poor that elementary education rather than technical training absorbs the time of instructors. The fall-out rate is high. Two other schools of this type are projected, one at Kapagere near Port Moresby to open in 1966 and the other in the highlands at Korn Farm near Mt. Hagen in 1967.

There will be a great temptation under existing planning and thinking to permit recruits with inadequate technical-level training (certificate) to enter the sub-professional grades of the Department of Agriculture—a situation that could cause considerable embarrassment later when

properly qualified personnel (diploma) become available. The temptation should be strongly resisted in favor of looking out for personnel of
adequate educational background.

One diploma-level agricultural college is under construction at Vudal
near Rabaul and is expected to be functioning in 1965. The entrance
requirement is to be Form 3 for a three-year diploma course. An annual
intake of 30 students a year is planned. This institution also is under
Department of Agriculture control.

These proposals fall far short of needs. The number of sub-diploma-level
intermediaries required for the implementation of the agricultural
development programs recommended by the Mission is estimated at
1,400 over the next eight to ten years. To this must be added a normal
growth requirement of the Department of Agriculture of about 600 in the
same period. Assuming a 30 percent fall-out, which is not unreasonable,
the three sub-diploma schools are unlikely to provide more than about
400 trainees, by 1974, against the about 2,000 needed.

Similarly, Vudal Agricultural College, with a planned output of only
20 diploma-level graduates a year, cannot make any substantial contribution to the sub-professional level of service for a very long time.
Approximately 100 diplomates may be turned out by 1974, after the first
graduating class of eight in 1968.[63] Several times this number could be
readily absorbed both in government and in the private sector.

These projections and comparisons suggest that a re-appraisal of
present plans is essential. The Mission believes that consideration should
be given to the abandonment of sub-diploma level technical education
in agriculture in favor of recruitment of this class of worker directly
from the comprehensive secondary-school system recommended by the
Mission (see Chapter 6). This would necessitate subsequent in-post training for particular needs. Training in the basic sciences has been recommended for the comprehensive secondary schools. Agricultural services
should be able to attract a high proportion of the output. If this line of
approach is accepted, the Popondetta School could be converted into a
comprehensive secondary school. The schools proposed for Kapagere and
Korn Farm, if opened, would be comprehensive secondary schools.

For the diploma-level activity must be stepped up. Trainees of this
level are needed urgently. The capacity of Vudal should be expanded
in line with the availability of entrants to turn out at least 60 diplomates
a year, which would require an annual intake of 90.

The Mission also holds the view that a second diploma-level institution should be established as quickly as possible. This should be located
in the highlands, since the Vudal environment will fit graduates more

[63] Assuming an intake in 1965 of 12 and a fall-out rate of one-third.

for service in lowland districts. It should be about the same size as Vudal. In the section on Forestry, the Mission suggests that the highlands diploma-level institution provide training in both agriculture and forestry. The cost of a second institution could well come from the savings made from the abandoment of the Kapagere, Korn Farm, Popondetta and Bulolo projects. In setting up diploma-level colleges, the Mission also holds the view that much good could come from placing such units under the administrative control of a corporate board of governors on which are represented agricultural and commercial interests as well as the Departments of Agriculture and Education. Finance through the Departments of Agriculture and Forests should ensure adequate orientation of training to departmental needs. This arrangement would create a favorable environment for recruitment and operation of teaching and research staff more easily than under direct departmental control. It would also pave the way for eventual inclusion of the two colleges in the National University, when this is established, facilitating thereby the eventual raising of agricultural technical training to the professional level.

There are many reasons why it is important that special efforts should be made to train indigenes to enter the professional ranks of agricultural service. These efforts should not await the establishment of a university in the Territory. Even if the university were to begin operations within a few years, it is likely that an agricultural faculty would follow and not precede the basic faculties of arts and sciences which must take many years to establish and consolidate.

In the meantime, selected qualified students should be sent abroad for training. Basic training at a level necessary to meet university entrance is essential. The numbers of indigenes with this background are woefully small at present but these will increase rapidly as the secondary-school program progresses. Despite the intense competition from other branches of the Administration and the private sector, agriculture must have a claim on a number of those available and provide them with scholarships to appropriate overseas institutions. In this regard tropical, rather than Australian, centers would be likely to turn out more useful graduates in a shorter time. The Philippines, Malaysia and Thailand now have agricultural faculties of reasonable caliber. Of the Australian universities, only the Brisbane environment approaches tropical conditions in agriculture. Veterinary science needs are not so circumscribed.

Assuming two such scholarships are awarded in 1964, four in 1965, eight in 1966 and 16 in 1967, and assuming that 75 percent of these graduate, a useful nucleus of indigenous professional officers could join the service from 1969 onward. This would be a reasonable start toward eventual long-term staffing with substantial numbers of local people at the highest levels.

Agricultural Research. The Mission is impressed with much of the applied research that has backed up agricultural extension work. With even a shorter history than that of the advisory services, and under the handicap of inadequate staff in both numbers and experience, the effort has been quite remarkable. Agricultural research in the Territory has not been slow to take advantage of research and its application in other tropical countries. It has shown imagination and skill in adapting techniques of agricultural production to the special environments with which it has been faced. Research workers have been able to pass their findings on to extension officers, and implementation by both European and indigenous farmers has paid handsome dividends.

The Mission disagrees with the view expressed in some circles that less, not more, research is required in agriculture. Throughout this presentation of the status and potentials of primary production, reference has been made at every stage to gaps in knowledge that must be filled for continued progress. It is true that sufficient is known to provide guidelines to sound development; it is equally true that much more must be known to increase efficiency of existing methods to develop new techniques, and to widen the scope of existing forms of production.

At present, responsibility for agricultural research is vested mainly in the Plant Industry Division of the Department of Agriculture. A certain amount is also carried out by the Division of Animal Industry in respect to animal and pasture production, and by the Fisheries Division in its special sphere of interest.

The Plant Industry Division operates seven main experimental centers. One, at Keravat, concentrates on cocoa, coconuts, Robusta coffee and the lowland crops. Another, at Aiyura, handles highland interest in Arabica coffee, pyrethrum and tobacco. A plant quarantine station at Laloki controls plant introductions. In addition, there are specialist centers at Epo for annual crops, Bisianumu for rubber, Garaina for tea, and Yambi for the special problems of land use in the Sepik.[64] At a new headquarters in Port Moresby, staff and laboratories handle soil survey investigations and provide services in plant pathology and chemistry.

The Animal Industry Division controls diagnostic and servicing laboratories at Kila Kila near Port Moresby and investigates problems of animal-breeding, animal husbandry, animal health and pasture production at its various livestock centers. The Erap unit tends to specialize in following up the various problems of animal production that have

[64] This unit is serving no useful purpose and should be closed.

become evident from field experience. Moitaka in the lowlands and Baiyer River in the highlands are concerned mainly with cattle-breeding. The Fisheries Division maintains a marine biological station near Port Moresby (not yet completed), together with several small vessels for marine work. Pond fisheries are also under study.

In addition, the Commonwealth Scientific and Industrial Research Organization (CSIRO) of Australia provides assistance, partly in an advisory capacity as in the field of cattle-breeding investigations, and partly by carrying out specific investigations. The more important of these involve land capability studies of selected areas. It has also conducted fishery surveys. In the more sophisticated research field, the National University of Canberra, through its School of Pacific Studies, provides specialists to cover more academic approaches in anthropology, botany, geology, geography, tenure systems and the like. Many of these studies have some relevance to practical agriculture.

Valuable as have been the contributions to date, the time has arrived for stepping up the tempo and quality of Territory agricultural research. The Mission has been impressed with the current dearth of sufficiently trained personnel. It has ncted the losses in staff of recent years and the slowing down or cessation of effort in consequence. It is somewhat critical of the extent of direct supervision of the research activities of individuals from headquarters which perhaps arises from this situation. It is very critical of the division of research responsibility among different segments of the Department of Agriculture with little effective coordination or cooperation where this is badly needed.

All research centers are now quite inadequately staffed, both in numbers and quality. Some have no professionally qualified personnel or only one such officer. This has been due in part to losses and partly to the over-all problem of recruitment. It is also not good enough to expect staff without formal training in research to undertake research. Possible ways and means of handling recruitment are dealt with later in discussing staffing of the Department of Agriculture. One angle not applicable to the general problem but special to research personnel is the question of supervision. Although research needs to be well organized, and should be oriented toward defined objectives, especially when requirements relative to resources are great, the research worker does not generally perform well when under too much detailed direction. A tendency to design all experiments as well as policy in Port Moresby has been noted. This method leaves little initiative to the scientist in the field. If this tendency has arisen because of the caliber of staff available in the field, it provides yet another reason for raising the standard of recruits to a level involving trained scientists capable of operating as independent workers. There are several areas where division of research responsibility and liaison could be improved. The Division of Plant Industry, for instance, introduces new pasture plants but has no livestock on its stations being used for testing and evaluating these, and the Animal Industry Division engages in pastoral improvement but has no agrostologist to handle the many problems involved. The consequence is that progress in this area is limited to the contributions of enthusiastic veterinarians and their lay staff who have not been trained in pasture production. This situation must be remedied if the livestock industry is to be soundly developed.

The senior administration of the Department of Agriculture is not unaware of these general problems. Its plans for reorganization as the first step toward their solution are to be commended. The setting up of a Research and Development Division to handle all primary industry research is a move in the right direction. Under good leadership, the necessary research climate could be created within such a major division not only for good research but for the recruitment of the staff required.

The terms of reference of this new division should emphasize the priority of research designed to capitalize to the maximum degree possible existing knowledge of tropical agriculture. Its program should also be oriented in the direction of the recommendations in respect to the development of subsistence and commercial farming and appropriate farming systems. Basic research should not be ignored, but at this stage should be limited to the solution of those local problems of land use which cannot be solved without more fundamental study. The areas (both applied and basic), in which major gaps exist, have been indicated in appropriate parts of this report in the discussion on subsistence and commercial farming.

In tackling the research needs, consideration should be given to enlisting the cooperation of the CSIRO to an even greater degree. Territory welfare should be a legitimate responsibility of this experienced, well-organized, well-staffed and internationally famous institution. Cooperation should not be restricted to intermittent assistance with special problems. It should involve a continuing partnership such that CSIRO participates in planning the over-all research approach in all fields; provides direct aid by secondment of staff urgently needed, aids in recruitment and training of new staff and recognizes research service in the Territory as equivalent to service in Australia from a career viewpoint.

Growers' associations should play a greater role by contributing financially and providing support and guidance for biological, technical and marketing research. Until recently, the Administration concentrated an estimated 85 percent of its agronomic research efforts on cocoa and coffee. Growers benefited greatly. Now that these industries have grown to maturity and strength they should raise funds in support of a more aggressive research program. A greater measure of self-sustained research in cocoa and coffee would enable the Administration to develop a broader program of applied research to cover rubber, tea, oil crops, cereals and other crops.

Finally, the Administration should not be loath to approach the many international organizations, foundations, and universities with a view to securing their interest and participation in research related to the primary industries in Papua and New Guinea. There is potential scope for enlisting the cooperation of the United Nations specialized agencies such as FAO and the Special Fund. The Ford, Rockefeller and Carnegie foundations and the Agricultural Development Council of New York, as well as others, might also be approached.

Agricultural Credit. The need for agricultural credit has been described under each commodity program. Institutional aspects such as source of funds, organization and operation of a Territory Development Finance Company are covered elsewhere.[65] The peculiar social and economic conditions of farming in the Territory, which require deviations from normally accepted banking standards and methods of providing agricultural credit, need consideration here.

The question of the extent to which credit can be expected to function as an incentive to agricultural development is important. Insofar as the large and dominant native sector is concerned, this is by no means as clear as in many other countries. Having been exposed only recently to the monetary economy, many indigenes do not place a high value on money. Their wants so far have been simple. Traditionally these wants have been met from their own gardens or by trading without the use of money in the modern sense. More recently there has been increasing need for cash to acquire store goods, but these wants have generally been met by small cash incomes. "One lap-lap is wardrobe enough" is a common attitude. Again the use of credit is complicated by traditional involvement of the extended family with village groups in transactions involving livelihood, objects of value as well as money. This situation imposes serious limitations on the incentive role of credit. Despite these aspects, however, the Mission has the impression that farming for cash income is rapidly being accepted by indigenes as an inevitable part of their new way of life and that in these circumstances credit could be a strong motivating factor in increasing production.

The need for credit is particularly urgent for the still small but in-

[65] Money, Banking, Credit and Public Revenue (Chapter 8).

creasing number of native entrepreneurs. Their scale of operation requires employment of hired labor and purchase of capital equipment. Their progress is vital for the economic future. Without access to development credit, they can hardly be expected to succeed.

In the European sector, availability of development capital on reasonable terms is likely to be the vital factor determining the rate and extent of improvement and development. This is specially the case under the present investment climate. A development-oriented credit program could be a decisive factor in re-establishing confidence of Europeans in the future of the Territory. Without this confidence the contribution of European producers is more likely to decline than increase.

In providing for the credit needs of native farming, the greatest problem which will confront the proposed Territory Development Finance Company arises from the lack of orthodox security for loans granted. Except for farmers on organized settlement units, and for some entrepreneurs leasing land from the Administration, native smallholders are likely to farm communally owned land to which they have no individual title of record. In these circumstances, the land cannot be used as security.

Wherever possible, loans should be limited to individuals who are able to secure approval of native councils or village authorities for land use of the area involved and for the purpose desired. Based on this approval, it should be possible to secure the acceptance of some responsibility by the appropriate group authority for disciplinary action in the event of default or performance failure by individuals concerned.

Most loan requirements of native farmers involve only small amounts of the order of £A100 to £A200. Finance is needed for tools, planting materials, spraying equipment, chemicals and processing facilities. Apart from insistence that as much as possible of the cost of these be covered by contributions from the individual concerned, no cash need pass, the goods being provided through normal trade channels on official orders. Disbursement in this way should be made as required. Disbursement would involve several years in the case of most crops so that credit provision can be linked to the development progress being made. As experience is gained by both the lender and the borrower, cash can pass to the borrower if that is desirable.

All borrowers should provide written agreements to repay. Loan terms should be such as to provide realistic periods of grace for capital repayment determined by the time before the developments being financed become productive. Repayments must be insisted upon, a strict collection policy being instituted from the outset. Once even a few smallholders are permitted to default—in cases other than from losses due to *force majeur*—the over-all rate of loan repayment could fall below acceptable standards and borrowers begin to confuse loans with grants. For this reason it is especially important that as a rule interest payments be not subject to grace periods. Where cooperatives are developed to handle processing and marketing, the repayment problem and the logistics of collection might well be eased by the technique of securing payment through the cooperatives.

In all transactions, the concept of supervision at all stages should be implemented. As previously indicated, this responsibility should be tied to the activities of extension workers initiating each smallholder development. Smallholders will need assistance, guidance and supervision, not only in a technical farming sense, but also in respect to their credit needs and obligations, to which they will be equally new. The logistics of dealing with very large numbers of small loans are complicated as well as costly. It would be unrealistic to expect the proposed Territory Development Finance Company to set up complete and separate national machinery for this purpose. The finance company should have a staff to review, approve and collect the payments but at least in the beginning it will unavoidably have to rely on the extension officers for appraisal and follow-up on credits.

The problem of acceptable collateral does arise with the European sector. However, here also, realistic periods of grace for capital repayment should be the policy.

The total credit needs of the recommended program in both amounts and phasing are summarized in Table 32.[66] They total about £A17.9 million for the ten-year term, with £A4.9 million for the indigenous farmer and £A13 million for the European. Requirements during the first five-year phase could amount to £A9 million. It will be noted that credit needs for the indigenous farmer rise only gradually. This will help in gaining the requisite experience of operating credit in this sector.

No specific allowance has been made in the table for possible credit needs in the forestry sector, in view of the difficulties involved in providing a meaningful estimate. Credit requirements for the forestry sector, therefore, should be considered as a contingency item.

Land Settlement. Land settlement, as a major weapon in agricultural development, looms large in current administrative planning. It is argued that commercial agriculture has reached the stage where growth is likely to be severely impeded, unless special measures are taken to concentrate services and resources in particularly favorable regions with sparse population in association with a transfer of population to these regions. The arguments assume that rapid growth requires a combination

[66] Details on a year-by-year basis for the individual programs are given in the Statistical Appendix, Table 18.

TABLE 32: Summary of Credit Requirements (Ten-Year Term)

(£A million)

Years	Indigenous Farmers	European Farmers	Total
1	0.237	1.082	1.319
2	0.280	1.325	1.605
3	0.367	1.501	1.868
4	0.412	1.551	1.963
5	0.459	1.701	2.160
Total	1.875[a]	7.160	9.035[a]
6	0.466	1.161	1.627
7	0.513	1.161	1.674
8	0.554	1.161	1.715
9	0.597	1.161	1.758
10	0.662	1.161	1.823
Total	3.010[b]	5.805	8.815[b]
Grand Total	4.885	12.965	17.850

[a] Including £A0.12 million for the cocoa program not allocated to individual years.
[b] Including £A0.218 million for the cocoa program not allocated to individual years.

of reasonably concentrated and suitably motivated population with a particularly favorable environment of soils and climate. These considerations are combined with a belief that further effective participation by Europeans in the next decade is likely to be politically unacceptable, and that the traditional village environment is not conducive to efficient cash cropping. Further, the case for land settlement as a development technique is supported by arguments involving the political and social need to cope with areas subject to high population density, the greater economy of concentrated versus dispersed infrastructures and administrative services, and the desirability from the viewpoint of nation-building of mixing peoples of different tribes and locations. Finally, it is argued that farming on an individual rather than on a communal basis has little or no prospect in the traditional village environment; hence the need for transplanting properly motivated individuals and families into a new environment: the settlement.

The Mission has carefully considered these views. From what has already been recommended it will be obvious that it believes the development of the agricultural potential can be tackled more effectively, rapidly and economically in other ways. A major criticism of the settlement approach by government is that world-wide experience has shown it to be a most expensive technique, expecially when it is taken for granted that all basic costs must be supplied by the State. Examination of the proposals of the Administration with respect to its first settlement schemes near the north coast of New Britain and in the Northern District reinforces this contention.

The project in New Britain, which was the subject of concentrated study by a special planning committee of the Administration while the Mission was in the Territory, envisages the settling of about 3,000 native farmers on some 80,000 acres at a total cost estimated at £A7.25 million. This figure does not include overhead administrative costs of execution and supervision of agricultural development. The road costs used are subject to question as being far too low. Nor does the figure quoted include the capital need of an additional £A1 million for forest exploitation necessary as a prerequisite to land clearing and efficient land use. The total cost over a 25-year term to be used for a comparison of economic costs and benefits is more likely to be of the order of £A10 million. Over the first ten years, costs could total at least £A6.5 million or about £A2,000 per settler, exclusive of forestry costs. Credit requirements are estimated at £A600 per settler. While the project could be economically viable on a cost/benefit basis, the Mission considers it difficult to justify the expenditure of such a large amount of capital on so few farmers under circumstances where capital supply of the Administration is limited, and where the same amount invested, without the need for expensive infrastructures, could benefit many more farmers.

The problem in the Territory is one of improving the cash economy not of 3,000 farmers but of some 400,000 farmers. Acceptance of the settlement approach, even though the rate of development be stepped up to 10,000 farmers, would cost between £A20 and £A30 million and still deal with but a fraction of the problem.

It is for this basic reason that the Mission favors the concentration of effort and resources on the approaches it has recommended. In addition, there is insufficient evidence that substantial transfer of people from their traditional homes will be acceptable. Unless this kind of shift is acceptable, much of the political and social justification is lost. Further, the Mission is impressed with the fact that the Administration has had but little experience of the practical problems of land settlement. By no means have all its ventures into this field been successful.[67]

For these general and specific reasons, the Mission is of the opinion that it is far too early for the Administration to commit itself to land settlement as a major method of agricultural development. For the same reasons, the Mission strongly recommends that land settlement be

[67] In 12 districts, 634 settlement leases have been organized. Poor results have been recorded on 151 holdings at Cape Rodney and in several other areas.

the subject of planned trials as a development technique.[68] Suitable areas should be selected. Within these, alternative approaches to settlement should be explored. The number of such trials should be limited only by the priority need to introduce cash crop farming more intensively and extensively to natives in their existing locations. In addition, all such trials should be geared to attainment of the production targets that have been recommended for the different commodities. When the results indicate the basis for a more fundamental decision, the Administration can chart its course accordingly.

Marketing. Implementation of the Mission's recommendations, in respect to improvement of subsistence agriculture, will depend partly on the development of satisfactory exchange or marketing arrangements for food crops. This requires intensive activity by the proposed Development and Marketing Division of the Department of Agriculture. Insofar as the export crops are concerned, the problems are less acute. The major agricultural export commodities are handled through well-established marketing arrangements. Australian producers and traders are experienced and able so that direct State participation is unnecessary. State aid is required mainly through support on trade policy issues, cooperation with producer boards and through the maintenance of quality control services which are already well established.

With respect to the subsistence sector there is need to establish many more village markets under official guidance and support to provide better opportunities for sale or exchange of produce. There is also need to develop marketing facilities for perishable fruit and vegetable products to supply the urban centers. One possibility, which the Mission submits for consideration by the leading trade stores, is the gradual establishment by the latter of units in their stores for the marketing of local produce. The stores might find it useful to assist the producers in planning production, selection of varieties, standards of quality and packaging. Concurrently, there should be a much wider development of trade stores with goods of use to indigenes and of good quality and reasonably priced so as to increase the tempo of motivation in the direction of farming for cash. The existing activity of the Department of Agriculture in purchasing surplus produce from native farmers in areas where no regular alternative outlet exists is sound and should be continued. To an increasing degree, this operation should be geared to increasing use of local foods by all government departments involved in group feeding responsibilities. Research is needed on subsistence crops, particularly with respect to im-

---

[68] By trials, the Mission envisages blocks involving 100 to 300 smallholder units in areas near existing centers and facilities rather than large-scale operations of the type planned in New Britain.

proving storability of perishables and developing better storage and transport facilities, so as to make marketing to more distant centers feasible.

Of particular importance are cooperative and rural progress societies amongst indigenes. These are of key importance to group processing, quality control and orderly marketing, of both local and export crops. Many more are needed.

Export commodity crops face fewer marketing problems than do food crops. They are all storable after farm processing. On the whole their marketing on behalf of both European and indigenes is well organized, particularly in respect to copra by the Copra Marketing Board and to rubber by the Growers' Association. In negotiations for international commodity agreements, the Territory's interests have been ably represented by delegates from the Administration and from Australia. The Mission has only a few observations for improvement.

Special effort is needed to persuade native producers to harvest coconuts at present not marketed. Better transport services and better coverage by cooperatives to handle processing and marketing would be action in the right direction. Currently, cooperatives handle only 25 percent of indigenous copra and 7 percent of all copra. These figures might be stepped up with material benefits to the indigenous farmers concerned as well as to the economy.

Rubber is marketed by an organization of European growers who face no real problems in view of the favorable trade arrangements with Australia. As smallholder rubber production comes into being, a new factor will be injected. The Administration will have to work out ways and means of marketing their output. The cooperative approach probably holds the greatest promise of providing a workable technique.

Coffee and cocoa differ materially in their marketing needs from copra and rubber. The latter are salable on the international markets according to well-recognized grades. There is no need to preserve the identity of individual lots of the same grade so that bulk-handling is possible. In the case of coffee and cocoa, the position is radically different. Apart from minimum requirements in respect to size of bean, color and freedom from impurities, grade does not reveal finer quality characteristics. Sale is often by sample or on the reputation of previous sales. Identity of shipments has to be preserved until they reach the end-user whose price is related to quality aspects meeting his special needs. Rewards for quality can be substantial. The search for end-users who will pay for quality and the establishment of new markets are functions quite different from that of marketing bulk-type commodities to which the marketing board approach is well suited. Cocoa and coffee appear to be sold most satisfactorily through private merchants or agents on a competitive basis. This is the current system in use in the Territory. It should be continued.[69] However, the Department of Agriculture, through its involvement in production and processing amongst indigenes, has a definite role to play in the marketing of native output. Specific references to needs and possibilities in this connection have already been advanced when dealing with these commodities.[70]

Organization and Staffing. Administrative and technical responsibility for primary industry (except forestry) is vested in the Department of Agriculture, Stock and Fisheries. The strengthening of this body is one of the most crucial needs for implementation of the agricultural recommendations of the Mission.

The department is presently organized in five divisions: Administration, Plant Industry, Animal Industry, Extension and Marketing, and Fisheries. While this sub-division of activities and responsibilities is capable of meeting functional requirements, weaknesses have become apparent in recent years as the work of the department has grown and the pattern of farming has changed in extent and complexity.

There is considerable imbalance in the functions and support of the major divisions. Fisheries is very small, yet enjoys divisional status. Costs and staffing of this division and of the Animal Industry Division, which by comparison is substantially bigger, are fractional relative to the only large division, Extension and Marketing, which absorbs about 65 percent of staff and finance. Each division tends to operate independently at headquarters and particularly at the district level. Each conducts its own research, development and extension programs. Much greater coordination is required in areas such as grassland research and development, agricultural extension and inland fisheries. Investigational and advisory activities are directed toward the objectives of each division with little or no over-all planning or evaluation.

Too many functions and responsibilities are vested exclusively in the director. He must be able to delegate both responsibility and authority to one or more assistant directors, particularly in the operational field. Policy decisions should be considered by a top-level policy committee of assistant directors in council with the director. By virtue of his position, as administrative head of the largest industry, the director is

[69] Legislation for the establishment of a Coffee Marketing Board was passed in 1963. This board will, *inter alia*, have powers to buy and sell coffee and later may be directly involved in the trading of coffee.

[70] Also, the Administration should be prompt and flexible in meeting special requirements of the trade. The Mission was informed by several farmers and traders that lack of regulation for a standard bag for the shipment of cocoa beans had caused marketing difficulties and resulted in loss of export revenue.

necessarily involved in a large number of functions only indirectly affecting his own organization. These leave him little time to exercise directly his full executive responsibilities.

Recognizing these weaknesses, the Administration is currently considering fundamental changes in the organizational structure. The Mission strongly endorses changes of the type envisaged. The accompanying organizational chart illustrates a suitable new organizational pattern. While substantially similar to that being considered by the director, it incorporates some modifications which the Mission considers worthy of attention.

Essentially the proposal is for reduction of divisions to three well-balanced technical units each with higher status through leadership at assistant director level. Each assistant director would have a dual function. As a member of a top-level policy committee he would participate with the director in defining development objectives and in formulating major programs. As the administrative head of his own division he would be responsible for program implementation through his division and for coordination with the other two divisional units.

The Mission suggests that the proposed Research Planning and Evaluation Division should absorb most of the functions of the existing Plant Industry Division, and would include sections to handle animal and fisheries research and general science services which are currently the responsibility of other divisions. It would develop new sections to handle resource inventory and program planning and to give adequate attention to rural economics, particularly in the field of commodity research and marketing. The new division is planned to embrace staff with broadly comparable creative interests and thereby to provide an environment for fruitful work by competent scientific personnel.

The Animal Industry Division would continue all its present functions with the exception of animal research. Its animal husbandry section would be significantly enlarged to enable it to implement the extensive cattle program which has been recommended. At least for the initial ten years of the development phase of the program, it would be responsible also for the extension aspects of livestock production and training. At a later stage, this function might well be transferred to the Development and Marketing Division in the interest of maximum coordination of advisory work.

The Development and Marketing Division would be responsible for implementing all development programs in agriculture as well as fisheries. It would have an enlarged education and training section to cater for the rapidly increasing needs in this sector. Location of this particular unit within Development and Marketing is somewhat debatable. There would

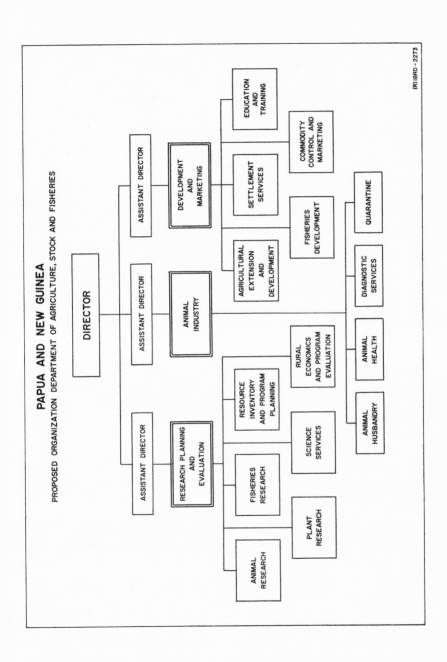

PAPUA AND NEW GUINEA

PROPOSED ORGANIZATION DEPARTMENT OF AGRICULTURE, STOCK AND FISHERIES

(R)IBRD - 2273

be an advantage in aligning training with development work and problems, but on the other hand it might be easier to attract a competent
teaching faculty to a more science-oriented environment such as that of
the Research Planning and Evaluation Division. Tying training to research also would have educational advantages. In deciding which unit
should be administratively responsible for education and training, this
aspect should be appraised in the light of local attitudes and more
specialized knowledge of conditions.

The Mission suggests the elimination of the Fisheries Division. It is
logical to place all research functions on the one hand and all extension
functions on the other in the same specialized units, especially where
the total size of the operations concerned is so small. In the event of a
substantial expansion in the size of the fishing industry, subsequent re-
establishment under separate control should be considered.

Of major importance to the efficiency of the department is the adequacy of staff in number and quality. Analysis of the existing staff
position (1963) shows that problems exist in filling established positions.
Table 33 compares the number of positions for which places have been
established with the positions actually filled.

The divisions of Animal Industry, Plant Industry and Fisheries depend
largely on professional staff. Almost half the positions were vacant. In
contrast, the Division of Extension and Marketing, where most of the
staff carry only diploma-level qualifications, had over 70 percent of its
positions filled. Over-all, about one-third of professional and technical
level posts were vacant.

These weaknesses stand out more clearly if the situation with respect
to selected categories is examined. Of senior posts, which require mainly

TABLE 33: Professional and Sub-professional Positions, Established and
Filled[a]

Division	Established Positions	Filled Positions	Percent Filled
Headquarters	4	3	75
Animal Industry	53	30	57
Plant Industry	86	48	56
Fisheries	12	6	50
Extension and Marketing	229	162	71
Cadets	27	23	85
Total	411	272	66

[a] Not including Department of Forests. See Forestry.

SOURCE: Department of Agriculture, Stock and Fisheries, 1962/63.

professional qualifications, only 35 percent were filled. Of junior posts involving either diploma holders or recent graduates, 87 percent were filled.

It is obvious that the department has difficulties in recruiting staff. Serious as this is, the difficulty of retaining qualified professional specialist and senior staff is even more serious. Policies affecting recruitment and retention need appraisal with a view to correcting these weaknesses. This is essential not only to bring the department up to strength but to attract the additional staff required to implement the development program.

Basic to the problems, particularly with respect to retention, are defects stemming from the structure of service categories and career prospects. The existing structure does not differentiate sufficiently between professional, sub-professional, intermediary and support categories. Support staff are largely recruited as field workers from the better indigenous farmer trainees of the farm-training program. Many trainees have insufficient education and many field workers are illiterate. Yet field workers, qualified at the most for support categories, have been promoted to intermediate positions. Certificate holders of schools of the Popondetta type are slated to commence service as assistant agricultural officers, and under the existing system could advance to the sub-professional grade. Diploma holders, though entering service at lower commencing salaries and qualifying for first promotion later than university graduates, have the same career opportunities as university graduates with advanced degrees. This latter situation is especially disturbing to young graduates who are not happy with a service which can make them subservient to diploma holders.

There is a strong case for upgrading the quality of the service and the first step in this direction would appear to be to place a limit on the career opportunity of diploma-level staff so as to make it quite clear that only university graduates can proceed to the senior grades save in exceptional circumstances. Similarly, bars to advancement at lower levels should be clearly defined. A suggested new staffing pattern of service categories, designations and entrance requirements is shown in the accompanying chart. Reorganization along these lines is recommended. The particular designations suggested fit primarily the proposed new division of Development and Marketing, but little modification is needed to apply the principles to the other divisions.

Professional staff can only be attracted and retained if there is greater opportunity for professional improvement. Research and other forms of academic improvement should be encouraged, through correspondence courses, participation in research, provision for accumulating and timing

PROPOSED SERVICE CATEGORIES AND CAREERS
FOR THE DEPARTMENT OF AGRICULTURE, STOCK AND FISHERIES

SERVICE CATEGORY	DESIGNATION	GRADE	ENTRANCE REQUIREMENT
PROFESSIONAL:	DIRECTOR, DIVISION CHIEF		UNIVERSITY DEGREE
	PRINCIPAL AGRICULTURAL OFFICER		
	SENIOR AGRICULTURAL OFFICER	III	
		II	
		I	
PROFESSIONAL AND SUB-PROFESSIONAL:	AGRICULTURAL OFFICER	III	
		II	UNIVERSITY DEGREE
		I	OVERSEAS DIPLOMA
INTERMEDIARY:	AGRICULTURAL INSTRUCTOR	III	
		II	LOCAL DIPLOMA a/
		I	
	ASSISTANT AGRICULTURAL INSTRUCTOR	III	
		II	
		I	SECONDARY SCHOOL FORM 3 TO 6
SUPPORT:	FIELD WORKER	III	
		II	COMPLETION OF FIELD WORKER TRAINING
		I	COMPLETION OF FARMER TRAINING
	FARMER TRAINEE		—

Exceptional Career ....   Normal Career

a/ Local Diploma holders will start at upper grades of intermediary until the standards of local training equal those of overseas training.

(R) IBRD-2355

vacations for longer periods of study leave, credit for time spent on academic improvement as for time rendered in the service, etc. These are examples of policy measures that could contribute markedly to an ever-increasing competence and to a greater service morale of the professional staff. Diploma holders entering at the sub-professional level could also be encouraged to participate in this effort of self-improvement.

For effective upgrading to occur, more and a higher proportion of graduate-level personnel must be recruited. One of the main difficulties here springs from the fact that the link between Territory service and comparable Australian public services, both Commonwealth and State, is far too nebulous. While theoretically there is no bar to agricultural specialists transferring to Australia, this is difficult in practice and becomes more so the longer it is delayed. There is a widespread belief amongst staff and potential staff that there is a gentleman's agreement to the effect that Australian departments will not recruit in the Territory, so that acceptance of a post there virtually cuts out a career opportunity in the wider Australian field. Many young and promising staff members, committed to Territory service in consequence of bursary assistance, return to Australia to seek work as soon as the bond period is completed.

From discussion with department professional staff at all levels, the Mission formed the view that ways and means should be sought to link Territory and Australian public service in a practical way. If the professional and sub-professional staff could be assured of adequate position and seniority in the Australian services, the present disincentives to Territory service would largely disappear, and the necessary climate would be created to permit much more extensive recruitment and retention. In addition, secondment of staff by both Commonwealth and State agricultural services would be a means of quickly building the professional staff to needed levels until such time as the improved recruitment conditions begin to have an impact.

Even though such changes in career opportunity are introduced, the vacancies cannot be filled overnight. As a means of meeting the inevitable time lag, the Administration should also introduce a system of short-term contracts whereby candidates at the professional level are offered specific posts under sufficiently attractive salary and transportation terms. The Mission believes that there are young agriculturists in many countries who would be prepared to consider contracts for periods of two or three years as a means of broadening their experience, although they would be unwilling to cut themselves off from their homeland for an indefinite term. This approach would allow the Territory to draw staff from outside Australia, as an example, from New Zealand and various European countries.

In close consultation with senior officials of the department, the Mission has estimated the extra staff needs of its proposed development program. These are set out in Table 34.

TABLE 34: Staff Requirements for Development Program

	Research, Instruction and Administration[a]	Field Officers, Junior Research, Instruction and Extension Officers[b]	Project Managers and Produce Inspectors[c]
Cocoa	5	40	20
Coconut	3	20	6
Rubber	3	20	6
Tea	2	10	5
Cattle	15	40	18
Farmer-training Officers	2	15	—
Diploma-level Training	16	10	—
Land Settlement	2	10	—
Fisheries	—[d]	—[d]	—[d]
Sub-total of Professional	50[e]	85[e]	—
Sub-total of Sub-professional	—	85[e]	55
Total	50[e]	170[e]	55

[a] Research and top level Administration: all professional staff.
[b] Field officers, etc.: half professional.
[c] Project managers, etc.: all sub-professional.
[d] Additional fisheries officers are assumed to be covered by the increase of 100 officers referred to in text below.
[e] Rounded figures.

The total needs come to about 275 professional and sub-professional officers in approximately equal numbers. In addition, the departmental administration considers that the present in-post establishment would need to be increased by 100 officers to permit normal growth in sectors outside the individual commodity programs. The Mission considers this estimate to be reasonable. With approximately 250 officers in-post, the total departmental staff in the professional and sub-professional categories should rise to 625. This is an increase of 240 or about 65 percent over the existing establishment, and 375 or 150 percent over existing staff. The bulk of the additional staff of 375 would need to be recruited over the next six years. Allowing for normal losses, this means an average recruitment rate of about 80 officers annually over this period.

The feasibility of obtaining this number is all important. From data supplied by Australian Commonwealth authorities, the annual output of agricultural graduates from all States in Australia is likely to average about 160 to 180 over the next few years, the figures showing a rising trend. In addition, there are, of course, the many agricultural and science graduates now employed in government or private industry in Australia. From these sources the annual need of the Territory is about 40. With regard to agricultural diplomates the annual output based on recent enrollments is likely to be about 200. The Territory's annual need again is about 40. Although sources outside Australia can be expected to contribute some staff, especially if the basis of recruitment is improved and broadened along the lines suggested, the main burden must fall upon Australia. If economic development is to be achieved on any worthwhile scale, the Australian Government will have to assign the highest priority to recruitment and secondment of Australian personnel for service in agriculture in the Territory and take the necessary measures to make such service financially and professionally attractive.

No mention has been made of clerical, intermediary and supporting staff. At present these number some 3,000. The department has indicated that the program would require the doubling of this figure. Undoubtedly some increase would be necessary but in view of the rapidly increasing standard of education of the indigenous people, the Mission has some doubts as to the validity of this projection. The present average caliber of indigenous employees is very low. It should rise substantially once the products of secondary schools come onto the labor market and if the department claims a realistic proportion of these. A strong supporting staff, not so much in numbers as in quality, is necessary. The Mission cautions against a tendency to inflate the payroll without sufficient regard to real needs.

Summary of Proposed Expenditures

A summary of proposed expenditures by the Administration during the next five years resulting from the programs recommended in the fields of agriculture, livestock, forestry and fisheries is given in Table 35. These estimates pretend to be no more than global indications of the likely orders of magnitude, since the Mission was not in a position to make more detailed expenditure projections.

TABLE 35: Summary of Projected Expenditures for Agriculture, Livestock, Forestry and Fisheries Programs, 1964/65–1968/69[a]

(£A thousand)

	1964/65–1968/69	
	Total	Annual Average
Current Expenditures		
Agriculture, Stock and Fisheries		
Total Expenditures of Department[b]	12,250	2,450
Vocabulary Stores	1,300	260
Forests		
Total Expenditures of Department[b]	2,700	540
Vocabulary Stores	350	70
Sub-total	16,600	3,320
Capital Expenditures		
Livestock Development	450[c]	90
Forestry Development	5,225	1,045
Fisheries Development	100	20
Other Building Requirements, Department of Agriculture, Stock and Fisheries		
Agricultural Colleges, Vudal and Highlands	800[d]	160
Extension Stations	150	30
Various Buildings	150	30
Agricultural Machinery	160	32
Sub-total	7,035	1,407
Grand Total	23,635	4,727

[a] This summary is not intended to be exhaustive. In addition to the items listed, allowance has to be made for overheads like housing, air charters, motor and water transport, maintenance of buildings and equipment and minor new works. These overheads have been included by the Mission in its budget projection for all departments combined (see Chapter 2).

[b] No correction has been made for some small items included in the budget of the department which are of a capital rather than a recurrent nature.

[c] Exclusive of cattle freight subsidy, which is included among total expenditures of the Department of Agriculture, Stock and Fisheries.

[d] On the assumption that about £A100,000 for Vudal will have been spent during 1963/64, as anticipated in the Works Program, 1963/64.

As indicated earlier, the Mission proposes, for the Department of Agriculture, Stock and Fisheries as a whole, an expansion in professional and sub-professional staff from the total of positions actually filled during 1962/63 of about 250 (excluding cadets) to 625, an increase of about 150 percent. The Mission envisages that in order to accommodate this increase the total budget of the department during the next five years would have to rise on average by about £A350,000 annually, 25 percent of the level budgeted for 1963/64 (of almost £A1.4 million).[71] Thus, a total of £A12.25 million would be needed over the five years, corresponding to an annual average of £A2.45 million.[72]

Expenditures on vocabulary stores for the Department of Agriculture, Stock and Fisheries have been assumed to rise from a budgeted level of £A200,000 in 1963/64 by £A20,000 a year.

Anticipated current expenditures of the Department of Forests were already mentioned in the Forestry section.

Among capital expenditures the requirements for livestock and forestry development likewise were already commented upon in the respective sections. In respect of the Department of Agriculture, Stock and Fisheries, the Mission projects that capital expenditures in addition to those listed in the Livestock section might total about £A1.2 million.[73] This projection assumes that the total cost of the agricultural colleges in Vudal (to be expanded as recommended) and in the highlands would be about £A900,000 and that, in accordance with the Mission's general approach, additional extension stations would be simple structures consisting partly of local materials; otherwise costs no doubt are bound to be substantially higher.[74]

The projection for agricultural machinery is in line with past requirements and estimates provided by the department.

[71] Further assumptions underlying this estimate are that the rise in professional and sub-professional staff during the five-year period would be somewhat less than one and a half times the 1962/63 number of staff; that the rise in subordinate staff would be proportionately smaller, thus reducing the total rise in salaries and wages over the five years to 125 percent; and, that the ratio between salaries and wages and other expenditures of the department would remain about 2:1 as at present.

[72] These amounts include current expenditures for the livestock program already mentioned in the section on this subject.

[73] No allowance has been made for the agricultural schools at sub-diploma level at Popondetta, Kapagere and Korn Farm. Since the Mission recommends that the school in Popondetta be converted into a comprehensive secondary school and those at Kapagere and Korn Farm, if established, likewise be comprehensive schools, the expenditures involved would be part of the costs of the education program, discussed elsewhere.

[74] The Agriculture Department estimates the costs of extension stations built from imported materials about three times as high.

SECONDARY INDUSTRY

The Growth and Structure of Industry

Secondary industry in the pre-World War II economy was limited to simple copra driers on plantations, small sawmills and a few plants engaged in making soft drinks, bakery goods and desiccated coconut, and shipbuilding and repair. After the war, with the still small and highly fragmented local market, the major developments were oriented initially to the processing of local raw materials for the export market. A coconut oil plant was opened in 1951, and plywood manufacture and passion fruit processing for export began in 1953. Since that time the emphasis has shifted more to industries serving the growing internal market and, for the most part, processing imported raw materials. A brewery was opened in 1952 and this has been followed by plants producing twist tobacco, furniture, paints, concrete products and cigarettes. The output of soft drinks and bakery products has increased substantially, and there has been a fast growth in metal-working and in repair and maintenance work.

Manufacturing statistics have been collected only since 1956. The available data on the growth of secondary industries are shown in Table 1. Between 1955/56 and 1962/63 the total number of factories increased from 123 to 331; value added increased from £A2 million to £A5.6 million. These figures somewhat overstate the rise in output because of improvements in statistical coverage. Nevertheless, the growth of industry has been rapid. It has kept pace with the fast rise in government spending and in total domestic expenditures in the money economy, and has exceeded the rate of growth of domestic exports. At present, manufacturing probably contributes about 10 percent of the Gross Domestic Product in the money economy, but well under 5 percent if the output of the subsistence economy is also taken into account.

Employment figures give further data on the structure of industry. The plywood plant of Commonwealth-New Guinea Timbers Ltd. at Bulolo is by far the largest employer, with about 350 persons when operating at capacity, plus substantial numbers in logging operations. Other sizable

TABLE 1: Industrial Production, 1955/56–1962/63

Class of Industry	Number of Factories	Total Average Weekly Employ- ment	Value of Salaries and Wages Paid	Value of Output	Value of Materials and Fuels Used	Value Added by Manu- facture
					(£A thousand)	
1955/56						
Metals, Machines, etc.[a]	40	610	205	549	168	381
Food and Drink[b]	28	398	87	544	297	247
Sawmills and Joineries[c]	45	1,988	541	1,978	752	1,226
Other Manufacturing[d]	10	398	88	1,392	1,208	184
Total	123	3,394	921	4,463	2,425	2,038
1962/63						
Metals, Machines, etc.[a]	151	2,139	1,163	3,444	1,607	1,837
Food and Drink[b]	62	1,383	288	2,635	1,533	1,103
Sawmills and Joineries[c]	76	2,587	726	3,227	1,562	1,665
Other Manufacturing[d]	42	844	365	3,893	2,876	1,017
Total	331	6,953	2,543	13,199	7,577	5,622

[a] *Industrial Metals, Machines and Conveyances.* Includes general engineering, mechanical-repairing, welding, electrical and radio-repairing, sheet metal working, aircraft maintenance, ship and boat-building and repairing, motor vehicle repair workshops.

[b] *Food, Drink and Tobacco.* Includes bakeries, biscuits, aerated waters and cordials, breweries, tobacco manufacture, and central coffee processing plants.

[c] *Sawmills, Joineries, etc.* Includes sawmilling, plywood and veneer manufacture, carpentry and joinery workshops and furniture-making.

[d] *All Other Industries.* Includes tire retreading, paint manufacture, printing, coconut oil processing, powerhouses.

SOURCE: Department of the Administrator, Bureau of Statistics.

Note: Includes operations performed at government plants and shops.

employers are the twist tobacco plant at Port Moresby (about 170), the twist tobacco and cigarette plant at Madang (140), the coconut products plant at Rabaul (120), the veneer plant at Lae (112), and the brewery, bakery and concrete products operations at Port Moresby (75 to 80 each).

In 1962/63, there were 36 plants in the Territory that employed more than 50 persons; these gave work to about 46 percent of total manufacturing employment. The average firm is much smaller, however, with 238 of the 331 firms in 1962/63 having 20 or fewer employees. In recent years, the increase of 200 plants added 2,500 indigenous workmen—or an average of only 12 per plant—to employment in secondary industry. As of 1962/63, there was a total of 6,950 persons employed in secondary industry, composed of about 1,100 Europeans, 200 Asians and people of mixed race and 5,600 indigenes. The latter figure is small when compared with the 40,000 indigenes employed in primary production, and even smaller when related to the total population of 2 million. Reflecting the small size of the average plant, there were 143 working proprietors in 1962/63 who accounted for approximately 40 percent of the total establishments. Of the 143, 118 were European and the remainder mostly Asian; no indigene has entered secondary industry in an entrepreneurial or ownership role.

Most of the capital investment in secondary industry is Australian, although sizable blocks of capital have come from some other countries such as Canada (plywood) and Malaysia (brewing). The Commonwealth Government owns a 50 percent-plus interest (one share gives the Government a controlling interest) in the Commonwealth-New Guinea Timbers Ltd. Native enterprise is represented by several cocoa fermentaries owned and operated by Local Government Councils and financed via bank loans guaranteed by the Administration.

Prospects for the Growth of Industry

The production increases which are foreseen over the next ten years are primarily in agriculture, including livestock and forestry. The growth in output of copra, coffee, cocoa, rubber and cattle will require increases in processing capacity. Commercial production of tea and pyrethrum will also necessitate the construction of new processing plants. The prospects for these commodities are detailed in Chapter 3. In the field of manufacturing proper, an expansion in the output of coconut oil may be looked for as coconut production increases over the next ten years and there should be a favorable opportunity to re-establish desiccated coconut manufacture. There is also a potential for processing peanuts into butter and oil. Exports of wood veneers and plywood should also expand, particularly if freer access to the Australian market can be secured.

Apart from the processing of agricultural and forest products, the prospects for developing manufacturing for the export market are limited. With the possible exception of its natural gas and the potential for hydroelectric power, the Territory does not possess rich natural resources which could provide a basis for large-scale industry. Even if raw materials could be imported there is no large reserve of skilled labor and capital. The mass of the indigenous population is still mostly uneducated and lacks even rudimentary industrial skills. The enterprise, capital and skill required by industries so far established have been provided wholly by small Australian and Asian communities or have been imported from abroad.

The Territory does not possess the natural advantages to enable it to manufacture on a large scale for export and in view of the small scale of the domestic market, the possibilities for producing items currently imported are limited. Nevertheless, it is in production for the domestic market that the best prospects for the development of manufacturing lie. Such development can hardly be spectacular, as the domestic market is still small and fragmented. But with rising incomes from the fast growth projected for agriculture, livestock and forestry and with a continued increase in government spending, the growing domestic market will provide the opportunity for expanding the production of many of the items already produced in the Territory and for manufacturing other items which are now imported.

The non-indigenous community of some 25,000 provides the greater part of the demand for consumption goods. Personal incomes of the non-indigenous community were estimated at about £A28 million in 1962/63 while those of the indigenous community were estimated at £A16 million. The non-indigenous demand is, however, spread over a very wide range of relatively high-quality products, most of which could not be manufactured economically. By contrast, the demands from indigenous consumers whose average incomes are small are concentrated on a very limited range of products which, apart from a few items of foodstuffs, consist of simple clothing, beer, tobacco and cigarettes, simple tools and household utensils, trinkets and other small luxuries. These are bought in relatively large quantities, and it is the "mass market" provided by the indigenous people that offers the best prospects for developing the manufacture of consumer goods in the next several years. Already the production of cigarettes is rapidly expanding and, with the repeal of restrictions on the consumption of alcoholic drinks by indigenes, the demand for and production of the local beer has increased very sharply. Good possibilities appear to be the production of simple clothing, footwear, metal bowls and other household utensils, laundry soap and cheap luggage. These are items requiring an unsophisticated technology and modest capital outlays, and experience has shown that the indigene can be trained to perform well at the levels of skill required in such operations.

While the indigenes are likely to provide the main market for local manufactures of consumer goods, the non-indigenous market will be important for some items. The indigenes are the consumers of the large quantities of canned meat and fish currently imported but the non-indigenous community provides the main market for fresh, frozen and chilled meat. As pointed out in Chapter 3, the Territory can produce its fresh meat requirements, and with the construction of the new abattoir at Lae, and other abattoirs as required, manufacture of by-products—sausages, blood and bone meals, tallow, etc.—will be possible. The non-indigenous community also provides an important part of the demand for bakery products, beer and cigarettes, and would probably do so for certain types of clothing and food items which could suitably be manufactured and processed.

An expansion of demand for producer goods—notably concrete products, bricks, paints, joinery—can also be looked for as the economy expands and as expenditures by the Administration on new capital works continue to rise. As the plantation economy grows under projected programs, the demand for repair and maintenance services for processing plants and transport equipment will rise. The implementation of the recommended program for coastal shipping should lead to a major expansion in ship-building and repair. The manufacture of oil drums and other containers has been investigated by private interests and the production of lime in simple vertical kilns offers a reasonably good potential, especially in the highlands where cement is expensive.

There is also a need for small service industries. As the economy develops, so will the need for such industries as shoe repair shops, tailors, barber shops, laundries, dry cleaners and repair shops of all kinds. The Department of Trade and Industry is aware of the needs, and the Mission would encourage the department to find ways and means of helping the indigene, by training and advice, to operate small service industries.

These are some of the more promising potentials for the development of manufacturing. There will be others as the economy develops. One is the exploitation of the as yet undetermined reserves of natural gas. The gas may be exported through either liquefaction or pipeline transportation. A variety of products can be derived from a natural gas base, with perhaps the most appropriate being hydrocarbons for conversion into urea (for nitrogenous fertilizer usage). Use of the gas as a low-cost fuel for cement manufacture is another possibility. Comprehensive studies of the commercial potentials, carried out in 1961/62 under joint financing by the Administration and a private company, indicated that an investment under current circumstances would not be attractive, especially since the assumed extent of the reserves would have to be proved. However, the natural gas reserves represent a major fuel potential as well as a raw material source for future industrial use.

If present and future potentials are to be realized, capital, management and labor must be mobilized. The managerial experience of the European will be needed to continue the operation of existing industry and to plan and operate new industry. Labor, both unskilled and semi-skilled, is likely to be available in ample quantity (see Chapter 6). With the expansion of education, especially technical education, as recommended in Chapter 6, there should be a rapid growth in the availability of labor with a good technical background for acquiring further skills in industry.

For the highest levels of skill, local industry will have to rely in the near future on high-cost imported manpower, but this dependence should gradually lessen if the programs of education and training recommended by the Mission are vigorously implemented. In general, therefore, labor should not be a major obstacle to industrial growth.

The mobilization of capital and enterprise is much more problematical. The sources of these will be the non-indigenous community in the Territory, and foreign investors and businessmen chiefly in Australia. Factors to be considered by new investors are those associated with establishing manufacturing plants in most if not all underdeveloped countries—for example the lack of a well-developed infrastructure, difficulties and delays in obtaining imported materials and parts with the consequential increase in costs, and the risks inherent in breaking into new markets. These problems loom the larger because of the favorable opportunities for investment in the fast growing Australian economy. Moreover, with the fragmentation of the Territory market and transport difficulties, industry located in one of the larger centers is so isolated from other centers that it has little advantage over industry located in Australia considering the longer shipping distance to the Territory. A further factor, which has been increasingly important in recent years, is uncertainty about the political future of the Territory. This uncertainty resulted in recent years in an unwillingness of some people with money to invest it in the Territory, and an outflow of capital (see Chapter 1).

Despite these various problems, experience indicates that investment in well-conceived and well-operated ventures offers potentially high rewards. To attract management and capital to take an interest in the opportunities that exist, the Administration, together with the Government of Australia, should adopt and implement policies which will encourage investment both by the people now in the Territory and by investors from outside. There are a number of problems and policy issues which if clarified the Mission believes will help create a feeling of greater confidence among investors.

Government Policies

Access to the Australian Market. The Australian Tariff Board has extended limited free-entry privileges to specific Territorial products, based on a policy that Australian producers should be protected against undue competition. Thus the free entry of plywood from the Territory, was accorded by Australia to the limit of 16 million square feet ($\frac{3}{16}$-inch basis) of highly moisture-resistant plywood per year. Quantities above this limit, and all imports of other types such as "waterproof," are subject to a duty of 32½ percent *ad valorem*. Passion fruit pulp has been permitted free entry of a certain amount per year, with duty of 8/3d per gallon (approximately 33 percent) prevailing for amounts above that. The free entry limit was increased in 1960 from 25,000 to 45,000 gallons a year, with the new limit prevailing for three years; policy covering 1964 and beyond had not been announced at the time this report was written. Since the imposition of the duty on passion fruit adds some 8/3d to the price per gallon, it would appear to be a significant factor in the demand for the product. It is clear that the economic growth of the Territory would be benefited by the liberalization of entry of Territorial products into Australia. Australia is now paying a very high portion of the bill for the development of the Territory. Policies which would permit the expansion of the market in Australia for products of the Territory could, over the years, indirectly decrease the volume of direct assistance from Australia, and the Mission urges sympathetic consideration by the Commonwealth Government for the adoption of such policies.

Competition from Australia. Australian manufacturers exporting to the Territory qualify for the Commonwealth's Export Incentives Scheme. For every £A1 spent on export promotion, Australian producers receive a double deduction of £A2 from income assessable under Australian income tax. And for increases in exports over a base period, a firm receives a rebate on payroll tax depending on the labor content of the product, which in numerous examples amounts to a rebate equal to anywhere from 2.5 to 15 percent of the value of increased exports. In addition, an exporting producer can spend three times the amount of his payroll tax rebate on additional market promotion with after-tax cost remaining unchanged. It would be difficult to determine to what extent the Export Incentives Scheme has affected the sales of existing firms in the Territory, which do not enjoy such tax deductions, but the Mission believes that the scheme operates to the competitive disadvantage of the Territory. Also the Australian manufacturer may profit enough by exporting to the Territory under the scheme to discourage his investing in the Territory.

As the Territory is administered by Australia, it is questionable whether it should be included within the scope of the Export Incentives Scheme any more than, for example, the Northern Territory. In case of exclusion of the Territory there might, however, be a tendency for the prices of imports from Australia to rise for the range of products which the Territory could not itself produce. The Mission recommends, therefore, that a more selective approach should be adopted. The advantages gained from the scheme, by Australian producers of items which the Territory has a good chance of producing economically, should be offset by appropriate tariff protection in the Territory market. This procedure should, in appropriate cases, also be applied to strengthen the incentive for Australian producers to set up a plant in the Territory rather than to export the product from the mainland.

Tariff Policy. The Administration has taken a number of positive steps to encourage industry. In 1959, action was taken to remove the 10 percent tariff that had previously been levied on imports of machinery used for many operations in mining, manufacturing, sawmilling and agriculture. Since then, further tariff action has been taken to assist specific industries as follows:

a. The tariff on imported beer was recently raised from 7/6d to 9/6d per gallon, providing increased protection to the brewing industry.

b. Twist tobacco manufacturers have been aided by a reduction of the tariff on imports of unmanufactured tobacco from 12/6d per lb. to 6d per lb. (even less on a graduated scale down to 1d depending on percentages of locally raised tobaccos that are used).

c. The new factory producing cigarettes was given free entry for two years (from June 6, 1963), of partially processed tobacco (normal duty is 12/6d per lb.) and certain specified cigarette wrapping materials, gums, and filter tips used in the manufacture of cigarettes, together with exemption for one year from the excise tax on cigarettes. The tariff on imported cigarettes is 30/-d per lb.

The Mission is in accord with the direction taken by Administration tariff policy. Infant industries with good promise for healthy growth merit protection and assistance in the form of direct tariffs on imported competitive products, and the free entry of equipment, raw materials and semi-manufactures used by Territorial producers. The granting of anticipatory tariffs—that is, the announcement of a tariff that will go into effect when production of the goods commences—and other measures to give protection should also be explored.

Tax Policy. The rate of income tax levied on public, non-profit and cooperative companies is 4/-d in the £A (or 20 percent), half the predominant rate for public companies in Australia. Private companies that have distributed a certain portion of earnings are taxed at the rate of 2/6d in the £A (12.5 percent) on the first £A5,000 of taxable income and 3/6d in the £A (17.5 percent) on the balance of taxable income. In case of private companies that have earned profits but have not distributed at the minimum rate, a tax at the rate of 6/8d in the £A (33⅓ percent) is levied on the insufficient distribution. Deductions are generally allowed on expenses incurred in gaining or producing assessable income, including deductions (subject to certain conditions) on losses over the previous seven years and write-offs of bad debts. Depreciation on plant and equipment owned and used in the production of assessable income is deductible at rates generally higher than in Australia.

The Mission suggests that a stronger emphasis should be put on the incentive aspects of tax policy. One such incentive could be in the form of exemption from Territory income tax for approved "pioneer" industries for a period of, say, five years from the start of commercial operations. At present, profits on operations which are remitted to Australia are taxed at the Australian rate (i.e., double the Territory rate). In this way the incentive provided by the lower rates of taxation is lost. The Mission suggests to the Australian authorities that profits remitted to Australia from pioneer industries incorporated in the Territory, whether or not they are subsidiaries of Australian firms, should be exempted from Australian taxation. The Mission also believes that dividends received by Territory residents from pioneer companies should be exempt from taxation during the tax holiday.

The depreciation provisions in the income tax structure should be modified to permit accelerated depreciation of plant and equipment over, say, a five-year period. Such allowances would apply to new plants and to equipment used in the expansion of industries presently located in the Territory. Another step in the right direction would be to lower the tax, or to raise the exemption, on undistributed profits applicable to private companies to encourage use of earnings in expanding and/or modernizing plant and equipment of companies now operating in the Territory.

The cumulative effect of the various tax concessions recommended in the previous paragraphs would generally be smaller than the sum of the individual concessions. For instance, a tax holiday would mean an additional concession only to the extent that profits would remain after application of the already existing carry forward of losses. Similarly, a tax holiday would in relation to accelerated depreciation amount to an additional tax advantage only if profits subject to tax remained after deduction of the higher depreciation amounts from gross profits. The Mission is nevertheless of the opinion that the various incentives in combination might well contribute substantially toward providing the necessary fillip to get a number of additional industries off the ground. Also, in the long run, after expiration of the periods of special concessions, the Treasury would start reaping the benefits if new, profitable industries would have come into existence.

The Mission also suggests that the introduction of additional tax concessions along the lines indicated be preceded by a careful study to delimit the field to which they might usefully apply; for reasons of revenue the tendency should be resisted to make the field of application too wide.

Industrial Estates. Under the existing policy, the Administration has sole authority to purchase land from native owners. The Mission believes that where sites for industry are not available in urban areas, the Administration should take steps to acquire land suitable for industrial development, and should plan to provide, at cost, the necessary servicing facilities. If land for such purposes cannot be purchased, the Administration should, as the responsible government, proceed to exercise its sovereign powers and acquire the land through the courts with payment of just compensation. In the larger towns where there is a potential for industrial expansion, the Administration should acquire sufficient land for industrial estates or parks. The estate system could be important in helping new industries. Provision should be made for facilities needed to make the industrial estates effective but the Mission would suggest that the Administration stop short of the actual erection of buildings until there is a clear justification for these as part of an industrial estate.

Power and Fuel. Elsewhere in the report the Mission points out the possibilities of exploiting known gas reserves and of finding oil resources. There are no known commercial deposits of coal in the Territory. Electric power is supplied from hydro stations supplemented by diesel capacity. The present system, which is being expanded to meet projected demand, provides relatively expensive power in terms of world prices. Since power prices generally play a minor role in the cost structure of industry, the Mission does not consider that they constitute a serious deterrent to the industrial development. There are potential major sources of low-cost power when the demand develops.

Industrial Finance. Other than the participation of the Commonwealth Government in financing the plywood plant in 1953, government financial assistance to secondary industry has been limited to Administration guarantees on repayment of bank loans for several central cocoa fermentaries operated by Local Government Councils. As far as the Mission could determine, short-term bank credit has not generally been a serious bottleneck for well-established industries. Longer-term loans have not been so readily available. The Commonwealth Development Bank has made four loans to industry in the Territory but these have been small in amount, averaging only £A11,000 each. The Bank cannot lend at less than 6 percent, and normally requires as security a first mortgage on land with individual recorded title. The Development Bank has no staff in the Territory but operates through the Commonwealth Trading Bank. These conditions have limited its role as a lender to new industrial ventures.

There are substantial private savings, but as mentioned earlier these have in recent years to a considerable extent been drained away in the outflow of capital to Australia. There is a clear need to encourage a greater use of these funds in industry and to attract new private capital from abroad. Private investments can be encouraged by the prospect of high returns, and these may be secured if outside capital on favorable terms can be obtained to finance a major part of the projected investment. The Mission believes that the provision of such capital would stimulate private industrial investments in the Territory, and the Mission recommends elsewhere in this report, the establishment of a Territory Development Finance Company (see Chapter 8). It would be the responsibility of this organization to encourage the participation of private investment in industrial development, and to participate in the financing of enterprises unable to obtain needed funds on reasonable terms from normal banking or commercial finance sources.[1]

Research and Promotion. The Department of Trade and Industry has divisions that are concerned with industrial development and trade promotion. Its services are available to companies that wish to investigate the possibilities of establishing new industries in the Territory. The department has also undertaken a systematic investigation of possibilities for import substitution. Much material has already been gathered.

Potential investors often have little knowledge about resources and investment opportunities. This fact, coupled with the strong desire of the Administration to accelerate development by private investment, makes it necessary in the opinion of the Mission for the Administration to take the initiative to promote industrial investment and development by the private sector. To this end, the Mission recommends that the department should be strengthened to enable it to initiate or make studies of promising new industries; to interest investors to consider participating in these industries; to cooperate with other departments of the Administration in recommending what assistance, including tax and tariff concessions, might be given to new and expanding industries; and to recommend the setting up of industrial estates and to administer such estates. The department should also develop an appropriate inventory of basic information on resources, transport costs and markets.

The staff requirements needed to carry out this expanded program over the next five years will have to be adjusted in the light of experience obtained and accomplishments of the department. The staff of the divisions of industrial development and of trade promotion will have to work closely with the proposed Territory Development Finance Company. Staffing needs of the department and of the finance company, therefore,

[1] The Bank should also be equipped to provide finance to small enterprises, such as service industries.

will have to be coordinated to obtain optimum results and avoid duplication of effort. The investment in staff to undertake this program could bring substantial returns to the Territory.

In addition to the efforts of the Administration, the trade stores and companies generally can further promote the production of items such as simple furniture, handicrafts, shoes and soap, for marketing through their stores. The economy of the Territory is small. Its growth can be accelerated by efforts on a small as well as on a large scale. Every new small enterprise or producer means added employment and greater purchasing power.

In this connection it was noted that trade stores, large and small, contained almost no local produce. One exception was coffee from the highlands, but this is found in only a comparatively few stores. There were indications that some of the trading groups have discouraged local production of items that might be in competition with those imported on the grounds of quality, unreliability of production, costs, etc. These may well be valid points but the trade stores could and should help find satisfactory solutions. The Mission believes that the trade stores, with their substantial volume of business and outlets, could contribute more than they are now doing to stimulate development.

The Mission suggests, therefore, that the trade stores and appropriate businesses owned by Europeans and other non-indigenes consider ways and means of encouraging local production and marketing. Encouragement could take the form of assurance of markets to the producers, assistance in planning production, in design, in maintenance of standards and quality and possibly even in financing. Efforts along these lines could make a very useful contribution over the years to the economy of the Territory, and also be of benefit to the financial position and general status of those making such efforts.

Training. At present, the skilled talent necessary to operate manufacturing enterprises, especially management, technical and "white collar" skills, is scarce, expensive and mostly non-indigenous. Technical training of indigenes—both junior training programs and the important pre-apprenticeship training for technical trades—is the responsibility of the Department of Education. Mission schools also contribute to this training, as do numerous other departments. These are discussed in the chapter on Education and elsewhere.

In addition to the training and education in the schools and the extension services, private business can make a definite contribution to the training and development of the indigene. The European has technical skills and managerial experience which the indigene does not have. If the indigene is to learn these skills and the management of industries, trade stores or other forms of enterprise, he must be employed, trained and given opportunities. The European, under the conditions of the Territory, should assume the responsibility to employ and train the native as rapidly as the educational standards of the indigene and sound business permit. Training should not be limited to the lower-level positions but should include the higher-level positions as well. Such in-service training programs may appear expensive and troublesome, but experience elsewhere has proved that the effort and cost frequently bring high returns.

Cooperative Societies

The Registry of Cooperative Societies is maintained by the Department of Trade and Industry. Cooperatives have shown a strong interest in both consumer and producer activities, the latter in connection with marketing agricultural products.

As of June 30, 1963, there was a total of 267 cooperative societies, with a membership of over 85,000 (see Table 2). Most perform the dual function of marketing agricultural produce (mainly copra) for indigenes and operating trade stores. They are owned and managed by indigenes, and thus comprise an important mechanism for increasing indigenous participation in the business economy. The stock of consumer goods—depending on how attractive or useful the goods are—also serves as incentive for the indigene to work more and produce more in order to have money with which to purchase the things he sees and wants. It is important that goods be made available to consumers at the lowest possible prices, and the cooperatives, if well run, can play an important part in keeping down the costs of marketing and distribution. Trade store operations accounted for 61 percent of the £A1.144 million total turnover in 1962/63, while copra marketing represented 33 percent. The remainder was mainly accounted for by marketing of Robusta coffee, crocodile skins, and some rice and cocoa.

There has been a relatively slow growth in the cooperative societies in recent years due in considerable part to limitations of government staff available to accomplish the tasks of organizing, training, advising, auditing, and inspecting the groups and their operations. Efforts have been concentrated on consolidation and strengthening of already established areas and on retrieval of lost ground, with expansion activities relegated to a very minor role.

The Mission believes that the Registry of Cooperative Societies in the Department of Trade and Industry should be strengthened to permit the carrying out of a program to expand both the number and improve the efficiency of operation of cooperative societies and supporting associations.

TABLE 2: Salient Data on Cooperative Societies and Associations (for year ending March 31, 1963)

| Type | Number | Member-ship | Capital | Turnover (£A) | | | | Rebates to Members (£A) | Total Fixed Assets (£A) |
				Store	Copra	Other	Total		
Consumer Societies[a]	22	2,630	39,445	126,584	—	—	126,584	3,227	19,040
Producer Societies[a]	30	17,621	49,318	—	18,155	34,824	52,979	857	10,831
Dual-purpose Societies	215	64,981	524,865	574,296	354,982	34,781	964,059	28,731	125,214
Total Societies	267	85,232	613,628	700,880	373,137	69,605	1,143,622	32,815	155,085
Associations[b]	13	226	295,082	556,341	4,999	4,521	565,861	6,135	155,310
Federation[c]	1	7	54,914	224,590	—	—	224,590	100	60,818

[a] "Consumer" refers to trade store operation and "Producer" to operation of marketing agricultural produce.
[b] Secondary organizations operating as procurement and marketing agencies for primary organizations (member societies).
[c] Federation of associations (tertiary organizations).

SOURCE: Department of Trade and Industry—Registry of Cooperative Societies.

To strengthen the Registry group there should be an increase in both European and indigenous staff. The Mission does not have sufficient knowledge of the potentials of the cooperative program to be specific as to the number of Europeans and indigenes needed. In the chapter on Education, the Mission endorses the plan to replace the present training program by training facilities at the college level which will represent important assistance to staffing for the cooperative societies.

Building Construction

Because of the importance of building construction in the economy, the Administration has taken an active interest in seeking ways of improving the efficiency of the industry and possibilities for utilizing more local materials. The Administration itself is the largest customer for building construction, having spent a total of £A4.2 million in 1962/63 on buildings, exclusive of repairs and maintenance, or almost 50 percent of its total capital expenditures that year. This represented 75 to 80 percent of total building construction (excluding bush construction by indigenes). As of September 1961, employment in construction amounted to about 3,400 persons, of which 2,700 were indigenes.

A major part of the building construction is handled by a relatively few large contracting firms headquartered in coastal cities, mainly Port Moresby. Smaller European contractors in all urban centers account for most of the remainder, with indigenous contractors handling only a small part of the work.

A number of special studies have been made recently of various aspects of building construction,[2] including the utilization of more local materials at probable cost savings, and the Mission places a high priority on continued research in this field.

The housing census of 1961 showed that about 80 percent of the outer walls of dwellings then occupied (excluding those occupied solely by indigenous persons) were constructed of wood (47 percent) or fibro-cement (33 percent). All of the fibro-cement was imported. In the last few years, cement block and brick for office and commercial buildings have been used in increasing amounts. Building construction costs, with use of imported materials (fibro-cement, steel and iron), are high and

[2] Alcock, A. E. S., and Richards, H. M., Report on the Building and Construction Industry in Papua and New Guinea, 1962; Ballantyne, E. R., Building in the Territory of Papua and New Guinea, C.S.I.R.O., Division of Building Research, 1962; Saini, B. S., Tropical Building Research, Territory of Papua and New Guinea, Preliminary Report, 1963; Hosking, J. S., Limestone and Lime in Territory of Papua and New Guinea, C.S.I.R.O., Division of Building Research, 1963; Hueber, H. V., Lime Kilns for Territory of Papua and New Guinea, C.S.I.R.O., Division of Building Research, 1963.

especially so in the interior areas involving costly air transport. The Mission believes that much greater use should be made of local materials —combined in appropriate cases with modern plumbing, flooring, windows and doors, and lighting—for simpler and much less costly buildings for schools, aid posts, hospitals, patrol posts, staff housing, etc. Pressure treatment or adequate brush treatment of timbers with appropriate wood preservatives should be adopted much more widely, and tests should be made to confirm experiments made elsewhere on usage of chemical treatment of thatch for roof and walls of native buildings to impart fire resistance and to greatly extend their life. Limestone and locally made lime make very satisfactory material for building stone, aggregate for cement, and lime-stabilized bricks and blocks. Various types of bricks and cement blocks can be made from local materials with a minimum of imports.

The greater use of such local materials would encourage investment in processing facilities and create more local employment. It would tend to discourage private importation of building materials and assist the balance of payments. It would reduce the gap between the European and native cultures and would be more in keeping with the ability of the Territory to provide from its own resources. It is important to lend every reasonable encouragement to the organization of small business and to increase employment opportunities. If tariffs are necessary for the protection of local groups processing local materials the Mission would encourage the Administration to take appropriate action.

HANDICRAFTS

Papua and New Guinea have a great wealth and variety of handicrafts, but relatively little has been done to promote production and less has been done to develop overseas markets. From the Sepik River in the west to the Trobriand Islands in the east and from the south coast of Papua to the northernmost islands, handicrafts of one kind or another are being produced by the natives. The ancestral masks, carved figures and crocodiles of the Sepik, the skilled wood carvings of the Trobriand Islands, the stone axes and bark belts of the highlands, baskets from Buka, the food bowls, woven ware, carrying bags and fish traps are some of the many items.

Handicrafts present an opportunity for village people to enter into the cash economy. The Mission believes that their production should be encouraged. However, there are problems in the production and marketing of handicrafts. If the product is to have a steady market it must have quality of materials and workmanship. Shoddy handicrafts will not sell. Much of the handicraft now produced is unique and this quality should be maintained. Also, not all handicrafts have value outside the village; some items have only a limited market. Changes in design and materials should make some items more attractive and salable. Expert assistance is needed for such guidance.

The marketing of handicrafts undoubtedly would be facilitated by increased tourist visits, and attractive local outlets might be set up in cooperation with the proposed tourist bureau. Some effective work already has been done by the Girl Guides' Association and the Boy Scouts in developing local markets. Missions, native local government councils and private traders provide outlets in the bush areas, with museum collectors also active periodically. It might be possible to interest the cooperative societies and trade stores in playing a part in marketing handicrafts. Australia would seem the logical market to begin a promotional effort, assuming that a satisfactory *modus operandi* can be worked out to make possible export to Australia within quarantine regulations.

The Mission recommends that the Department of Trade and Industry include on its staff a person with experience and ability to give undivided attention to this subject with the expectation that an organized handicrafts program could be developed for consideration by the Administration.

TOURISM

Historically, the Administration has not encouraged tourists. Until recently substantial areas had not been under control and, therefore, were not safe. The Administration also feared the detrimental effect tourists might have on the indigene. With the advance of law and order, coupled with the progress of the indigenous people, the Administration has shown greater interest in attracting tourists to the Territory. The Mission agrees that a positive policy toward tourism is now called for, including the active promotion of a tourist industry. While only a modest increase in tourist earnings can be expected over the next few years, tourism could become an important source of income as the Territory becomes less isolated and better known.

The Territory has an unusual variety of attractions in the hundreds of tropical islands, and a mainland with one of the world's great mountain ranges. The climate along the coast and in the islands is warm and generally not unpleasant. In the highlands, it is cool with frost in the higher valleys and even light snow on the high peaks. Lush forests, brilliant tropical flowers, birds of paradise, coral and sandy coasts, great rivers and lovely islands afford a great variety of scenery. Culturally, the people of the Territory have only recently emerged from the Stone Age, and their celebrations, shows, fairs, sing-sings, customs and way of life are extraordinarily colorful and almost unique. The people, the fauna, the flora and the location in the South Seas all add up to a fascinating setting which can provide a pleasant, interesting and even exciting experience for tourists. The coastal waters afford good fishing—in some areas sport fishing—as well as the magnificent scenery of the South Sea Islands.

The Territory is fortunate in having major shipping and airlines with experience not only in the Territory but throughout the South Pacific. The Administration and the private sector should cooperate in examining the potential, planning for acceleration and taking the action needed to realize the potential for increasing the tourist trade. It is clear to the Mission, however, that the Administration must take the lead in creating an atmosphere which will attract tourists. As a first step, the procedure for admission and travel to Papua and New Guinea should be simplified. Tourists should be made to feel welcome.

As another step forward, the Department of Trade and Industry might give thought to working out basic tour plans or patterns and ensuring that basic accommodations and other facilities are adequate at key locations. It is the Mission's view that hotel facilities should maintain the atmosphere of the South Sea Islands, while providing the amenities. Local materials and designs should be used whenever possible. Fortunately, air transport is quite well prepared by experience and equipment to accommodate tourists, but the industry should keep in mind the possibility that increasing numbers of tourists will be visiting the mainland and the islands. With the improvement of the roads some sections are now open to tourists but appropriate motor transport will be needed at various places.

Australia is at present the main source of tourists, and efforts should be made to promote this interest. The tourist traveling around the world and inter-area tourists and businessmen offer major visitor potentials. Special effort is needed to tap such sources, as the Territory is off the principal travel routes. The Honiara service connecting with Fiji and the service to the west connecting with Indonesia provide only a limited entry. The Territory suffers from a lack of direct connections with the Far East and Europe and with North America. Travelers from outside Australia visiting the Territory must first go to Australia and again return through Australia. A jet air service between Sydney and Manila with a stop in the Territory would make it convenient for both businessmen and tourists to visit the Territory. The Mission, in Chapter 5, recommends a cost/benefit study of airport improvement to international jet standards for the airports at Port Moresby and Lae with the possible restoration of the Qantas Australia-New Guinea-Manila service, discontinued in 1960. Passengers traveling to and from Australia by this route could take advantage of a stop in Papua and New Guinea. The restoration of this service might do more than any other single step to boost tourism.

Expenditures by the Administration to promote tourism should include the overhead for a Bureau of Tourism, plus loans for improvement of and for new accommodations as well as for necessary transport equipment. The Mission would suggest that administrative and promotion expenses be limited to, say, £A15,000 to £A20,000 a year to begin with. The capitalization of the proposed Territory Development Finance Company (see Chapter 8) should recognize the possible need for loans to the tourist industry. Private interests should play their part by investing a substantial share of the funds required for hotels, transportation and other facilities.

Summary of Proposed Expenditures

The responsibilities of the Administration in respect of the activities examined in the preceding sections on secondary industry, handicrafts and tourism are, with the exception of building construction, all concentrated in the Department of Trade and Industry. Various proposals to increase expenditures were already made. As indicated, the Mission advocates a strengthening of the staff of the Department of Trade and Industry to stimulate the development of secondary industry, to expand the cooperative program and to promote handicrafts and tourism. On account of other activities performed by the department which the Mission did not review in detail, including matters concerning customs, migration and marine, some additional expenditures will no doubt also be required.

Although the Mission is not in a position to substantiate detailed expenditure proposals, it has on a global basis projected a rise in total expenditures of the Department of Trade and Industry from almost £A600,000 estimated in the budget for 1963/64 by an average of about £A60,000 a year, to £A900,000 in 1968/69. The Mission believes that spending of this order of magnitude can be justified in principle and in the light of its basic recommendation to emphasize as much as possible activities that tend to increase the productive potential. At the same time, the Mission wants to stress that, considering the Territory's revenue position, expenditures of the recommended order should only be made if they are found necessary for the purposes indicated.

Reasonable amounts should also be allocated among Purchase of Capital Assets and General Maintenance for the various types of vessels operated by the Department.[3]

MINING

The outlook for the development of mineral resources is not encouraging. Gold output, which has accounted for 98 percent of the total recorded value of mineral production to date, has been steadily declining since the post-war peak of £A2,150,000 worth mined in 1953. Unless recent reports of possible new lode deposits are substantiated, gold output is expected to fall to about 25,000 ounces per year—worth about £A400,000—when the last alluvial dredge at Bulolo stops operating within a few years. Gold mining has produced some £A40 million worth of metal[4]—most of it since rich deposits were developed in the Bulolo area during the 1930s.

The greatest hopes in the mineral sector rest on general geological indications that the Territory, and western Papua in particular, may contain major petroleum fields. The search for petroleum has been disappointing, with 22 deep-test wells having been drilled, mainly since World War II. However, exploration efforts are continuing but at a slower rate than in past years. There are proved indications of probably large natural gas reserves of an extent yet to be determined.

Geological indications are not bright for other metals. Large deposits of nickeliferous ore in eastern Papua and adjacent parts of the Morobe District of New Guinea have been investigated in recent years by exploration parties for Bulolo Gold Dredging Ltd., International Nickel Company of Canada, Ltd., and for a joint undertaking by Hanna Mining Company and Homestake Mining Company. Results to date show the presence of nickel over sizable areas but in amounts much too small to permit economic recovery—especially under the high-cost transport conditions prevailing in these locations. There are relatively good grade— 40 to 56 percent—bauxite deposits on Manus Island, but of small size (estimated at a half million tons) and difficult accessibility. Government geologists have recently completed reconnaissance surveys for bauxite in the Fly and Bamu rivers area of western Papua and of the high plateau area near Sogeri, east of Port Moresby. Results are not encouraging. A

---

[3] Elsewhere in the report, the Mission recommends that the Administration fleet should become a responsibility of the Treasury Department, in which case the expenditures concerned would become part of the budget of this department. We have made no allowance for this transfer in our projections.

[4] This figure makes no allowance for change in the price of gold over time.

very rich assay for silver was recently obtained from lode material at Porgera 50 miles west of Wabag in the Western Highlands.

The rugged topography and heavy rainfall deter laterite accumulation of minerals such as bauxite and nickel. The general difficulty of accessibility, the heavy forest cover, the dearth of rock outcrops, and the mountainous terrain make exploration costs high. Deposits must be high grade to permit costly development and transport to market.

There are substantial deposits of non-metallic minerals such as sand and gravel, limestone and clay. Relatively little systematic exploration for these minerals has been done because their occurrence is very widespread, and their use depends largely on local needs. They are used for aggregate in cement products and concrete, for road metal, and in Goroka for making burnt brick. Limestone and other weathered rock could also be used for making lime in small plants at a few locations, and possibly eventually for making cement. Small deposits of phosphate rock are known on some of the small islands of the Admiralty Group, and small sulfur deposits have been found near some of the recent volcanoes. Low-grade deposits of coal have also been investigated but none are of commercial size.

Gold and By-products of Gold Mining

Gold has dominated the mineral output, accounting for about 98 percent of the total recorded value—£A41.7 million—of cumulative mineral production through 1962/63.

Until the early 1920s, gold mining was confined to Papua where annual output ranged in value between £A43,000 and £A89,000 from 1896 to World War I. During this period, most of the output came from alluvial workings in the Misima, Woodlark, Lakekamu, Yodda and Milne Bay gold fields, with reef or lode production (also important) from Misima and Woodlark.

With the discovery of rich alluvial gold in the Bulolo Valley in 1922, production in New Guinea was initiated. Most of the output has come from extensive dredging operations by Bulolo Gold Dredging Ltd., a subsidiary of the Canadian company Placer Development Ltd. At first, supplies and equipment had to be carried in over rough mountain tracks, a back-breaking job. Then small airstrips were constructed to accommodate shipments by plane. These airfields made possible the dramatic airlift of eight huge gold dredges (in components that were later assembled), each dredge weighing about 2,000 tons. Annual output ranged between £A900,000 and £A2,954,000 during the period 1932–57, excepting the war years and post-war years, 1942–47, during which production ceased. The peak year was 1940. Since 1954 production has steadily declined (see Table 3). This is due to the working out of known payable areas, working of lower-grade ores, and progressive abandonment of areas of marginal value due to rising costs. Yield per cubic yard of gravel treated also has been going down. Combined dredging and sluicing operations by Bulolo for the year ending May 31, 1962, resulted in recovery of gold (and minor amounts of silver) worth about 12 cents (US) per cubic yard of gravel treated. Bulolo now estimates that by the closure time of the one dredge still in operation (probably within about three years), it is probable that total dredging operations will have handled some 260 million cubic yards of gravel for a return of 2.1 million ounces of gold. At a value of US$35 per ounce, this would amount to an average of about 28 cents (US) per cubic yard, far above the 12 cents (US) average realized in 1961/62. This is striking evidence of the lowering tenor of ore mined in the latter years of this operation.

In the year 1961/62, Bulolo Gold Dredging Ltd. produced slightly under half the total output of the Territory. Next largest producer was New Guinea Goldfields Ltd., with about a quarter of the total. Of the total New Guinea value of gold output, 38 percent came from dredging, 36 percent from alluvial workings (sluicing, hydraulicing, etc.) and 26 percent from lode mining.

Minor amounts of silver and platinum metals have been produced as by-products of gold production, and small quantities of copper and

TABLE 3: Production of Gold in the Territory, 1950–1963 (years ending June 30)

Year	Quantity Fine Ounces	Value (£A)
1950	85,746	1,221,100
1951	87,841	1,360,677
1952	110,360	1,709,587
1953	138,781	2,149,817
1954	91,137	1,414,265
1955	86,791	1,356,021
1956	72,010	1,125,158
1957	79,253	1,238,336
1958	50,369	787,010
1959	45,690	713,913
1960	45,256	707,119
1961	42,848	669,503
1962	42,149	658,570
1963	41,956	655,565

SOURCE: Department of Territories—Economic and Statistical Branch.

manganese ores valued at a few thousand pounds per year have been produced sporadically, mainly from the Astrolabe and Rigo deposits, respectively, a short distance east and southeast of Port Moresby.

Continued explorations for gold by private parties have centered on finding additional alluvial deposits. The valleys have been pretty thoroughly scoured by individual prospectors and exploration parties. In addition, much prospecting has been done to find new lode deposits. Results of most of these efforts have been quite disappointing. Optimistic reports on recent underground exploration of the old Misima lode deposit, released in 1963 by Pacific Island Mines, Ltd., require confirmation.

While gold mining has been dominated by foreign-owned companies, indigenous miners also produce a considerable quantity. It is the policy of the Administration to develop a strong force of native prospectors, and to this end special officers have been appointed to assist and advise the indigenous miners on the working of their holdings. Output by indigenes from their own sluicing and panning operations, some of which is carried out on a royalty basis with the claim owner, rose from 2,892 ounces to 5,669 ounces between 1957/58–1961/62, and value of the output rose to a level close to £A90,000. In 1962, there were about 3,000 indigenes mining alluvial deposits. Some of them work full time at mining, but most mine only part time to supplement subsistence farming. By providing a mechanism for bringing a substantial number of people into the cash economy, gold mining has made and continues to make an important contribution to the economy over and above the value of output.

The Commonwealth Government pays a subsidy to small miners of gold—both indigenous and non-indigenous—amounting to £A2/8/- per fine ounce. A subsidy of up to £A3/5/- per fine ounce is paid to large producers (over 500 ounces per year), with the limitation that the subsidy plus the profits do not exceed 10 percent per annum on capital employed. This payment is applicable to mining throughout the Commonwealth. It is estimated that some £A60,000 per year might be paid by the Commonwealth Government as a subsidy to gold miners in the Territory during the next five years.

Petroleum and Natural Gas

Petroleum. Explorations in western Papua, where the general geologic pattern is promising for petroleum deposits, have been going on since 1912, but efforts up through 1937 were confined largely to surface geologic mapping, and the drilling of a few shallow test wells. Intensive exploratory activities were started by two major exploration companies in 1938, namely, Australasian Petroleum Company (Anglo-Iranian Oil Company, Vacuum Oil Company, and Oil Search Limited) formed to investigate extensive exploration permits held by Oil Search Limited, an Australian company; and Island Exploration Company (Anglo-Iranian Oil Company and Vacuum Oil Company) formed to continue investigations already started by Vacuum on its own permits in both Papua and New Guinea. Expenditures by these two companies—represented largely by British and United States capital—have accounted for probably close to 90 percent of oil exploration expenditures in the Territory, estimated at about £A40 million.

Investigations in western Papua have included extensive air photo surveys, regional and local detailed geologic mapping, extensive gravity meter and ground magnetometer traverses, much seismic refaction work, and the drilling of 22 deep-test wells. The rough locations of these wells are shown on the map facing page 228.

Results have been disappointing in terms of oil discovery, although definite strikes of gas in four wells, plus shows of oil and gas in most of the other test wells, evidenced the presence of hydrocarbons. An encouraging initial oil flow at Puri quickly declined and turned to brine; a good initial gas flow in the same well also declined severely under prolonged test.

Since 1961, the tempo of exploration has slowed considerably. In that year arrangements were made for Oil Search Limited to become the major owner of the Australasian Petroleum Company and Island Exploration Company under an agreement that Oil Search Limited would spend £A3 million on exploration and/or exploitation work in Papua during a five-year period starting in May 1961.

Oil Search Limited scheduled the drilling of a new well (Mutari No. 1) a short distance south of the Fly River near its mouth starting late in 1963, with further seismic work scheduled for areas near the coast along the northwest and north shore of the Gulf of Papua. Financing of this program (about £A2 million to be spent from about August 1963 through May 1966) is to be handled with their own funds.

Two American companies (Marathon Oil Company and Continental Oil Company), after taking over and studying a large permit in the southeastern part of the Papuan basin region, have extended their permit to June 1965 and plan seismic work on two surface anticlinal structures close to the coast. If the seismic work indicates sufficient downward continuation of the structures, wells may be drilled to test them.

High exploration costs—ranging between two and three times those in Australia—place the Territory in a less favored position compared with many other areas in the world in competing for petroleum exploration funds. Commonwealth government policy has recognized this fact since 1957 by the payment of substantial subsidies, under authorization of the Petroleum Search Subsidy Act, to the private companies exploring for petroleum (the act also applies to Australia). The subsidy covers 30 percent (reduced from 50 percent in 1962) of the cost of drilling on structures and of geophysical surveying, and 40 percent (reduced from 66⅔ percent in 1962) of the cost of stratigraphic drilling. Payments to Territory companies during the years 1958 to 1963 under the subsidy program amounted to £A968,000, close to half of which was expended during the 1960/61 year. On the assumption that Papua remains a high-potential oil region, the Mission endorses the continuation of subsidy payments at a level high enough to offer an inducement to private industry to continue petroleum explorations to the fullest extent justified.

The outlook for increased exploration efforts is clouded by the present over-supply situation in the world petroleum market. However, the possibility that oil production costs will increase in oil fields in South East Asia may draw renewed interest in the possibility of opening a major new source of supply in Papua. The large and growing Australian petroleum market will also continue as a strong inducement for seeking *large* fields in the Territory; on the other hand, any major successes in the strong oil exploration program in Australia, encouraged by the recent discovery in Queensland at Richmond Downs, could deter interest in the Territory.

Natural Gas. Substantial quantities of natural gas have been found in four wells on separate structures in western Papua—Barikewa, Kuru No. 1, Bwata and Iehi. Initial open-flow gas tests on these four wells (see map) indicated 90 million cubic feet per day for Barikewa, an esti-mated 50 to 100 million cubic feet per day for Kuru No. 1 (went out of control and had to be flooded), 43 million cubic feet per day for Bwata, and 33 million cubic feet per day for Iehi. These are very sizable gas flows and indicate the probable presence of large gas reserves.

Special studies of the Barikewa gas well were made in connection with a comprehensive study on possible markets for natural gas. These studies produced estimates of reserves at that location which varied from 40 billion cubic feet to 530 billion cubic feet due to the impossibility of making accurate estimates from one well. From existing data it is quite impossible to estimate any meaningful figure for total gas reserves at the four gas well locations, except that they are probably large.

Additional drilling, costing many millions of pounds, would be needed to assess their size and productive capabilities prior to planning for any large-scale use of the gas. Possibilities for using natural gas are discussed under Secondary Industry.

The Role of Government

Government policy is one of strong encouragement and assistance to mining. Liberal subsidies have been granted by the Commonwealth Government to encourage petroleum exploration and to support gold mining. A program of general assistance to mining is carried out by the Division of Mines, Department of Lands, Surveys and Mines. Much geological work has been done by both Commonwealth and Territorial organizations. Legislation and regulations bearing on mining contribute to a favorable climate for mineral exploration and development, including concessions to mining profits in the income tax. The Mission was favorably impressed by the Government's efforts to encourage mining.

The prospecting and mining of minerals are governed by various mining ordinances which provide controls relative to the granting of leases and agreements, the registration of agreements, the payment of royalties and other fees, and the physical operations involved in mining with respect to safety and health. Title to all minerals in Papua is vested in the Crown and in New Guinea in the Administration. Royalty is payable at the rate of $1\frac{1}{4}$ percent of the value of all gold and other minerals produced. Petroleum and natural gas are subject to a royalty of 10 percent of the gross value of all crude oil or natural gas produced. Non-metallic minerals such as limestone, clays, guano phosphates, sulfur, etc., are not considered minerals under the mining ordinances. Such deposits on lands owned by the Administration are leased as lands by the Lands Division under special provisions applying to each case.

Expenditures in the general program of assistance to the mining industry allow for financial advances on a matching basis to persons engaged in developmental mining; assistance for the test drilling of favorable mineral deposits; financial assistance for crosscutting for further occurrences, providing water supplies, drainage, or road-making; free assays; and the establishment of custom treatment plants. As has been noted, assistance and advice is also given to indigenous miners on the working of their holdings. The Mission believes that the programs of assistance to mining should be continued at about the same level.

The Mission also endorses the Government's policy of encouraging mining through tax concessions. Mining companies are subject, of course, to payment of the income tax imposed in the Territory. However, exemptions from income tax include profits from mining principally for gold, and in some circumstances for gold and copper; 20 percent of profits derived from mining certain metals or minerals, e.g., tin, copper, pyrites, bauxite, and income derived by a bona fide prospector from the sale of rights to mine a particular area for gold or other prescribed metals and

MINERAL RESOURCES & POWER POTENTIAL

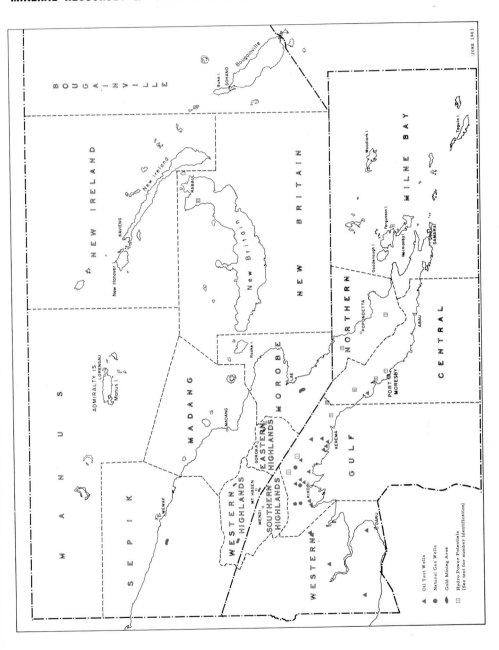

JUNE 1963

minerals; also, expenditures on exploration or prospecting, plant development etc., may be written off under conditions specified in the Territory Income Tax Ordinance.

Geological activities are carried out by geologists seconded from the Australian Bureau of Mineral Resources to the Geological Branch of the Department of Lands, Surveys and Mines. They provide geological supervision of drilling programs for mine development assistance being carried out by the Division of Mines of the same department and provide similar help in engineering geology involved in surface investigations and exploratory drilling for dam sites, tunnels, etc. The Geological Branch is conducting a progressive regional survey and geologists from the branch assist in making local geological studies of specific areas. The Geological Branch also carries out important programs in vulcanology and geophysics aimed at predicting volcanic activity.

The Mission believes that the staff of the Geological Branch, now composed of eight geologists, will require augmentation if it is to meet the growing demands for its advisory services to other departments of government, and at the same time to continue its geological mapping activities and assistance to the Mines Division. To the Geological Branch falls the task of carrying out geological investigations related to hydroelectric power developments and potentials; water supply problems; the locations of bridge sites, roadways and road metal sources for the recommended highway program; and materials for building construction. Thus, the Mission recommends that three engineering geologists be added to the Geological Branch.

The program for the detailed study of present vulcanism is aimed at developing methods for predicting volcanic activity that may be dangerous to inhabitants, so that adequate warnings can be issued for evacuation if necessary. Work and equipment are centered at the observatory at Rabaul, and regional vulcanological stations are at Manus Island and Esa-ala, Normanby Island. Seismic and tilt measurements, supplemented by investigations on vent temperatures and gas compositions in the field when necessary, are all used to locate and assess the severity of activity centers. The addition of staff needed to carry out the expanded program in vulcanism—three technical personnel—is considered by the Mission to be justified.

In addition to the vulcanism activities described above, a geophysical observatory at Port Moresby is operated directly by the Commonwealth Bureau of Mineral Resources. Recordings are made of routine seismological, geomagnetic, and ionospheric data for continuous distribution on a world-wide basis. New seismic equipment received from the United States Government will permit observations for inclusion in the world-wide standard seismic network. Analysis of the seismic activity has resulted in development of a provisional method of zoning the Territory into regions of differing seismic risk.

Proposed Expenditures

It is estimated that as a result of the increase in staff, the total operating budget of the geological branch would be increased from about £A34,000 in 1963/64 to £A58,000 in 1968/69. Expenditures on a yearly basis are estimated in Australian pounds as follows:

1963/64	*1964/65*	*1965/66*	*1966/67*	*1967/68*	*1968/69*
34,000	40,000	48,000	54,000	58,000	58,000

POWER

Known fossil fuel resources are confined to the probably large deposits of natural gas in western Papua, but these are far from power consuming centers. Petroleum potentials are still unconfirmed. There is no evidence of commercial coal deposits. However, the many rivers and high rainfall provide a source of power for many small hydroelectric plants and a limited number of larger ones. While the high mountains and very heavy rainfall imply a large potential for hydroelectric power, the topography is such that very high heads are generally available only far up the rivers where catchments become restricted and the flow relatively small. Storage areas for regulating the flow of water are limited. There are large seasonal variations in the flow of the rivers. Consequently, except where there are areas for storage, the firm power is limited by dry-weather flow which generally is only a fraction of the average flow.

Studies have been made of the hydroelectric potentials of several of the main rivers, and rough estimates of the hydroelectric potential of other rivers have been made without the benefit of studies. These estimates,

TABLE 4: Hydroelectric Power Potentials[a]

1. Purari River: Wabo Site	1,000 MW	6. Vanapa River	40 MW
2. Purari River: Pio Site	550 MW	7. Laloki River	40 MW
3. Musa River	200 MW[b]	8. Angabunga River	33 MW
4. Ramu River (full		9. Tauri River	30 MW
development)	200 MW	10. Oreba River	22 MW
5. Mambare River	100 MW[b]	11. Pondo-Towanokoko River	10 MW

[a] Numbers ahead of river names refer to locations (see map facing page 228).
[b] Potential may be larger.

SOURCES: Commonwealth Department of Works and private information.

shown in Table 4, indicate that there are a number of rivers with substantial hydroelectric power potential. More detailed studies would be justified when there are potential markets for power near specific site potentials. Other studies have been made of numerous small hydro potentials measured in hundreds of kilowatts.

Current Developments

The electric power industry is small. Total capacity is 21.5 MW (megawatts). But the Territory, with its many rivers and high rainfall, is fortunate in that small and moderate-sized hydro plants are relatively cheap to build because suitably sized run-of-river plants can be built without the need to construct reservoir storage. On the other hand, the cost of imported diesel fuel oil is high. Nevertheless, due to the geographical demand pattern for power, thermal has shared more or less equally with hydro in the increase in total capacity since 1954/55, the earliest year for which figures are available. Capacity is now about equally divided, with 11.4 MW of hydro and 10.1 MW of thermal power. Of the hydroelectric power 5.5 MW belongs to Bulolo Gold Dredging Ltd., which sells small amounts of power locally. Additional amounts of private power are generated by plantations, missions, and by Coconut Products Ltd., at Rabaul. Otherwise the Electricity Commission, created by Territory Ordinance in 1961, has the responsibility for generation, transmission, distribution and sale of all public power. These commission functions and responsibilities were generally performed previously by the Electricity Undertakings Branch of the Department of Public Works. The commission started operations officially on July 1, 1963.

The commission's largest hydro station is on the Laloki River at Rouna near Port Moresby. This plant began operation in 1956/57 with 3 MW capacity which was increased to 5.5 MW in 1960/61. A storage dam above the station at Sirinumu, completed in 1963, provides a regulated flow to increase hydro production during the dry seasons. As described below, the facilities at Rouna are to be expanded. The other stations are much smaller.

Operating data for the major stations indicate the cost superiority of hydro power. Average cost in 1962/63 at Port Moresby, served mainly by the 5.5 MW hydro station, was 2.8d per KWH sold. This compares with thermal power costs of 7.3d at Lae, 6.5d at Madang, 7.0d at Rabaul and 8.7d at Wewak. Diesel fuel costs 2/9d per gallon at principal towns and up to 3/7d in outlying centers.

With respect to capacity versus demand at major centers as of mid-1963, there were several tight spots—mainly at Madang, Wewak and Mt.

Hagen. Plans for additional diesel units at these locations and a small hydro plant at Mt. Hagen, plus more diesels at Goroka, Lae, Rabaul and Port Moresby, should provide capacities adequate to meet estimated requirements of these centers.

Projected Demand and Programs to Supply

In projecting future power demands in long-range plans for providing facilities to meet them, the Electricity Commission has used a uniform increase of 11 percent per year, compounded, for seasonal maximum demands. These projected demands are shown in Table 5. The increase of 11 percent is the general rate of increase during the past three years. Considering the potential demand increases for commercial and residential air conditioning, for processing tea, coffee and pyrethrum, and for chilling slaughtered beef in the Mission's agricultural development recommendations, and for increases needed for education, health, commerce and industry developments as foreseen by the Mission, these projected peak-demand estimates appear on the whole reasonable and perhaps on the low side.[5] The Electricity Commission will, of course, keep abreast of factors which will affect the demand for power and make the necessary adjustments.

To meet the expected increase in demand in the Port Moresby area, the Electricity Commission has scheduled additions to the Rouna Hydro Scheme. In the first stage a new power station (Rouna No. 2), to be completed in 1967, will add 12 MW to the Port Moresby system. This station will be capable of expansion to a capacity of 30 MW. The first stage, including construction of a new 66 KV transmission line, is estimated to cost £A2.3 million.

A second hydro system has been planned by the Commonwealth Department of Works, to provide power for the important section of the Territory now supplied largely by thermal power, extending from the highlands to Lae and Madang on the coast. The power station would be on the Upper Ramu River, near Kainantu, and would have an ultimate capacity of 48 MW (installed), with 66 KV transmission lines supplying power to Lae (90 miles), Madang (96 miles), Kainantu (10 miles), Goroka (55 miles) and Mt. Hagen (120 miles), as well as smaller outstations along the route of the lines. The first stage would have an installed capacity of 16 MW, consisting of two 8 MW units, at an estimated total

[5] A special case is Goroka where special additional demands for the planned teachers-training college and hospital have been programed. As explained elsewhere in this report, the Mission has not included these buildings in its recommended development program.

TABLE 5: Projected Seasonal Maximum Demands for Electric Power in Major Centers, 1963/64 through 1968/69

(kilowatts)

Center	1963/64	1964/65	1965/66	1966/67	1967/68	1968/69
Port Moresby	7,200	8,400	9,900	10,700	11,900	13,200
Lae	1,620	1,800	2,000	2,200	2,480	2,760
Madang	890	1,080	1,230	1,410	1,535	1,690
Goroka	360	420	480	740	820	930
Rabaul	1,840	2,050	2,270	2,520	2,800	3,100
Wewak	490	540	1,030	1,030	1,100	1,170

SOURCE: Papua and New Guinea Electricity Commission.

cost of £A6.4 million, including transmission lines and sub-stations, rural extensions, resumptions, residences for staff, and engineering and design. The cost per KW for the first stage of 16 MW are high but they include the cost of construction of much of the civil works for the ultimate capacity of 48 MW (installed). Even at this high cost, however, hydro power would compare favorably with an alternative thermal installation because of the high fuel costs. It is estimated that the centers and rural areas to be served by this system will have a maximum demand in 1970 of about 7.8 MW, almost equal to the initial firm capacity of the station.

At a system demand of 7 MW, the cost per KWH delivered is estimated at 2.5d for Lae, 2.6d at Goroka and 3.5d at Madang, as compared with present costs of about 7.3d at Lae, 6d at Goroka and 6.5d at Madang. Distribution to consumers from the main sub-station would add about 1.55d to the above figures. As the system load increases, as expected, and additional capacity is installed in the power station, it is anticipated that costs of production will be reduced. As demand increases to 18.3 MW, cost per KWH would be about 1.3d at Lae, 1.4d at Goroka and 1.7d at Madang. These cost estimates are based on the assumption of an annual load factor of 45 percent, interest rate of 5.5 percent, life of main civil engineering works of 50 years, and life of mechanical and electrical works of 30 years. The Mission views the Upper Ramu Scheme as a desirable undertaking to supply hydro power, at a lower cost than that of power generated by an alternative thermal installation, to the growing economy of the highlands and important coastal areas at Lae and Madang. Assumptions and estimates made in the many recent studies appear on the whole reasonable.

The Electricity Commission has plans for the construction of a number of smaller hydro and thermal units in other parts of the Territory. The commission also plans to shift excess diesel units from centers that will be served in the future by the two hydro schemes just described to other major centers.

A capital works budget including power generation, transmission and distribution, as proposed by the Electricity Commission for the years 1963/64 through 1969/70, is shown in Table 6. These estimates include £A5.2 million for completing the first stage of the Upper Ramu Scheme, the first small expenditures occurring in 1966/67 and large payments being made in 1968/69 and the following year, when the project would be scheduled for operation. The Mission feels that the over-all capital works budget outlined by the commission, including late additions discussed in the footnote to Table 6, appears to cover power needs adequately through the assumed completion of Stage I of the Upper Ramu Scheme in 1970.

TABLE 6: Estimated Capital Expenditures for Proposed Electricity Programs, 1963/64–1969/70 [a]

(£A thousand)

	Electricity Commission [b]	Administration [b]	Total
1963/64	380	264	644
1964/65	863	281	1,144
1965/66	1,928	219	2,147
1966/67	1,100	149	1,249
1967/68	931	147	1,078
1968/69	3,506	130	3,636
1969/70	3,499	130	3,629

[a] As submitted by the commission, there was included a total of £A5.2 million during the period 1966/67–1969/70 to cover construction of Stage I of the Upper Ramu Scheme, including transmission lines and sub-stations to carry power to Mt. Hagen. This compares with a total of £A4.4 million (excluding the Mt. Hagen line) shown in the October 1963 Commonwealth Department of Works report from which estimated power costs at Lae, Goroka and Madang, discussed above, were computed by Commonwealth engineers. Neither of these estimates included costs for land resumptions, rural supply lines, cost of engineering design and construction supervision, and costs of staff-living accommodations. These latter costs were estimated by the commission late in 1963, and brought total costs of Stage I up to £A6.4 million. The difference in capital expenditures of £A1.2 million (commission estimates) has been divided equally between fiscal years 1968/69 and 1969/70, and added to data originally submitted to the Mission by the commission. Inclusion of these cost increases in the power-cost estimates would increase them substantially.

[b] The Electricity Commission operates all government-owned generating plants. However, there are a number of so-called minor centers, of which 117 were operating in 1962/63 (generating units totaled 163 with capacities ranging from 2 to 75 KVA), which are operated for the Administration by the Electricity Commission with funds provided by the Administration: thus the breakdown in capital costs between the Electricity Commission and the Administration.

SOURCE: Papua and New Guinea Electricity Commission.

Rate-making Policy

Revenue forecasts prepared by the Electricity Commission, as shown in Table 7, assume that revenues will increase at 11 percent per year on the basis of existing rates. These forecasts indicate that the present level of rates should produce revenues sufficient to cover operating expenses, including all overhead and capital charges during the period under consideration.

TABLE 7: Estimated Expenditures, Revenue and Trading Position for Electricity Commission, 1963/64–1970/71 [a]

(£A thousand)

	Total Operating Expenditures	Revenue[b]	Profit or Loss	Progressive Position
1963/64	883	924	+41	+41
1964/65	942	1,025	+83	+124
1965/66	1,138	1,152	+14	+138
1966/67	1,282	1,277	−5	+133
1967/68	1,368	1,415	+48	+181
1968/69	1,673	1,571	−102	+79
1969/70	1,958	1,757	−201	−122
1970/71	1,749	2,005	+256	+134

[a] As submitted to the Mission by the commission, the trading position estimates did not include the additional cost of estimates for the Upper Ramu Scheme mentioned in footnote (a) of Table 6. Capital charges against these additional costs during 1968/69 and 1969/70, amounting to about £A42,000 per year, have been added to the expenditure column in this table.

[b] Revenue originating in minor centers is collected directly by the Administration and is not included in the table showing revenue collected by the Electricity Commission.

SOURCE: Papua and New Guinea Electricity Commission.

The Mission recommends that an examination of the present rate structure should be made to ensure that rates are comparable with the cost of providing supplies to different categories of consumers. The domestic supply rate, for example, is applied to private residences but also hospitals, schools and charitable homes. Commerical and industrial consumers are all charged at a general supply rate which appears to be somewhat higher than the domestic rate, except in Port Moresby.

When considering rate structures the relatively heavy capital investments over the period 1967–71, in connection with the Upper Ramu Scheme, should be taken into account and rates adjusted so that revenues should be sufficient to cover all operating and capital charges and also a reasonable proportion of future development expenditures.

Technical Training

The commission has its own technical-training program for power house operators, linesmen and electrical mechanics, with a total of about 140 trainees enrolled by mid-1963. The Mission endorses these efforts and suggests that modifications be planned and implemented to fit employment needs as projected for operations under the Rouna No. 2 and Upper Ramu schemes.

Proposed Expenditures

Estimated capital expenditures for the proposed electricity programs are indicated in Table 6. Total financial requirements of the Electricity Commission during 1964/65–1968/69 would amount to £A8.328 million and those of the Administration itself to £A926,000. Total borrowing needs of the Electricity Commission over the period might be slightly less if the projected surplus of revenue over operating expenditures would materialize, but in view of the smallness of the surplus it appears prudent to ignore it.

TRANSPORT

The transport system is not at present adequate to meet the developmental needs of the country. The lack of sufficient transport facilities hampers the efficient provision of administrative and social services and the movement of exports and supplies. Transport costs are often high due to the extremely difficult terrain over much of the country and the small volumes of traffic moved. These adverse factors are only partly compensated by relatively short hauls to overseas ports.

Most marketed production is exported. The transportation links which have, therefore, been of prime importance to the Territory have been the overseas shipping services to markets in Europe and Australia and the internal links connecting centers of production with the principal ports. The internal links have been of three kinds: coastal shipping, roads and air services. There are no railroads.

The main centers of production are the coastal areas of mainland New Guinea and the New Guinea Islands. Rabaul is the principal port of export, handling the copra and cocoa of New Britain and a substantial share of the copra and cocoa produced in New Ireland and Bougainville. Madang serves the main centers of production of the north coast of the New Guinea mainland and is also the principal port for the highlands. The bulk of the Territory's exports of processed forest products, mainly from Bulolo, passes through Lae. Rubber and copra from the south coast of Papua are shipped from Port Moresby and Samarai. The total tonnage of export traffic in 1962/63 was 217,000 tons. Import traffic totaled about 330,000 tons. Over 90 percent of imports are handled by the four major ports (Port Moresby, Rabaul, Madang and Lae), Port Moresby alone accounting for more than one-third of the total.

More than 95 percent of exports are carried to the overseas ports by road and coastal shipping, and this traffic is divided more or less equally between them. Copra, cocoa and timber produced in northern New Britain move mainly by road to Rabaul. Road transport also handles the timber traffic from the Wau/Bulolo area to Lae, copra-moving from coastal plantations to Madang and a substantial part of the New Ireland copra exported through Kavieng. Rubber from Sogeri also moves by road to Port Moresby.

Coastal shipping serves the inter-island traffic, principally between New Britain, New Ireland and Bougainville, but also from Karkar Island to Madang and from the Louisiade and D'Entrecasteaux Islands to Samarai. Substantial quantities of timber are carried by water along the New Britain coast to Rabaul and of copra along the New Guinea coast to Madang. Copra also moves by water along the Papuan coast to Port Moresby and Samarai.

Air transport is important in the export trade only for the movement of coffee from the highlands, mainly to Madang. The quantities involved, though rising rapidly, are still small. In 1962/63, about 5,000 tons of coffee were flown out of the highlands, equal to only 2 to 3 percent of the total quantity of exports.

The broad pattern of freight movements to and from the Territory is shown in the map on the facing page, together with the movements of exports from producing areas to the principal ports.

In contrast to freight transport, passenger transport is overwhelmingly by air, both within the Territory and between the Territory and other countries. The most heavily traveled route is that between Sydney, Brisbane, Port Moresby and Lae. Passenger travel between the New Guinea mainland and the islands is also heavy, due partly to the movement of migratory labor from the highlands and the Sepik District to the island plantations. Public road passenger transport is as yet little developed except in the Gazelle Peninsula and in and around Port Moresby. There is some movement of passengers on coastal ships, but the total number involved is still relatively small.

It is apparent that transport problems are complex and require a pragmatic approach. Thus, the Mission attaches great importance to the planning and coordinating of the transport system as a whole. No one solution to the transport problem is possible: in some areas a coastal shipping service combined with local access roads to coastal anchorages will provide the best solution; in other areas a combination of air services and local roads will be most suitable; in others an integrated system of trunk and feeder roads will best meet the requirements. The transport program must be closely coordinated with programs for the primary industries, and for extending and strengthening the health, education and other services. However, it is clear where the emphasis should be placed during the period ahead.

The major transport deficiencies at present are in port facilities, particularly at Rabaul, Lae and Madang, and in coastal shipping services. The first priorities in the development of transport services over the next five years should therefore be the expansion of major ports and the modernization and reorganization of coastal shipping.

MAJOR TRAFFIC FLOWS

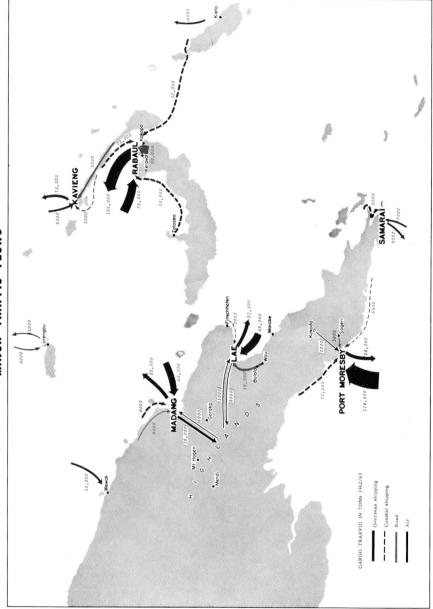

CARGO TRAFFIC IN TONS 1962/63

Overseas shipping
Coastal shipping
Road
Air

With the completion of the trunk road from Lae to Goroka some time in 1966/67, there will be for the first time an all-weather road linking the highlands with the coast. Road construction in the period ahead should concentrate on an improvement program to open up new areas for agricultural and livestock development and to obtain access to areas of exploitable forest. In particular, new feeder roads to link with trunk roads, airstrips and coastal anchorages will be a high priority.

Air services are generally well developed for the small amount of freight traffic carried. With the prospective improvement in road transport, some of the tasks performed by air carriers will be taken over by road haulers. Nevertheless, it is quite clear that for many years to come some parts of the country will continue to depend mainly on air transport, and in the transport of passengers the air services will continue to take first place. The emphasis in the period ahead should be on increasing the efficiency of air transport.

In considering transport services in the Territory, the problem of providing such services below costs or investing in transport facilities which cannot be recouped through user charges must necessarily arise. The Mission believes that as far as practicable transport services should be self-supporting in the long run. But there will be situations where investments should be made which cannot be justified solely on economic grounds. The question should be: would the investment or service substantially contribute to the acceleration of economic and social development, or is the lack or high cost of a service or facility responsible for serious under-utilization of production potentials or high costs of production or of administrative services?

No system of large-scale operating subsidies to internal services is recommended. The Mission believes that a program of improving basic facilities, combined with equipment modernization would be sufficient to assure a reasonably efficient transport system and lower the existing transport charges to more economic levels. A system of subsidies of the internal transport services would probably introduce further distortions in the Territory's cost structure. A subsidy once established tends to become a permanent feature and its subsequent removal results in painful readjustments. A subsidy should not be adopted lightly under a policy that aims at financial self-sufficiency.

Water Transport

Overseas Shipping. For commodity movements (both imports and exports) between the Territory, Australia and overseas countries, sea transport is far more important than air transport. The Territory is on the main trade routes between Australia, Europe and the Far East. Overseas shipping services on these routes are quite satisfactory, much better than the low volume of Papua and New Guinea trade would justify. It does not enjoy equally good service with North America which adversely affects the development of exports to that market.

The Territory depends almost entirely on foreign markets for the sale of its products and on imports to supply its requirements. It was frequently stated to the Mission that the economy is adversely affected by high shipping rates, particularly to and from Australia which takes about 50 percent of the Territory's exports and supplies almost 60 percent of its imports. To test this opinion the Mission made a comparative analysis of the general pattern of rates in the South Pacific region and those applicable to Papua and New Guinea. The general conclusion was that their rates for traffic are not inconsistent with the structure of shipping rates in the region (see Annex IV). Nevertheless, the Territory's development may be adversely affected by the burden of shipping rates, especially rates to and from Australia. The main factors which influence the level of these rates are operating costs, directional imbalance of traffic, the state of port facilities and the efficiency of stevedoring services which affect the rate of cargo-handling.

Operating Costs. The leading operator on the Australia/Territory route is an Australian company with a long tradition of operations and with large trade store and plantation interests in the Territory, the Burns Philp & Co. Ltd. Burns Philp is the only regular line on this route operating vessels registered in Australia and manned by Australian crews. In order to compensate the company for higher costs inherent in this operation, the Government of Australia pays Burns Philp an annual subvention of £A150,000. The company also has the sole right to carry copra from the Territory to Australia (which provides valuable backload); it has berthing priority for one boat in Territory ports and some priority in obtaining government cargo. These measures of assistance to Burns Philp make it possible to maintain an Australian shipping service without restricting international competition in shipping between Australian ports and the Territory.[1] These same factors result in Burns Philp being the price (or rate) leader.

Since the institutional factors are largely under the control of the Government of Australia (copra shipment arrangements, subsidy), it is apparent that the Commonwealth Government can exercise a strong influence over rate levels and rate structure on the Australia/Territory

---

[1] Operations between Australia and the Territory are exempted from the provisions of the Navigation Act by Order-in-Council (August 27, 1925). If this exemption had not been granted Australia/Papua and New Guinea trade would be reserved to Australian ships with higher operating costs.

route. A more active policy in this respect appears to be justified on grounds of economy for the Administration and others using such shipping facilities in the Territory. The prerequisite to a more active policy would be a change from the compensation type payment for the employment of Australian ships and crews to a subsidy for the provision of certain services under specified conditions with explicit control over the level and structure of shipping rates of the subsidized operation.

The Mission believes that it would be to the benefit of the Territory to change the basis of the subsidy now paid to Burns Philp to a service subsidy with control over the level and structure of rates and frequency of service, and that this subsidy should be administered jointly by a committee appointed by the Commonwealth of Australia, Department of Shipping and Transport and by the Administration.

Directional Imbalance of Traffic. Another factor influencing the level of overseas shipping rates is the heavy directional imbalance of traffic. Since 1950, the ratio of the volume of import to export traffic has varied from 1.22:1 to 1.65:1, with a worsening trend. This imbalance is especially heavy in the case of the Australia/Territory route where the ratio of inbound to outbound traffic is estimated at 3.7:1.[2] Unfortunately, little opportunity exists for compensating for the deficiency of outbound traffic by loading at other ports on the route.

In theory this situation could help the Territory exporter if the shipping lines would offer promotional rates on (bulky) exports. In practice, this has not happened. The possibilities of improving the present situation by means of direct government intervention are limited. However, it is likely that some long-range improvements may be achieved through closer liaison and consultation between the shipping lines and the exporters and that exports may be promoted through rate concessions. Such concessions can only be negotiated if the shipping lines and the exporters are fully aware of the possibilities of trade expansion through lower rates which implies close liaison between carriers and shippers; the maintenance of such a close liaison is a highly specialized task.

The Mission recommends that an officer be designated to review overseas shipping tariffs and schedules and advise the Administration and the shippers of any tariff changes or possible rate concessions, to maintain liaison with the Commonwealth of Australia, Department of Shipping and Transport and with the shipping lines and to assist the shippers in negotiating tariff concessions and service changes. Such liaison and consultation has proved advantageous in other countries.

[2] Estimated by the Mission from Overseas Trade Statistics and data supplied by the Office of the Chief Collector of Customs, Department of Trade and Industry, Territory of Papua and New Guinea.

Overseas Ports. In view of the heavy dependence on foreign trade, the efficient functioning of the ports is of major importance. The Port Moresby, Samarai and Kavieng overseas port facilities are the only ones adequate to handle present traffic. The total volume of traffic at the overseas ports during the 12 months ending June 30, 1963, is shown in Table 1.

A measure of the utilization of port capacity is provided by an analysis of the distribution of the arrivals and departures of vessels. The results are summarized in Table 2.

This analysis does not show differences in the quality of berthing facilities or the efficiency of traffic-handling operations. For example, one of the two wharves at Rabaul and the wharf at Madang are much inferior to the modern facility at Lae. Consequently, the utilization data understates port problems at Rabaul and Madang.

Port development has been on an *ad hoc* basis, the urgent problems being handled with little attention given to the longer-term requirements. This is understandable. During the immediate post-war years, the most urgent task was to reconstruct the destroyed port facilities and keep the

TABLE 1: Traffic Handled by Territory Ports, 1962/63 [a]

(tons)

Port	Cargo Unloaded		Cargo Loaded		Total Cargo Handled		
	Overseas	Internal Handled by Overseas Ships [b]	Overseas	Internal Handled by Overseas Ships [b]	Overseas	Internal Handled by Overseas Ships [b]	Total
Port Moresby	113,617	7,098	23,933	5,809	137,550	12,907	150,457
Samarai	7,257	562	8,099	318	15,356	880	16,236
Rabaul	74,467	1,937	105,679	4,368	180,146	6,305	186,451
Lae	49,016	2,784	21,182	4,831	70,198	7,615	77,813
Madang	50,569	2,392	21,883	1,223	72,452	3,615	76,067
Kavieng	5,544	1,012	12,714	157	18,258	1,169	19,427
Lorengau	2,680	264	1,824	51	4,504	315	4,819
Wewak	9,964	1,285	237	655	10,201	1,940	12,141
Total	313,114	17,334	195,551 [c]	17,412	508,665	34,746	543,411

[a] Coastal shipping cargo is excluded since this type of shipping does not use overseas wharf facilities.

[b] Internal (i.e., intra-Territory) cargo handled by overseas ships estimated from sample survey.

[c] In addition, small quantities of exports are shipped directly from Manus and Bougainville.

SOURCE: Office of Chief Collector of Customs, Territory of Papua and New Guinea.

TABLE 2: Utilization of Territory Ports

Port	Number of Days when there were							Percentage of Days when the Port Facilities were		
	0	1	2	3	4	5	6 or more	Under-utilized	Fully Utilized	Congested
	Overseas Ships in Port									
Port Moresby	83	166	69	32	8	6	1	87.2	8.7	4.1
Rabaul	41	104	122	55	29	11	3	39.7	41.1	19.2
Lae	162	120	63	16	4	—	—	44.4	41.4	14.2
Madang	173	116	57	12	7	—	—	47.4	39.4	13.2
Kavieng	285	69	10	—	1	—	—	78.1	20.3	1.6
Samarai	235	89	30	11	—	—	—	64.4	28.5	7.1
Lorengau	349	14	2	—	—	—	—	n.a.	n.a.	n.a.
Wewak	289	48	23	4	1	—	—	n.a.	n.a.	n.a.

SOURCE: Listing of arrivals and departures of overseas vessels prepared for the Mission by Collector of Customs.

Note: n.a., Not applicable. No reasonable berthing facilities available at these ports.

flow of exports and supplies moving. However, the adverse effects of the lack of forward planning have become apparent. With the exception of Lae, the access to port areas is generally poor and results in unnecessary congestion, loss of time and inefficiency; also the space available for port area development (storage space, warehouse sites, sites for parking and maintenance of traffic-handling equipment, etc.) is insufficient, and warehousing space is either inadequate or barely adequate. The future extensions of berthing facilities and their utilization and location, in relation to the routing of traffic from the areas of production, have not received adequate attention. Transshipment of cargo between coastal vessels and overseas ships is often handicapped by the lack of an easy direct access between overseas and coastal wharves.

It is clear to the Mission that certain improvements at Rabaul, Lae and Madang should be undertaken without delay. These are summarized as Stage I in Table 3. Sound port development requires, however, that each step taken should fit into a scheme to meet the Territory's long-term port requirements. The Mission recommends, therefore, that before the completion of Stage I long-range development plans for all overseas ports, including land utilization and land acquisition programs, development of access roads and organization of traffic flows in the harbor areas and adjacent town districts, should be prepared. Such plans should be formulated by specialized port planning consultants in cooperation with the government departments and agencies concerned, including the proposed Harbor Authority (see page 245).

TABLE 3: Port Improvements at Rabaul, Lae and Madang

Rabaul	Lae	Madang
Stage I		
Construction of the second permanent wharf for overseas vessels. Acquisition of land in the port area. Improvement and extension of access road network in the port area.	Construction of the second overseas berth.[a]	Construction of a permanent wharf (one berth).[b] Acquisition of land in the port area. Improvement of berthage and transshipment facilities for coastal vessels. Improvement of access roads. Timber wharf.[c]
Stage II		
Removal of the "wreck wharf" to provide site for the third berth. Construction of a separate discharge facility for bulk fuel-handling. Improvement of coastal ship berthage and transshipment facilities.	Construction of a separate bulk fuel-handling facility. Modernization of the small ship wharf and provision of adequate transshipment facilities.	Construction of the second permanent wharf. Construction of a separate facility for bulk fuel-handling.
Stage III		
Further improvement of harbor facilities along the lines recommended in the long-range development plan. Construction of the third berth.	Further improvement of harbor facilities along the lines recommended in the long-range development plan. The third overseas berth may be required.	Further improvement of harbor facilities along the lines recommended in the long-range development plan. The third overseas berth may be required.

[a] This berth is now under construction.

[b] Project approved by the Administration and construction anticipated to commence at the end of 1964.

[c] The necessity of a separate wharf and timber yard will depend on the progress of timber exploitation in Gogol.

Note: Stage I should be undertaken without delay but the improvements in Stages II and III are recommended subject to their being included in the long-range development plans to be prepared by the port consultants.

Small Ports. Small ports tend to be inefficient and the utilization of the facilities poor, as the freight volumes do not justify the employment of modern traffic-handling equipment, and short peak periods are usually followed by days of low or no utilization. Costs are higher if ocean-going ships have to call at a multiplicity of ports, each generating a small volume of traffic. These higher costs must be reflected in rates. At present the rates for freight between Australia and the smaller ports are some 16 to 20 percent higher than between Australia and the major ports of the Territory. If traffic were concentrated at the major ports, the greater efficiency which could be achieved by handling larger traffic volumes could result in lower rates. While it would not be realistic to expect that the number of ports serving ocean-going ships could be decreased nevertheless, in planning future port facilities, the built-in disadvantages of increasing the number of overseas ports must be considered. The complementary improvement of coastal shipping as described later will be essential.

The Mission recommends that no new overseas ports be developed during the next five years with the exception of completing the port development at Kieta and the possible construction of an overseas wharf at Wewak, if such a wharf should be considered necessary in view of broader policy objectives. Other new port developments should be restricted to specific needs of large-scale forest exploitation and export schemes where floating or lightering of logs is impracticable and where additional concession revenues fully cover the costs of such facilities. The development of new overseas ports at Oro Bay and on the north shore of New Britain is not at this stage recommended. The traffic in prospect would not justify the investments in such facilities, and it could be handled more economically by the existing ports of Lae, Samarai and Rabaul.

Port Management-Proposed Harbors Board. At present, no special organization exists for the management and operation of ports. The Mission supports the Administration's proposal to establish a Harbors Board and Port Advisory Committees representing port interests and users at each port. The board would have full authority for port management and control. It would have its own staff and its organization, functions and powers would parallel similar instrumentalities in Australia.

The revenue of the board would come from wharfage, berthing and mooring charges, storage dues, rents and profits of land vested in the board and grants or subsidies appropriated by the Administration. The past trends of port and harbor revenues show a reasonable improvement over the years, consistent with the growth of traffic. However, no attempts have been made to seek revenues from harbor concessions, rentals and land leases. The revenue potential should be fully exploited.

On the basis of past revenue trends, the harbors board would enjoy a surplus on operating account (before meeting capital charges), but would require special grants for major capital works required for port modernization and necessary land acquisition. The Mission recommends that after the completion of Stage I of the major port construction program, the board should be responsible for meeting amortization and depreciation costs of new harbor works in major ports. As minor ports have often been created for administrative or other non-economic reasons and are unlikely to become financially viable, the Administration should continue to bear the costs of capital works at such ports.

Stevedoring Services. The efficiency of stevedoring services affects the cost of terminal operations of overseas ships and thus, in the long run, the level of shipping rates. In most ports, stevedoring services are provided by a number of organizations; usually there are more stevedoring groups than the maximum number of ships which can be handled at the same time. The splitting of the low volume of total traffic between different organizations results in poor utilization of equipment which, in turn, acts as a disincentive to acquiring specialized equipment. The efficiency of different stevedoring services varies from very good to poor. The Mission recommends that the proposed harbors board should have authority to license stevedoring services. This should lead to increased efficiency and lower costs.

Coastal Shipping. The total volume of traffic carried by internal shipping services has been relatively stable over the last few years (see Table 4). The frequency of coastal shipping is shown in the map facing page 252.

TABLE 4: Internal Shipping Cargoes Handled by Principal Papua/New Guinea Ports [a]

(thousand tons)

Year [b]	Unloaded	Loaded	Total Tonnage Handled
1960/61	117.6	89.2	206.8
1961/62	122.1	78.5	200.6
1962/63	119.2	87.7	206.9

[a] Port Moresby, Samarai, Rabaul, Lae, Madang, Kavieng, Lorengau, Wewak.
[b] Year ending June 30.
SOURCE: Territory of Papua, Territory of New Guinea, Annual Report.

Water transport between ports is provided by overseas ships (on an "incidental traffic" basis) and by coastal vessels. Overseas vessels carry practically all the traffic between Port Moresby and the ports on the north shore of New Guinea and the New Guinea Islands and a significant proportion of traffic between ports in the Territory of New Guinea. This high degree of participation of overseas vessels in Territory trade has adversely affected the development of a strong and efficient coastal shipping industry.

In some parts of the Territory, the coastal trade is dominated by coastal vessels operated by the large trading and plantation companies which are geared primarily to the satisfaction of their own needs rather than to providing a public service. In addition to large trading companies, coastal vessels are operated by a number of small companies acting as owners, charterers, agents, etc. Some of these companies are starved for capital; their equipment is obsolete and their operating costs are high.

These factors together with a shortage of qualified indigenous masters and inadequate loading and unloading facilities at small ports and anchorages make coastal shipping operations relatively expensive. Operating costs of coastal vessels are estimated to vary between 4d and 6d per ton-mile for larger and more modern vessles and between 6d and 11d for smaller and old vessels (calculations are based on the assumption of a 75 percent load factor).

The coastal shipping fleet in mid-1963 consisted of 207 vessels of which 180 were capable of carrying only 50 net tons or less. This fleet is not adequate for the current needs of the coastal trade. In some areas, the lack of regular shipping services has adversely affected the production and marketing of cash crops. With the expected increases in agricultural production, the coastal shipping service will become increasingly inadequate unless a comprehensive program of rationalization and modernization is adopted.

The Mission recommends the reorganization of the industry through the introduction of economic regulations, re-equipment, training of personnel, especially indigenes, and construction of small wharves and jetties and the necessary access roads. These measures will require action by the Administration, which has, under the Shipping Ordinance (1951–1960), powers of licensing, control and fare regulation of local shipping.

A system of economic regulation of the internal shipping industry should be introduced comprising both route or service licensing and rate control. Under this system, responsible carriers would be licensed for the operation of the specified routes. In the granting of licenses for local routes, priority should be given to independent operators with the financial resources to undertake fleet modernization, to operators who are willing and able to develop more extensive inter-regional services and to operators with good operating records.

The route licenses should not be exclusive; a degree of competition should be encouraged. The primary purpose of the route regulation would be to grant a degree of protection to responsible operators who are able and willing to modernize their equipment and provide essential services. Granting profitable routes to good operators will help them to obtain new capital and make it possible to allocate to them "development" routes (i.e., those which are considered to be in the public interest but which could not be operated without protection).

Parallel with the strengthening and rationalization of coastal shipping there should be a gradual phasing out of overseas vessels from coastal shipping operations. Although this would result in overseas vessels losing marginal revenues from intra-Territory trade, these losses would be compensated by cost savings resulting from the avoidance of numerous intermediate stops at secondary ports.

The coastal shipping industry should be given temporary assistance for fleet expansion and modernization. This assistance should include credit for re-equipment. Free design services to develop economical models for coastal services should be provided, if possible, through the facilities of the Shipbuilding Board in Australia. These design studies should be coordinated with research into problems of corrosion in tropical waters, since corrosion is a major factor increasing maintenance costs. To assure the economics of standardization it is suggested that not more than two types or sizes of vessels be developed. To familiarize operators with the advantages of using modern vessels, model or prototype boats should be put into service preferably under a special contract with a selected operator or as a part of the Administration's fleet. The new vessels should include provision for refrigeration and freezer space as well as other equipment essential to meet the distribution needs of the cattle, fishing and agricultural industries.

The present training programs for indigenous masters, engineers and seamen should be continued and if necessary expanded. The Sea School of the Marine Branch impressed the Mission as a well-conceived training institution. Its success will depend on the willingness of the industry to employ the trainees and the Mission urges that the industry lend encouragement to the school and use its graduates. The graduates in the long run should become the operators and owners of a substantial portion of the shipping industry.

Finally, a program for the construction of local loading and unloading facilities coordinated with local access road systems should be developed. In view of the fact that such improvements would primarily generate local benefits, the program should be based on cost-sharing arrangements between the Administration, local government councils and plantation owners.

The Mission wishes to stress that the success of the program recommended will depend to a large extent on the response of shipping interests and on the ability and willingness of the independent local operators to improve and expand their services. However, the possibility must be faced that an orderly and progressive development of services over certain routes or in certain areas could not be achieved on the necessary scale or within the desirable period, either by the present operators or by other private interests. Should this happen it would be essential to supplement the existing services by a new enterprise partially or wholly owned by the Government. Such an enterprise should be run on commercial lines and submitted to the discipline of profit and loss accounting. The role of this organization would be to supplement and not to replace privately owned companies, and it should enjoy neither special consideration in route licensing nor monopoly privileges.

Estimated Expenditures for Water Transport Facilities. The first priority in the program for developing water transport facilities is the improvement of major ports. The Mission estimates that during the first two years of the five-year program, appropriations for port improvement should be at a level of about £A550,000 annually. Thereafter, it should be possible to gradually reduce the annual appropriation as major works are completed. There will, however, be a continuing need for the development of small ports. The Mission estimates that appropriations of about £A450,000 in 1966/67 and about £A350,000 in 1967/68 and 1968/69 should be sufficient to meet the cost of all port improvements. In the absence of detailed information, these estimates must be considered as orders of magnitude.

With the establishment of the harbors board, the responsibility for maintenance of harbor works will no longer fall on the Administration. The costs of maintenance will be met by the board. These are estimated to rise from about £A45,000 in 1964/65 to £A60,000 in 1968/69.

A second high priority is the reorganization and modernization of coastal shipping. The total investment in new and reconditioned ships and ancillary facilities is estimated at roughly £A6 million. It is doubtful whether the industry will be able to finance such expenditures without assistance, and the Mission recommends that the proposed Territory Development Finance Company be prepared to provide credit to assist in financing this program. Other costs will fall on the Administration directly, such as the costs of ship design, the production of model vessels, and the provision of local loading and unloading facilities at coastal anchorages. Together these are estimated to cost about £A700,000 over the five-year period.

Air Transport

Australia/Papua and New Guinea Services. On the Australia/ Papua and New Guinea route, air transport is the most widely used form of passenger transport. It is only a secondary means of cargo carriage

but an important one. The smallness of the Territory market and its
geographical fragmentation make the maintenance of satisfactory stores
of spare parts and specialized goods very difficult; under these circumstances rapid air delivery is essential for the efficient workings of many
enterprises.

Service between Australia, the Territory and the Philippines (Manila),
the latter providing a connection with services to the Far East, Europe
and North America, was operated until July 1960 by Qantas Empire
Airways. At that time the Australia/Territory route was taken over from
Qantas by the two major Australian domestic air carriers, Trans-Australia
Airlines (TAA) and Ansett-ANA, and the service between the Territory
and Manila came to an end.

The two airlines fly DC 6Bs on this route but with the growth in traffic,
summarized in Table 5, they plan to replace them with Lockheed Electras
as soon as the airports at Port Moresby and Lae are brought to Electra
standards. The planned extensions of the two airports to Electra standards
are justified by the expected traffic growth.

TABLE 5: Air Transport Traffic, Australia/Papua and New Guinea,
1959–62

Year	Passenger-miles million	In-crease %	Cargo (Ton-miles) thousand	In-crease %	Mail (Ton-miles) thousand	In-crease %	Load factor Passenger %	Load factor Weight %
1959	38.2		923		203		63.5	55.3
		14.1		23.2		23.2		
1960	43.6		1,137		250		63.7	54.5
		17.7		7.1		26.0		
1961	51.3		1,218		315		60.9	51.4
		11.3		0.9		11.4		
1962	57.1		1,229		351		62.0	57.9

SOURCE: Commonwealth of Australia, Department of Civil Aviation, Statistics of Australian Regular Air Services.

Overseas Services. As there are no direct air connections between the
Territory, the Far East, North America and Europe, all traffic is channeled
via Australia.[3] The lack of such an international service is a major deterrent
to the development of tourist traffic and has an unmeasurable but negative

[3] TAA on behalf of Qantas operates a service to Kota Baru in West Irian from Lae
and to Honiara in the British Solomon Islands also from Lae. A Garuda service
operates between Kota Baru and Lae.

effect upon travel by others with possible interests in the Territory as well as upon shipment of spare parts and other speciality items. The restoration of the services to Manila depends on several factors, including bringing either Port Moresby or Lae airport to jet standards. It may also require suitable traffic-pooling arrangements between Qantas and TAA over the Territory/Sydney section which would make a Territory stop economically justifiable.

The second condition should be possible of solution: both airlines are government-owned and are subject to government policy. Whether the up-grading of Port Moresby (or Lae) airport to jet standards is economically justified or not depends on the prospects for the development of the international tourist industry as well as on other benefits of a direct overseas link. The necessary cost-benefit analysis is complex and could not be made by the Mission in the time available. It should be undertaken jointly by the Department of Civil Aviation and the Administration, and should it indicate that the airport extension would be justified economically, the Qantas service between Australia, the Territory and Manila should be restored as soon as possible. In this analysis, account should be taken of the many long-term benefits of tourism and other travel in the Territory, as well as of immediate financial results (see page 220).

Internal Air Services. Air transport in Papua and New Guinea has had a long, colorful and distinguished history. The early growth was associated with gold mining activities where the high value of the product, limited volume and the short haul made this means of transport economical. Basically, the same factors were responsible for the use of air transport to serve the coffee industry in the highlands and rubber and beef in the Kokoda Valley. The airplane also made it possible to open up highland and other interior areas where the only alternative was travel by foot.

At present, three scheduled airlines, TAA, Ansett-MAL and Papuan Airline Transport (Patair) as well as small charter services, operate in the Territory.

The analysis of air traffic development is difficult because of the inadequacy of statistics relating to charter traffic which forms a large proportion of total transport flying. More than 50 percent of air transport revenues in 1962 were earned by charter flying. Consequently, the pattern of traffic development must be deduced from available statistics on regular (scheduled) air services and from airport activity data. These statistics show substantial increases in traffic over the past three years (see Table 6). Air traffic flows for passenger and cargo in 1962/63 are shown in the map facing page 252.

TABLE 6: Airport Traffic: Major Airports, Scheduled and Non-scheduled Traffic (years ending June 30)

Airport	1960/61		1961/62		1962/63	
	Out[a]	In[a]	Out	In	Out	In
Passengers	(numbers)					
Port Moresby	19,524	13,098	15,166	17,643	22,432	20,756
Lae	17,892	16,020	21,090	20,676	23,275	25,576
Rabaul	13,368	14,244	14,376	16,187	15,516	16,583
Madang	12,918	13,194	13,742	14,390	17,312	15,325
Goroka	7,623	8,831	9,200	9,890	16,924	16,768
Wewak	6,468	6,678	7,877	8,257	8,415	7,605
Mt. Hagen	5,298	5,388	4,949	5,850	8,385	8,975
Popondetta	1,272	1,764	2,399	2,566	3,268	3,386
Cargo	(short tons)					
Port Moresby	1,947.9	1,120.6	2,357.4	1,218.7	2,428.5	1,253.0
Lae	4,090.2	823.4	4,445.7	1,204.8	4,066.9	1,174.9
Rabaul	238.6	120.8	152.2	148.7	191.7	198.5
Madang	13,855.6	2,620.0	14,060.1	3,120.4	17,986.8	5,229.7
Goroka	2,237.4	5,401.8	2,426.0	7,435.8	3,179.5	9,507.0
Wewak	252.8	92.4	619.4	142.1	726.2	185.6
Mt. Hagen	822.9	3,912.6	1,353.7	4,223.4	2,209.2	5,689.6
Popondetta	101.8	283.9	86.5	299.4	92.7	254.5

[a] Estimated traffic (information incomplete).

SOURCE: Commonwealth of Australia, Department of Civil Aviation.

Most of the travel in the Territory is by air. In addition to the movements of non-indigenous personnel and their families and of indigenes traveling individually, there is a large movement by air of migratory labor, chiefly from the highlands and the Sepik and Morobe districts to the New Guinea Islands. Migratory labor movements generate more than 20,000 trips a year, of which over two-thirds are by air.

With cargo traffic, the most important flow is between the ports of Madang and Lae (chiefly Madang) and the highlands. This traffic is highly directional: traffic to the highlands exceeded highlands export traffic, mostly coffee, in the ratio of 3:1 in 1960/61 and 2.8:1 in 1962/63. The directional imbalance should decrease as coffee plantations come into full production. Charter transport predominates on these routes.

The average load over most routes is small. The total traffic volume originating in or destined to an area is often split among a large number of points, due mainly to the multiplicity of small airstrips, a heritage from the time when individual pockets of development were considerably more isolated than they are today. Concentration of traffic points, now made possible by the improvement of local road systems, might make economic the use of larger aircraft and so reduce air transport costs.

FREQUENCY OF COASTAL SHIPPING

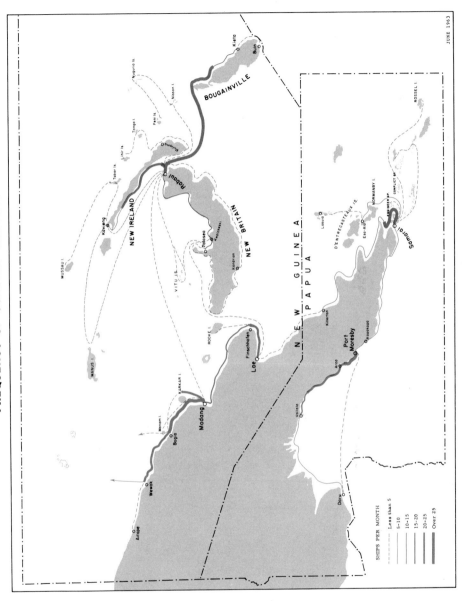

JUNE 1963

SHIPS PER MONTH

Less than 5
5-10
10-15
15-20
20-25
Over 25

AIR TRAFFIC FLOWS

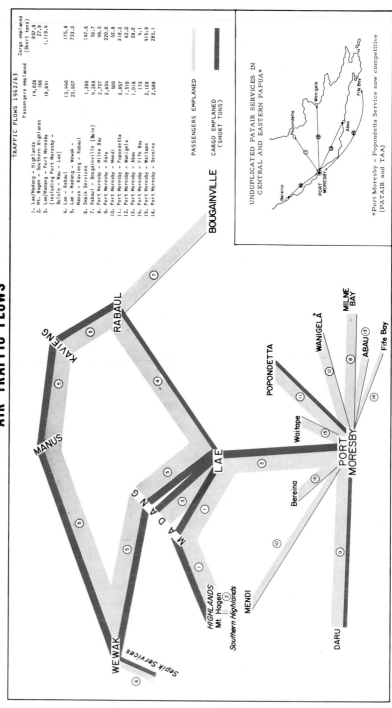

TRAFFIC FLOWS 1962/63	Passengers emplaned	Cargo emplaned (Short tons)
1. Lae/Madang - Highlands	14,026	857.9
2. Mt. Hagen - Southern Highlands	166	27.9
3. Lae/Madang - Port Moresby (including Port Moresby - Bulolo - Wau - Lae)	19,641	1,119.4
4. Lae - Rabaul	13,440	175.8
5. Lae - Madang - Wewak - Manus - Kavieng - Rabaul	23,907	733.3
6. Sepik Services	1,390	147.6
7. Rabaul - Bougainville (Buin)	4,288	53.7
8. Port Moresby - Milne Bay	2,737	48.5
9. Port Moresby - Daru	3,604	220.0
10. Port Moresby - Mendi	509	52.8
11. Port Moresby - Popondetta	3,857	318.3
12. Port Moresby - Wanigela	1,518	62.0
13. Port Moresby - Abau	1,018	28.0
14. Port Moresby - Fife Bay	173	4.1
15. Port Moresby - Waitape	2,128	415.8
16. Port Moresby - Bereina	2,689	285.1

PASSENGERS EMPLANED

CARGO EMPLANED (SHORT TONS)

UNDUPLICATED PATAIR SERVICES IN
CENTRAL AND EASTERN PAPUA*

*Port Moresby - Popondetta Service now competitive
(PATAIR and TAA)

SCHEDULED AIRLINE ROUTES

JUNE 1963

ROADS

JUNE 1963

Existing trunk roads
Road Program
Territorial boundaries
District boundaries

MILES
50 0 50 100 150 200

Pattern of Services and Government Regulation. Air transport in New Guinea is strictly regulated by the Commonwealth Government. These regulations are identical with Australian air transport regulations; they reflect the Australian air transport policy on the mainland and are administered by the Commonwealth Department of Civil Aviation (CDCA). This system has many advantages: the resources of an established department of world reputation can be applied; high safety standards of Australian civil aviation, consistent with the International Civil Aviation Organization (ICAO) agreements and recommendations, are maintained; and coordination is achieved between operational (technical) and economic regulations.

Airline policy in the Territory is the extension of the "two airline policy" adopted in Australia. Under this policy most routes are served by two airlines, TAA and Ansett-MAL Airlines, but Patair and TAA serve several low-traffic density routes in Papua. The routes operated by the scheduled airlines are shown on the map. Under this system the airlines are virtually assured equal (or almost equal) shares of the markets, and their scheduling, capacity and rate policies are strictly controlled. The regular airlines also operate charter flights on their routes, but other charter operators have been restricted.

It is often assumed that charter services play an important part during the developmental period only and that their substitution by regular schedule services is both natural and desirable. This theory is contradicted by the actual air transport development in a number of countries where aviation plays an important role. Charter and schedule services should not be considered as different stages of service development nor should schedule services be regarded as necessarily superior. In any transport situation, a special balance between scheduled, semi-regular and irregular bulk transport services exists. Although, as a rule, the development of scheduled services should be encouraged and some degree of protection for a scheduled operator is justified to achieve a useful standard of frequency, the optimum balance cannot be determined by a government agency alone and considerable leeway should be left to the reasonably free play of market forces and consumer preferences.

The three independent small aircraft charter operators are Stol Air Services (based at Port Moresby and serving Papua), Crowley Airways (based at Lae and serving Morobe and New Guinea Islands) and Territory Airlines (based at Goroka and serving the highlands). In addition, a number of missions operate their own light aircraft, and where authorized provide some commercial services. The airline companies themselves (TAA, Ansett-MAL and Patair) also engage in light aircraft operations, especially Ansett-MAL.

The Mission observed a shortage of small aircraft which is quite critical in some areas. The impression appears to exist that the CDCA would not approve the expansion of capacity and operations of the independent charter operators but the Mission was assured by the senior department officers that a reasonable request for fleet expansion would be favorably considered. The small aircraft operators are reluctant, however, to develop subsidiary bases as they fear they may be forced out of some areas in case of further extensions of protected routes of the airlines.

The Mission has carefully considered the organization of air transport regulating functions and the scope of the regulations. The question was raised whether the organization regulating air transport should be locally based. The Mission is aware of the very difficult problem of recruiting qualified personnel that would arise if the control of civil aviation were to be transferred to the Administration. Moreover, even if this were done the obligations imposed by international civil aviation conventions, together with their complexity, would make it necessary for the CDCA to preserve certain important responsibilities. The Mission believes, therefore, that there are good reasons for the CDCA, at least for the time being, to continue its economic and operational regulatory authority. The Mission endorses the plan to expand and grant an increasing degree of autonomy to the regional organization of the department which, the Mission understands, is being considered by the department. The economic regulatory functions should continue to be performed in close cooperation with the Administration.

The control of the independent operators of small aircraft may have been too restrictive. With its low initial cost and operational flexibility, the small aircraft has an important role under Territory conditions: it is often the only medium of communication with isolated posts; it is the only air transport medium which can assure any degree of service frequency at points of low traffic volume; it provides a useful supplement to scheduled services, especially where only indirect routings exist; and, it provides a rapid means of visiting a number of points for an administration officer or a businessman who cannot be tied to a fixed schedule.

While recognizing that scheduled services require a degree of protection, the Mission recommends that the position of the light aircraft operators should be reviewed; the independent carriers should be given more expansion opportunities; and the introduction of new aircraft and the establishment of subsidiary bases should be encouraged. Where the costs to the Administration of administrative services can be reduced by a locally based aircraft, such arrangements should be made with the Administration guaranteeing to the operator a minimum of revenue.

Consideration should also be given to the granting of supplementary airline licenses to independent carriers for the operation of low traffic density routes which could be economically performed by light aircraft in coordination with charter activities. In order to assure adequate safety and service standards as well as reasonable coordination with airline services, the possibility of associateship agreements between the airlines and independent operators should be explored.[4]

The Mission also recommends that, to achieve better coordination between the aviation authority, the airlines, the Administration and the air transport users in the Territory, an air transport officer should be appointed to the proposed Department of Transport described later in this chapter. His functions would be: to maintain liaison between the Administration and the CDCA on matters relating to airline regulations; to conduct economic studies on new airport development and maintain liaison with CDCA on matters relating to airport development; to advise the Administration on airline rate matters; and to work with the users and the airlines on rate revisions, etc.

Rate and Cost Structure. In view of the importance of air transport services to the economy of the Territory, the problem of airline rates assumes a special importance. The general level of rates and the rate structure is largely left to the airlines to determine, subject to over-all supervision of the CDCA. There is reason to question whether the rates reflect faithfully the costs of provision of service.

The influence of the limited competition over the level and structure of rates is very slight. As rate changes involve inter-airline consultations, the present system does not favor rate experimentations or promotional rates. An analysis of airline rates and costs is shown in Annex V. The general conclusion of the Mission is that the level of rates is rather high.

It must be remembered, however, that the burden of air cargo costs on the user is much lighter than in most other parts of the world where conditions are somewhat similar to those in the Territory, namely, isolation and poor development of surface transport facilities with air carriage the main transport medium. While costs per ton-mile are high, the distances flown are relatively short. The cost per ton to the transport user is, therefore, often quite moderate.

Airline costs are increased by a number of factors. Difficult operating conditions severely restrict the number of available flying hours and the regularity of service, especially on the important routes to the highlands

---

[4] Associate carrier arrangements have been successfully experimented with in a number of countries. These arrangements, always under the over-all supervision of government authorities, may cover coordination of maintenance, traffic-handling and scheduling, technical advice and supervision by technical departments of larger airlines, etc.

and across the New Guinea Islands; the costs of the non-indigenous personnel, employed not only as pilots and in key technical or managerial positions, but also at relatively low levels, e.g., tradesmen, traffic clerks, etc.,[5] are high; traffic-handling operations are marked by high costs and unsatisfactory quality; and the lack of supporting services, which force the airlines to provide, for example, employee housing, local transport, etc., makes for high overhead costs.

The standards of operation and maintenance are satisfactory. This is due to the aggressive promotion of airline services and strict enforcement of operating and safety regulations by the CDCA as well as to the efforts of the airlines themselves which have invested relatively large funds in the Territory. The quality of management is satisfactory.

Like any other group of regional carriers, the airlines face a re-equipment problem. The equipment now used (DC 3s and Bristol Freighters) has high and increasing operating costs and must be regarded as obsolete, but because of short-haul and daylight restriction, the airlines must necessarily employ aircraft with low standing costs (depreciation, finance charges, etc.). The solution appears to be the replacement of some of the cargo aircraft by larger secondhand planes, for example, DC 4s, with lower unit costs and low-standing costs. This solution presupposes traffic concentration at fewer airports which should be brought up to DC 4 standards.

All means of reducing airline costs, consistent with the preservation of satisfactory safety and operational standards, should be carefully examined. In addition to the introduction of larger aircraft to replace, on some routes at least, the present equipment, special attention should be given to the improvement of ground traffic-handling. In order to achieve these improvements the Mission recommends the following steps: smaller strips which, because of good road connections, are no longer justified, should be closed; air strips at points generating larger traffic volumes should be brought up to DC 4 standards (after the new Mt. Hagen airport and Goroka runway extensions are completed, cost/benefit studies may indicate that some other airport extensions are justified); and the duplication of traffic-handling establishments should be eliminated. With relatively small traffic volumes, the maintenance of two traffic-handling organizations, two storage facilities, two sets of vehicles and loading equipment, is a luxury for which the users of air transport services should not be required to pay. The lack of mechanical equipment not only results in slow turn-around of aircraft and excessive

[5] Considerable cost reduction could be achieved by employing indigenes to perform many of the functions. This will be increasingly possible with the rapid expansion and upgrading of education.

loading crews but also results in poor handling of cargo, high rates of damage, etc.

The Mission also recommends that the present route structure should be reviewed to achieve a greater rationalization of ground services and connecting flights. Route duplication at least on low-traffic-density routes should be eliminated. The training of indigenous airline and CDCA personnel should be intensified, and to achieve this goal the establishment of a joint airlines/CDCA training center should be considered.

Airports. Practically all the flying operations in the Territory are performed with wheel equipment. In spite of development along the coasts and the potential contribution of amphibious aircraft, this type of equipment is not used with the exception of a single Catalina (PBY). The relatively low costs of airstrip construction relieve the economic pressure for the use of amphibious aircraft. Consequently, the development of air transport depends, and is likely to continue to depend, on the provision of airstrips. An extensive network of airstrips has been developed (see Table 7).

In most areas, airfield facilities can be considered adequate for the existing needs. Where, however, a particular area depends entirely for its supplies on air transport and where only a "C" or "D" category strip exists, the construction of at least a "B" category strip may be justified by the resulting savings in costs and time of air shipments. In some areas—especially in the islands region—the lack of airstrips suitable

TABLE 7: Airports and Aerodromes in Papua and New Guinea (June 1963)

Aircraft Category[a]	Government			Total
	Department of Civil Aviation	Administration	Private	
Viscount, DC 6	3	—	—	3
A	15	26	5	46
B	—	33	9	42
C	—	19	8	27
D	—	16	122	138
Total	18	94	144	256

[a] Aerodromes are classified by the maximum size of aircraft they can accommodate, viz: "A Category" DC 3 or equivalent; "B" Norseman, Piaggio P166; "C" DHC 3, DHC 2 and equivalent; "D" Cessna 190, 180, 170 or equivalent.

SOURCE: Compiled from listing of aerodromes supplied by the Department of Civil Aviation, Commonwealth of Australia.

for light twin aircraft is a serious obstacle to the organization of a more efficient personnel and supplies network. The most obvious case is the Milne Bay District, where the district personnel have to rely on slow-moving water transport. Here efforts should be made to develop airstrips at key points.

Estimated Expenditures. The Administration will have to incur expenditures on the construction and upgrading of minor airports and airstrips. The costs of major extensions will be met by the CDCA.

In order to bring the more important minor airports up to DC 4 standards as quickly as possible, the Mission recommends that appropriations in the Administration's budget should be stepped up from £A150,000 in 1962/63 to a level of about £A200,000 a year until 1966/67. By then the major works should have been completed, and the Mission estimates that annual appropriations for new capital works over the remainder of the five-year period could be reduced to about £A100,000.

On the maintenance side, expenditures can be expected to rise steadily as more and larger airports are brought into commission. The Mission estimates that the provision for airport maintenance by the Administration should be increased gradually to £A150,000 in 1968/69 as compared with actual expenditures of just over £A80,000 in 1962/63.

Road Transport

Road Systems. For reasons of geography, the existing roads do not form a national road system but are a series of unconnected regional or local systems. Most of the roads have gradually evolved from bush tracks originally constructed by patrol officers with the help of local villagers. The original tracks were located to provide access to villages and were first used to establish administrative control and to bring medical help. None of these roads were engineered. Most had an ungraded earth surface passable only by four-wheel drive vehicles.

The total length of the road system in June 1963 was about 7,000 miles. A regional distribution of roads and a classification as to their suitability for heavy-and-medium and for light traffic is shown in Table 8. The mileage figures can be considered only approximations since they include track roads of which the exact length is unknown, and adjustments are constantly required to take into account improvements and new construction. Classification for heavy-and-medium, and light traffic must also be considered only a rough approximation. The geographical location of the road systems is shown on the map facing page 252.

The relative importance to the economy of the different road systems is indicated by the traffic movements over them. Although the mileage

TABLE 8: Mileages and Classification of the Road System, June 1963

| Districts | Total Mileage | By Type of Traffic | |
		Heavy-and-Medium Traffic	Light Traffic
Papua			
Southern Highlands	308	5	303
Western	50	5	45
Gulf	123	41	82
Central	814	344	470
Milne Bay	213	174	39
Northern	302	199	103
Total	1,810	768	1,042
New Guinea			
Eastern Highlands	1,027	819	208
Western Highlands	650	350	300
Sepik	834	354	480
Madang	326	293	33
Morobe	823	717	106
New Britain	498	336	162
New Ireland	452	221	231
Bougainville	626	414	212
Manus	45	45	—
Total	5,281	3,549	1,732
Total Papua and New Guinea	7,091	4,317	2,774

SOURCE: Transport and Communications Bulletin, Bureau of Statistics, and replies to Mission questionnaires to district commissioners.

of roads in New Britain accounts for only 7 percent of the total mileage in the Territory, the network in the highly productive Gazelle Peninsula is the most important economically. The roads in the Gazelle Peninsula have been a major factor in its development. Statistics of total road traffic are not available, but approximate figures are available for export traffic moving by road. The tonnages of export traffic moving over the Gazelle Peninsula roads to Rabaul were of the order of 60,000 tons in 1962/63, compared with 18,000 tons moving to Lae (almost all from Wau/Bulolo), 8,000 tons to Kavieng along the east-coast road in New Ireland, 6,000 tons along the north-coast road to Madang and 3,000 to Port Moresby, principally from Sogeri.

Taking into account import and local traffic movements, total goods traffic on these road networks was considerably greater. This is particularly true in the area of Port Moresby, the seat of government and the largest town. Nevertheless, the export figures provide a good indication of the relative importance of the different road systems. They also show clearly the still minor role of roads in other districts, particularly the highlands districts of the mainland. The small quantities of highlands export traffic (5,000 tons in 1962/63) move to coastal ports by air, and the roads of economic importance there are the feeder roads connecting coffee-growing areas with airstrips.

The other principal road networks are: the Kokoda-Popondetta-Oro Bay/Killerton road in the Northern District of Papua; the roads leading out of Wewak and Maprik in the Sepik District; the Buka Island and Kieta coastal roads in the Bougainville District and roads in the north-eastern corner of Manus Island.

These roads carry little traffic and with the exception of the first are of small economic importance. They have been developed primarily for administrative purposes. Traffic over the Northern District roads, though light at present, will increase substantially as the new cocoa plantations between Popondetta and the Kumusi River come into production.

Present Road Conditions. Given the present traffic volumes, the condition of the roads of major economic importance is generally satis-factory for freight movements and automobile travel. In the Gazelle Peninsula, the roads are, with few exceptions, all-weather roads. The most prevalent road construction material is pumice. This is an extremely light non-plastic material; it does not normally become boggy but main-tenance difficulties arise because, with the high rainfall, the light-weight pumice floats away, leaving large scars on the roads. Satisfactory road metal to stabilize the pumice surface has proved difficult to find, but possible deposits are being investigated.

The Lae-Bulolo-Wau road has been reconstructed to all-weather standards, all rivers are bridged and the condition of the road is good. Maintenance costs, however, are rather high by Territory standards. In the Madang District, the north-coast road to Dylup plantation and the Bogia Sub-district road are surfaced with coronus, a product of decom-posed coral, which has proved an ideal road material where traffic is light. Construction and maintenance costs are low. In New Ireland, the east-coast road between Kavieng and Namatanai is also being surfaced with coronus; its condition is good and maintenance costs are low. In and around Port Moresby the roads are generally satisfactory; the most im-portant, the road to Sogeri, has been constructed to adequate standards and is generally well maintained.

In other areas and particularly on the roads through high mountain passes, the condition of the roads is fair to poor. In the highlands the construction and maintenance of valley roads has been relatively easy and inexpensive. The roads through the passes, however, have been built in areas of geologically unstable terrain and high rainfall. The builders were forced to construct to low standards to avoid high construction costs. Frequent landslides and washouts result in high maintenance costs, and low population densities in the immediate vicinity of the passes restrict the possibility of using local effort on maintenance work. Thus, the Mt. Hagen-Goroka-Lae road on the sections through the passes is traversable only by four-wheel drive or heavy vehicles. The latter frequently get bogged, sometimes for days at a time.

Road Programs. The major road programs being undertaken by the Administration are: the reconstruction to all-weather standards of the road from Popondetta to Oro Bay; the construction of a road from Wewak to Maprik to connect a large concentration of population with the port and district administrative headquarters; the reconstruction and extension of the Gogol Valley road from Madang to an area of forest potential; the construction of the west-coast road in New Ireland, where economic development has been hampered because of the lack of good anchorages for coastal shipping; construction of the Watarais-Gusap-Dumpu road along the upper Ramu river valley to serve projected cattle developments in the upper Ramu and connecting with the Lae-Goroka road at Watarais; and the reconstruction of the Lae-Goroka road. The last is by far the largest road project at present under way.

After the penetration of the highlands by explorers and officers of the Administration traveling on foot, the first commercial links with coastal ports were provided by air transport. The first roads in the highlands were tracks connecting villages and plantations with airstrips. Over the years, the disconnected local roads were joined to form valley road systems. During the 1950s, the Administration decided to connect the highlands by road with Lae. Although a road from the highlands to Madang would have connected with a better harbor, the selection of the Lae route appears to have been justified on the grounds that the road passes through the Markham River valley, a potentially rich agricultural and cattle area, and construction appeared to be less difficult. The section from Lae to the Umi River (87 miles) is nearly completed, and the section from the Umi River to Watarais at the foot of the Kassim Pass (13 miles) is under construction. The remaining sections—Watarais to Kainantu (23 miles) and Kainantu to Goroka (56 miles)—are scheduled for completion by 1966/67.

With the possible exception of the road from Wewak to Maprik, being built by the military, the Mission believes that the road projects now under way in lowland areas are justified from the viewpoint of the prospective increases in production and traffic. They should be implemented as scheduled. In addition to these projects, other road construction and improvements in lowland areas will be required to enable the agricultural and forestry programs recommended by the Mission to be implemented. A considerable part of the projected increase in output of copra, cocoa and rubber is expected to come from existing plantations. This will require the improvement and extension of existing road networks, for example, in northern New Britain, New Ireland and the Northern District of Papua. In addition, new agricultural areas will have to be opened up and new roads built. In particular, new feeder roads to connect producing areas with coastal anchorages will be required.

For the livestock program, the Watarais-Gusap-Dumpu road is of high priority as is the reconstruction of the Watarais-Goroka road. Further, road improvements in the upper Wahgi and Baiyer river valleys in the highlands will be needed as well as an extension to the upper Jimmi River valley to connect with slaughter facilities at Mt. Hagen. Other road improvements in the Highlands will be required for the tea and pyrethrum programs: some existing feeder roads will have to be upgraded and new ones built.

Whether the output of coffee, tea and pyrethrum would move by road to Lae for export, assuming the completion of the Lae-Goroka road, is uncertain. From its study of air transport costs in the Territory and having regard to the quantities of traffic involved, the Mission believes that air transport will probably continue to be the most economical means of moving much of the traffic, particularly if air transport economies are gained as the result of introducing DC 4 aircrafts, as recommended elsewhere in this chapter.

The small traffic flows in prospect from the highlands throw doubt on the economic justification for the very heavy expenditures on the reconstruction of the Watarais-Goroka road scheduled for the next three years (about £A3 million). This will not materially change even after the existing coffee plantations come into full production and the tea, pyrethrum and cattle programs recommended by the Mission are implemented. However, the highlands are heavily populated containing approximately 40 percent of the total population of the Territory. The absence of an adequate road link with the coast has kept the area in a state of isolation, and has undoubtedly increased the costs of administration and slowed economic growth. While air transport has brought pocket development to the highlands, it cannot in the long run fully develop the area, and there is no doubt that sooner or later a good road or roads from the highlands to the coast must be provided. The question, therefore, is one of timing.

On balance, there appears to be a reasonable case for going ahead with the road as scheduled. By the time it is completed, the agricultural and cattle programs recommended for the highlands should be well established, and there will be an increasing flow of traffic to the coast from Goroka and points east. As the highlands' economy and the services of the Administration there expand, the flow of traffic to the highlands will grow even more rapidly. The road could also become an important tourist route, and particularly so if the resumption of international air services to Manila is found to be economically justified. For these reasons the Mission supports the timing proposed for the reconstruction of the Watarais-Goroka road.

A road connection exists between Goroka and Mt. Hagen through the Wahgi Valley. The sections of this road over the passes are inadequate for the movement of freight traffic. Even after the reconstruction of the Lae-Goroka road is completed, the extension to Mt. Hagen would not serve as a satisfactory link between the Western Highlands and the coast unless the Goroka-Mt. Hagen road were completely reconstructed at heavy cost. Even if this were done, the relative distances from Mt. Hagen by road to Lae and by air to Madang would probably make a change from air to road transport uneconomic for the small volumes of traffic involved. Thus, major reconstruction does not appear justified within the next five years. Nevertheless, there are good reasons for continuing the present maintenance work and for making improvements in this road, as it provides a valuable administrative link and connects important local road systems.

At a later stage, a road link between the Western Highlands and Madang may become essential. This road will, however, be very costly and given the prospective traffic flows its construction does not appear to be economically justified within the next five years. This does not preclude further work on the project. Alternative routings should be surveyed and a feasibility study should be started at an early date covering technical and economic aspects. The possibility of incorporating the Mt. Hagen-Jimmi River valley road, required for the cattle program, into the Mt. Hagen-Madang road should be considered, as well as a connection with the planned Ramu River valley road.

A special problem exists in isolated parts of the interior, notably in the western part of the Western Highlands District and in the Southern Highlands. In these areas there has been little development beyond the establishment of law and order. Geographical factors make the linking by road of these areas with the more developed parts of the highlands prohibitively expensive. Numerous small runways have been built and air services can carry the essential supplies needed by the Administration in maintaining law and order, and in bringing medical help and education to the isolated tribes. Effort in these areas should, therefore, be concentrated on the construction of feeder roads connecting villages with existing airstrips.

Road Standards. Standards of road construction vary considerably among regions according to the grade of road, the availability of road-building materials, and to the choice of standards by regional and district engineers. Most of the non-urban roads are one-lane roads. Where graveled, the surface width varies from 12 to 18 feet with two shoulders of four to six feet.

Discussions on the adoption of uniform design standards have been going on for some time, and at present the following specifications are being proposed:

a. *Primary or Trunk Roads*
   Design speed: not less than 25 miles per hour and not greater than 50 miles per hour, depending upon topographic conditions.
   Width of road bed: 20 feet.
   Width of pavement: 12 feet (single lane).
   Type of pavement: untreated gravel, constructed to a standard satisfactory for commercial vehicles up to Australian load limits.
   Bridges: single lane; H 20-S 16 loading.

b. *Secondary or Feeder Roads*
   Same standards apply as for trunk roads except that feeder roads will essentially be graded earth roads, graveled only where needed and with width reduced where required due to topographic conditions.

These standards are satisfactory except for bridge design, where H 15-S 12 loading would be more in line with future traffic. Rights-of-way of 120 feet should be reserved for future widening.

The Mission recommends the adoption of design standards for use throughout the Territory. It recommends also that road-planning should be based on the principle of stage construction, i.e., roads should be planned to permit gradual upgrading as traffic grows without abandonment of the original road. Techniques should be adopted to enable widening of single- to two-lane roads at some future date. For example, bridges and drainage structures should be designed to allow subsequent widening of the road at minimum additional cost. It is important in planning new roads that adequate rights-of-way for future widenings and for transmission and communication lines should be reserved.

Because of the numerous rivers and streams, bridge-building is one of the important problems of highway construction. Although some permanent bridges have been built, the majority of the existing bridges are of temporary timber construction, which have to be periodically replaced at increasing cost. Prolonged rains or landslides often result in the collapse of bridges and the blockage of traffic. The only satisfactory solution to the problem appears to be the development of a simple permanent but inexpensive bridge which could be easily erected from prefabricated parts. Both the Commonwealth Department of Works (CDW) and the Territory Department of Public Works (PWD) are engaged in the development of a suitable design. Obviously, these efforts should be coordinated.

The standards of road maintenance also vary considerably. Roads which are the responsibility of CDW are well maintained. The conditions under which PWD operates are not conducive to the maintenance of uniform standards, which vary from one district to another, depending on the availability of maintenance equipment, allocation of maintenance funds and the quality of local supervision as well as on the interest and assistance given by the district administration. Consequently, the standards vary from good to poor.

In general, the traffic volume is so small that damage due to vehicular traffic is negligible; however, even at present a heavily loaded conventional-drive truck operating with chains after a heavy rain can do considerable damage to the road. With the further growth of traffic, increased use of roads with a subsequent increase in road damage may be expected. Having regard to expected traffic flows and the greater costs of building roads to higher standards, the Mission recommends that vehicle-load and axle-weight regulations be strongly enforced and, if necessary, the present regulations strengthened. Consideration should be given to the introduction of a system of seasonal load-limit reductions to prevent road damage during the periods of heavy rains.

Execution of Road Projects—Government Organization. The responsibility for construction and maintenance of roads is divided between CDW and PWD. The existence of the two public works organizations dates from the post World War II period when, with the large volume of urgent reconstruction work to be done and a shortage of professional staff in PWD, CDW was invited to come to the Territory and take over certain public works.

With its large resources the Commonwealth Department, the largest organization of this type in Australia, was able to move in with a minimum of delay and establish a sizable organization in the Territory. It can draw on the resources of the Australian organization; it can offer professional personnel career opportunities in the Territory and in Australia; it operates a cadetship system, and because of its size and professional reputation it is considered a good place for an engineer to work.

PWD has encountered difficulty in staffing technical positions due to the hesitancy of qualified engineers to make a career of public service in the Territory. There is a shortage of engineers in Australia and those interested in government service are more attracted by organizations such as CDW. As a result, the number of professional engineers employed by PWD is inadequate.

The division of work between PWD and CDW is not well defined and is decided project by project. In general, CDW is responsible for the construction and maintenance of major works, but the criteria for dividing the work sometimes appear to be based on PWD's more intimate knowledge of local conditions due to its close cooperation with local administration officials and in the case of CDW on its larger and more experienced professional staff. The division of work is sometimes awkward and has led in some instances to unnecessary and costly duplication of manpower and equipment. For instance, the road from Port Moresby to Sogeri is maintained by CDW but the extension of this road is maintained by PWD; the road from Lae through the Markham Valley is maintained by CDW, while a temporary road across the Umi River in the Markham Valley is maintained by PWD; on New Ireland the road on the east coast is being constructed and maintained by CDW while the road on the west coast and the extension of the east-coast road are being constructed by PWD.

Government policy requires both departments to execute the greater part of their programs by contract. The lack of long-range planning has made it difficult up to the present to execute road works efficiently and economically. Contracts are quite small and it has been impossible to interest competent construction firms from Australia to present bids. The announcements of these small projects have attracted only a few local contractors. Proposals have not always shown competitive pricing and CDW has in several cases had to execute projects with its own labor force, much against its preference. As a result, CDW has been forced to enlarge its construction organization, and at present has more highway construction equipment in the Territory than any of the local contractors.

The Mission recommends that responsibility for public works in the Territory should be organized to end the duplication and inefficiency resulting from the present organizational structure. While, it might be desirable at some future date to organize an independent highway department, the Mission believes that the road program envisioned for the next several years does not justify a separate department and recommends that the road program should be carried out by a Road Division organized within the PWD. This road division should be made up of design, construction and maintenance sections. Its staff should be held to a minimum by following the current policies of the Administration that large works should be designed by consulting engineers and constructed by contractors, and that day-labor forces should be used only where contractors are not available or where the work can be carried out by the Administration at significantly lower cost; all maintenance, on the other hand, should be carried out by the Road Division.

Based on the record in recruiting professional staff, the Mission agrees with the Administration that it will be difficult for PWD to staff a road division within a reasonable period of time. The Mission, therefore, recommends that the Administration ask the CDW to assume responsibility to staff the road division. The chief of the road division should be a CDW senior engineer of high professional standing with executive experience. CDW should assign professional employees as required to effectively staff the road division. The terms of assignment should be such as to attract and interest the professionals in CDW in an assignment for a period of years in the Territory. The length of assignment of the CDW professional staff in the Territory should be of sufficient duration for them to become acquainted with the problems and work, and to make a satisfactory contribution.

The Mission believes that the long-term objective should be to establish a road division which can stand on its own feet. This implies that CDW would provide professional staff until permanent career officers, either native or non-indigene, can be obtained. The chief of the road division, therefore, should, from the start, be made responsible for organizing a permanent staff of adequate quality. The PWD professional personnel now working on road projects in the Territory should be absorbed into the road division either by being employed by CDW or directly by the road division. As the permanent staff grows, the need for professional personnel, from CDW would be less until eventually the road division could operate without CDW personnel.

For non-professional staff, the objective should be to employ and train a permanent staff and only in exceptional cases should be it necessary for CDW to assign non-professional staff to work in the road division.

As yet there are no native professionals trained as engineers. As the education program grows and expands, provision will be made for the training of professional people. However, such a program will take many years. To accelerate the training of native professionals, the Mission believes that the road division should select indigenes who can be sent overseas for professional training with the understanding that they will be employed by the road division. It should be recognized, of course, that due to the level of education and experience of the indigene, it will take years before any reasonable number can be added to the professional staff. Indeed, it will take some years to recruit and train indigenes to take a larger part in the non-professional work of the road division. Only by positive effort will the indigene be infused into the work of the road division at a satisfactory rate.

The Australian Army Engineers are constructing the road between Wewak and Maprik and they were scheduled to take over the design and supervision of construction of roads in the Northern District of Papua late in 1963. The Army Engineers and the new road division should, of course, coordinate their activities.

Cost of the Road Program. With the difficulties of terrain, high labor costs, the very limited resources of local contractors and its relatively high standards of construction, the costs of roads are high. The CDW estimate for the single-lane Watarais-Kassim Pass road shows an average cost per mile of £A110,000 in very mountainous terrain, £A29,700 in mountainous terrain and £A17,900 in rolling terrain. These costs include drainage structures but do not include bridges.

The construction costs shown by PWD for various smaller works are considerably lower. PWD has constructed single-lane earth roads, graveled where necessary, at a maximum cost of £A10,000 per mile in mountainous terrain and at £A2,000 to £A3,000 per mile in flat terrain. It is very probable, however, that these average costs have been based on field costs of works where a large amount of free or cheap labor was obtained with the help of patrol and district officers. For estimating future costs, these averages should not be used since free labor is rapidly becoming a thing of the past in many parts of the Territory. The Mission believes that a realistic estimate of the cost of construction of single-lane graveled roads would average about £A6,000 per mile in flat terrain and £A18,000 per mile in rolling terrain, if gravel is available within reasonable hauling distance. The minimum cost in mountainous terrain would be about £A30,000 per mile, if earth work is balanced. These costs include cost of drainage structures but not the cost of forest clearing and bridges. A safe average cost for heavy forest clearing would be about £A1,000 per mile and for single-lane bridges about £A150 to £A200 per foot.

For maintenance costs, there are again considerable differences in the figures of the two departments, but again PWD costs should be used with caution since they may include much free labor in outlying districts. The PWD annual average is £A200 per mile. CDW annual maintenance costs fluctuate widely from £A250 per mile on the east-coast road on New Ireland to £A1,000 per mile on the road between Lae and Wau.

True maintenance costs are difficult to estimate since, in many cases, maintenance and betterment activities are undertaken simultaneously and the same locally based equipment, construction plant and personnel are used for new construction, betterment and maintenance. Nevertheless, the following limits are considered reasonable for estimating annual maintenance expenditures per mile: £A600 to £A1,000 for main roads, £A200 to £A300 for secondary roads and £A50 to £A100 for graded tracks.

The estimates of total costs of the road program over the next five years are provisional. The Mission has included in its recommended program provision for major projects plus a very approximate figure for other projects, chiefly feeder roads. The major projects include those recommended in the earlier section on road programs, plus provision for improvement and extension of the Port Moresby area and Gazelle Peninsula networks. Until work schedules are further advanced a precise allocation of total expenditures over each year of the program cannot be made, but new construction expenditures are anticipated to be largest during the first three years of the period, mainly on account of construction of the Watarais-Goroka road. An approximate allocation is shown in Table 9. The Mission has estimated that annual maintenance appropriations should be increased to about £A1.6 million.

As already noted, most local roads were constructed with a considerable local contribution of free labor by the native population. However, local interest throughout the Territory is not always the same, and a more uniform system of sharing the costs of local road construction is desirable. The Mission recommends that unless the construction of a particular road is urgently needed for administrative purposes, feeder roads should be constructed under a cost-sharing system. At least 50 percent of the costs of feeder-road construction should be borne by local communities and the balance by the Administration. Imputed cost of free labor should be taken into consideration. Rights-of-way should be

TABLE 9: Road Expenditures, 1963/64–1968/69

(£A thousand)

	1963/64[a]	1964/65	1965/66	1966/67	1967/68	1968/69	Total 1964/65– 1968/69
New Construction[b]	765[c]	2,300	2,000	1,900	1,500	1,300	9,000
Maintenance	1,233	1,600	1,600	1,600	1,600	1,600	8,000
Total	1,998	3,900	3,600	3,500	3,100	2,900	17,000

[a] Budget estimates.
[b] Including engineering and feasibility studies.
[c] Including special project Sepik District.

contributed by the local communities and the land vested in the Crown. The Administration should provide technical assistance in road location and construction. Administration funds should be allocated among districts taking into account population, percentage of the population accessible by existing roads, interest of local groups, availability of air-strips and coastal shipping, and planned administrative expenditure.

In view of the underdeveloped state of the road system, the problem of adequate user charges has not been a pressing one. Import duties on gasoline during most recent years were about 5 percent of total import duties and amounted to between £A125,000 and £A150,000 per year, a negligible amount when compared with funds required in the future for new road construction and adequate road maintenance. A re-assessment of the general approach to user charges is required because of the rela-tively high costs of new trunk road projects, and the increase in road maintenance cost. In addition, the development of some regional road systems has reached a level where new investments are required, not on grounds of general economic development, but on grounds of user benefits.

A system of regional user charges can be accomplished through special license fees imposed on the users of public roads in a particular area. In view of the geographic separation of regional road systems, such a scheme should be quite practicable and would be equivalent to a toll road system.

The Mission recommends that a regional system of user charges, possibly in the form of regional surcharges on vehicle license fees, be imposed for the purpose of financing a share of road improvements and maintenance costs, where the existing regional system is quite well developed. This system could be introduced, for instance, in the Gazelle Peninsula of New Britain to help meet the cost of surfacing the main roads. After the Lae-Goroka road is completed and traffic volume builds up, a similar system of user charges should be considered for vehicles using this road, and also the Lae-Wau road, to help meet the high maintenance costs.

Road Transportation. At the end of 1962, there were just over 10,220 vehicles, of which about 50 percent were automobiles, 44 percent commercial vehicles and 6 percent motorcycles. Since 1959, the total number of vehicles has increased on the average by 8.5 percent a year. Registrations are shown in Table 10.

The trucking industry is still little developed. The largest trucking firm with 40 vehicles is in New Britain. Its main business is transportation of copra products. There are three other companies operating over 20 trucks (one each in New Britain, Lae and Port Moresby). A major proportion of freight is moved by private vehicles or vehicles owned by local cooperatives. Most of the truck operators rely for the bulk of their

TABLE 10: Registrations of New Motor Vehicles, 1956–1962 [a]

	Calendar Years						
	1956	1957	1958	1959	1960	1961	1962
Automobiles	525	473	422	548	588	580	684
Commercial Vehicles	624	364	490	617	751	660	832
Motorcycles	183	89	111	104	132	95	95
Total	1,332	926	1,023	1,269	1,471	1,335	1,611

[a] Includes Commonwealth-owned vehicles, other than Defense Service vehicles.
SOURCE: Territory of Papua and New Guinea, Quarterly Summaries of Statistics.

business on renting trucks for construction work, or on government contracts.

Truck operating costs (to truckers) are high and vary greatly, depending upon region and class of road. Under the most favorable conditions, they average 11d per ton-mile, but in some areas are as high as 5/6d per ton-mile with the average costs in the interior ranging between 1/6d and 2/-d per ton-mile. These high costs are due to poor roads, inadequate supply of spare parts and high wages of good mechanics. With the development of the road system and growth of road haulage, average costs should decrease, probably to a range of 11d-1/5d per ton-mile. However, high labor costs are likely to persist until an adequate supply of trained indigenous mechanics is available. These operating costs are reflected in high rates, although where the trucks are used for passenger transport of indigenes and goods transport, the rate per ton-mile may be lower than the fully allocated costs of truck operations.

The improvement of roads should, by lowering truck operating costs, result in considerable growth of the trucking industry and lower costs to shippers. The carriers will, of course, have to expand their operations and acquire larger equipment. In the case of most operators, such an expansion will be dependent on the availability of credit.

A breakdown of freight-carrying vehicles by areas and by vehicle weight is given in Table 11.

In view of the potential importance of the road transport industry, the Administration should maintain close liaison with road transport operators and help in the dissemination of technical and managerial information among road haulers.

Transport Planning and Administration

During the last five years, transport expenditures (capital and current) of the Administration and the Commonwealth Government varied between 13 to 16 percent of total public expenditures. Of the expenditures

TABLE 11:   Freight-Carrying Vehicles, by Area and Vehicle Weight [a]
(mid-1963)

Area and Districts	Utilities, Panel Vans, Land Rovers, etc. (capacity under 30 cwt.)	Trucks (capacity 2–3 tons)	Trucks (capacity 4 tons & over)	Semi-trailers	Trailers
Port Moresby (Central)	546	84	78	23	87
Bulolo (Morobe)	33	8	23	—	—
Wau (Morobe)	67	16	14	—	—
Lae (Morobe)	388	39	161	—	95
Rabaul (New Britain)	991	208	191	6	51
Wewak (Sepik)	99	31	28 [b]	n.a.	—
Madang (Madang)	178	82	43	—	—
Mt. Hagen (W. Highlands)	9	7	10	—	—
Goroka (E. Highlands)	361	45	21	—	—
Kainantu (S. Highlands)	38	6	14 [b]	n.a.	—

[a] The areas included cover most of the truck population, although information on certain areas was not available.
[b] Including semi-trailers.
SOURCE: Royal Papua and New Guinea Constabulary.

of the Administration only, about 8 percent was spent for transport in 1962/63.

At present there is no department within the Administration which has the responsibility to coordinate, plan or think about the transport problems of the Territory as a whole. Responsibility is divided between several departments and offices of the Administration and the Commonwealth Government. An interdepartmental committee of the Administration was appointed to prepare an over-all transport plan or "Transportation Task," but no provision was made for a staff. Members of the committee have other responsibilities and have not been able to devote adequate time to transport problems. The planning and programing of actual expenditures on transport projects is coordinated, to some degree, during the budget determination stage.

The present organizational structure does not provide efficient long-range transport planning and administration. At this stage of the Territory's development, it is important that the problems in respect to road and air transport, ports and coastal/overseas shipping be considered as a whole. To varying degrees all are inter-related. To make sure that transport facilities meet the requirements of the Territory with the minimum of expenditure, the Mission recommends that a separate Department of Transport be established with the following functions: the preparation and revision of investment plans and programs to meet the transport requirements of shippers, consumers and government departments; administration of legislation relating to transport industries which are subject to the authority of the Administration; liaison with the Commonwealth of Australia's departments concerned with transport functions; provision of advisory services to other departments of the Administration whose planning involves transport; and provision of advisory services to transport users and to the carriers.

The functions of the proposed department would be similar to those of transport departments now existing in some countries. The departmental activities would be restricted to regulatory, economic planning and economic or business advisory functions; it would not be involved in operations, technical or engineering planning, or design.

The activities of the Marine Branch of the Department of Trade and Industry should be transferred to the new Department of Transport as should the planning functions of the existing inter-departmental committee on transport. The Administration fleet should become the responsibility of the Treasury Department which is the services department in the field of transport.

The Department of Transport should have three divisions with responsibilities as follows:

Marine: Supervision of safety regulations; economic regulation of coastal shipping; planning of coastal shipping wharves; re-equipment planning; and liaison with the Harbors Board and the Commonwealth Department of Shipping. The existing sea training school would come under this division.

Road Planning and Transport: The economic planning of road construction programs in cooperation with the Road Division of the Department of Public Works (the road division would be responsible for the technical or engineering planning and programing); liaison with road users and technical information dissemination; regulations relating to vehicle operating standards, load limits, etc. (this function should be performed in cooperation with the Departments of Public Works, Law and Police); preparation of user taxation proposals; and, advisory and liaison services with other departments of the Administration.

Economic Coordination: Liaison with Commonwealth Government and Administration departments including the Department of Civil Aviation; transport planning in general; administration of cost-sharing assistance funds; and, rate negotiations and liaison between the carriers and transport users (the overseas shipping rates officer would be in this branch). In view of the importance of the coordination aspect in airport construction, the air transport officer should also be a member of this branch. Economic planning by this department would be subject to the over-all coordination and supervision of the Central Policy and Planning Committee (see Chapter 2).

The proposed organization should not be large. The average size of a division should be three to four professional officers. Some of the functions of the new department would replace functions now performed on a full- or part-time basis by officers in other departments of the Administration and some of these officers should be transferred to the new department.

Summary of Proposed Expenditures

The expenditures on different elements of the transport program have been detailed in earlier sections of this chapter. A summary of recommended current and capital expenditures over the next five years is shown here, together with budgeted expenditures for 1963/64.

	1963/64	1964/65–1968/69	
	Budget	Total	Annual Average (£A thousand)
Current Expenditures			
Roads and Bridges	1,233	8,000	1,600
Aerodromes	85	625	125
Wharves and Beacons	46	260	52
Department of Transport	—	200	40
Total	1,364	9,085	1,817
Capital Expenditures			
Roads and Bridges	765	9,000	1,800
Aerodromes	70	800	160
Coastal Shipping	—	700	140
Harbors	192	2,250	450
Total	1,027	12,750	2,550

COMMUNICATIONS

The operation of the communication services suffers from the same basic problems as the transport systems—low volume of traffic, the requirement to serve widely scattered small centers and difficulties of terrain. By its very nature, communication facilities serve the demands of the Administration and of the small market sector, predominantly non-indigenous. Approximately 40 percent of all trunk calls are made over telephones in Administration and Commonwealth government offices. A few native cooperative societies have advanced to a stage where a telephone is necessary. At mid-1963 there were only two telephones rented by indigenes.

Organization

The Department of Posts and Telegraphs operates the internal public communication system geared to meeting the most pressing requirements. In addition, the Overseas Telecommunications Commission, the Department of Civil Aviation and the Postmaster General's Department of the Commonwealth Government perform certain functions in the field of communications in the Territory. The Australian Broadcasting Commission (ABC) and the Department of Information and Extension Services both have limited radio broadcasting systems also in the Territory (see Chapter 6). The relationship and functions of these agencies are illustrated in the chart on page 276.

The Department of Posts and Telegraphs is efficiently and competently run. The professional and executive staff of the department were for the most part trained and acquired their experience working for the Postmaster General's Department, which continues to provide technical and organizational advice. The training school run by the department to supply its needs for indigenous clerical and operating personnel has been quite successful.

Telephone Services

In 1963, there were 16 urban areas with local telephone exchanges[6] operated by the Department of Posts and Telegraphs and a private telephone exchange for 120 telephones in Bulolo. Good progress has been

[6] Port Moresby had four inter-connected telephone exchanges serving the urban area; thus the total number of Post Office exchanges in 1963 was 19 serving 16 urban areas. A small exchange at Toleap was temporarily withdrawn from service during the 1962/63 fiscal year and its subscribers connected through Rabaul. A new automatic exchange at Toleap is to be established during the fiscal year 1963/64.

DISTRIBUTION OF RESPONSIBILITIES FOR TELECOMMUNICATIONS SERVICES
IN THE TERRITORY OF PAPUA AND NEW GUINEA

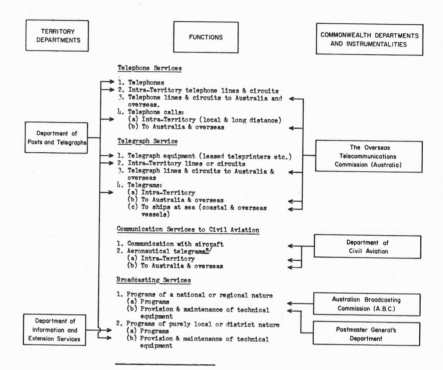

a/ By agreement, the Department of Civil Aviation handles "B" Class aeronautical telegrams (i.e., telegrams dealing with passenger bookings, freight, etc.) over the Aeronautical Fixed Telecommunications Network (A.F.T.N.). This service is used by Ansett and TAA only.

Notes: Lines and arrows indicate Department or Instrumentality performing the given function.
"Intra-Territory" - within the Territory of Papua and New Guinea.

made with mechanization as 80 percent of the local services are automatic. The growth of the telephone services during the last six years is summarized in Table 12.

TABLE 12: Telephone Services

Year Ending June 30	Number of Exchanges	Lines Connected	Instruments Connected	Number of Subscribers
1958	17	3,041	4,612	3,032
1959	18	3,350	5,133	3,336
1960	20	3,509	5,503	3,470
1961	20	3,664	6,172	3,721
1962	20	4,187	7,054	4,123
1963	19	4,635	7,994	4,599

SOURCE: Department of Posts and Telegraphs, Territory of Papua and New Guinea.

The trunk system is maintained by VHF and HF single channels with the exception of Port Moresby-Lae (VHF three-channel). In most cases, the connections are open during specified times of the day; e.g., the Madang-Mt. Hagen line is open between 9:30 a.m. and 9:45 a.m. (Monday to Saturday) and between 2:45 p.m. and 3:00 p.m. (Monday to Friday). Only few services (e.g., Port Moresby to Lae and Rabaul) operate on a 24-hour basis. The quality of service on HF channels is uneven. The growth in traffic is shown in Table 13.

TABLE 13: Trunk-Line Traffic (number of long-distance telephone calls)

Years	Outstations-Zone Center			Overseas			
	Originat- ing at Out- stations	Termi- nating at Out- stations	Total	Intra- Territory[a] Originat- ing Calls	Originat- ing in the Territory	Terminat- ing in the Territory	Total
1957/58	7,090	4,964	12,054	67,632	5,577	2,615	8,192
1958/59	11,605	6,970	18,575	86,819	7,444	3,691	11,125
1959/60	16,691	12,256	28,947	80,270	8,542	4,727	13,269
1960/61	24,704	13,731	38,435	61,575	10,588	7,574	18,162
1961/62	35,646	15,345	50,991	68,014	12,570	6,694	19,264
1962/63	40,695	18,370	59,065	78,541	13,126	7,548	20,674

[a] Inter-zone traffic.

SOURCE: Department of Posts and Telegraphs, Territory of Papua and New Guinea.

Telegraph Services

Most of the telegraph messages between the centers are handled by manual telegraphy using single-channel HF connections. Machine telegraphy is used between Port Moresby-Lae and Lae-Wau (VHF channels); in the Port Moresby area landlines are used; telegraphs between Lae and Bulolo are telephoned. The development of services is shown in Table 14.

TABLE 14: Development of Telegraph Services

Years	Number of Stations	Number of Messages Handled
1957/58	250	690,221
1958/59	281	842,854
1959/60	303	956,842
1960/61	366	1,133,953
1961/62	403	1,094,085
1962/63	513	1,172,143

SOURCE: Department of Posts and Telegraphs, Territory of Papua and New Guinea.

The factor which will determine any substantial future growth of demand for telecommunications will be the emergence of indigenous enterprise and the indigenous people into a modern economy. Then the demand for telecommunication services will no longer be restricted to a small proportion of the population. However, even under the most optimistic assumptions it is not probable that any significant demand for telephone services by the indigenous population can be generated within the next five years. With the implementation of the development program the demand should grow quite rapidly in the years thereafter.

A very high rate of growth of the volume of intra-zonal telephone connections can be observed. This growth is due to the increase in the number of outstations (increase of Administration services and of economic activities in the interior) and the greater use of communication facilities. The telecommunication outstations are in most cases local Administration posts which act as telegraph agencies and are credited with terminal fees. Many radio outstations are operated by private interests or missions acting *sui juris* for the Department of Posts and Telegraphs. There are very few private radio networks—Ansett and TAA being the most important exceptions.

Private versus Public Networks

The Department of Posts and Telegraphs has the responsibility of developing a strong public territory-wide network. Quite naturally, the department being revenue-conscious tends to look at the development of specialized private networks as a possible drain on potential revenues. At the same time, the officials of the department recognize that under certain circumstances private radio networks are probably justified on the grounds of efficiency of the enterprise. The development of coastal shipping and road haulage most likely will lead to new demands of the carriers for private radio networks. Similar developments are known throughout the world; in many countries with the public communication system better developed than in the Territory, a private communication network maintained by an airline, air charter company, a trucking enterprise or a coastal shipping line is considered an essential part of the transport organization. It would be most unfortunate if similar developments in the Territory were to be frustrated by over-restrictive licensing. At the present time, only a nominal fee of £A1 is charged for a license, which is hardly restrictive.

It is recommended that the Department of Posts and Telegraphs review the present licensing policy for private, limited-purpose communication networks in order to establish criteria for handling applications for the operation of such networks, priorities in frequency allocations and license fee determinations. Public carriers (airlines, licensed coastal-vessel operators and long-distance for-hire truck operators) requiring private radio-communication networks as a part of their service organizations should be given priority in the allocation of frequencies and license fees charged for the permit should be minimal.

Overseas Cable

During its visit to the Territory, the Mission was informed that it is most likely the overseas cable from Australia will be connected to a point on the north shore of New Guinea, probably at Madang. Should this development take place, the Territory will be able to enjoy adequate telecommunication connection with Australia, with which most of the overseas communication users in New Guinea have the primary community of interest. However, in order to achieve full benefits from this development the main routes connecting Madang, Lae and Port Moresby will have to be expanded beyond their present capacity of three channels.

The Mission understands that comprehensive studies of the alternative ways to best utilize this link are being conducted by experts from the Postmaster General's Department. It is not possible for the Mission to comment on the possible cost of the necessary changes.

Economic Criteria for Expansion

Charges for all services provided by the Department of Posts and Telegraphs are based on rates by the Postmaster General's Department of the Commonwealth Government in Australia. However, costs in the Territory are for the most part considerably higher than those applicable to the Postmaster General's Department in Australia with the result that communications in the Territory are substantially subsidized.

This raises the question of the economic criteria to be used under the prevailing circumstances in planning the improvements of the tele-communication system. In more advanced countries, the development of telecommunication systems can be related to the expected increase in demand for the services or to the general benefits from system extension to the present users which can be measured as justification for the invest-ment. In the Territory, the normal criteria of the more developed coun-tries for investment and expansion, and improvement hardly exists. Potential users, at least at this time, are limited primarily to the non-indigenous people who are scattered over a very wide area and the cost of providing services is high.

Undoubtedly, the strict rationing of time when long-distance telephone service is available would appear to impose a serious limitation on the value of service. However, even with the present limitations emergency calls can get through in most cases, and the users adjust themselves to the restrictive schedules. In some cases improvement of communications may produce significant savings of business travel. In some cases the business transactions or administrative decisions could be expedited; the tracing and redirecting of shipments could improve the flow of supplies. Furthermore, the feeling of isolation, present in some parts, could be counteracted by the availability of a better communication service. All these factors should be taken into account in evaluating costs and benefits of investment in telecommunications.

An indication of the importance of communication services to people in isolated areas is the fact that telephone calls originating at the out-stations exceeded the ones originating at the center by more than 2:1; similarly, on a different scale, overseas calls originating in the Territory exceeded substantially the number of calls coming into the Territory. If the ratio of originating to terminating calls is an indication of the importance of a communication service to a community, these statistics may be interpreted to show the relationship between the size of a com-munity and service benefits. This would appear to support the contention that the greatest benefits from the improved communications would accrue to smaller, isolated or semi-isolated communities and would increase the efficiency of the local services of the Administration and more isolated business enterprises. The inference is that in planning the development and pricing of the communication system, the Department of Posts and Telegraphs would be justified in adopting the policy of attempting to achieve financial self-sufficiency as far as the service at and between the main centers is concerned, and a sliding scale of subsidy for service to smaller centers and outposts.

It is clear that the Administration should provide reasonable communication services to the more remote areas primarily for administrative efficiency. Under these circumstances, there is no alternative to the Administration paying a substantial portion of the costs. However, in connection with the main routes and in urban centers the Mission recommends a policy of economic charges and the very minimum of subsidy.

MANPOWER

The employment pattern is for the non-indigenous population to supply the skilled workers and the managerial and administrative personnel, and for the indigenous population to supply the unskilled and semi-skilled workers. The small proportion of the indigenous population in employment, the low levels of skill and low wages of the majority of the indigenes in employment, and the relative scarcity and high cost of non-indigenous skilled workers are main features of the labor situation.

The employed labor force, totaling about 95,000 in 1963, reflects the level of economic development. The number of indigenes in reported employment at the end of March 1963 was 76,800, of whom 1,600 were women. If indigenes employed by other indigenes are added,[1] the total of indigenes in employment was probably about 80,000. This was little more than 13 percent of the estimated adult male population of 600,000. Furthermore, growth in employment of indigenes has also been slow, especially if viewed against the increase in population. Indigenes in employment increased from almost 30,000 in the middle 1920s to almost 57,000 by the outbreak of World War II, to about 66,000 by the early 1950s and there was a further increase of 10,000 over the past ten years. This rate of growth over the past decade is probably an overstatement because the statistical coverage over the period has improved.

Approximately half of the indigenes in employment are engaged in agriculture and forestry. Manufacturing accounts for a small proportion of the total (3.5 percent), and with the great decline in gold output in the past ten years the proportion of indigenes in mining has been sharply reduced to only 1.2 percent. Of the indigenes in employment, almost 30 percent are in government service.

Data on the non-indigenous population in employment are available for two census years, 1954, when just over 10,000 non-indigenes were at work and 1961, when nearly 14,000 were employed. Since 1961 there has been some increase in non-indigenous employment. Judging by the increase in the non-indigenous population, the increase in employment has probably been of the order of 1,000. The industrial distribution of the

---

[1] Their inclusion in data collection would provide only a minor improvement in statistics at considerable expense.

non-indigenous groups is markedly different from the distribution of indigenous workers; only 8 percent are engaged in agriculture and forestry, while 36 percent are in the professions, business and community services, commerce and finance. Manufacturing accounts for only 6 percent, mining for less than 2 percent. Approximately 40 percent are employed by the Government.

As a large employer, the Administration exerts influence over conditions of employment and the level of wages and salaries of indigenous as well as non-indigenous workers. In terms of labor laws, however, the Government has played a minor role in regulating the employment of non-indigenous workers, although it has enacted legislation in respect of workmen's compensation, industrial safety, etc., which is of general application. Its main concern has been the conditions of employment of native workers. Here the Government has played an active role in setting minimum wage rates, and laying down a comprehensive employment code.

Conditions of Employment

Faced with an indigenous population living at a low economic level and with little knowledge of the modern world, the Government has attempted to ensure adequate supplies of labor required for the expansion of the money economy while at the same time preserving, to the extent possible, the traditional way of life and social structure of the indigenous population. The assumption behind government policy has been that the great majority of the indigenes in employment are still intimately linked with their villages, and it has been part of the government policy to preserve this connection. The village cares for the dependents of the worker while he is away and on his return provides his means of livelihood and support in old age. In the absence of any more formalized social security system, this support, and hence the maintenance of ties with the village, is essential for the great majority.

The Government has distinguished in its employment regulations between workers employed on contracts, and casual workers. The casual workers now can be employed anywhere at their own discretion. Contract or agreement workers, normally for a two-year period, can be employed away from their home districts, but the employer has to undertake to pay for the transportation of the worker from his home to the place of employment and for subsequent repatriation, requirements not existing for casual workers. Unless accompanied by their wives, workers are required by law to return home after two years, and a substantial proportion of their wages must be withheld for payment upon return to their homes so that the families of migrant workers might share in the workers' earnings.

With the development of plantations and other economic activities in areas such as northern New Britain, New Ireland and Bougainville, where the population is either sparse or usually unwilling to work for the wages offered, there has been a very substantial movement of labor from other areas such as the Sepik District and the highlands where economic opportunities have been very limited. At present, 43,500 or more than half the indigenes in employment, are working outside their home districts, and half of these are agreement workers. The Government has encouraged the migratory system and maintains a recruiting service for highland labor. It has done this in order to protect the highlands from over-recruitment and to insure that effective steps are taken to protect highland workers from diseases, particularly tuberculosis, to which they will be exposed in the lowlands.

The migratory labor system gives the native workers the experience of working on a plantation where he is bound to acquire some skill and discipline. However, coconuts and cocoa, the crops of the islands and coastal areas, are not the crops of the highlands from whence he comes and upon returning home he may soon forget the little he has learned. Some workers sign up for a second and third period of service. But the system does not lend itself to the establishment of a more stable and perhaps more responsible labor force because, as the cost of transporting and maintaining the wife of a migrant has to be borne by the employer, very few of the migrant workers are accompanied by their wives. It should also be recognized that to the extent that the Administration recruits the labor from the highland areas for the planter, there is less incentive or reason for the planter to hire more local labor and to train labor to a higher degree of efficiency. Despite these disadvantages no radical and rapid change in the system seems likely for several reasons. As an economic mechanism, the system helps to reduce the imbalance of labor supply and demand. In the areas of greatest employment opportunity there is not sufficient labor available locally to supply the demand at anything approaching current wage levels: for example, in northern New Britain, the people of the area, being relatively prosperous producers of cash crops on their own account, are not as a rule attracted by the wages offered on the plantations. On the supply side, economic opportunities offered in the highlands from which the migratory labor comes are limited, and for some time to come there would seem to be little prospect of many of these people earning cash incomes unless they leave their home districts for work elsewhere.

Although the migration of agreement workers is likely to continue, the employment pattern is changing. Over the past ten years, the number of agreement workers has remained approximately constant while the increase in private wage employment has been almost entirely on account of casual workers, and the proportion of casual workers among those in private employment has risen from 45 percent ten years ago to 53 percent in March 1963. About two-thirds of the casual workers in employment are working in their home districts as compared with about a quarter of agreement workers and, although the available statistics do not provide conclusive evidence, there appears to be a trend toward the growth of a more settled labor force. In recent years, a system of piece work has been introduced on some plantations, which provides a return to the workers sufficient to attract labor from the surrounding areas, and many of these workers have remained for long periods with one plantation. Employees in this category, however, still form a very small part of the total labor force.

Wages

Wages for indigenous workers are determined by law. For workers outside the main towns, the minimum wage paid, including the share paid in kind, is officially valued at £A106 a year. This figure does not include other costs borne by the employer for hospital and medical attention, workers' compensation premiums and similar benefits, or the extra cost of food, clothing, accommodation and prescribed articles when a worker is accompanied by his dependents. The legal minimum cash wage for indigenous workers outside the main towns is £A1/10/- a lunar month during the first year of employment and £A1/15/- thereafter.

There are no price indices, so it is not possible to tell precisely how much rural cash wages have risen in real terms. From 1945 to 1956 the minimum cash wage was 15/-d per calendar month; in May 1956, it was raised to £A1/5/- to enable the worker to buy as much with his money as he could do in 1945; in January 1961, the minimum wage was raised to its present level. On the basis of a broad comparison with price trends in major supplying countries, it is almost certain that the real value of the minimum cash wage is now greater than it was in 1945, but the difference is probably quite small. This comparison with 1945 would be of less significance if a high proportion of indigenous workers were paid more than the minimum wage, but in fact over 55 percent of workers receive the minimum. By far the greater part of wages is paid in kind, and although the cash wage is low, there is no over-all shortage of labor offering at this wage. There is in fact more labor offering, particularly in the highlands, than there are jobs available.

For the first time in 1961, an urban minimum wage was set by agreement between representatives of employers and employees. A minimum of £A3 a week came into effect for Port Moresby, Rabaul and Lae, and a minimum wage of £A2/15/- was set for Madang. Workers employed in domestic service, stevedoring and shipping services, and primary production are excluded from this agreement and, if the employer supplies any part of the wage in kind, he is entitled to make deductions from the cash wage. By comparison with the rural wage, the urban wage appears high and seems to attract more labor, to the towns, than can find jobs. While the scale of the problem cannot be precisely determined due to the absence of unemployment figures, the small urban population would seem to indicate that the problem of urban unemployment is still minor.

The introduction of the urban wage was a step toward the payment of wages in cash, rather than partly in cash and partly in kind. The Administration favors this change and is itself considering the introduction of a full cash wage for its own indigenous employees. While recognizing that some workers coming from the more remote areas to work on plantations may not be equipped to spend their wages wisely if paid wholly in cash, the Mission believes that the earning and spending of cash wages is of great value in introducing the indigenous worker to a modern economy, and it strongly supports the movement toward the payment of a full-cash wage. The Mission believes that the Administration should encourage the more widespread payment of a full-cash wage, while recognizing that legislation to enforce such payment in all industries would not be justified at this time.

For most non-indigenous workers the level of wages and salaries is determined mainly by the wage and salary levels for comparable experience and skill in Australia. To attract personnel from Australia, the employer has to pay the Australian rate, and provide assisted passages to and from the Territory, free or subsidized housing and probably additional leave after an agreed period of service. Labor turnover in the case of expatriates is often high, adding to the cost. The labor is both expensive and difficult to obtain, for the fast growth of the Australian economy provides attractive opportunities within Australia.

Manpower Prospects

With almost half of the adult male population not yet engaged in the cash economy at all and with the population increasing, it is reasonable to expect that a substantial expansion in production for the market will be possible before any shortage of unskilled labor develops. This expansion will be partly from increased wage employment and partly from the further development of cash cropping by the indigenes on their own account.

It is also to be expected that skilled labor, if it has to be drawn from Australia, will continue to be expensive and in many cases difficult to obtain. In the opinion of the Mission, substantial forward progress in the economy will be dependent on the training of the indigenes in appropriate skills. The indigenes are being trained in technical trades, clerical work and other middle-grade positions, and there is every reason to believe that with appropriate education and training they will be able to fill more and more managerial, professional and administrative positions in due course. It is in the middle ranges where substantial numbers will be needed. The implications for education are discussed below. It is important to note that increased educational opportunities will create manpower problems as well as progress. Up to now, adolescents—and indeed young adults—with only a few years of primary schooling have, owing to the shortage of persons with even this amount of education, been accepted for training as teachers, agricultural field workers and aid-post orderlies or, being old enough, have gone into employment immediately. As it becomes more normal for enrollment in school to begin at six years of age, the average age of primary school completers entering the economy will drop sharply to the 13- or 14-year-old level. It is clear that though technical training needs to be considerably expanded, there will soon be more youngsters age 13 and 14 than can be taken into the training programs or absorbed into the economy as skilled and partly skilled tradesmen. They will be too young to find immediate employment.

It is important that the fullest and most economic use be made of what, for several years to come, will be small numbers of relatively educated and skilled human resources. To advise upon manpower requirements in both the public and the private sector and on the education and training appropriate to meet them, the Mission recommends the establishment of a Manpower Board composed of representatives of different departments of the Administration and of the private sector.

EDUCATION

Economic, social and political progress will depend upon the progress of the people themselves. A central role here falls to education, in providing ideals, objectives and motivation for progress, in changing attitudes, beliefs and practices which might hinder it, and in imparting the knowledge and skills needed to meet the demands of the Administration and economy for skilled indigenous manpower.

Among adult indigenes, the paucity of educated persons is extreme, under 1 percent having received a full primary education and probably less than a hundred having completed a full secondary course, while the first university graduate was expected at the end of 1964. Further, enrollment in the upper forms of secondary schools is still so small that it will be at least ten years before the Territory can count upon any substantial numbers of young adult indigenes, with a full secondary or university education, as a source from which its leaders may be drawn. There is need for the expansion and development of all levels and types of education and training, primary, secondary, technical, vocational, higher and adult, but the problem is to determine priorities.

Education has only recently reached a stage which requires that the needs for the further development of primary schooling be balanced against those for other levels and types of education, and that priorities be determined. Until the end of World War II, the Administration's educational activities, in both Papua and New Guinea, were very slight. Since the establishment of a Department of Education in 1946, however, the growth of the primary school system, both Administration and mission, has been rapid. Education policy, backed by increasingly heavy expenditures, has in recent years concentrated on getting more and more children into school at the appropriate age for starting, i.e., at about six years of age. Discounting inflated enrollments due to over-age pupils in the preparatory grade—the entry year of primary school—the Mission estimates roughly that over one-half of this age group now enters school each year, a high rate for a country so undeveloped and with so dispersed a population. The large enrollment already in the lower grades means that total primary enrollment will increase rapidly as the smaller classes now at the top of the primary pyramid are displaced by the larger groups at the bottom. First consideration must, therefore, be given to providing teachers and facilities for the mass of pupils who will be moving up, standard by standard, so that completion of a full primary course may become, as soon as possible, the normal terminal point of full-time education for the majority of pupils.

For an increasing minority of the pupils, provision for secondary schooling must be given high priority. Unless well-grounded pupils enter the secondary schools and continue in them to reach the levels required for entry into the various professional and sub-professional training courses and into the occupations basic to the Territory's economy, there can be no prospect for responsible positions to be occupied on a significant scale by indigenes. In 1963, there were only 14 pupils in Form 6,[2] the final year of secondary school, and less than 4 percent of the pupils were above the first three forms. Development of the secondary system is,

[2] In addition, there were 25 indigenes in their last year in Australian secondary schools.

therefore, a most urgent need. The most rapid rate of expansion feasible will not be too great during the next five years to fill the requirements for educated manpower. One important reason for a rapid expansion of secondary education is that it would then be possible to limit entry to primary teacher training to indigenous students who have had some years of secondary schooling, instead of having to accept as teachers persons with no more than a primary education. At the same time, recruitment of expatriate teachers for primary schools can be discontinued.

The Mission believes that the importance of agriculture should be adequately reflected by the attention given to it throughout the educational system. Unless education can be made meaningful, the indigenous peoples may turn against it as a promise unfulfilled. We consider it urgent to adjust the school curricula to better suit the conditions of the Territory and to meet its needs and to make the education given an effective instrument of cross-cultural understanding.

The development of the Territory cannot wait for the products of formal schooling alone. The adult population suffers from a serious circumscription of intellectual and aesthetic abilities. The mass of adults form an uneducated group which needs help in adapting itself to the impact of the inevitably increasing cultural contacts with other parts of the world, and in becoming more progressive in its approach to ways of gaining a livelihood. The social, economic, educational and political problems inherent in the indigenes' transition from their present state to the mid-twentieth century demand a system of adult education complementary to the school system.

Considering the high priority that selected educational development must have, the Mission believes its recommended program is appropriate in relation to expenditures proposed in other sectors and is within the capacity of the Administration to implement, and especially so, if the close cooperation between the Department of Education and the religious missions is maintained and extended over the period ahead. Most of the funds needed for increasing educational opportunities, and a large portion of the staff required will, in continuation of past and present practice, have to be provided from without. But the expenditures will in turn hasten the day when the Territory will be able to depend on its own resources with only a minimum of external assistance.

Primary Education

Before World War II, educational activity on the part of the Administration was negligible in both Papua and New Guinea. In Papua, the Administration limited its educational activities to assisting missions, which had been established as early as 1872, and the funds needed to subsidize mission schools were raised by local taxation. From 1921 to 1935 the total grants paid in Papua amounted to only £A59,109. In New Guinea on the other hand, the Administration set up its own system of education in addition to the mission schools but spent on the average only about £A8,000 annually during the 20 years before the last war.

The main developments in education occurred after World War II. A rapid growth in primary schooling, both Administration and mission, started at that time and has continued to be present. In 1948, the first Administration primary schools were opened in Papua with 246 pupils, making, with the 1,850 in schools in New Guinea, a total of only 2,100 for the whole Territory. By 1958, the numbers in Administration schools had increased to 16,000 and by 1963 to nearly 41,000, an average annual increase of more than 20 percent.

Mission school enrollments rose from 90,000 in 1948 to 130,000 in 1958 and to 166,000 in 1962. This increase was accompanied by a marked improvement in quality. The Education Ordinance, 1952–1957, set minimum standards for mission schools, dividing them into three groups, registered, recognized and exempt.[3] Regular inspections and classification of mission schools started in 1958 when there were 27,000 pupils in registered and recognized schools, and 121,000 in exempt ones. By 1962, the former group reached 95,000 (109,000 in 1963) while the latter had fallen to 71,000. At the same time, the numbers of exempt schools declined from 3,140 to 2,130. While total mission enrollment has remained almost stationary since 1959, the heavy swing from exempt to approved schools evidences a great improvement in standards.

The school enrollment tapers sharply from the base to the apex of the primary pyramid (see chart and Table 1). In Administration schools, 17 percent of the pupils are in the preparatory grade compared with 7 percent in Standard VI. The contrast is even more marked in mission schools in which the corresponding figures are 35 percent and 2 percent. This distribution is due partly to the rapid expansion of the primary system, with the concomitant increase in numbers at the base, and partly to drop-out. Over the seven-year course the drop-out rate is estimated to be 22 percent in Administration and 67 percent in mission schools, the

[3] Registered schools are those complying fully with the requirements concerning such matters as the constitution of the controlling authority, the management of the school, the suitability of the buildings, the numbers and qualifications of the teachers and the suitability of the curriculum. Recognized schools are those which, though not fully meeting the requirements, have reached a satisfactory standard. Exempt schools are those which do not come within either of the categories, and are granted exemption from the requirements for such a period as the Director of Education considers appropriate. Most exempt schools are in primitive areas, with untrained teachers of limited education themselves, and not teaching in English.

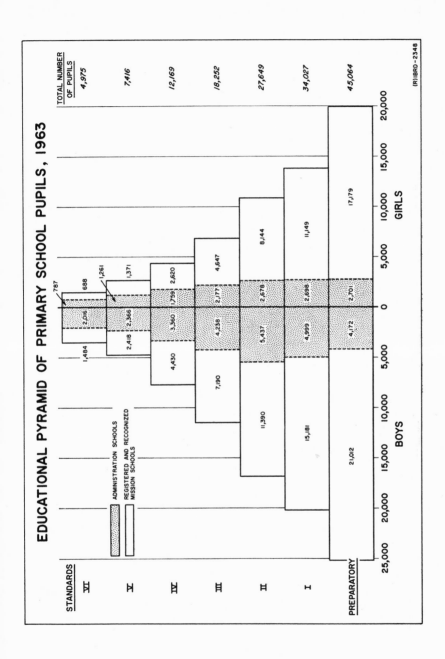

EDUCATIONAL PYRAMID OF PRIMARY SCHOOL PUPILS, 1963

TABLE 1: Projections of Primary Enrollment, 1964-69 [a]

Year	Preparatory	Progression %[b]	I	%	II	%	III	%	IV	%	V	%	VI	Total	Increase[c] Pupils	Increase[c] Teachers
Administration Schools																
1963	6,873	99	7,697	99	8,115	99	6,415	95	5,119	95	3,627	90	2,803	40,649	—	—
1964	8,500	99	6,804	99	7,620	99	8,034	95	6,094	95	4,863	90	3,264	45,179	4,530	151
1965	9,500	99	8,415	99	6,736	99	7,544	95	7,632	95	5,790	90	4,377	49,994	4,815	161
1966	10,500	99	9,405	99	8,331	99	6,669	95	7,167	95	7,250	90	5,211	54,533	4,539	151
1967	11,000	99	10,395	99	9,311	99	8,248	95	6,335	95	6,809	90	6,525	58,623	4,090	136
1968	11,500	99	10,890	99	10,291	99	9,218	95	7,836	95	6,018	90	6,128	61,881	3,258	109
1969	12,000	99	11,385	99	10,781	99	10,188	95	8,757	95	7,444	90	5,416	65,971	4,090	136
													Total	25,322	844
Mission Schools																
1963	38,191	75	26,330	90	19,534	75	11,837	75	7,050	90	3,789	90	2,172	108,903	—	—
1964	44,000	75	28,643	90	23,697	80	14,650	75	8,878	90	6,345	90	3,410	129,623	20,720	414
1965	44,000	75	33,000	95	25,779	80	18,958	75	10,987	90	7,990	90	5,710	146,424	16,801	405
1966	44,000	80	33,000	95	31,350	80	20,623	75	14,218	90	9,888	90	7,191	160,270	13,846	361
1967	44,000	80	35,200	95	31,350	80	25,080	75	15,467	90	12,796	90	8,899	172,792	12,522	313
1968	44,000	80	35,200	95	33,440	80	25,080	75	18,810	90	13,920	90	11,516	181,966	9,174	229
1969	44,000	—	35,200	—	33,440	—	26,752	—	18,810	—	16,929	—	12,528	187,659	5,693	142
													Total	78,756	1,864

[a] Figures are for school years starting in February.
[b] Progression rates are inflated by transfers from mission schools.
[c] Calculations for Administration schools are based on a teacher-pupil ratio of 1:30. Calculations for mission schools are based on the following teacher-pupil ratios: 1964, 1:50 and 1965-69, 1:40.

figures being somewhat affected by transfers from mission to Administration schools. The ratio of boys to girls is about 3:2. Girls are both actually and relatively more numerous in mission than in Administration schools; in the latter the boys outnumber them by about 2:1. As parents become more accustomed to the idea of girls attending school, it is expected that their numbers will tend to equal those of the boys without the need for special measures.

During the period 1959 to 1963, total primary enrollment in Administration and approved mission schools has risen by an average of about 18,000 a year. The Administration schools have increased by an average of about 4,500 pupils a year, but at an uneven rate, while the approved mission schools have expanded more regularly by about 13,500 pupils yearly. Enrollments may be expected to rise still further. Official estimates of the likely 1964 preparatory enrollments are 8,500 in Administration schools (against 6,873 in 1963) and no less than 44,000 in approved mission schools (against 38,191 in 1963).

The future growth of the primary enrollment will, of course, depend both upon the preparatory intake and upon the progression rates between standards. As regards the latter, in making projections of the enrollment in Administration schools, the Department of Education allows for a 1 percent decrease annually between preparatory and Standard III, 5 percent annually between Standards III and V and 10 percent between Standards V and VI, giving an over-all progression through the primary grades of somewhat less than 80 percent. The figures are inflated by transfers from mission schools. For these schools the department calculates on the lower and irregular progression rates of a 25 percent loss between preparatory and Standard I, 10 percent between Standards I and II, 25 percent annually between Standards II and IV and 10 percent annually between Standards IV and VI, giving an over-all retention rate for the whole course of somewhat more than 30 percent. The department expects that within the next two years the annual loss between preparatory and Standards I, II and III will decrease to 20, 5 and 20 percent, respectively.

The Administration schools have such advantages as a low pupil-teacher ratio, high proportions of qualified teachers, better premises and the prestige attaching to the Administration. Applications both for initial entry and for later transfer to them may therefore well increase at the cost of mission enrollment. Should any such tendency appear, the Mission believes the Administration should firmly limit entry to its schools, since otherwise it may find itself saddled with a financial burden for primary education excessive for the Territory's economy. The Mission recommends that new preparatory places provided in Administration schools should complement, not compete with, those in mission schools, and that acceptance of later transfers be limited, to avoid an increase of progression rates in Administration schools (including transfers) above those mentioned in the preceding paragraph.

In planning for the expansion of the primary system, first priority must clearly be given to the consolidation of the schools already started by adding to them year by year the necessary higher standards, until all pupils who have entered at the preparatory level have the opportunity of pursuing a full primary school course. The Mission believes that this should be the main target in the field of primary education in the years to come and beyond that additional enrollments should be limited. The Department of Education considers that the point has now been nearly reached at which a school has been started in every place where a full entry group of about 30 day-pupils will be available each year. If new schools are started, recourse may therefore have to be made to such techniques as one-teacher schools, multiple-class teaching and biennial entry.

The Mission has made projections, given in Table 1, of the possible growth of the primary school system during the period 1964–69. It considers as reasonable a gradual increase in Administration preparatory enrollment from its estimated level of 8,500 in 1964[4] to 12,000 in 1969. This increase would allow for the enrollment of additional pupils, due to population growth, in areas where schools are already in existence and would allow some, although modest, expansion of primary schools to areas where they do not yet exist. No subsequent increase has been projected over the estimated 1964 preparatory enrollment for approved mission schools since it is considered that the increase in enrollment, due to population growth in areas with existing schools plus incorporation pupils from new areas, will be balanced by the disappearance of over-aged pupils. Some fall in numbers may in fact be experienced. On the basis of these projections, total enrollment in Administration and approved mission schools by 1969 would be almost 254,000 or slightly over 10,000 more than total enrollment in 1963.[5]

[4] Figures for the actual 1964 enrollment in Administration schools, received since this was written, show a marked increase, both over the estimates produced in Table 1 and, in Standards I to III, over the 1963 enrollments in preparatory and Standards I and II, evidencing a significant influx of pupils from outside. The excess of the 1964 preparatory enrollment over that projected will, at a teacher-pupil ratio of 1:30, have called for about 60 extra teachers, who will be needed throughout the five-year period. Whether future preparatory intakes and transfers to other classes further raise enrollments and teacher requirements above those projected by the Mission will depend upon the policies adopted by the Administration.

[5] We would at the same time expect the enrollment in exempt mission schools to decrease further. This enrollment may perhaps be estimated to have declined, by the end of 1963, from its 1962 figure of 71,000 to around 50,000.

The Mission advocates, as a general approach to economic development in this report, concentration of effort during the five-year period on areas which are the most promising and already the more developed. As applied to education, this policy implies consolidation of the already existing primary schools by the addition of necessary higher standards and expansion, to the maximum possible extent, of secondary education. The proposed enrollment targets for primary schools would nevertheless allow for the addition of some schools in areas where, as yet, no school exists. The Mission considers this desirable because it believes that in practice it would be very difficult to ignore the interests of the at present less favored parts of the Territory completely.

The Mission recommends that in starting new schools and converting exempt mission schools to approved ones, priority be given to a redress of the present marked unevenness in the distribution of schools. In Bougainville and Manus, virtually all children of school age are enrolled in Administration or approved mission schools. The schools in these districts average one for every ten or less children of school entry age. The evidence indicates that the school system has to some extent permeated the whole of the districts, including some areas where the concentration of pupils is so low that recourse must be had to multiple-class teaching. By contrast, in the highlands and the Sepik, which contain half the Territory's population, rather less than 15 percent of the children of school age are in Administration or approved mission schools and rather more in exempt schools. There is a school of the former type for only about one in every 100 children of school entry age, or, if exempt schools are included, one for every 25. Opportunities in these districts for gaining an education are therefore much more restricted.

If one assumes that by 1969 there will be in total about 400,000 children of primary school age, our projections imply that by that time between 60–65 percent of this age bracket would be enrolled in primary schools. In later years this percentage would, at a constant preparatory enrollment level and assuming unchanged progression rates, become somewhat higher still. Considering the low stage of development and wide dispersal of population, the projected enrollment rate is, by comparable standards elsewhere, quite high.[6]

The Mission considered the possibility of a smaller primary school program but this would, apart from the possibility of reducing projected enrollments modestly by not allowing the start of new schools, require either denying access to some future pupils in areas where schools already exist, or disallowing pupils already in school to follow a full primary

[6] The percentage of 60 to 65 would be somewhat lower if the assumed number of children of primary school age by 1969 of 400,000 proves an underestimate. Even so the enrollment rate would, considering circumstances in the Territory, be high.

course. We concluded that these avenues were not desirable. Nevertheless, the Mission is of the opinion that the primary school program, on the basis of preparatory enrollments already reached in 1964, is somewhat out of balance with the pace of development in other sectors, and if the Administration should be pressed for funds it should give consideration to holding the line more firmly on the expansion of primary education. Priority should be given to building up secondary education until such time as substantial advancement in general economic development will have been reached.

Responsibility for Primary School Facilities. Formerly, when Administration schools were established outside the main towns, the local people were required to erect the school buildings. These were naturally constructed of bush materials and soon needed repair. Owing to the difficulties of persuading the local people to carry out maintenance, the Administration introduced a system of supplying a skeleton frame and a corrugated iron roof, sometimes leaving to the local people the responsibility of erection and finishing off with any additions of their choice, such as a concrete floor and cladding with such materials as bamboo poles or woven grass.

Two important questions are here involved: who should be responsible for the construction and maintenance of village primary schools, and of what materials should they be built? The answers to both will spring from that to a third and more basic question: what is to be the function of the primary schools? In the Territory, the village school will for many years to come be far more important than it is in developed countries as a focal point for the efforts and aspiration of the people, rather than being merely an instrument for passing on to the younger generation the traditions of the older. To the children who attend it by day and to the adults who meet in it, the school is the means by which new knowledge, ideas and practices are introduced and it is the place in which, especially, thought will be given to the problems caused by the intrusion of new ways upon the old.

Given the importance of the primary school to both children and adults, the erection and maintenance of school buildings affords a first-class opportunity for the Administration to pursue one of its major tasks— that of inducting the indigenes into the management of their own affairs and the development of the responsibilities of citizenship. If the indigenes are not prepared to construct and maintain a primary school, which is an essential without which they can have little hope of making progress, the prospects of fitting or persuading them to assume other responsibilities of a modern society are dim. Since rural communities are not sufficiently developed economically to afford imported materials, the normal practice should be to use local materials to the fullest extent possible in the construction of village schools.

The economic advantages of this are clear: the local materials can be provided at low cost, and positive economic gain may often result through the encouragement given to the development of local industries such as sawmilling, brick-making and building. The coolness and quietness of buildings so constructed makes them very suitable as classrooms. The use of local materials would also avoid the danger of unintentionally implanting the idea in the indigenes' minds that progress can come only by completely abandoning their own ways and wholly adopting those of the Europeans. The introduction of improvements and refinements to traditional types of building suggested by European construction methods—and there are several examples of this—would be a positive step toward achieving a "blending of the cultures."

Marked as the economic advantages would be, the use of local materials for rural primary schools would have other and no less important advantages. The personal participation of parents and villagers in the building and maintenance of schools can be a potent factor in arousing interest in the establishment and subsequent successful operation of a school. The cooperation between parents and the Administration, between members of the village, and among different villages where the school serves more than one, can be a valuable contribution to political development. Even the lack of durability of most of the buildings erected from local materials,[7] usually considered as their main drawback, may not be without its advantages. Since the school will need to be repaired from time to time and every few years will need replacement, there will be recurrent opportunities for cooperative endeavor, for the exercise of new skills and for making any changes in site or design that have become desirable.

There are enough examples to show that local communities will make great efforts to build schools, such is their eagerness for their children to be educated. It is also clear that the people of Papua and New Guinea are willing to have the Administration provide the building, if such is the policy. It is the belief of this Mission that the people will respond to a policy which makes them responsible for school building and maintenance, and that the resultant administrative problems which will no doubt be encountered upon occasion will be more than compensated for by the educative value to the communities of the assumption of this responsibility. The Mission, therefore, recommends that the local communities be made responsible for the supply, erection and maintenance of primary school buildings. Thus no provision for further supplies of steel frames or

---

[7] There are a few examples of schools erected in permanent materials such as local coronous or stabilized earth or cement brick.

corrugated iron is included in the recommended expenditures for primary education. The Mission recommends further that the local communities be made responsible for building and maintaining primary teachers' houses. The Administration should encourage assumption of greater responsibility by small financial grants and by paying for the so-called European amenities required for the teachers' houses.

Also, it will be advisable for the Administration to be prepared to continue providing some assistance in construction costs while the policy advocated is being made effective. Encouragement should be given to the communities to make increased use of more permanent local materials, such as stone, coronous and stabilized earth brick, sawn timber and shingles. Practical forms of such encouragement might be contributions by the Administration toward the cost of block-making and wood-working machines and of cement freight.

It has been Administration policy to require that school sites should be vested in the Administration even when the schools themselves have been erected by the local communities, the object being to guard against possible disputes arising as to the ownership of the premises. This requirement appears to be unnecessary. If local communities are to develop the capacity to manage their own affairs, they must learn to take such precautions as may be reasonable and practical to safeguard their interests, or to deal with the situations which arise if they do not.

The Mission is unconvinced of the desirability, at this stage of the Territory's development, of making school attendance compulsory in selected areas. For most parents in places where schools can be provided, the desire to secure an education for their children is so strong as to make compulsion unnecessary. Education is so generally regarded as a privilege to be eagerly desired that it would be a pity, for the sake of an easy administrative solution to the occasional problems posed by a small minority, to introduce regulations which might make the schools appear places children must be forced to enter.

Boarding Facilities. The dispersion of the population means that large numbers of children will be unable to attend school without boarding facilities. The Mission endorses the view of the Administration that the provision of these for primary school pupils is not a responsibility it should undertake. It believes that one of the simplest and potentially most rewarding ways in which local communities could assume part of the responsibility for education and could contribute to the unity of the inhabitants would be to offer boarding facilities, in the vicinity of schools, for children whose homes are too far away for them to attend daily.

No special accommodation would normally be required for this purpose; all that would be needed would be sleeping space in village huts.

Nor would food be a serious problem. The parents could bring in supplies from time to time, while the children could bring food from their homes if they returned there on weekends, and they could help to grow their own food in the village and school gardens. Since most of them will, after leaving school, live on the land, a certain amount of practical work in agriculture, horticulture and livestock keeping could be a useful complement to their studies.

In this connection, during its observations of both Administration and mission schools, the Mission noticed the contribution that the pupils themselves were making to their own support and to the conduct of the schools. In many cases not only do the pupils grow practically all their own food, but they prepare and cook it as well. They do the cleaning of the school premises and tend the school grounds. They do their own laundering and in some cases carry out school decorations, and assist in the making of furniture. In technical schools, the pupils have assisted in erecting buildings. This is a characteristic which should be preserved and developed not merely as a means of getting things done economically, but as an aspect of education of real value in the development of character and in the fitting of pupils for life. The Mission attaches importance to the development, by practical means, of a tradition among parents, citizens and pupils of making a contribution to the provision of education, in kind, in labor or in cash, according to local circumstance.

Primary School Curriculum. As the first Administration primary schools were started for Australian children, they naturally adopted an Australian curriculum, still to be found in the 49 "A" schools which are attended mainly by Australian children. The curriculum, however, did not meet the needs of the indigenes who had to learn English as a foreign language and lacked the background knowledge gained by Australian children from their environment. For the "T" schools, therefore, which are attended by indigenes, the curriculum has been adapted, especially at the lower levels, to take account of such differences, the latest revision being published in 1963.

While all children are freely admitted to "A" schools if their command of English and home environment would enable them to profit from a course designed for native speakers of English, the Mission recommends against separation of schooling on the basis of different curricula. The requirements of pupils who are and are not native speakers of English can easily be met within the same school, and the Mission recommends that the "A" and "T" schools be progressively merged.

The primary objective and result of the "T" curriculum is to give literacy in English and some proficiency in number work. These are the qualifications chiefly necessary for entry to secondary schools or teacher training, or for Administration or other paid employment—in which hitherto the small numbers leaving from the upper standards of the primary schools have mostly been absorbed. However, the recommended expansion of primary education can be justified only if accompanied by a marked reorientation and modification of the curriculum.

In the future, large numbers of those leaving from the apex of the primary pyramid will be unable to gain entry to secondary schools, while the lower age of entry to primary schools now becoming general means that few of them will be old enough to go straight from primary school to paid employment or vocational training. Thus, the future to be foreseen for increasing numbers of those completing primary education is life at home in the village. The basis of this life will for long continue to be subsistence agriculture, and the primary education received, supplemented as described later, should enable progressive improvements to be made in this, together with an increase in the production of cash crops and in the growth of a more modern economy.

Until it becomes possible to provide secondary education for all—and this will not be in the foreseeable future—the primary school must serve as a screen to separate those who will continue their schooling from those who will not. The latter, however, must not be regarded, or be given cause to regard themselves as failures, and it should be considered a normal thing for them to attend primary school as a preparation for village life. However, if this outlook is to become accepted and the boys and girls who are not selected for secondary schools or vocational training —and their parents—are not to feel disillusioned and dissatisfied, it appears that a new orientation needs to be given to the primary curriculum, since those who pursue the present one show little desire to remain in the villages.

For any change in this attitude, the primary school curriculum must fulfill two conditions. First, the grounding it gives in literacy and the other knowledge and skills required for entry to secondary school-training or employment must be so presented that such entry is not taken to be its only purpose, and failure to gain it thus means time and effort spent for nothing. On the contrary, the grounding must be so related to village life that its value in enriching this may be obvious to both pupils and parents. Much can be done in this respect by the use of reading material— especially in English teaching, nature study and social studies—and of mathematical exercises, based upon the assumption that the natural environment for a child is that of the village.

Second, increased emphasis needs to be given to crafts which would raise the standards of life in the village, for example, cane and grass weaving, decoration, plastic arts and needlework. The wide variety of subjects comprised in the term "nature study" needs to be orientated to the improvement of village life. School gardens may be used to accustom the children to the idea of new crops, or better ways of raising known ones. Livestock—pigs, goats, cows, poultry, pet birds, rabbits, guinea pigs, bees, etc.—may be kept at the school for similar purposes, as well as for their other educational value. The object would not be vocational training, though the knowledge and experience gained and interest aroused would greatly facilitate this later. The aim would be to impart a knowledge of, and foster a love for, plants and animals and to enrich village life so that it may be more satisfying to young people who have completed all or most of the primary grades.

For the more mature of the pupils likely to leave school at the end of the primary stage, there is a case for some attention, during the last two years of the seven-year course, to the application of their education to specific aspects of village life. Practical training at this level is now carried out in separate junior technical schools, a feature of which is work on projects which assist the community and call for practical application of knowledge and skills taught in the classroom and workshop. Pupils assist in building schools and in making furniture, water tanks and small boats. The Mission considers that junior technical schools should disappear as separate entities, but that appropriate elements of their curricula, with suitable additions, should be incorporated in those of the upper standards of primary schools.

A main factor in shaping the present curriculum has been the Administration's desire to provide the indigenes with a school system equated to Australian standards. The Mission considers that this policy should be reviewed, and that targets for attainment be more directly related to the conditions of the Territory. The latter's primary schools are now sufficiently widespread and firmly established for the Administration to cease to concern itself overmuch with the equality of standards between the Territory and elsewhere. The indigenous pupils labor under two severe handicaps, of having to learn as a foreign language the medium of instruction, which must necessarily delay their progress and, of not receiving the help in, and opportunities for, informal learning which Australian children receive from their much more advanced environment. Attempts to force standards toward equality with those in Australian schools are likely to result in emphasis being placed upon the subjects which are the more easy to teach and to examine, such as English and mathematics. Pupils may be forcefed with facts and drilled in mechanical responses, and insufficient attention may be paid to the development of mental abilities and habits.

There is urgent need for the establishment in the Department of Education of a research and production unit of some six professionals concerned with curricula, textbooks, and teaching materials and aids. The recent revision of the primary curriculum was carried out by officials with other full-time tasks. Departmental officials will not have the time to carry out the amount of work to be done if they are to give effective supervision to a growing school system, though the unit should include staff with some active engagement in teaching. Prime concerns of this unit will be the production of a primary curriculum rooted in the conditions of the Territory, and problems associated with the teaching of English.

The general approach now used to teach English has been well devised, but every available means should be explored in assisting pupils to learn English as rapidly and thoroughly as possible. Very effective use is being made of the radio, for instance, and its use could profitably be extended. The Mission believes that far more use could be made of the tape recorder, and extensive testing of this aid is recommended. Television offers a potential as a teaching aid that requires study, as will be discussed later.

Teacher Supply for the Primary Schools. The development of the primary system hitherto has been made possible largely by the work of European teachers, who form some 30 percent of the teachers in Administration primary schools and about 20 percent of those in approved mission schools. While the secondary and technical schools will have to continue to depend almost wholly upon Europeans for many years to come, the Mission believes that the stage has been reached at which they should play a diminishing part in primary schools.

One reason for this is that the annual cost of a European teacher is much higher than that of an indigenous one. At least as cogent a reason, however, is the desirability of having primary school teachers with close racial and environmental affinities with their pupils.

The difficulties of bridging the gap between the adult teacher and the pupils, especially those in the lower standards, is already great enough without the added complication of the two being of totally unrelated origins and backgrounds. The adults best equipped to teach young children are those who are able, out of their own experience, to understand the pupils' problems and to pass on to them the ideas, habits and attitudes which they think will be of the greatest benefit to them.

Since the present indigenous teachers are the first generation of their profession, many of them may not themselves be sufficiently well acquainted with European culture to be able to differentiate in importance between its elements, to make a satisfactory blending of it with their own cultures, or to select what to pass on to their pupils, and determine the

best ways in which to do it. They will, therefore, need continuing association with European teachers, who can be especially useful in setting
standards, and who have a particularly valuable contribution to make in
the teaching of English. The present 800 or so Europeans in the primary
schools are ample to provide the necessary contacts, and the Mission,
therefore, recommends that after 1964 the training and recruitment of
expatriate teachers for primary schools should be discontinued.

The Mission recommends also the discontinuation, at the end of 1964,
of the "A" course of primary teacher-training, which takes its entry from
those who have completed Standards VI or VII. Teachers trained in this
course, who form half the teaching force in Administrative schools, and
rather more in approved mission schools, have rendered invaluable
service, and the development of the primary system would have been
impossible without them. However, the employment as teachers of those
who have had no more than a primary education themselves, and whose
professional training has perforce had to be directed largely to drill in
classroom techniques, can be justified only as a temporary measure. Now
that adequate numbers can be foreseen as entering the secondary schools
and subsequently becoming available for training as teachers, the Mission
believes it will be possible to meet the needs for new primary teachers
during the next five years from persons who have completed at least
Form 2 of the secondary schools.

The Mission considers that as soon as it becomes possible, the minimum
educational and professional requirements for appointment as a primary
teacher should be those held by the present "C" course teachers—that is,
an intermediate certificate (three years of high school) followed by a
two-year course of professional training. As an interim measure, however,
to secure the numbers of new teachers which will be required during the
next five years, the Mission recommends the institution of a one-year
course of training at the end of Form 2 of the secondary school, replacing
the present two-year "B" course.

The numbers of additional teachers required for the primary expansion
envisaged will depend on the pupil-teacher ratio. In Administration
schools the ratio is 30:1, and although this is very favorable compared
with other developing countries, the Mission hopes that it can be adhered
to in view of its educational advantages. In mission schools, the ratio is
more than 50:1. This the Mission considers too high for satisfactory
progress, except with above average teachers, and recommends that the
conditions of payment of grants-in-aid be modified to bring about a
reduction from 1965 onward, to a ratio nearer 40:1.

On the basis of these ratios, the Mission calculates that during 1964–69
an addition of some 850 teachers will be needed in Administration and of

about 1,860 in mission schools, the total annual requirements diminishing from about 570 in both 1964 and 1965 to some 280 in 1969. Of the total 2,710, about 675 will have been added by training and recruitment in 1963, and a further 850 may be expected by the end of 1964, leaving somewhat less than 1,200 to be trained during 1965–68 (see Table 1). The foregoing figures do not allow for wastage, but this is very low at this stage of the Territory's development.

The quantities of trainees required will be well within the capacity of the secondary schools to supply (see Table 2). Some reorganization of the training facilities may be needed (in particular, some of the smaller of the 26 mission colleges could be amalgamated with considerable benefit), but the capacity of the present facilities, Administration and mission, amounting to about 800 places, is more than adequate to the task. No capital costs or additional recurrent expenditures should, therefore, be required during the period under review; this implies that the Mission recommends against the construction of new teacher-training colleges.

If possible, the numbers of females going into primary teacher training should be increased. The teaching force is overwhelmingly male and the shortage of women teachers causes grave difficulties in the development of girls' education. It means also that the youngest children, who should normally be taught by women, have to be taught by men. Among the students at present in training, men outnumber women by three to one so that there is no early remedy in sight for this situation.

The pre-service and in-service training of primary teachers needs to be extended to prepare them for a more active role in village life. For several years to come there will be very few persons in the villages with more than a primary education, while large numbers will not have had even that. The primary teachers, therefore, will be in a position to provide leadership and to help guide the villages in their development. While the activities of the primary teachers must remain related primarily to the education of children, they should be equipped and expected to work very closely with those responsible for the various aspects of adult education, and for promoting a rise in the standards of living. Amongst other things the primary teachers should be given some training in the teaching of handicrafts, and they should study the nature of local life, practical possibilities for its improvement, and the basic forms which a blending of the cultures might most felicitously take.

Teacher Housing. The policy has been to construct houses for primary teachers of a European type and from pre-fabricated or partly prefabricated materials. Sometimes these have been made in Australia but use has been made of facilities which the Territory affords for the provision of materials such as timber and plywood. The official costing figures used are £A1,000 for an indigenous teacher's house, £A1,600 for an expatriate unmarried teacher's house, and £A6,000 for an expatriate married teacher's house. The actual cost often far exceeds this, especially in the highlands to which the transport of material and pre-fabricated sections has to be made by airplane. Here the cost for an expatriate married teacher's house may be £A10,000 or more.

A well-built house of local materials, of a durability comparable to that of the type of house now being constructed, costs about £A300. Even if built to standards fully suitable for European occupation, equipped with electric light and modern plumbing it could be erected for a fraction of the cost of the present type of housing. A very significant financial saving would thus be achieved by the use of local materials for teachers' houses, but even more important would be the effect it would have upon the indigenes' conception of what is meant by advancement and how it can be made.

This matter acquires urgency as increasing numbers of indigenous teachers come into service. By being housed in a markedly different way from those whom they are expected to teach, by both precept and example, these teachers are being sharply divided from the people whom they are to educate. This distinction could hamper their work. In addition, the example and incentive for village people to improve their own housing conditions would be lost. The present type of construction is too far removed from the indigenes' experience and capacities to serve as an incentive to emulation. If, on the other hand, the teachers' houses were built of local materials, but with improved techniques and to higher standards, they could be both symbols of and stimuli to progress.

Most of the new houses, with the ending of expatriate training and recruitment as teachers for primary schools, will be for occupation by indigenous teachers. The fact, however, that they are of native materials should not be permitted to become an obstacle to their occupation by Europeans, should it be necessary to transfer Europeans to staff the schools where such houses are available. A strong impetus to local development could be given by such occupation. If the Europeans show that the advanced development they represent does not require complete rejection of traditional ways, the indigenes will receive an encouragement to progress by using their local resources.

Pre-schools. As indicated in the chapter on Health, the Mission considers that pre-schools are more properly the concern of the Department of Education than that of Health, and recommends their transfer to the former. The Mission believes these schools can help in improving conditions in the social sector in areas, such as Hanuabada, in which the growth of urban conditions causes problems among the indigenous population. The Mission considers, however, that Administration support for pre-schools should be limited to such areas, and sees no justification for public expenditure, at this stage of the Territory's development, on pre-schools in other areas and for more advanced segments of the population. Continued expenditure at the current level is recommended during the five-year period.

Administration Expenditures for Primary Expansion. The capital costs of the expansion of the primary system during 1964–69 will be slight. If the construction and maintenance of school buildings and teachers' houses is undertaken by the local communities, the only capital cost to the Administration will be the supply of furniture and equipment, officially estimated at £A3 per pupil. The cost for the 25,000 extra pupils would thus be £A75,000. It would be advisable, however, to allow for some modest capital expenditure—say, £A100,000—on primary school buildings by the Administration while the policy advocating transfer of responsibility for these to the local communities is being introduced. This amount should also cover small financial grants, to be provided to local communities as an incentive, and the cost of the so-called European amenities required for the teachers' houses which the Administration should be prepared to continue to pay, as discussed before. The present recurrent cost of £A30 per annum per pupil in Administration schools includes the cost of expatriate teachers, who are costed at £A1,600 (not including housing, travel, etc.) each per annum against the native teacher's £A200–£A400 according to qualifications. Since native teachers will be used for the additional pupils, a lower figure may be used. If £A25 is used as a unit cost, the increase in recurrent costs would amount to about £A575,000 per annum by 1968/69, with a total increase during 1964/65–1968/69 of approximately £A1.935 million.[8]

Grants-in-Aid to Mission Schools. In recognition of the importance of the mission schools and to help improve the quality of their education, the Administration provides subventions in the form of grants-in-aid for trained teachers and for the provision of textbook and teaching materials. The grants for teachers are made on a six-point scale ranging from a maximum of £A500 per annum for a fully certificated expatriate teacher down to £A100 per annum for an "A" course indigenous teacher. In 1963, grants were made for 2,264 teachers, including 480 expatriates.

It is most important that the cooperation of the missions in education of the indigenes should be continued and extended. The missions substantially share with the Administration the burden in providing education—

---

[8] Based on enrollment figures as projected in Table 1. The school year corresponds roughly with the calendar year. The amounts mentioned here have been recalculated to a fiscal-year basis.

enrollment in mission schools outnumbers that in Administration schools by nearly 3:1.

The subsidy to mission primary schools amounted to £A340,000 in 1962/63, or approximately £A3 per pupil enrolled in registered and recognized schools (as compared with a cost per pupil of £A30 in Administration primary schools). In the future this figure appears likely to be insufficient. The discontinuance of the "A" course of training will result in higher costs for new teachers trained in the "B" and "C" courses, while the reduction in the size of new classes from 50 to about 40 pupils will also involve greater expenditure. If a tentative figure of £A4 per pupil is assumed for costing purposes, subsidies to mission education would rise to about £A740,000 or by about £A400,000 per annum by 1968/69, with a total extra expenditure during 1964/65–1968/69 of £A1.645 million.[9]

Secondary Education

There was no secondary education in the Territory before World War II and its development since has been slow. There are now 68 secondary schools, of which 58 are junior high schools offering three years of study and ten full high schools offering six years. All schools are single stream. Of the total, the missions operate 40 schools, mostly very small—the average being 26 pupils per school—but a few of the missionary secondary schools are large and well endowed with buildings, grounds and equipment, and the teaching is of a high order.

The numbers of pupils enrolled are still very small, totaling only 3,800 in 1963; 2,250 in Administration and 1,550 in mission schools, a ratio approaching 2:1.[10] The enrollment in both types of school is concentrated in the lower forms (see Table 2). In Administration schools, boys outnumber girls approximately 3:1. Entry to secondary school is by means of an examination, taken by pupils from Standard VI and VII. The latter is an intermediate year which amounts practically to a repetition of Standard VI though it is usually conducted on secondary school premises. Secondary pupils are enrolled in the most convenient school for them in either part of the Territory. Scholarships are awarded to 20 pupils each year to attend secondary schools in Australia, 90 such pupils being there in any one year.

The six-year high school course follows an Australian syllabus, and pupils sit for the New South Wales Leaving Certificate. The high schools

[9] Based on enrollment figures as projected in Table 1.
[10] Enrollments mentioned here do not include those in technical schools, discussed later.

TABLE 2: Secondary Education Projections of Enrollment, 1964–69 [a]

	Standards				Forms											Total VII-6	Increase	
Year	VI	P.%[b]	VII	%	1	%	2	%	3	%	4	%	5	%	6		Pupils	Teachers[c]
							A. Administration Schools											
1963	2,803	30 40	547	40	1,010	100	378	60	204	70	66	95	25	95	14	2,244	—	—
1964	3,264	20 50	841	35	219 1,121 1,340	100	1,010	70	227	60	143	95	63	95	24	3,648	1,404	70
1965	4,377	20 50	653	30	294 1,632 1,926	100	1,340	80	707	40	136	95	136	95	60	4,958	1,310	66
1966	5,211	10 60	875	25	196 2,189 2,385	100	1,926	85	1,072	30	283	95	129	95	129	6,799	1,841	92
1967	6,525	10 60	521	20	219 3,127 3,346	100	2,385	85	1,637	30	322	95	269	95	123	8,603	1,804	90
1968	6,128	10 60	652	20	104 3,915 4,019	100	3,346	85	2,027	30	491	95	306	95	256	11,097	2,494	125
1969	—	— —	613	—	130 3,677 3,807	—	4,019	—	2,844	—	608	—	466	—	290	12,647	1,550	77
															Total		10,403	520

B. Mission Schools[d]

	Pupils	Rate	Rate	Teachers	Rate	Total	Rate	Pupils	Rate	Pupils	Rate	Teachers	Total VII-4	Increase Pupils	Increase Teachers
1963	2,172	20	30	550	30	681	60	246	40	46	50	11	1,534	—	—
1964	3,410	20	30	434	30	817 (165; 652)	70	409	50	98	30	23	1,781	247	12
1965	5,710	10	40	682	15	1,153 (130; 1,023)	75	572	50	205	20	29	2,641	860	43
1966	7,191	10	50	571	10	2,386 (102; 2,284)	80	865	50	286	20	41	4,149	1,508	75
1967	8,899	10	50	719	10	3,653 (57; 3,596)	80	1,909	50	432	20	57	6,770	2,621	131
1968	11,516	10	50	890	10	4,522 (72; 4,450)	80	2,922	50	955	20	86	9,375	2,605	130
1969	—	—	—	1,151	—	5,847 (89; 5,758)	—	3,618	—	1,461	—	191	12,268	2,893	145
Total														10,734	536

[a] Figures are for school years starting in February. Technical schools not included.
[b] Progression rates (%) are shown between columns and two rates show progression to Standard VII and Form 1.
[c] Calculations are based on a teacher-pupil ratio of 1:20.
[d] No figures are given for Forms 5 and 6 as it is doubtful whether they will be developed by 1969. The few pupils who might be ready to progress to them could transfer to Administration schools.

are both residential and non-residential. Both are open to all races but, in fact, the residential schools have been normally attended entirely by indigenes. They are single-sex schools, unlike the non-residential schools, which are coeducational. The junior high schools offer a three- to four-year course terminating at the New South Wales Intermediate level, and they cater for pupils who, while not considered capable of proceeding to more advanced secondary studies and matriculating at Australian levels, are yet above average ability. Pupils of the requisite ability may transfer to full high schools.

There are also three Administration technical schools, at Port Moresby, Lae and Rabaul, which are separate secondary institutions, with about 470 pupils. Most of these are pupils who failed to gain entry to a high school or junior high school. The basic course of two years, about 75 percent of which is devoted to academic subjects, leads to an apprenticeship in the first-class trades, such as carpentry, mechanics and plumbing, those remaining for the third and fourth years are trained to become first-class trade assistants. In addition, the Department of Agriculture conducts a secondary agricultural school at Popondetta.

There is thus a sharp distinction among the different types of secondary schools. This has marked disadvantages. It entails a selection of pupils for different courses, leading to different occupations, at a stage too early for the selective processes to have any real prognostic value. By separating those pursuing academic studies from those pursuing practical ones, it obstructs the growth of unity among the pupils and recognition of the value of the many different but interdependent forms of skilled activity upon which a modern economy rests. It restricts the pupils' opportunities to change from one course to another should their interest alter or their aptitudes emerge. It limits the richness and diversity of knowledge and skill to be found among the teaching staff, and also limits the opportunities for both staff and pupils to broaden their interests and outlook. It is uneconomic, since the schools are too small for the maximum value to be obtained from the overhead expenses.

The Mission considers that comprehensive secondary schools would better suit the Territory's needs and conditions than the present system, and recommends that at least the first three years of secondary education of all types, academic, agricultural, industrial and commercial, should be given in such schools which should have a multiple stream entry.

The 1963 enrollment in the upper forms of secondary schools is extremely small, with 14 pupils in Form 6, 25 in Form 5, and 77 in Form 4. Clearly, it will be several years before substantial numbers of indigenes with an education above the lower secondary level can be looked for (see Table 3). At the same time, a much greater output is needed from this

TABLE 3: Secondary Education Projections of Output, 1964–69

End of School Year	Ex Standard VII	Ex Forms					
		1	2	3	4a	5	6b
		Administration and Mission Schools					
	547	—	303	91	7	3	24
1964	851 304 457	245	507 204 268	160 69 424	30 23 7	7	60
1965	1,037 580 656	288	554 286 289	588 164 750	36 29 14	6	129
1966	1,170 514 417	477	722 433 358	979 229 1,146	55 41 16	13	123
1967	1,064 647 522	731	1,312 954 502	1,492 346 1,419	73 57 25	16	256
1968	1,323 801	904	1,961 1,461	2,183 764	111 86	—	—

a Mission figures include those who may transfer to Administration schools.
b Including those continuing full-time education.

Note: Top figures in columns are numbers of those leaving Administration schools and lower figures are those leaving mission schools. Figures on right of columns are totals.

level to meet the requirements for manpower now in short supply, such as qualified primary school teachers. Fortunately, the enrollment at the earliest stages of the course is comparatively heavy, there being in 1963— 1,691 in Form 1, 624 in Form 2, and 250 in Form 3.

How much the secondary system can or will expand during 1964–69 will depend in the first place on the number of pupils who would enter secondary schools from the primary ones if places are offered, and on the progression rates within the schools. These latter will, of course, be largely affected by the extent to which employment possibilities may induce pupils to leave school. With so few pupils previously in secondary schools, and, therefore, with so little experience to serve as a guide, no confident predictions can be made on this matter. However, the Department of Education is planning on substantial numbers of pupils going on from primary schools and continuing at a high rate of progression through the secondary system. The Mission considers development of the secondary system the most urgent educational need and therefore supports a policy of the most rapid expansion possible during the five-year period of its program.

On the basis of estimates of entry and progression rates supplied by the Department of Education, the Mission has projected the possible growth during 1964–69 of enrollment in Administration and mission secondary schools. In the Administration schools, numbers would grow from 2,700 (including Standard VII and technical schools) in 1963 to 12,650 in 1969, and in the mission schools from 1,900 in 1963 to 12,270 in 1969. Rapid as such a total five to sixfold increase would be, there is no doubt of the need for it if it can be managed, and it would, in fact, amount to only about 6 percent of the age group if this would be about 400,000. The Mission recommends that the expansion program for secondary education be aimed at attaining the projected increase in enrollment of more than 20,000 by 1968/69.

As a consequence of the Mission's recommendation that technical education at the secondary level be amalgamated with the academic courses, the projections above include enrollment destined for the technical program. In a society that is moving so rapidly from a primitive economy into a cash economy with the consequent need for all types of skilled manpower, it has not been possible to estimate with any degree of accuracy what numbers and skills are needed. The Administration will have to keep the question under continuous study and make appropriate adjustments in the school program. It is reasonable to assume, however, that an increased enrollment by 1969 of 3,000 pupils or more in the technical stream would be required.

The dispersion of the school population and the numbers, small compared with the total population of potential entrants to secondary schools, mean that a high percentage of pupils in the latter must for some years be boarders. The Department of Education estimates that until 1970 the schools will contain 80 percent boarders, at an annual maintenance cost per pupil of £A70. Paradoxically, the capital costs of boarding schools are lower than those of day schools, the costs per place being estimated at £A216 and £A200, respectively. This is due to the day schools being in towns, in which buildings are required to be of a higher standard.

The Department of Education sees major advantages in boarding schools over day schools at the secondary level, the four main being that it is easier to teach English in a completely controlled environment, that better facilities for study can be provided than the pupils would have if they lived at home, that it is easier to develop social training and extra-curricular activities and, that boarding schools help to break down tribal animosities and to build a national spirit. These advantages do not, however, clearly outweigh the dangers regarding too thorough an uprooting of pupils from their home environments, and the reduced opportunities of influencing the latter through the pupils, and the Mission recommends that nonresidential secondary schools should be established as rapidly as the supply of potential entrants permits.

Teacher Supply for Secondary Schools. Schools at the secondary level are staffed almost entirely by Europeans. In Administration schools these form 75 percent of the teachers in junior high schools, 100 percent of those in full secondary schools and teacher-training colleges, and 85 percent of those in technical schools. In mission schools they form 100 percent of the teachers in junior high, secondary and technical schools and 95 percent of those in teacher colleges. The present small enrollments in secondary schools make it clear that virtually no indigenous teachers above the primary level will become available during the next five years. There is, as yet no provision for training such teachers owing to the lack of students with necessary educational qualifications. However, from 1966 onward it should be possible to start training small numbers. No capital provision will need to be made during the five-year program period for this purpose, as use can be made of the facilities left available by the diminishing numbers of primary teachers in training.

During 1964–69, virtually the whole of the secondary teaching force will have to be made up of expatriates. Thus the most difficult problem in the expansion of secondary education will undoubtedly be the recruitment of enough qualified teachers. The numbers needed will depend on the pupil-teacher ratio, which at present is 16:1. With more and larger schools, this might be expected to increase to, say, 20:1. At this rate, the projected increase in enrollment would require a total of about 1,050 additional secondary teachers (520 for Administration and 530 for mission schools [see Table 2]). The need would begin with about 80 for 1964 and rise to about 220 for 1969. Some small part of the need could probably be met by suitably qualified Europeans now teaching in primary schools who could be replaced in these by indigenous teachers, but even so it appears that up to 1,000 new secondary teachers will need to be recruited over the five-year period.

The Department of Education calculates the staffing needs for technical education on a teacher-pupil ratio of 1:16, this latter being the maximum number of pupils whom it is considered a teacher can adequately supervise in a workshop. With the development of comprehensive schools the smaller size of workshop classes, as compared with academic ones, will not significantly affect the general secondary teacher-pupil ratio of 1:20 that has been assumed for the Mission's projection. The numbers of technical teachers needed will depend upon the enrollment in the technical streams. If this were 15 percent of the total, and the pupils' time were equally divided between general and technical classes, of the more than 1,000 additional teachers required for secondary expansion, about 75 would need to be teachers of technical subjects.

Arrangements for the secondment of teachers exist with the Australian States, but in 1963 only 40 teachers were so seconded.[11] There is no surplus of secondary teachers in the Australian States, which are themselves said to be short of them. The prospects and conditions offered by service in the Territory do not seem to have caught the imagination of secondary teachers sufficiently to lure them from Australia. Secondments normally last for up to two periods of two years each. There is no guarantee that as secondments terminate new teachers will be available, and in fact it is stated that Victoria is not in practice making new secondments.

A recruiting mission visited Great Britain in the winter of 1963/64 in the hopes of contracting 50 teachers. A possible source of recruitment which has not yet been considered are some of the Asian countries, which are often stated to have a surplus of graduates. Teachers from such countries might make a valuable contribution to the education and development of indigenes by extending the latter's knowledge of the forms which cultural advancement may take. However, Australia must remain the primary source from which teachers come.

The most practical possibility appears to be a firm program of secondment of secondary teachers by the Australian States, perhaps in proportion to their own teaching strength. As there are 27,000 secondary teachers in Australia, and a further 12,000 in vocational schools, to supply the whole

[11] Of these 16 came from New South Wales, 11 from Victoria, six each from Queensland and Western Australia and one each from South Australia and Tasmania.

1,000 teachers required would take only 2½ percent of the Australian States' teaching force, while if the missions prove able to meet their needs from other sources, the proportion would drop to little over 1 percent. The Commonwealth Government has directed the attention of its States to the responsibilities which Australia has undertaken in connection with the Territory and the need for skilled manpower to develop the secondary school program. If the secondary school program is to grow at a rate essential to the development of the Territory the Australian States will have to supply the teachers. The Mission therefore recommends that the Commonwealth Government work out a program whereby the State Governments will provide the additional teachers required for the secondary expansion program.

Secondary School Curricula. The secondary schools have hitherto used Australian-type syllabuses with local adaptations, but basic revision to suit local needs has now begun, and it is hoped to develop courses which will have certain regional biases or specialities, with due attention to agriculture, industry, commerce and Territory economics. In the lower forms of the comprehensive schools recommended by the Mission, academic and technical streams should not be sharply segregated, owing both to the amount of academic work, especially in English and mathematics, that the pupils in the latter will have to do, and to the need for those in the former to gain some experience in practical courses.[12] Such experience is important not only for the benefit it brings to the pupils, but for the effect it may have in preventing the growth of too sharp a distinction later between the white-collar workers and those engaged in practical occupations.

The Mission urges that, in the amalgamation of the present three varieties of schools, the importance of agriculture should be reflected by the attention paid to it in the comprehensive schools. In a Territory in which agriculture is, and for as far ahead as can be foreseen will be the mainstay of the economy and the sector in which the greater part of the people will be employed, the lack of any but an insignificant measure of agricultural orientation and education in the secondary schools is a striking omission. What is needed is not instruction in agricultural techniques, which may more properly be done in training institutions established specifically for that purpose, but, as has already been suggested earlier in connection with the curriculum of the primary school, the orientation of the school curriculum, especially in science, mathematics and social studies, to take account of this basic factor of life in the Territory. The core of orientation on agriculture at this stage will be science—

[12] To some extent this is already being done. There are 16 manual arts annexes (eight of them under native teachers) attached to post-primary and secondary schools.

botany, biology and soil chemistry—treated so as to show the general principles underlying the phenomena observable in the Territory and the practical applications and manifestations of such principles. The school grounds should be of sufficient size for practical work and demonstrations.

The Technical Stream.[13] For the development of the country's economy and the raising of the standards of living, there is no doubt of the need for an increase in education and training in technical subjects and trades of all types. This is indispensable for efficient operations, whether in building, manufacturing, storekeeping, maintaining vehicles and mechanical installations, or running a business, plantation or hospital. At present skilled and semi-skilled workers are almost all non-indigenes, mostly Australian. The resultant cost is high. Not only is the pay for technical or business employees higher in Australia than would be appropriate for similar levels of work in the developing economy of the Territory, but their cost in the latter is much higher than in Australia when the additional expenses on travel, housing, paid vacations, children's education, etc., are taken into account. The lack of indigenous skilled and semi-skilled personnel, and the high cost of expatriate clerks, salesmen and saleswomen, stenographers, typists, bookkeepers, foremen, tradesmen, etc., is a serious obstacle to the development of a viable business and manufacturing economy.

It is important, however, that the technical courses given should be specially designed to meet the needs of the emergent indigenes and not merely revised versions of courses in developed countries, in which the needs are likely to be very different. Attention must be paid not only to the introduction of new skills, but also to the conservation of existing and traditional skills and their development and adaptation to meet new needs. The technical curricula must not be concerned only with the trades of developed societies, although these will have an important place in them. They must take into account the basic occupations of the indigenes, namely farming and fishing, and seek to improve the productivity and the conditions under which these take place. This is to be done not only by the introduction of alien trades and skills, but by progressively improving indigenous forms of, for example, house and boat-building, bridging, decoration, wood carving, etc., introducing innovations while preserving the continuity of tradition.

Pupils now enter technical schools from Standard VI or above, most of the entrants being pupils who failed to gain entry to a secondary school.

---

[13] In addition to the technical education given in schools, the Departments of Agriculture, Stock and Fisheries, Forests, Public Health, Trade and Industry, Native Affairs, Post and Telegraphs and the Electricity Commission conduct courses relevant to their own activities. These are dealt with in appropriate sections of this report.

This fact is often lamented by protagonists of technical education. However, not only is it inevitable that the above-average pupils should be attracted to the more academic courses by the better ultimate prospects they offer but it is right that they should go to them since they are the avenue to the higher levels of all subjects, technical ones included. It must therefore be accepted that those who enter the technical streams are likely to be, for the most part, the less capable academically.

A substantial proportion of the pupils in technical courses is, and will continue to be, formed of apprentices, of whom, in 1963, there were 321 in training. Of the 142 placements made that year, 75 percent were in government work, and 25 percent in the private sector. Carpenters and joiners formed about one-third of the total, and diesel mechanics were a poor second, followed by plumbers and electricians. Notified vacancies numbered 186. Those who complete their apprenticeship and take the final trade examinations receive certificates qualifying them as skilled tradesmen, at standards approximating those in Australia.

While there must be some tradesmen with the highest levels of skill, it will only hold back development of the Territory's economy if standards similar to those in advanced countries are required for recognition as skilled tradesmen. The Mission therefore recommends careful consideration of how closely the standards of skilled tradesmen in the Territory should be related to those in Australia, with a view of determining the minimum standards acceptable at the present stage of development.

Additional Expenditures on Secondary Education. If the capital cost per place in a secondary school is taken as being £A210, the 9,000 additional places[14] recommended in Administration schools will require an investment of £A1.890 million. To this must be added the cost of teachers' houses, which are officially costed at £A6,000 for married quarters and £A1,600 for single ones. On the assumption that equal numbers of each would be needed, giving an average of £A3,800, housing for the 450 additional teachers[15] needed for Administration schools would amount to £A1.710 million making a total capital expenditure of £A3.6 million. The construction of a fair number of these houses from local materials with appropriate European improvements could result in substantial savings over the above estimates.

In 1962/63, the Education Department's recurrent expenditure on secondary education was £A695,100. This included £A20,450 grants-in-

[14] Excluding 1,400 places in 1964, for which we have assumed that provision will have been made before the start of the five-year period 1964/65–1968/69.

[15] Excluding 70 additional teachers in 1964, for which we have assumed that accommodation will have been provided before the start of the five-year period 1964/65–1968/69.

aid to missions. If this is deducted and allowance made for the part of the expenditure of £A350,370 for bursaries, subsidies and scholarships overseas which is not attributable to Administration secondary schools, it appears that, with a 1963 enrollment of 2,344 pupils, the average recurrent cost of a pupil in an Administration secondary school was about £A250 per year.[16] At this figure the increase in enrollment of 10,400 as projected above, would involve a rise during 1968/69 of approximately £A2.4 million in the recurrent costs of Administration secondary education, the total additional expenditure during 1964/65–1968/69 being £A7.1 million.[17]

The direct grants-in-aid paid to missions in support of secondary schools amounted to approximately £A13 per pupil in 1963. If account is taken of payments for maintenance of pupils and for books and equipment the total payment was probably about £A40. The Mission believes that a continued subvention of this order will not prove sufficient to induce or enable the missions to expand their secondary schools to the extent projected by the Department of Education. The choice would seem to be between raising the subvention to the mission schools to an adequate level or providing many of the places by increasing enrollment in Administration schools instead; it may be necessary to follow both courses of action.

There is a danger of underestimating the cost of the expansion program if the estimates are calculated at the present cost to the Administration of £A40 per mission-school pupil. Until this matter is clarified the Mission suggests a tentative cost of £A60 per pupil for the increased enrollment projected for mission secondary schools. On this basis, the cost to the Administration for the additional enrollment of 10,700 would be about £A550,000 by 1968/69. To this would need to be added about £A30,000 a year increased subvention in respect of the 1,534 pupils in mission secondary schools in 1963. The total additional subvention paid during 1964/65–1968/69 would be about £A1.5 million.[18] For the total secondary expansion program for both Administration and mission schools, the total additional recurrent expenditure during 1964/65–1968/69 thus amounts to approximately £A8.6 million.

With the expansion of secondary education, the practice of awarding 20 scholarships a year to mixed race and indigenous pupils to attend

[16] With an average enrollment of 828 in Administration technical schools the recurrent cost per pupil comes to £A225 per annum, or very similar to the cost of one in a secondary school.

[17] On the basis of enrollments as projected in Table 2; the amounts are on a fiscal-year basis as distinct from a school-year basis.

[18] On the basis of enrollments as projected in Table 2; the amounts are on a fiscal-year basis as distinct from a school-year basis.

secondary schools in Australia should be reviewed. The scholars are selected by competitive examination, so that the Territory secondary schools are deprived of the best of their potential entrants without any clear gain to the latter, there being no evidence that so radical a change of environment at a young age is of benefit to the pupils. In the years ahead, the need for scholarships will shift to the university level and it is the Mission's view that funds would be better spent on awards for post-secondary education.

In 1962, allowances were paid to assist about 1,250 non-indigenous children to attend secondary schools in Australia. With the increase in opportunities for secondary education in the Territory, the Mission recommends that the system of allowances be reviewed so that these become payable only when suitable education cannot be provided in the Territory.

Higher Education

There are no institutions at present giving what might properly be described as higher education, although the Papuan Medical College, with five students in its fourth year, is growing up to higher education status. An agricultural college at Vudal is planned for 1965. These two colleges are discussed in the chapters of the Mission's report on Health and Agriculture. Proposed Administrative and Co-operative Colleges are discussed below. Higher technical courses will be developed as entrants become available, and a considerable increase in correspondence courses, at the post-secondary level, will undoubtedly take place. The scarcity of numbers in the upper forms of secondary schools makes it clear that there can be no large-scale development of higher education during 1964–69, but a steady increase is to be expected.

A Higher Education Commission was appointed in 1963 and studied exhaustively the potentialities for the development of higher education. With a present population of over 2 million, and with a growth rate expected to rise above the present estimated rate of somewhat more than 2 percent, the Territory will ultimately have enough potential students to require a university. Pending publication of the Commission's report it would be premature to comment on the university itself. However, the Mission believes that there is nothing more central to the future progress of the Territory than leadership of a high caliber, some of which the staff and graduates of the university may be expected to provide. The Mission endorses the attention that is being devoted to the problems of higher education.

Two special institutions of a staff college nature are planned for Port Moresby; a Co-operative College and an Administrative College. The co-operative college for 150 students, to be conducted by the Department of Trade and Industry, is planned to take over and develop the work now being done by the Co-operative Educational Center. The college is to train cooperative officers, inspectors and other staff for the cooperatives and also provide training for bookkeepers, secretaries, clerks and store-keepers for both the public and private sectors. The capital cost is esti-mated at about £A200,000 and construction is scheduled for 1966/67. Recurrent expenditure for operations is estimated at £A60,000 per annum. The co-operative societies may be interested in assisting this training program by contributing annually 25 percent of the recurrent costs.

At the same time, plans are proceeding for an Administrative College for about 300 students to take over and expand the work of the present Public Service Institute. Courses in public administration, law, civics, land use, court procedures, local government, management and super-vision, community development and welfare work will be given. There will be courses in basic subjects such as English, mathematics, history, geography, clerical work, bookkeeping, shorthand and typing. But the preliminary plans also provide for the training of cooperative officers and the clerical courses appear to be of the same general type as those to be given by the co-operative college.

The need for training in the skills planned by both colleges is clear, and the Mission recommends that the Administration proceed to implement the programs. However, the Mission questions the need to establish two separate colleges with two separate sets of administrators, separate physical facilities and separate faculties. It is difficult to recruit qualified teachers, and the plans for two colleges appear not only wasteful of the teachers but unduly expensive. The Mission recommends that the Administration review the plans for the two colleges with the objective of merging the programs into one larger and stronger institution. In pro-jecting costs for the program, the Mission has used the estimated cost for the administrative college given as £A650,000 for the physical facilities plus a recurrent expenditure through 1968/69 of £A400,000. These costs should be reviewed and revised if the Mission's recommendation for one college rather than two is accepted.

Adult Education

Plans for educating the people would be incomplete if limited to the schools and related institutions. Substantial provision needs to be made, for assistance to young people and adults who have received no education or so little as to have gained no lasting benefit from it, to those who have had less than a full primary education, and to those who have completed the primary course or more but who should be encouraged to extend their education. Except for the last group, adult education will usually be closely related to the main sectors of indigenous life, and particularly to the preparation and execution of various projects to improve living standards. In the true sense these will be development projects, and relating adult education to development will have a double value; it will assist the execution of the projects and it will help the indigenes to learn. The fixing of clear objectives will provide incentives to effort and learning, while knowledge and skills can be transmitted more easily and effectively if their relevance to daily life and experience is obvious.

Adult education, as thus conceived, is only partially the responsibility of the Department of Education. The efforts will require the combined forces of many different government agencies, such as the Departments of Agriculture, Health, Native Affairs, Information and Extension Services and others, as well as the aid of private organizations. For the adults of the middle educational level—such people as field workers, trained farmers, aid post orderlies, and semi-skilled tradesmen—the educational effort should be related to their occupations and designed to encourage their progress and to assist them in overcoming local inertia. The education of this group would be in English, Pidgin English or Police Motu; written material would mostly need to be specially prepared. For the uneducated group—which at present comprises the mass of adults— education and training would center upon specific local development projects and largely take the form of on-the-job training and informal explanation and discussion, accompanied by information on achievements elsewhere. A major objective would be to arouse and maintain interest in development. For this group Pidgin English, Police Motu or vernaculars would be used.

The main objectives would be primarily utilitarian, but aesthetic activities should not be neglected; pride in the aesthetic qualities of home and village can be a valuable civilizing influence. In agriculture, the main items of interest would be land use and care, permanent, annual, sub- sistence and cash crops, forestry, livestock, tools, machinery, installations, transport and marketing. In health, attention would be paid to pre- vention, simple remedies, sanitation, hygiene, nutrition and child care. In housing, better uses of local materials would be shown and taught, together with the possibilities of making domestic life more comfortable by the use of furniture, mats and utensils which the indigenes could make for themselves. Homecrafts such as cooking, sewing and weaving would have a prominent place.

In formulating a policy to govern the effort to influence the economic, social and political advance of the indigenes, two major adult educational problems are the questions of what motivation may be employed, and of how existing beliefs which obstruct progress may be overcome. Since in their traditional societies the indigenes have few possessions, and even of these the most valuable are generally owned not by individuals but by groups, acquisitiveness may not be a strong enough trait to call forth the effort needed to raise standards of living above the traditional levels. Cargo cults and the ubiquitous belief in magic, through the expectation they foster of fulfillment of desire by supernatural means, deter from laborious effort, and obstruct the introduction of new ways and new ideas.

As motivation to effort and change, it would be unfortunate if only the incentive of personal gain came to be adopted. A supporting incentive might be to build upon the widespread native tradition of acquiring status by giving gifts. This tradition might be transformed into a concept of prestige through social service, the gift-giving being extended beyond the traditional items of shells and pigs to include services—such as those rendered by teachers, nurses, extension workers and others. The belief in magic will require the combined efforts of science and religion to eradicate and replace by more rational and enlightened concepts.

Example will be more effective than precept in stimulating the indigenes to progress out of their traditional ways, and in showing them how to do this. Several programs of the sort this Mission has in mind are already under way: the Department of Agriculture, for instance, has a training program for farmers who, upon their return to their homes, are expected to set an example to their fellow villagers. Proposals for the strengthening and expansion of this program are made in this report in Chapter 3, dealing with Agriculture.

Another means already employed of helping the uneducated or partly educated is the community technical school, of which two are operated by the Administration, one in New Britain and the other near Wewak. These do not require any fixed standard of entry—even literacy—and aim to give youths and adults training in any skills a community may feel it needs, such as building better homes of local materials, brick and furniture-making and vehicle repair. They do not have elaborate facilities, and when the need is met in one area the staff may be transferred elsewhere. The Mission would like to see this type of activity extended as soon as indigenous staff become available.

With the similar objective of introducing into the villages improved standards in housing and domestic life, a training program for selected married couples has been undertaken by the Department of Native Affairs. The Mission believes that this program, if organized on a larger and broader scale, and linked to other programs of the types just described, offers a promising potential as a prime mechanism for stimulating village development. The Mission can envisage the expansion of this training to include all the main aspects of village life, including agriculture, livestock, health, hygiene, nutrition, child care, housing, water supply and cooking.

The Mission can visualize a dedicated corps of men and women—perhaps even called a Development Corps—whose full-time duties would be to promote at village level economic, political, social and personal development. It can conceive of training institutions for this corps which would reproduce the conditions of village life, with family gardens and houses of local materials, though built to higher standards. The Mission puts forward such a scheme as being worthy of serious consideration, and would urge appropriate experimentation to test its feasibility and, if this is proved, to work out the details of a practical program.

To the Mission, the most logical approach would be to plan the program around groups of primary schools, each group being served by a development corps member. Where a primary school exists, there is need for a continuation center, which would be both the cultural focus of the area served by the school and the local forum for the planning and discussion of development projects and related topics. The primary school teachers could be expected to take an active part in the work of the centers, but normally they probably would not be in sole charge of them. To do so might make calls upon their time which would unduly curtail their school activities, and they would often, not having progressed beyond primary school themselves, lack the education as well as the training needed to run such centers. It is conceivable that, on an average, each development corps member could serve five centers a week, spending one evening a week in each. On this basis a program, to cover the full population served by Administration or approved mission schools, would require some 350–375 corps members or couples within five years.

Experimentation will be needed to discover what sort of person would be most suitable for such a corps. In the beginning, at least, the Mission suggests the most appropriate level of education and training would be Form 3 of high school (i.e., ten years of schooling) followed by perhaps a one-year course of training. An essential part of such training should be personal confrontation with examples of development among analogous peoples and conditions. Such an experience both gives guidance in practice and stimulates the imagination to set objectives and to work for their achievement. Until some parts of the Territory have advanced sufficiently to serve as centers for such visits, recourse must be had to areas overseas. Fortunately, there are suitable places not far removed from the Territory—Malaya, Samoa, Fiji, for example—so that the transport expenses involved would not be high.

For young people and adults who have had a complete primary education or more—a group to be found mostly in professional and semi-professional occupations such as medical assistants, teachers and extension workers—the great need is for reading matter. Public libraries are but little developed, there being a central library in Port Moresby and 11 branches throughout the Territory with a total of 54,000 volumes—about one book per 40 inhabitants. Estimated expenditure on library books and periodicals amounted to only £A8,800 in 1963/64. Adequate supplies of reading material are indispensable if those leaving primary school are not to relapse into illiteracy. The Mission recommends the spending of £A20,000 per year on the purchase of books for public libraries, the provision of 6 mobile services, and the establishment of 25 branch libraries and 60 new village centers, during the five-year period.

Coordination of Adult Education. The importance of adult education and the variety of its ramifications were recognized by the establishment in June 1963 of an Adult Education Council, composed of representatives of the Department of Education, Native Affairs, the Administrator, Information and Extension Services, the Public Service Commissioner, indigenous groups and voluntary organizations. Among other duties, the council is given responsibility for developing adult education and for coordinating all Administration activities in this field. The Departments of Agriculture and Health, which are not only active in adult education but represent two of the most important segments of the work which needs to be done, are not represented on the council.

The time is appropriate for reconsideration of policy and activities in the field of adult education. As a first step, the Mission recommends that representatives of the Departments of Agriculture and Health be added to the Adult Education Council, and that this council be made responsible for advising on budget requirements for adult education activities of the various departments concerned. The council should serve as a forum for the exchange of ideas and for the suggestion of lines along which coordinated development might take place.

The council should not, however, be given the responsibility for coordinating the educational and training aspects of projects in the field. Neither should any one operating department have such responsibility, since all facets of indigenous life will be involved and much of the educational effort will be directly related to practical projects which may involve several interests. It is the Mission's recommendation that the District Commissioner should assume responsibility for the education and training associated with development projects in his district. The Mission recommends further the appointment in each district of an adult-education officer responsible to the District Commissioner, and charged with the coordination of adult-educational work associated with development projects. This officer will need assistance in achieving the inter-departmental coordination involved, as well as that between the public and the private sectors. It is possible that the Native Affairs Department might be organized and oriented to provide the assistance needed, calling upon the resources of the other departments.

Radio and Television

Printed matter is of no use with illiterates; films can be shown only in the few parts in which the transport of projectors and generators is easy and economic; and personal contact is by its nature restricted and would thus be limited even if adequate numbers of trained staff were available— which they are not. With transistor receivers, however, broadcasts can be heard easily, and as the only universal means of ready communication with the indigenes throughout the Territory, radio has clearly therefore a great potential for adult and school educational purposes.

This potential is already being exploited. Broadcasting is carried out by the Australian Broadcasting Corporation (ABC) and by the Administration. The ABC operates a 10 KW transmitter at Port Moresby and also a 2 KW transmitter at Rabaul which is due to be replaced by one of 10 KW. It employs a staff of 70 and operated in 1962/63 on a budget of £A109,000. Until recently, the ABC's broadcasts were intended mainly for the Europeans in the Territory and the programs were of the type which Australians would expect in their own country. During the last year or so, much more attention has been paid to broadcasting for the indigenes. News broadcasts are made in Pidgin English and in Police Motu as well as in English. There are programs of native music and regular broadcasts to schools. The programs for these are devised by the Department of Education and are very valuable in the teaching of such subjects as English and Music.

Apart from these broadcasts, the Administration has felt the need for broadcasts in local languages so that indigenes who do not speak English, Pidgin English or Police Motu might be informed of matters both within the Territory and outside it which might be of interest and concern to them. Use is, therefore, being made of the Department of Posts and Telegraphs' transmitters at Rabaul and Wewak after normal working hours. During 1964–69, the Department of Information and Extension Services, which is responsible for the Administration broadcasts, proposes to increase its activities until it offers 20 different programs.[19]

[19] The additional stations envisaged are: Kerema, Mt. Hagen (two channels), Daru, Goroka (two channels), Madang, Vanimo, Lae, Milne Bay, Bougainville, Popondetta, Mendi, Kavieng, Kainantu, Central District, Talasea and Wabag.

In addition to the ABC and the Administration, some of the missions desire to establish broadcasting services and there is a possibility that commercial enterprises might also become interested. A proposal is therefor under consideration for the establishment of a Territory Broadcasting Control Board which would be responsible for establishing new stations where the need exists, particularly in areas now served inadequately by the ABC, for the allocation of frequencies, for the licensing of stations and for the control of programs from those stations not operated by the ABC or the Administration.

In respect of this last objective, the Mission considers it important that the possibility of reaching the indigenes at the local level should not be restricted to official programs. As the sole means of widespread communication among an almost illiterate adult population, radio is clearly of primary importance as a means of conveying information and of forming public opinion. As such, a free radio is of the same importance as a free press in literate countries. It cannot be denied that problems will result if diverse and perhaps conflicting statements and ideas are put out by stations operated by different interests. The way to solve these, however, is not by control of programs. The way to make the indigenes develop mental alertness and critical abilities, so that they will be able to make good judgments for themselves, is not to restrict their experience to approved versions of facts and ideas. It is rather to exercise them in comparing and weighing differing versions, and attempting to discern the truth or error of each. Even if programs within the Territory were controlled, those emanating from outside it could not be, while the establishment of a virtual monopoly of the only universal means of communication does not appear prudent.

This Mission supports in principle the establishment of a network of radio stations capable of giving better coverage than can be obtained with the present installations. It considers that the ABC and the Administration have complementary roles to play in the production of broadcast programs, and that effective machinery for consultation between them should be established to ensure that in the installation and operation of transmitters the resources of both bodies should be used in the most economic and effective manner.

Even the radio, however, able as it is to reach all parts of the Territory, is of limited effect. The impact is solely aural and, if attention on the part of the listeners is not to lag, a very high proportion of the time in the programs must be given to entertainment. Experience seems to suggest that only a few minutes of talk at a time can be given if the indigenes' attention is to be retained. By contrast, television has both a visual and an aural impact and its attractive power is enormously greater than that of radio.

Television does not yet exist and there are no plans for installing it. Just because television is one of the most recent developments of life in advanced countries, however, it should not be thought of as a service to be expected only in such countries. In transport, the Territory uses the most modern means—the airplane—on a large scale, in the most primitive areas and for the most mundane purposes. If television is able to do, in the field of communication of knowledge and ideas, the sort of work which the airplane has done in transport, then there is no reason why it should not be introduced even in the most primitive areas.

A great gulf exists between the knowledge, customs and ideas of the indigenes of the Territory and those of advanced countries. If this gulf is to be bridged only by personal communication or, as education touches more and more of the people, by the spread of print and pictorial matter, decades must pass before any significant development occurs amongst the majority of the indigenes. Television would be particularly valuable in the schools. It could contribute to an improvement in the quality of the teachers by enabling them to see how material was handled by experts. It would bring to every pupil the best teaching available and it would introduce to the pupils facts and concepts difficult or impossible to impart otherwise.

Experience with the use of television in education is rapidly being gained in many countries, notably in the United States, Italy and Japan, and enough confidence in the medium has been established for the United States Government to go ahead with plans to set up a schools television network in American Samoa, with the object of presenting the complete core of the curriculum by this means. These facts warrant serious consideration being given to the possibilities of employing television in the Territory.

The practical difficulties and costs of establishing television coverage for the schools cannot at this stage be assessed. Some parts of the Territory, such as the Gazelle Peninsula, the Port Moresby area, Manus and parts of the Sepik River valley offer a high concentration of population without natural obstacles to transmission and reception. There are prospects for the future development of larger battery-powered receivers than are at present available. The Mission recommends that a technical survey of the television potential be made and that, if the results in any way justify it, one or more pilot projects be started.

Organization

The organization of the Administration's educational activities is efficient and the Mission has only a few modifications to suggest. The recommended transfer of responsibility for pre-school education to the

Department of Education from that of Health will involve some minor adjustments in staffing, while development of comprehensive secondary schools will call for some measure of integration between the secondary and technical divisions of the Department of Education.

There is a great need for research into the problems of educating the people of Papua and New Guinea. Reference has been made in the discussion of primary education to the need for the establishment in the Department of Education of a research and production unit to deal with curricula, textbooks and teaching material and aids. The work of this unit should not be limited to primary education but should cover secondary and adult education as well. It should also promote educational research in general into, for example, the knowledge, beliefs, attitudes, motivations, etc., of the native people; material outside the latter's environment which is of particular relevance in their development; and methods and media of communicating knowledge and skills to the indigenes and of stimulating activity on their part. In collaboration with the teacher-training division, the unit could assist European teachers in gaining an understanding of the beliefs, customs and languages of the people among whom they work. Acquaintance with these will make the teachers' work among both children and adults easier and more effective.

The present system of ranking teachers in the same grades as other members of the Public Service, and having them theoretically subject to the same regulations, appears to need some modification. The Public Service working hours do not fit with the school timetables nor with the practice, normal among teachers, of preparing lessons at home and of taking home exercises to correct in the evening. The Public Service leave arrangements do not suit the requirements of the school calendar and the Administration has already found it necessary to offer expatriate teachers an annual passage to Australia to avoid the disruption of school work which would be caused if any large number of them followed the normal Public Service leave pattern—as they are entitled to do—and were absent for three months every two years. Nor does it seem that the Public Service salary scales are always appropriate. The Mission therefore recommends that a Teachers' Branch be established within the Public Service, with appropriate regulations as to salary, leave, working dates and hours, and duties.

Also, some reorganization of the system of inspection appears desirable. At present the primary, secondary and technical divisions of the Department of Education all maintain their own inspectorial staff and are responsible for the inspection of schools pertaining to their divisions. A unified Inspectorate would effect savings, not only in travel, but in the time of the limited numbers of highly qualified specialists in the Department of Education. The savings would be particularly noticeable as comprehensive schools are developed. Such an inspectorate would rest upon recognition of the basic fact that in most cases an inspector need not be a specialist in the subject taught in order to form an opinion of whether the teacher is reasonably competent or whether he is exceptionally good or otherwise. It is in either of the last two cases that inspection is needed by a specialist. At the district level, the District Education Officer should be the senior general inspector as well as the senior administrative officer for schools and education of all levels and types; in most cases it will be necessary to supply him with an administrative assistant. The Mission recommends the creation of a unified inspectorate, and the assumption by the District Education Officer of the ultimate responsibility, to the District Commissioner and to the Director of Education, for all educational institutions in his area.

Summary of Proposed Expenditures

The expansion of the educational system, as recommended herein, will lead in particular to a rise in current expenditures; a summary of these expenditures is provided in Table 4. The item "Existing Level" represents total budget expenditures of the Department of Education for 1963/64.

In the context of secondary education, we recommend the abolition of scholarships for attending secondary schools in Australia; this might result in a reduction of expenditures of about £A50,000 a year, and this adjustment is reflected in the figures in Table 4.

In view of the substantial expansion of the educational system, the Mission anticipates an expansion of the administrative division at headquarters; to allow for this and for the recommended research and production unit, we have assumed for planning purposes that by 1968/69 expenditures would have risen by one half over the level of 1963/64 of about £A360,000. Assuming further that this increase would occur regularly over the period, this implies an average annual additional requirement of £A108,000, as compared to 1963/64.

Not all current expenditures for education are included in the budget of the Department of Education. The most important exception is Vocabulary Stores, the budget estimate for which was £A320,000 in 1963/64.[20] The Mission has no firm basis for projecting this item, but has, for planning purposes, assumed once more that the level might rise by one half by 1968/69; this estimate, like that for Administration headquarters, may in due course require substantial revision. We have also

[20] Included in the budget of the Treasury Department, Stores and Supply Branch.

TABLE 4: Current Expenditures on Education

(£A thousand)

	1963/64 (Budget)	1968/69	1964/65–1968/69 Total	1964/65–1968/69 Annual Average
Existing Level	4,150	4,150	20,750	4,150
Pre-school Program	40	40	200	40
Additional:				
Primary Education				
Administration Schools		575	1,935	387
Mission Schools		400	1,645	329
Secondary Education				
Administration Schools		2,400	7,100	1,420
Mission Schools		580	1,500	300
Abolition Scholarships		−50	−250	−50
Administration Headquarters		180	540	108
Total Department of Education	4,190	8,275	33,420	6,684
Vocabulary Stores	320	480	2,080	416
Library Books	9	20	100	20
Total	4,519	8,775	35,600	7,120

added £A20,000 annually for library books in accordance with our recommendation.[21]

The additional expenditures for primary and secondary education have been discussed earlier in this chapter.

The Mission has not attempted to make a specific budgetary allowance for a possible Development Corps. We believe it would be premature before the Administration will have had an opportunity to consider the merits of the proposed program of adult education.

Capital expenditures on education by the Administration have been summarized in Table 5. The basis of the various estimates has been explained earlier.

In this chapter we also mentioned the plans for the establishment of an Administrative College, involving capital expenditures of £A650,000 and current expenditures of £A400,000 over the five-year period. We have not included these amounts under education, a procedure also followed for other colleges that will be established.[22]

[21] To be included in the budget of the Department of Information and Extension Services.

[22] Current expenditures will be included in the budget of the Department of the Public Service Commissioner and capital expenditures will appear under Capital Works and Services.

TABLE 5: Capital Expenditures on Education

(£A thousand)

	1964/65–1968/69	
	Total	Annual Average
Primary Education		
Schools and Ancillary Buildings	100	20
Furniture and Equipment	75	15
Secondary Education		
Schools	1,890	378
Teacher Houses	1,710	342
Total	3,775	755

CHAPTER 7 *HEALTH, HOUSING, WATER SUPPLY AND SEWERAGE*

HEALTH

Health services, and especially curative services, have been given high priority by the Administration in the allocation of resources—personnel and funds. This policy coupled with the initiative and drive of the highly skilled staff of the Department of Public Health has produced an extensive public health service. The department is the Administration's largest employer of personnel and its share of the Administration's expenditure has, in many years since World War II, exceeded or approached one-fifth of the total. During recent years, the proportion has been going down from 16 percent in 1958/59 to 14 percent in 1962/63; the estimate for 1963/64 works out about 12 percent.[1] In spite of the falling trend, expenditure on health is still very substantial compared to that on other activities.

Although it is recognized that health services, especially effective health services, are expensive, the Mission believes that programs to improve health conditions deserve a continued high priority. However, these considerations in themselves cannot justify expansion at the rate of recent years. In the present context, the department must be considered in competition with others for funds and trained manpower. To accomplish the objective of making the Territory better able to stand on its own feet economically greater attention must now be given to increasing productive capacity. The costs of public health must be geared more realistically to the future ability of the native population to pay a substantial part of the costs of the medical program. Under these criteria, the question of whether additional physical facilities are needed requires careful consideration. In the Mission's opinion the building of additional hospital facilities should stop. The Department of Public Health should make do with the existing hospital facilities and should continue to give priority to the training of personnel and to programs aimed at preventing disease.

[1] The percentages include expenditures on health not included in the budget of the Department of Public Health, but do not or not fully include drawings on Vocabulary Stores (various supplies), for which 1 to 2 percent has to be added in each year.

Present Health Conditions

Comprehensive vital statistics are understandably lacking but it is estimated that the crude birth rate has been between 40 to 50 per thousand, the crude death rate between 30 to 40 per thousand, and the expectation of life from 30 to 40 years. The over-all rate of population increase is now estimated at about 2 percent annually, but in areas where special effort has been made to improve health and nutrition it has reached 5 percent. The infant mortality rate, which is generally regarded as a sensitive index of the state of public health, is not known for the Territory as a whole but there are wide local variations. In Port Moresby, it is less than 40 per 1,000 live births, whereas in rural areas it is seldom less than 100, usually between 200 and 300, and higher in isolated areas. Fifty percent of all deaths are reported to occur in children under five years of age.

As regards physical health, which is improving but still leaves much to be desired, the Territory is entirely free from the six quarantinable diseases: plague, cholera, yellow fever, smallpox, relapsing fever and typhus.

The lack of comprehensive health statistics renders impossible an accurate estimate of the incidence and prevalance of major diseases but sufficient knowledge is available to give a good general picture. In the Territory as a whole, malaria is the greatest single public health problem and the most important cause of ill health. An estimated two-thirds of the population live in areas where the disease is endemic and most of the remainder in areas where it may occur in epidemic form. Respiratory diseases such as tuberculosis, pneumonia, bronchitis, and influenza come next, and the third important group includes those commonly associated with ignorance of elementary hygiene such as leprosy, malnutrition, skin diseases, trachoma and various kinds of gastroenteritis, dysentery and intestinal parasitism including hookworm. Many infectious diseases are notifiable by law, those most commonly reported being, in order of frequency: influenza, infantile diarrhea, measles, pulmonary tuberculosis, chickenpox, unclassified dysenteries and whooping cough.

In general, the diet is deficient in protein, especially animal protein. In some areas, gross nutritional disorders are most often found in young children, especially after weaning, and in child-bearing women who seldom receive the additional nourishment their condition requires and from whom the little available meat is actually sometimes withheld because of taboos.

There is one disease peculiar to the Territory, kuru, a degenerative disease of the nervous system which affects mostly women and children in one particular tribe of some 20,000 people. It is always fatal and kills about 1 percent of the women in the tribe each year. Necrotizing jejunitis, an uncommon but highly dangerous disease of the intestine which appears to follow the eating of decomposing pig meat, is also found in the Territory. Research on both is continuing.

Despite the continued widespread occurrence of disease, there have been significant advances in public health since World War II. With the spread of health services and education there is developing in the native people a growing confidence in the power of scientific medicine to deal with conditions which were formerly treated, if at all, by traditional means such as benign sorcery. Yaws, which in many areas affected large numbers of children in the immediate post-war years, has been almost eradicated. The prevalence of tropical ulcer has been greatly reduced by aid posts and other facilities which provide prompt first aid for cuts and wounds and other gross skin diseases have greatly diminished; 550,000 people live in areas protected against malaria; the infant mortality rate has been reduced in some areas and a systematic attempt to improve rural water supplies has commenced.

A general conclusion is difficult to formulate because of the extreme variations between different parts of the Territory. It can be said, however, that the state of the public health, which was very poor in 1945, has improved to the point where it is neither markedly worse nor markedly better than in most developing countries.

Organization of Health Services

Health services are provided primarily by the Administration, supplemented by the work of the Christian Missions. Central direction comes from the Department of Public Health in Port Moresby. The Territory is divided into four regions, each administered by a Regional Medical Officer (RMO) and each having a large base hospital. The RMO's are responsible to the Director, but have the authority and responsibility to conduct the day-to-day medical and health services of their regions on their own initiative.

The regions in turn are divided into three, four or five districts, each under a District Medical Officer (DMO) who has the responsibility of providing an integrated service in his district, both curative and preventive. Each district headquarters has a hospital with at least one doctor and some trained nurses. The curative services reach the grassroots through a network of sub-district and rural hospitals which are simple in design and service, and a large number of medical aid posts which are even simpler. The preventive services operate partly through these static units but also through half a dozen rural health centers, 15 static infant welfare clinics, and a large number of mobile teams.

The Hospital Program

At the end of World War II, civilian medical and health services had virtually ceased to exist and hardly any pre-war hospital buildings remained. The Territory had been an active theater of war and materials from some military hospitals were re-used for civilian hospitals. In the smaller centers of population the urgent need for curative services was met by rapid construction of native-material buildings; the roof and walls of grass, the floor of beaten earth and with wooden trestles or sleeping platforms in place of beds.

By 1947, within two years of the formation of the Department of Public Health, 55 Administration hospitals were in existence including five European and three Asian for paying patients. Some 121,000 persons were admitted during the year. The commonest causes of admission were skin diseases many of which could have been treated on an out-patient basis if roads had existed and the patients could have moved back and forth from their villages to the hospital. By 1952, there were 75 hospitals, including 13 paying hospitals (ten European and three Asian) and some 95,000 persons were in-patients.

In 1951, a hospital rebuilding plan was formulated to replace the native-material buildings with more permanent structures which would have a longer life, which could more easily be kept clean and free from vermin, and in which better scientific and more hygienic treatment could be given. During the latter half of the 1950s, many of the native-material hospitals were replaced with permanent buildings and equipment and, at the same time, new hospitals were built, some with native materials. By 1962 there were 100 Administration hospitals, 89 general and 11 special, total admissions were 104,000 and the daily average number of in-patients was 7,700.

Three of the four base hospitals—Port Moresby, Rabaul (Nonga) and Lae—have been completely rebuilt since 1955. The fourth base hospital, for the Highlands District, is at Goroka. The Administration plans to replace this old hospital which was constructed mainly of local materials. The plan calls for construction based on standards equal to the other three at a cost of about £A870,000.

There are also 11 district hospitals (there are, in fact, 15 districts but the base hospitals serve the other four districts). The hospitals at Madang, Wewak and Daru have been completely rebuilt in recent years, and the rebuilding of three others as well as minor works on the remainder is planned. Except for specialists, a district hospital normally provides the same services as a base hospital, though supposedly on a more modest scale. However, both Madang (336 beds) and Wewak possess self-contained operating blocks including three operating theaters and the full range of ancillary rooms, the theaters being air-conditioned, and Wewak Hospital with 376 beds, completed in 1962 at a cost of £A768,500, exceeds Rabaul base hospital in bed capacity and cost.

There are 36 hospitals located at sub-district headquarters which are much smaller and simpler than the district hospitals. About half have an X-ray unit and have a doctor in charge. The 38 other hospitals are simple rural hospitals built of native materials and each is in the charge of a medical assistant.

Out-patients attending Administration general hospitals have increased very substantially and the totals for 1947, 1952, 1957 and 1962 were reported as: 66,500, 89,900, 191,950 and 418,100, respectively.

For each of the four regions the base hospital provides specialist services such as surgery, medicine, pathology, opthalmology and radiology (the Port Moresby General Hospital only provides specialized radiology services), the specialists acting both within the hospital and as consultants to other hospitals in the region. The Port Moresby General Hospital was completed as two wings in 1957 and 1958 at a cost of £A1.2 million. It has 412 beds, and provides additional specialist services for the whole Territory in pediatrics, radiotherapy, psychiatry, and anesthetics and is the teaching hospital for the Papuan Medical College. The base hospital at Rabaul was completed in 1958 at a cost of £A522,000 and has beds for 316 non-paying patients, plus an old annex for paying patients which it is planned will be replaced by a new wing. The base hospital at Lae, to be completed in 1964, has 412 beds and the final cost will be close to £A1 million. All three are well planned, constructed to European standards and have the departments usual in major hospitals such as operating theaters, X-ray departments, laboratories, etc. Each includes a training school for nurses.

There are also 11 Administration special hospitals, one for mental cases and the remainder for leprosy and long-term tuberculosis patients, which are staffed and operated by the Christian Missions but the expenses of which are met by the Administration. On June 30, 1963, it was reported that these 11 hospitals had 3,260 beds in all, roughly two-thirds of them being housed in permanent buildings.

Supplementing the Administration's installations are 88 general hospitals, and five special hospitals for leprosy and tuberculosis patients maintained by the Christian Missions. Practically all of them receive Administration subsidies for trained staff, drugs and dressings, but a subsidy is granted only when the Administration is satisfied that the hospital is located where a real need exists and where Administration services will not be duplicated. Normally, therefore, mission hospitals are established after prior consultation.

Traditionally, mission medical services have operated on the concept of the hospital or fixed unit and their work has been almost entirely curative. It is estimated that the missions do approximately 30 percent of all the curative work, toward the cost of which the Administration contributes about 10 percent of the Department of Public Health's budget. Only in the last few years have the missions developed preventive health programs on a significant scale.

The mission hospitals vary widely, from modern very well-equipped buildings of European standard to native-material huts where missionaries, who are not doctors, do useful work with a minimum of equipment. That the latter is by far the larger category is shown by the fact that, although all the large hospitals have a doctor (except a few which are attempting to obtain one), there were only 18 mission doctors on June 30, 1963.

Perhaps because of the lack of medical personnel, the available statistical returns of the number of in-patients and out-patients handled by the mission hospitals appears unreliable, but it is estimated that the number of out-patients at mission hospitals may have been in the region of half a million in 1962/63.

Review of the Hospital Program

The heavy backlog of untreated disease at the end of World War II necessitated that the emphasis should be on curative services. The Department of Public Health's success in the face of tremendous difficulties in quickly covering the Territory with a network of health installations, using the materials at hand, was a remarkable achievement.

The seemingly large number of rural hospitals is due to the absence of roads, which often made the provision of many small units the only alternative to doing nothing. A large number of people were admitted as patients because it was physically impossible for them to receive treatment as out-patients. However, the erection of buildings should not outstrip the availability of trained staff: each sub-district hospital should have a doctor or assistant medical officer (AMO) and each rural hospital at least a medical assistant together with other trained personnel. In mid-1963, 15 of the sub-district hospitals, one of which had 160 beds, were without a doctor.

Until recent years, any figure for the total number of hospital beds would have been largely fictitious and the department preferred to record the number of persons treated rather than the number of beds. This was because the sleeping platforms accommodated varying numbers of patients and, to complicate the picture, a patient's family would often move into the hospital with him. However, the department has estimated that in September 1963 there were in the Administration hospitals, 7,240 beds and in the hospitals of the Christian Missions, 3,500, a total of some 10,740. There was, therefore, one hospital bed for each 186 of the population, a ratio that is about the same as in Greece and far exceeds that in most African countries, the Philippines (810), Indonesia (1,280) and India (2,000).

It may, however, be questioned whether all beds should be counted. Of the 89 Administration general hospitals, 38 are classed as rural. They are by intention simple buildings giving minimum service, have no doctor in charge and in most countries would be called dispensaries. In addition, 12 sub-district hospitals with approximately 800 beds are in rural areas and classified as dispensary beds. But even when their bed capacity (estimated at 2,700 in all) and the bed capacity of comparable mission hospitals (estimated at about 2,000) are deducted from the total, a ratio of one bed to each 330 people is obtained. The conclusion seems inescapable that Papua and New Guinea possess, in respect to coverage and ratio of beds to population, a medical service more closely approximating European rather than South East Asian standards.

The Mission believes that there has been over-building of hospitals and an extension of hospital facilities at a rate faster than could be properly staffed and effectively used. The Mission also believes that the adoption of Australian standards for the larger new hospitals was not appropriate in the conditions: these buildings are luxurious, unrelated to the standards of most of the people, and the costs are very high, much higher than the Territory without substantial aid has any prospect of being able to afford in the future. The elaborate new hospitals at Madang, Wewak and Daru could have been simpler structures built at considerably less cost.

While recognizing that hospital facilities are not everywhere satisfactory and that improvements are required, the Mission recommends that in the future the standards of hospital construction should be related not to those demanded in Australia but to standards that would be acceptable in the Territory and which in the longer run it would be able to afford.

In the light of the foregoing, it is the opinion of the Mission that the best interests of the Territory would be served by a policy of constraint in regard to hospital capacity, and the Mission recommends that there should in general be no expansion of hospital capacity during the next five years. In particular, the reconstruction of the Goroka Hospital to the standards proposed does not seem warranted, but more modest improvements there and at other centers will be needed. The Mission recommends that capital expenditures on hospital improvements should be limited to about £A100,000 annually over the next five years. This sum does not include expenditures on capital works which are now in the course of construction, nor does it include the new paying wing at the Port Moresby General Hospital, whose construction is linked with the provision of facilities for the Papuan Medical College. Expenditures under these two headings are estimated at £A310,000 and £A210,000, respectively, and the Mission recommends that these amounts should also be provided in the development program.

The Mission also recognizes that for social and political reasons the Administration may wish to proceed with the reconstruction of the Goroka Hospital to the standards of the other base hospitals, and with the construction of the Laloki Mental Hospital to serve the Territory as a whole. Consideration is also being given to the Donadabu Hospital (for hansenide and tuberculosis patients) near Port Moresby. In the context of the program for economic development, the Mission is unable to endorse these projects for the reasons given above. If, however, they are implemented, additional expenditures of about £A1.5 million will be incurred over the period of the program.

Charges for Medical Services

All hospital services in the Territory are free except in the annexes for paying patients, which originally were reserved for the non-indigenous population but which for some years have been open to all patients who can and wish to pay. The Administration and the Department of Public Health have given considerable thought to the problem of formulating a payment scheme for the hospital system as a whole, but so far none of the plans put forward have been tested in action.

The hospital and medical program is expensive and absorbs a substantial part of the total budget. The cost will continue to climb and will take a greater proportion of the budget unless action is taken to hold the line on the medical program. Also the native people, in addition to the Europeans, should begin to make some form of payment for the services and drugs they receive. The budget of the Department of Public Health for 1963/64 included £A495,000 for drugs and dressings; in addition, £A603,000 was allocated in the budget of the Treasury Department among Vocabulary Stores for use by the Department of Public Health and the missions. Payment for any portion of supplies provided directly to patients will represent a saving. The native people pay little or no taxes but they have the benefit of the very high-standard medical program. The Mission believes that it is important in the development of responsibilities in a modern society that the native people should not be led increasingly to expect that all services provided by government should be free. To the contrary the Administration, in the development of the people for the time when they will determine their political future, should place greater responsibility on them for the payment of services they receive from the State. The Mission believes that all people who are now earning money by working or producing cash crops should pay a reasonable charge for hospital services and drugs. The Mission also believes that most of the indigenes who do not have cash can and should make a payment in kind for hospital services and drugs. These payments in cash or kind may be small at first but should be more proportional to the cost as the economic position of the people improves. The Mission has a firm belief that the objective justifies every reasonable effort to think through and evolve a practicable system of payment.

The Mission recognizes that there are difficulties involved in such a scheme. When payment is required the people may urge higher standards of public health facilities or they may, at first, resent payment and turn against the Administration. The Mission suggests, therefore, that the payment scheme be tested in one or more areas before it is adopted as a Territory policy. This will afford an opportunity to gain experience in the formula to be used and in meeting the administrative problems that are certain to arise.

Health Centers

A recent development in the health services has been the establishment of rural health centers from which trained workers can bring problems of public health and preventive medicine to the people. The Department of Public Health plans to establish a chain of such centers throughout the Territory, progressively transforming rural hospitals into health centers. The Mission supports this concept. The health centers are intended to have a minimum staff of one AMO or one medical assistant, two infant welfare nurses, and one assistant sanitary inspector. It is the policy of the Administration to have the local communities provide the land and buildings and to have the Local Government Councils in proportion to their resources, take the responsibility for a growing share of the costs of operating the centers. This policy gives the local communities and councils the opportunity of assuming not only more responsibility but greater participation in the affairs of government. The Mission wholeheartedly endorses this policy.

By mid-1963, six rural health centers were in successful operation, one in New Ireland, two in New Britain near Rabaul, two in the Eastern Highlands and the sixth on the south coast of Papua. These centers have rightly been located where a network of access roads exists and have been provided with their own transport. The Administration's target for expansion is about five each year for the next five years. In addition to the contributions from the local communities and councils, the cost to the Administration would be about £A85,000.

Besides the rural health centers, the Department of Public Health is planning to establish health centers in the principal towns to provide the basis for services such as health education, child care, etc., and considering the expected growth of population in the towns, the Mission supports the establishment of such centers. A center for Rabaul is scheduled for 1964/65, to be followed by a center for Lae. It is tentatively estimated that each center will cost about £A60,000.

Aid Posts

At the base of the pyramid of health installations are the aid posts, of which there were on June 30, 1963, almost 1,900 including those maintained by the missions. The aid post consists typically of native material buildings: a dispensary, a storehouse, a residence for the Aid Post Orderly (APO) and a few beds for sick persons. Normally the community is expected to provide the land and buildings, i.e., an aid post is established only when there is to some extent a felt need.

The APO is typically a young man with a few years of primary education who receives 18 months' special training in a school for APO's and is then assigned to an aid post. His duties are to provide first aid, give simple treatment for common disease (malaria, gastroenteritis, bronchitis, skin diseases, etc.), refer more difficult cases to the nearest hospital and set an example to the community in sanitation and elementary hygiene. He returns to a rural hospital once a month for more drugs and dressings and is meant to be supervised in his own aid post once every three months by the medical assistant in charge of the hospital, but in practice this has sometimes proved impossible owing to lack of communications. He is expected to be always available to the community but is actually a part-time worker as he spends a portion of his time working in his garden to produce the food he eats.

As more rural health centers are established, the present system of aid posts will gradually become subordinate to the health center program. Although most of the work of the APO's has, until now, been curative, it is intended that they should be integrated into the preventive health service. As more rural health centers are established, some aid posts in the corresponding areas will become redundant while others can become outposts of the health centers.

By themselves the aid posts do not provide an adequate rural health network to support an effective health program. This has been due partly to inadequate training of the APO's and partly to the impossibility of providing effective supervision everywhere.

The Mission is aware that steps have been taken to improve the APO system. Four years of primary education are now the minimum entry requirement in many areas, and refresher courses are given—although they are, understandably, too brief and too few for the large number of APO's who need them. A new method under trial is to appoint a competent APO as aid post inspector or supervisor of a group of eight to ten aid posts.

The target was to increase the number of aid posts to a total of over 2,000 by mid-1967 (approximately one for each thousand of population) as compared with the 1,800 existing in June 1963. While recognizing that only the Departments of Public Health and Native Affairs, who are fully familiar with all the details, can decide the merits of individual cases, the Mission believes the following principles should be followed in planning the future of the aid post system: no new aid posts should be established unless adequate supervision can be provided; present aid posts, which do not receive supervision at reasonable intervals owing to lack of access roads or other means of communications, should be closed until adequate communications are provided; there should be increased supervision for the aid posts retained, and more refresher courses for the APO; the Local Government Councils should take a greater responsibility for aid posts, the responsibility being graded according to the councils' resources with the Administration paying the balance. The subsidy for aid posts maintained by the missions and for mission training of APO's should be continued.

Preventive Health Programs

Health Education. The Health Education section, which was established on paper in 1959 and commenced effective work in January 1963, has produced a considerable amount of media, has held three training courses for medical, health center and malaria staff, and has commenced to decentralize into the regions. Its field work has been concentrated almost entirely on two specialized programs: malaria control and a pilot project to popularize peanuts as a weaning food for infants. The Mission endorses the department's plans to provide training courses for senior aid post and hospital orderlies, a seminar for teachers, in-service courses for medical assistants and infant welfare nurses, and courses at teacher-training colleges.

A qualified educator heads the section and there are two European and seven indigenous assistants who have received in-service training. Another European is taking a diploma course overseas. The aim should be to have one fully qualified person (indigenous whenever practical) in each region by mid-1969. The Mission is in agreement with the plan to have two in-service trained indigenes in each of the 57 sub-districts by the end of 1965.

It is difficult to estimate how much the expanded program of health education will cost. The Mission suggests that the small budget for the section could well be doubled within the next three to five years.

Environmental Sanitation. The great need for better sanitation at the village level is being met in part by a graduated-subsidy scheme to Local Government Councils. In the short time since it was introduced in January 1962, the response has been very encouraging as regards improved drinking water supplies, and by mid-1963, 237 safe water schemes had been completed. Some are single tanks, others larger reticulated systems, while new wells have been sunk and old ones protected, small dams have been constructed, etc.

Patrol officers play an important part in stimulating this work, but prime responsibility for recommending new facilities and inspecting existing ones falls upon the Department of Public Health, i.e., the patrolling medical assistant. In areas where each community has a latrine with a lid to keep out flies, a rubbish hold and a clean stream reserved for drinking water, for example, the patrol inspects these facilities and ensures that they are in good order and are being used. It is precisely at the village or community level that improved sanitation is most needed and the addition of an assistant health inspector to the staff of each health center, expansion of the health education campaign and more mobile infant welfare clinics can be expected gradually to bring it about. In the main urban areas, there is routine milk sampling, inspection of food and food premises, condemnation of unsatisfactory foodstuffs, inspection of barbershops, eradication of mosquitos and other pests.

Infant, Child and Maternal Health (ICMH). The ICMH service is carried out through 24 fixed and 528 mobile clinics. The latter are operated by staff who travel by road weekly or fortnightly from the nearest fixed clinic or rural health center. Antenatal care is given and expectant mothers are advised to use the hospital when an abnormal birth is expected; advice is given on hygienics, sanitation, nutrition, etc.; children are examined and immunization given against whooping cough, diptheria and tuberculosis. In selected areas, vaccination against polio-myelitis and smallpox has been done.

In the year ending June 30, 1963, Administration clinics reported 124,577 attendances by children under one year and 262,653 by children aged one to five, while 5,918 women registered for antenatal care. Other activities of the service included a school health program in which 30,000 children were examined medically and nurses were provided for urban schools, an experimental family planning project in Port Moresby and a pilot project for training indigenous midwives in Manus.

The ICMH service was staffed at mid-1963 by one part-time and three full-time doctors, 50 expatriate nurses and 98 indigenous trained nurses and assistants. Infant welfare nurses are well trained in a special school at Minj in the Western Highlands where a three-year course is given to new entrants and a post-graduate course for Territorial nurses. These girls, all indigenous, should be the backbone of the service in years to come.

In the last few years, the Christian Missions have extended their medical work by organizing mobile clinics to carry the work to the people. They are encouraged to do this by a traveling allowance from the Administration and are helped in many cases by assistant nurses trained in their own schools. In the year ending March 31, 1962, the missions reported[2] 418,195 attendances by children (all ages), and almost 4,000 women registered for antenatal care with 57,904 attendances. The statistics indicate an important volume of work but are not comparable with the department's figures owing to different methods of reporting and in some cases, incomplete returns.

The very young children and women of child-bearing age are the groups most prone to malnutrition and undernutrition, and the ICMH is making efforts to improve nutrition. The indigenous child, if it survives the hazards of the first month, usually does well while breast fed but often languishes after weaning due to lack of suitable food. The Depart-ment of Public Health, developing and improving a process originated by the missions, has produced a paste consisting of ground peanuts which has been successful in pilot trials and which will, if some obstacles in the way of its widespread use can be overcome, help to solve the problem

[2] Reports to the General Assembly of the U. N., 1961–1962, on the Administration of Papua (Appendix XIX, Tables 14 and 15) and of New Guinea (Appendix XIX, Tables 15 and 16).

of a weaning food for infants. Kwashiorkor and other diseases due to lack of dietary protein occur in children in some areas. Among adults, symptoms of protein deficiency are not so obvious but can be precipitated by stress (severe anaemia, childbirth, the withholding of food from old people). There is no doubt that more dietary protein would improve the health of the population. This applies especially to milk for children in the highlands where a high potential for milk production exists and to the use of fresh meat throughout the Territory. In Chapter 3, the Mission discusses ways and means to provide more protein for the diet but there remains the problem of gradually educating the village women to make better use of foods which are available. The Mission recommends that a home economist be employed to teach infant welfare nurses, health center staff, and others what to teach the village women. Overseas training should be given to one or more indigenous nurses who demonstrate particular interests and talents.

Malaria Control. While malaria control activities date back many years, the current program has been in operation for only six years in part of the Sepik District and for a shorter time in New Britain, New Ireland and Bougainville. There are about 550,000 persons in the protected areas, and an estimated 1.4 million people who live in the highly endemic malarious areas. Malaria peters out at altitudes around 7,000 feet. The methods employed have been residual spraying with DDT twice yearly and the provision of drugs twice yearly at the time of spraying. In some of the islands, interruption of transmission of malaria has been achieved. In the Sepik, however, where the parasite rate in children has been reduced from 80 percent to about 8 percent, interruption of transmission by this method is not in sight and continued spraying for an indefinite period will be necessary unless new methods are evolved. Pilot trials of drugs are being tried with some success. The long-acting malaria suppressant (C1501) will undergo field trials in the Territory during 1964.

Personnel employed on the program include three doctors, one regional supervisor, 23 field supervisors and 40 field assistants trained in the malaria school of Kundiawa, and a much larger number of subordinate workers including 500 spray men.

Tuberculosis Control. The incidence of tuberculosis is directly proportional to the degree and duration of the indigenous peoples' contact with Europeans and to the degree of urbanization and culture change. Thus, it is maximal on the coast and minimal in the highlands, and the increasing ease with which people move from one zone to the other has rendered it impossible, in practice, to prevent its inland spread. The department has, therefore, aimed at the widest possible protection with

BCG vaccination of the highland people, while isolating and treating as many infectious cases as possible in all regions and undertaking a special preventive program in urban schools.

The control program is at present operated by four doctors, including the specialist in charge, five medical assistants, three radiographers, and a larger number of subordinate staff. Four teams, one in each region, undertake mass survey examinations, give BCG vaccination to protect those not yet infected and refer for treatment the patients who are discovered. By June 30, 1963, more than 600,000 persons had been surveyed or resurveyed. In the year ending June 30, 1963, 181,350 were surveyed, 38,100 examined by X-ray, and 101,000 received BCG vaccination. On the same date 2,350 patients were receiving in-patient treatment, 1,750 out-patient treatment and something like 2,000 school children preventive treatment. About 4,000 have been discharged from treatment and are kept under supervision so far as communications allow.

Leprosy. In contrast to tuberculosis, leprosy is much more a rural than urban disease and this fact has posed great problems. Leprosy appears to be endemic in most parts but its distribution is patchy and it tends to occur in pockets. Surveys have enabled the Department of Public Health to estimate that there are some 10,000 cases in the whole Territory.

The control program is directed by a specialist medical officer assisted by a small staff. Out-patient treatment, especially for non-infectious patients has been encouraged and in 1963, it was reported that 2,854 were receiving treatments from a large number of treatment centers (aid posts, clinics, hospitals, etc.). Although modern drugs are easy to administer even under primitive conditions, the universal experience has been repeated, namely, that they can be administered effectively only when adequate supervision is available.

The institutional component consists of six Administration and five mission leprosy hospitals or colonies, together with some special wards in general hospitals. Very few patients were discharged from such institutions in the pre-war years, but with modern drugs it was reported that 3,113 patients were discharged in the last complete year. Nevertheless, the end is not yet in sight; the problem of accessible population again arises, and less than half the 10,000 cases have as yet been treated.

Other Preventive Programs. Although cholera and smallpox do not exist in Papua and New Guinea, precautions have been taken lest they should at a later date be imported. Anti-cholera measures can be brought into operation within 24 hours should occasion arise, and a smallpox vaccination campaign covering 850,000 persons has been carried out in the areas believed to be most vulnerable. Smallpox vaccinations should be extended gradually throughout the Territory.

Analysis of the Preventive Programs

Health education and rural environmental sanitation work are proceeding along satisfactory lines and the field programs in malaria, infant, child and maternal health, tuberculosis and leprosy are ably conducted by well-qualified personnel. The greatest uncertainty arises not from the organization of the preventive programs, but in relation to the rate at which further progress can be made.

World-wide experience with field programs has demonstrated the validity of certain principles which are relevant to Papua and New Guinea: surveys are not justified unless treatment programs follow; treatment programs which follow surveys must rely mainly on domiciliary treatment; domiciliary treatment is effective only when it is supervised regularly and well; effective supervision can be given only when an infrastructure (e.g., a health center system) exists; and the latter can function effectively only when trained staff are available and where transport can be provided, i.e., where the population is accessible. Only then can significant expansion of the field programs be expected to justify the manpower, money and time spent on them.

Within the framework of these principles the Mission believes that the Administration's targets are on the optimistic side without an excessive expenditure of funds. Specifically the target for leprosy—all cases to be surveyed and placed under treatment by mid-1967—is much too optimistic. The target for malaria—1.3 million people to be protected by the same date—even with very substantial manpower and expenditure of money would be difficult to maintain, even if momentarily achieved. The proposed increase in the number of women receiving antenatal care from 20 percent to about 60 percent by the end of 1967 was not well based because the accessible population at the relevant date was, and still is, unknown. The target for tuberculosis, to survey or resurvey 1.25 million keeping all cases under treatment, is too ambitious with prevailing conditions.

The Mission recommends that for each field program the department should draw up a plan of operations including the objectives of the program, the means to be used to achieve the objectives, an estimate of the accessible population, the personnel, physical facilities, equipment, supplies and transport required, a timetable for operations, an estimate of costs, and the methods to be used to evaluate the program at intervals. This plan, when accepted by the Director of the Department of Public Health and by the Administration, would be each program director's guide.

The Mission fully endorses the department's intention to increase preventive medicine's share of total health expenditures by technically sound steps.

Personnel and Training Requirements

To meet the needs of the health program, not over the next five but the succeeding years as well, more trained indigenous personnel are required. At present there are no indigenous doctors with the equivalent of an Australian medical degree, nor any in training. At mid-1963 there were 13 indigenous AMO's graduated from the Fiji School of Medicine for Assistant Medical Officers. These AMO's substantially do the work of doctors and have the courtesy title of doctor, but they are not registrable to practice medicine in Australia and are not eligible to sit for post-graduate diplomas overseas.

Enrollment of new students at Fiji has ceased though three still in training will complete their studies; otherwise training now takes place wholly at the Papuan Medical College. The college provides a five-year course for AMO's and the first class of five will complete this course in 1964. The normal entry requirement for the course is 11 years' schooling, although students have been accepted with only ten and given a year of pre-medical training. The five-year course is followed by a mandatory internship. On the basis of the enrollment in 1963, plus the enrollment at Fiji, the number of AMO's available for internship will be 6 in 1964, 12 in 1965, 13 in 1966, and 10 in 1967. The college expected to take in 25 new students in 1963/64 who would be available for internship in 1968. Counting the 13 already in service, the maximum cadre of qualified AMO's by the end of 1969 will be 79—assuming no attrition.

At mid-1963, there were 110 fully qualified doctors in the Department of Public Health.[3] In order to obtain Australian trained doctors for the Territory, the Administration pays the cost of cadet medical training for young Australians on condition that they serve for at least five years after graduation. At mid-1963, there were 28 cadets in training. Despite the cadet system and vigorous efforts at recruitment, the number of expatriate doctors has not increased significantly in the last several years. There has been a steady wastage due to resignations and retirements.

The number of AMO's needed by 1969 includes the 123 doctors/AMO's now available, plus one for each of 15 sub-district hospitals now without an AMO, and one AMO for each new health center. For prediction purposes the Mission estimated this at 20. Thus, without any allowance for contingencies, the output of AMO's would be just adequate for the needs of the service if the number of expatriate doctors can be kept

[3] Excluding 8 private practitioners, 18 mission doctors, and one each in the Army, Navy and Red Cross.

up to the 100 mark, which appears improbable. No increase in the out-put of AMO's by 1969 can be expected, given the length of the training period, but the department plans to expand the intake of students year-by-year to reach 60 in 1969. While expatriate doctors will be needed as senior specialists for many years, AMO's can be expected progressively to take over junior specialist posts (public health officer, tuberculosis officer in the regions, malariologist, etc.) and some should be given post-graduate studies abroad.

The more basic question, however, is whether the medical service should be staffed with less than foreign trained degree doctors. Arguments can be advanced against the principle of training substandard doctors anywhere: they lack full professional status, are not eligible for post-graduate university diplomas, can only become fully qualified later by going back to the beginning, and are liable to become discontented, or even embittered as a result.

But the Mission is in agreement with the Administration that the drawbacks must be accepted, for the alternative is even less attractive. A medical service cannot be run without doctors. There are too few now, the numbers from overseas are expected to fall, and the training in Australia or other countries of substantial numbers of indigenous doctors will take many years. At best, one or two may be trained by 1973 and a few more in the next ten years. AMO's will be needed for decades and training in their home environment is more satisfactory than any other.

The time must come when the indigenous doctor qualified by, say, Australian standards will appear, but the Mission believes that such training should be undertaken overseas for the foreseeable future. Quite apart from the difficulty of obtaining qualified teaching staff, the cost of establishing medical training at university level in the Territory itself would not be justified.

Medical Assistants. At mid-1963, there were 128 European medical assistants but recruitment ceased in 1962 and the total is expected to dwindle to less than 100 by mid-1969. A three-year course of under-graduate training for indigenous medical assistants commenced at the Papuan Medical College in 1962/63. The entry requirement is nine years' schooling, and 13 students are taking the course. The special one-year post-graduate course for health workers who already have the necessary experience (e.g., male nurses) continued and eight have obtained the Medical Assistant Certificate in 1962/63, making 16 in all. The projected intake for the three-year course of training is 15 each for 1964 and 1965, increasing to 20 in 1966 and then to 30, 40 and 45 in the three years up to 1969. On the basis of these projections, the number of qualified indi-genous medical assistants should be about 80 by 1969, excluding any medical workers who may qualify after taking the one-year post-graduate course.

More medical assistants are and will be needed in the preventive services and in smaller hospitals where the one medical assistant now in charge is so tied to his in-patients that he has little or no time for patrolling. Also, the medical assistant is a career man who may later specialize in some branch of medicine such as health education, teaching or hospital administration. The Mission recommends that the future requirement for medical assistants be re-examined to determine whether the planned training program should be expanded. With the expected substantial increase of students in secondary schools (see Chapter 6) enough recruits for an expanded training program should be available.

Nurses and Subordinate Staff. There is a great need for more indigenous trained nurses both for the preventive and curative services. In 1963, there were about 100 indigenous nurses. Present training plans envisage an intake of 60 nursing students in 1964, 80 in 1965, 100 in each of the next two years and 110 in 1969. Taking account of the nurses at present in training, there should be over 500 indigenous trained nurses by 1969 and the service will be better staffed than it is today.

Nurses training is carried out as an adjunct to the Administration base hospitals. The minimum entry requirement is seven years schooling and the basic training course is three years which includes some instruction in health education and elementary public health. A 12-month post-graduate course in midwifery (10 students at mid-1963) and a six-month course in public health nursing (32 students) are given. The missions also train a number of nurses for their own work. Training facilities for nurses are generally adequate except at Rabaul where the department plans to build a new training school starting in 1967/68.

A Nursing Council is in the process of formation. It will in future be responsible for nurse training and will unify the curriculum, examinations, etc., of Administration and mission training schools.

Large numbers of hospital and nursing assistants, infant welfare assistants, infant welfare orderlies, hospital orderlies, etc., are trained in all the large hospitals, where they do the work which is carried out in more advanced countries by nurses or nursing aides. These individuals are trained on the in-service principle and are, at the present stage of development, indispensable to the continued operation of both the preventive and curative services. The specialized field programs train their own staff, some on the in-service principle and others in special schools, the malaria schools at Kundiawa and Rabaul being examples of the latter. There are also training programs for technical assistants in radiography, laboratory techniques and dentistry.

Headquarters Organization

The organization of medical services on a regional basis, which has meant the decentralization and delegation of responsibility, has worked well since its adoption in 1958. Nevertheless, the responsibilities remaining with the head office of the Department of Public Health are heavy, and the department has been concerned with how to streamline its administration in Port Moresby.

The department is organized into seven divisions: Medical Services, Preventive Medicine, Medical Training, Medical Research, Mental Health, Infant, Child and Maternal Health, and Administration. Each division is headed by an assistant director who is responsible to the Director. Two special sections for health education and statistics also report to the Director and his office is represented on several boards and councils. Headquarters responsibilities include policy, central administration, advisory services to the regions, planning and execution of surveys, planning and supervision of the specialized programs (ICMH, malaria, tuberculosis, leprosy, etc.), the training program, recruitment and personnel management, accounting and the preparation of reports, budget estimates, etc.

The organizational structure has been recognized by the department as unsatisfactory in relation to the wide range of responsibilities. The Mission concurs in this conclusion and recommends that the organizational structure be streamlined. Specifically, the Mission recommends that a Deputy Director be appointed to strengthen the central administration and permit the Director and the Deputy, alternately, to make tours of inspection, to attend international conferences and perform other duties away from the office without denuding the central office. The number of divisions could be reduced and the Mission suggests a grouping of the various activities into four main functions, namely: Medical Services, Preventive Medicine, Medical Training and Administration. In accordance with the findings of the Papua/New Guinea Medical Research Advisory Committee, the Medical Research Division should be transformed into an independent institute for medical research which should receive an operating subsidy from the Administration but would also be eligible for research grants from external sources and could accept donations from individuals and trusts. The Department of Education should assume responsibility for the pre-school program.

Summary of Proposed Expenditures

As mentioned earlier in this report, the expenditures on health services have in past years represented a high proportion—in some years 20 percent or more—of Administration expenditures, and the rate of growth of spending on health has been high. Although the share of all health expenditures in total Administration expenditures has been falling in recent years, nevertheless expenditures included in the budget of the Department of Public Health have on average increased by 13 percent annually in the past five years.

The health services have now, by the standards of most undeveloped countries, been brought to an advanced level and, in the light of the Mission's view that future government spending should emphasize economic development rather than social services, the Mission recommends that spending on health should grow much more slowly than in the past.

It has not been possible to calculate precisely the financial impact of all the Mission's recommendations on health services, but the Mission believes that a rate of growth corresponding to about 5 percent annually in the spending of the Department of Public Health would enable a reasonable expansion and improvement of services to take place in accordance with the nature of its recommendations. This rate of growth would mean a much slower expansion of health expenditures than in the past.

It is envisaged that the increase in expenditures over the period to 1968/69 would be primarily related to expansion of programs of preventive medicine and medical training. The Mission has recommended that medical research should be transferred to an independent institute but envisages that the Administration would make through the Department of Public Health an annual grant to the institute, not exceeding £A60,000. The Mission has also recommended that the pre-school program of the Department of Public Health should become the responsibility of the Department of Education. The costs of this program—about £A40,000 annually—would then be transferred to the Department of Education's budget.

The budget of the Department of Public Health does not include all current expenditures on health. In addition to this budget, account has to be taken of the items Vocabulary Stores (included with the expenditures of the Treasury Department, Stores and Supply Branch, and representing a wide variety of supplies used by the Department of Public Health) and Hospital Engineering (in the budget part of the expenditures on General Maintenance). Estimated expenditures on these items during 1963/64 were £A603,000 for Vocabulary Stores (including £A106,000 for mission hospitals) and £A65,000 for Hospital Engineering. For purposes of planning we have assumed that, as in the case of current expenditures made directly by the Department of Public Health, a rise corresponding to about 5 percent annually would be sufficient to accommodate reasonable requirements. On this assumption, total amounts required for Vocabulary Stores and Hospital Engineering during the five-year period 1964/65–1968/69 would be about £A3,500,000 and £A380,000, respectively, corresponding to annual averages of £A700,000 and £A76,000.

In summary, current expenditures on health by the Administration would be as follows:

(£A thousand)

	1963/64 (Budget)	1964/65–1968/69 Total	1964/65–1968/69 Annual Average
Department of Public Health	3,600[a]	20,900	4,180
Vocabulary Stores	603	3,500	700
Hospital Engineering	65	380	76
Total	4,268	24,780	4,956

[a] Exclusive of expenditures for pre-school program.

The financial implications of the Mission's recommendations on capital works may be summarized as follows:

Projected Capital Expenditures on Health Installations

(£A thousand)

	1964/65	1965/66	1966/67	1967/68	1968/69	Total 1964/65–1968/69
Work in Progress[a]	260	50	—	—	—	310
New Works						
Hospital Improvements	100	100	100	100	100	500
Port Moresby General Hospital: Paying Wing	100	110	—	—	—	210
Health Centers	75	15	15	80	20	205
Papuan Medical College (Stage 2)	120	40	160	—	160	480
Rabaul Nursing School	—	—	—	20	80	100
Total	655	315	275	200	360	1,805

[a] Estimated expenditure for various projects included in the Works Program, 1963/64.

In addition to capital expenditures on health installations, allowance has to be made for hospital and medical equipment, on which £A83,500 was spent during 1963/64. For purposes of planning, we have again assumed a rise corresponding to about 5 percent annually; this would imply a total requirement of about £A485,000 during the next five years, i.e., £A97,000 per year on average.

In most recent years long-term loans and grants have been provided to missions for capital expenditures on health (the 1963/64 budget includes total expenditures of about £A60,000 for this purpose). In accordance with our view that it is desirable to bring capital expenditures on health installations back to a lower level, we have made no special allowance for this item for the next five years.

In total, capital expenditures on health by the Administration would be as follows:

(£A thousand)

	1963/64 (Budget)	1964/65–1968/69	
		Total	Annual Average
Health Installations	617	1,805	361
Hospital and Medical Equipment	83	485	97
Total	700	2,290	458

HOUSING

Over 96 percent of the population live in rural areas and for the most part provide their own housing. Employers normally provide housing for their European staffs, for migratory labor and for most indigenous workers in urban areas. The provision of such housing has been costly. In the case of the Administration, staff housing has absorbed more than 25 percent of investment expenditures in recent years. The Mission believes that in the long run, employees should normally be responsible for housing themselves. Steps should be taken to make this possible, especially in urban areas where the need will be more acute and less easily met than in the countryside. The scale of the urban housing problem is still small, but the issues are quite complex. With the growth of urban populations to be expected in the future, it is important that solutions should be adopted which will not in the long run impose excessive financial burdens on the Administration.

The standards of housing in rural areas are very simple. The typical hut is built of local materials—pole timber, bamboo, grass, pit-pit, canes and palm leaves. In a few areas, there has been some improvement in standards: sawn timber has been used in doors, windows and floors, thatched roofs have been replaced by galvanized iron or aluminum roofing and grass walls by platted canes or more permanent materials, but the number of houses of this kind is still a very small fraction of the total.

In urban areas, standards of housing are generally higher, almost all houses being built of permanent materials. Most houses are built of wood or fibro-cement panels on a wooden frame, with an iron or aluminum roof. Concrete blocks have been used increasingly in recent years. A substantial proportion of such building materials is imported. Most housing, both for indigenes and expatriates, is provided by employers though in Port Moresby there are several villages within the urban area where a substantial number of the native people live in their own houses, or in accommodation rented from other natives. Also, in Port Moresby squatter shacks have been built in several areas, mostly with very inadequate provision of essential services such as water, sanitation, or access roads.

With the rapid growth in the non-indigenous population following World War II, new houses have been built in increasing numbers and, although exact figures are not available, probably about 80 percent of all non-indigenous housing has been built since the war. The Administration has just on 2,500 dwellings used by the European staff plus 1,200 married quarters for natives, together with hostel accommodation for about 300 European staff and dormitories for a much greater number of single indigenous employees. No comprehensive data are available on non-indigenous housing since the census of June 1961, when there were just over 7,000 non-indigenous dwellings, but it is probable that the Administration now owns almost one-third of all such dwellings.

The standards of non-indigenous housing compare favorably with those in Australia although they are more costly in the Territory due to higher labor and material transport costs.

The provision of housing by employers, both government and private, has been essential to attract qualified staff from Australia. The lack of suitable housing in adequate quantity is said to have hampered the expansion of government services in recent years.

The Mission recognizes that in the present circumstances where most of the Administration's professional, semi-professional and clerical staff is recruited from abroad and is subject to frequent transfer between districts, the Administration will have to continue to provide housing or otherwise ensure that housing is available for a large proportion of its personnel. Private employers also will have to continue to ensure that housing for their European staff is available. Nevertheless, the Mission believes that in the longer term, and particularly as the indigenes form a growing proportion of the skilled work force, employees should be expected increasingly to provide their own accommodation. This change can only come slowly, and employers, as in more advanced countries, will have to continue to provide housing in special circumstances, for example in remote areas or for migratory labor. But, as the economy matures and a more settled work force develops, it is desirable that private home ownership, with its accompanying economic and social benefits, should be encouraged and employers should be relieved of the heavy capital costs and administrative burden of providing employee accommodation.

As the first step in the direction of divesting itself of responsibility for staff housing, the Mission recommends that the Administration introduce economic rents for staff housing as soon as possible. At present, only nominal rents are charged. A typical rent on expatriate housing is £A48 a year for a house costing £A5,000 to £A7,000. The rents on housing for indigenous staff, for example £A31 a year for married quarters costing £A1,250, while more closely related to costs, are still uneconomic.

The introduction of economic rents for staff housing would have to be compensated by salary adjustments for public servants. The charging of economic rents and the payment of higher salaries would remove a strong disincentive to public servants to acquire their own houses. It might also create a demand for housing for purchase or rent from private owners. Such a development could be stimulated by the provision of credit on suitable terms.

The Mission recommends that the Administration should be prepared to sell its houses to public servants, and should assist those public servants wishing to acquire their own houses by extending the scope of its present housing loans scheme. Alternatively, the employee might borrow directly from the savings banks. In any case there would appear to be ample funds available in the savings banks to meet any prospective increase in the demand for housing loans.

The Mission believes that private employers should consider adopting similar policies. It is in the employer's interest to encourage non-indigenous staff to put down roots, and the Mission believes that financial arrangements could be worked out which would benefit both the employer and the employee, by relieving the former of the capital and maintenance costs of providing staff housing and by giving the latter an addition to income which he could use to acquire an equity in his own house.

The introduction of economic rents is related also to the question of housing standards, particularly for the indigenous public servants. Some thought has been given within the Administration to building houses which are adequate for expatriates, and on which an economic rent could be paid by indigenes as more reach higher levels of the public service. The cost of such a house would be about £A2,500, as compared with about £A1,250 for the married quarters now being built for Administration servants and £A5,000 to £A7,000 for most expatriate housing. As more indigenous public servants move into higher positions with more pay, they will presumably take over houses formerly occupied by expatriates, but they will not be able to afford to pay economic rents for the larger houses. If the rents of larger houses have to be subsidized, it will then be difficult to resist claims for subsidized rents on smaller houses. From this point of view, it is desirable that the Administration should aim to provide more housing at a cost which the indigenes will be able to afford to buy or rent in the future.

The standards of Administration housing in the more remote areas also attracted the Mission's attention. Before World War II, the houses of officers of the Administration in out-stations were frequently built of native materials. These houses cost very little but as a rule lasted for only a few years. Since the war, most houses in out-stations have been built of permanent materials, which in many places have been brought in by air from the nearest port or center of supply. The advantages of using permanent materials have greatly reduced maintenance work and sometimes speed of construction, but due to transportation of materials and labor the initial costs of such houses have been substantially above costs in the main centers, and several times the cost of houses built with local materials. The Administration has been aware of the need to reduce building costs and has commissioned several studies which have considered, *inter alia*, the possibility of using local materials—e.g., bricks, cement blocks, timber, grass, reeds and bamboo in house construction. These studies have concluded that by better selection and by using preservatives where appropriate, the life of local materials such as timber, grass, reeds and bamboo can be greatly extended, and the savings in initial costs of construction resulting from the use of these materials and of cement and coral blocks promise to be large. The Mission urges that greater use should be made in Administration housing of local materials, both to save costs and to stimulate the development of local skills and local employment in supplying and using these materials. This would also have an important educational value in demonstrating to people outside government and, particularly to the indigenous people, how local materials could be better used in their own housing; how in effect the European gets his good house.

Besides housing many of its own staff, the Administration has provided housing in urban areas for indigenes generally. The majority of natives working in urban areas are still housed by their employers, but with the trend toward the introduction of a full cash wage, native workers may be expected increasingly to want to find their own accommodation.

Where the employer does not provide accommodation, native workers may live in their own houses, in rooms rented from other natives, live with friends and relatives or they may erect a shack with or without the permission of the owners of the land chosen for this purpose.

The Administration has been aware of the need to provide housing in urban areas in addition to that supplied by employers and has built, at a cost of more than £A250,000 about 220 houses in Port Moresby, Rabaul, Lae and Madang for sale or lease to suitable indigenes. None had been sold when the Mission was in the Territory. The rents, ranging from £A1/14- to £A2/6/5 a week in Port Moresby, are high in relation to the wage of £A3 a week for most urban workers. Within the past year, the Administration has built cheaper one and two-roomed houses in Port Moresby, which will rent for approximately 18/6d a week, but even this would appear to be beyond the reach of the majority.

Accurate statistics of the indigenous population of urban areas are not available, but it is estimated that the indigenous population in Port Moresby has risen by roughly 10 percent annually in recent years and the population in other centers has also increased. Further growth can be expected, and many of the newcomers will continue to be unskilled or semi-skilled workers, wishing to maintain their links with rural areas to which they will expect to return. These workers are unaccustomed to spending much on housing in their villages, and while in town would probably prefer the bare minimum of shelter to paying for better accommodation. Experience in African countries suggests that in these circumstances either accommodation has to be subsidized by the employer or the government or a local authority bearing or sharing the burden, or arrangements have to be made to allow self-help housing to be built on a controlled basis with provision of the minimum services—water, sanitation, access roads and street lighting—required to maintain public health, and law and order.

For the migratory worker, unaccompanied by wife and family, who stays in town for only a year or two before returning to his village, it will probably be necessary to provide hostel or other suitable accommodation on a subsidized basis. Experience in some African countries suggests that the costs of subsidizing this type of accommodation, though heavy, are manageable. Such accommodation is, however, quite unsuited to the needs of the worker accompanied by his family, and this type of worker will have to be attracted to the towns in increasing numbers if a stable, increasingly skilled urban work force is to be built up. It is just in this area of providing family housing that the problem becomes particularly difficult. Urban wages of the indigenous worker are generally low in relation to family needs, and he can, therefore, afford to pay little for accommodation. But his need for space is much greater than that of the single man, and if housing of a standard comparable with that so far built by the Administration is provided, the subsidy per worker has to be much larger. Here again, African experience suggests that the costs of subsidizing family housing on this basis become so great as to be unmanageable in the longer term as the urban population grows, and that, at least until urban wages rise appreciably, the only practical alternative is the provision of housing on a self-help basis. Even this may involve some element of subsidy, but the costs should be relatively small.

Self-help housing should be built on demarcated plots, supplied with the minimum of essential services. Minimum standards of construction should be laid down (e.g., buildings should not cause serious fire hazard), and financial and technical help may be needed by the house builders. It may also be appropriate to assist with the supply of materials and in actual construction. The object should be to provide plot-holders with security of tenure, so that they can improve their houses as resources become available, and sell them if they wish. The Mission believes that in the longer terms self-help housing is likely to prove the only practical means of providing family accommodation in urban areas in adequate quantity, and commends this approach to the Administration.

The Mission believes that the creation of a single housing authority with responsibility for housing Administration staff and for housing programs in urban centers would provide the most effective and economical organization and recommends that such an authority should be established. The authority should have the responsibility for all Administration houses. Responsibility for construction and maintenance should be transferred to the authority from the Commonwealth Department of Works (CDW) and the Public Works Department (PWD), but the actual work of construction would be done, as at present, mostly by contractors. Responsibility for leasing should be transferred from the Treasury Department. The Administration would have to provide capital funds, but the housing authority should be financially self-supporting. The rents it charges should be sufficient to cover the capital charges payable to the Administration, plus maintenance and administrative costs. If the authority were required to provide housing at less than an economic rent, the Administration or the private employer should make up the difference.

The work of the housing authority would gradually change. As urban areas grow and as increasing numbers of public servants acquire their own housing, the housing authority would become increasingly concerned with urban housing generally rather than with housing for Administration personnel. The authority might also broaden its responsibilities to assist in improving housing standards in rural areas, but initially it should concern itself with Administration urban housing.

The total investment in Administration housing is not known, but over the five fiscal years 1958/59–1962/63, £A8.4 million were spent on housing for expatriate and indigenous staff, and this accounted for more than one-quarter of all investment expenditures of the Administration during this period. Budgeted expenditures on housing in 1963/64 total £A1.8 million, somewhat greater than the average of the past five years.

The costs of housing to be financed by the Administration over the next five years will be heavy. The programs recommended for Agriculture, Forestry and Education envisage the employment of about 950 additional European officers by the Administration during this period. Accommodation must be provided for these officers. Expansion in other departments of the Administration will require additional housing and progress must be made in catching up on the present housing backlog as a step toward reducing the losses by resignation of existing personnel. While it is impossible to estimate all housing requirements precisely, approximately 2,000 additional housing units for European officers will be required over the next five years, if the programs recommended by the Mission are to be implemented and the necessary expansion of other public services is to take place. Almost 60 percent of the existing Administration housing for European officers consists of family dwellings. If the same proportion is applied to new construction, the capital costs of the 2,000 new units would approximate to £A8 million if all are built in permanent materials. This sum has been provided in the development plan, but the Mission would again stress the desirability of encouraging the Administration's European officers to buy or build their own houses, of adopting simpler housing standards, and of making greater use of local materials. If progress is made along these lines, the cost to the Administration of housing its additional European staff over the next five years could be substantially less than the figure shown above.

The Mission has noted that the Administration now provides housing for approximately 40 percent of its indigenous staff. To a large extent, therefore, the indigenous staff already provide their own housing. The Mission recommends that the Administration should, whenever practicable, aim to help its indigenous staff to acquire their own housing rather than attempt to house them itself. The Mission recognizes that there will continue to be circumstances where indigenous staff will be working far from their home districts and will be subject to perhaps frequent transfer between districts. In many of these cases the Administration may have to provide housing as in the case of its European staff. The Mission recommends, however, that in urban areas the housing of Administration indigenous staff should be considered as part of the wider problem of housing indigenous urban workers. Given progress with self-help housing and with the greater use of local materials, experience in the Territory and in other countries indicates that accommodation of acceptable standards can be provided at quite moderate costs, but until urban housing needs have been assessed (preferably by the proposed housing authority) no realistic estimate of the cost of urban housing for indignes can be made. Nor is it possible, from the data available to the Mission, to estimate the costs of housing those members of the Administration's indigenous staff who cannot reasonably be expected to find their own accommodation. The Mission has, therefore, made no specific provision for indigenous housing in the development plan.

WATER SUPPLY AND SEWERAGE

With its abundant rainfall and numerous rivers and streams, water is generally available for human use throughout the Territory. In rural areas where over 96 percent of the population live, water is obtained from bores, wells, rivers and streams. For a few indigenes and for most of the non-indigenous population, roof catchments provide water for domestic use. The only major exception to this is Port Moresby, which lies in a relatively dry area, and which has a fully reticulated water supply. Partial systems exist in Lae and Popondetta, and in most towns there are wells or bores from which supplies are obtained when water is short during periods of dry weather. Only in Port Moresby is a charge made for water supplied.

Port Moresby is also the only center with a developed sewerage system. In other centers septic tanks or a sanitation service are used. Lae and Rabaul have sewerage systems serving large government installations such as hospitals or labor compounds to which other users may be connected in the next few years. As of mid-1963 no charges were being made for sewerage services in any center, but the Administration was planning to introduce charges in Port Moresby. Charges have been levied for sanitation services.

Local Government Councils have been encouraged by the Administration to take an interest in water for villages and over the past ten years the councils have spent increasing sums on the improvement of water supplies in more than 500 villages. These improvements have taken the form of new bores or wells, the construction of underground or overhead tanks and the protection of wells. The work has been done under the supervision of the Department of Health and in the past two years the Administration has given subsidies to local government councils to help meet the cost of these improvements.

Total capital and current expenditures by the Administration on water and sewerage (current expenditures also include costs of sanitation services) over the past five years have been as follows:

(£A)

	1958/59	1959/60	1960/61	1961/62	1962/63
Capital Expenditures	410,000	169,000	133,000	135,000	128,000
Current Expenditures	176,000	178,000	197,000	220,000	238,000

Spending by the local government councils has risen from £A5,000 in 1958/59 to £A22,000 in 1962/63. The heavy expenditures incurred in 1958/59 were on account of major additions to the water supply system in Port Moresby.

The charges levied for water in Port Moresby and for sanitation services in all centers are such that the Administration incurs substantial losses on both these services as well as on the sewerage service in Port Moresby. The position in Port Moresby is indicated by the financial results for the year 1962/63 which are set out in Table 1.

TABLE 1: Port Moresby Water, Sewerage and Sanitation Services, Financial Results, 1962/63

(£A)

	Water Service	Sewerage Service	Sanitation and Garbage	Total
Revenue	48,000	—	29,800	77,800
Operating and Maintenance Costs	81,400	16,506	40,862	138,768
Capital Charges [a]				
Depreciation	31,000	15,300	—	46,300
Interest	55,000	24,200	—	79,200
Total Costs	167,400	56,006	40,862	264,268
Loss	119,400	56,006	11,062	186,468

[a] These charges are approximate only as the records of past investment are incomplete and no up-to-date valuation of the existing water and sewerage systems has been made.
SOURCE: Treasury: data supplied to the Mission.

It appears that calculating interest at 5.5 percent and allowing for depreciation on the existing and new installations projected for the next five years as calculated by the CDW at 3 percent per annum, the losses on the water and sewerage system in Port Moresby would increase from £A119,400 and £A56,000 in 1962/63 to £A214,000 and £A61,500 in 1968/69. If the present user charges of 1/-d to 2/-d per thousand gallons for water and £A12 per sewerage connection were increased to 3/6d and £A30 respectively the two services could break even in 1968/69, based on present projections.

There being no plans to the contrary, rain water catchment will continue to meet the needs of most users in the urban areas, with the exception of Port Moresby. As a result, most of the expenditures projected for the five-year period will be on account of expansions to the water system in Port Moresby, though some improvements in public reticulated supplies in Lae and Rabaul are envisaged, and an expansion of the water system in Wewak is projected for 1965/66 on account of the probable build-up of defense installations in the area.

Similarly no major new sewerage schemes are envisaged during the period of the plan, and projected expenditures will be almost wholly on account of extensions to the Port Moresby system.

The demand for water in Port Moresby has risen at a rate of approximately 10 percent a year during the past four years, and the CDW is projecting future demand at the same rate of growth. On this basis, the department has projected a water consumption in Port Moresby of 1,600 million gallons in 1968/69 as compared with 968 million gallons in 1962/63. The peak daily demand is expected to rise over this period from slightly more than 3 million gallons per day to about 6 million gallons per day.

The achievement of such a rate of growth in demand will clearly depend to a large extent upon a continued expansion of government operations and of a consequential growth in the population of Port Moresby. It will also depend in part on the maintenance of the present uneconomic charges for water used. By charging such a rate, the Administration encourages the increased use of water. By comparison with consumption levels in some other tropical countries, the average daily consumption per capita in Port Moresby at almost 80 Imperial gallons is high, especially having regard to the fact that about three-quarters of the town's population are indigenes. The Mission can see no good reason why water, sewerage and sanitation services should be heavily subsidized. Rather it believes and recommends that in the interests of a more rational allocation of resources the prices charged for these services should be brought up to economic levels.

The introduction of economic charges for reticulated water is likely to have an impact on the demand for water and hence on the growth of consumption. This would in turn affect the assumptions on which the projected expansion of the Port Moresby water undertaking has been based. For this reason the Mission cannot fully endorse the plan for expansion prepared by the CDW. Nevertheless, elements of the plan are flexible and to this extent expenditures can be adjusted if the actual increase in demand for water is faster or slower than projected.

The total capital expenditures on water supplies projected for the five-year period amount to £A1.589 million. Of this, £A977,000 are expected to be spent on the system for Port Moresby, where a new pumping station and water-treatment plant, new town reservoirs and a steady expansion of the reticulation system are planned. Expenditures envisaged on the water system in Lae over the period of the plan are small, totaling less than £A60,000. Most of this will be on account of modest extensions to the reticulation system. In Rabaul new bores and pumping stations will be installed and a new reservoir built, provided that exploratory drilling for water in the area of the town is successful. Modest extensions to the reticulation system are envisaged but unless a suitable source of water can be found it is doubtful whether these will be built. The installations envisaged for Wewak include trunk mains, a water-treatment plant, a reservoir and a reticulation system.

A similar distribution of expenditures is envisaged for expansions to sewerage systems. In Port Moresby trunk sewers and the reticulation system will be extended, and a small amount of money will be spent on a new treatment plant. Expenditures in other centers will be very small. Of the total capital expenditures on sewerage of £A642,000 over the five-year period, £A585,000 will be spent in Port Moresby.

The projected distribution of capital expenditures over the period of the plan is shown in Table 2.

TABLE 2: Projected Capital Expenditures, 1964/65–1968/69

(£A)

	1964/65	1965/66	1966/67	1967/68	1968/69	Five-Year Total
Water (CDW)	513,000	421,000	205,000	265,000	185,000	1,589,000
Sewerage (CDW)	287,000	112,000	80,000	83,000	80,000	642,000
Minor Works (PWD)	20,000	20,000	20,000	20,000	20,000	100,000
Total	820,000	553,000	305,000	368,000	285,000	2,331,000

SOURCES: CDW and PWD: data supplied to the Mission.

As indicated in the table, expenditures at Rabaul are contingent upon the discovery of a satisfactory source of water. If this is not found, expenditures projected for 1965/66 and 1966/67 could be approximately £A80,000 and £A60,000 below the figures shown in Table 2.

The operation and maintenance costs of water, sewerage and sanitation services over the period of the plan have been projected in Table 3. These are gross expenditures without taking into account any revenues from water, sewerage and sanitation charges.

TABLE 3: Projected Operation and Maintenance Expenditures, 1964/65–1968/69

(£A)

	1964/65	1965/66	1966/67	1967/68	1968/69	Five-Year Total
Water (CDW)	124,000	134,000	144,000	155,000	166,000	723,000
Sewerage (CDW)	24,000	26,000	19,000	20,000	20,000	109,000
Sanitation	95,000	100,000	105,000	110,000	115,000	525,000
Water Services in Minor Centers (PWD)	30,000	33,000	36,000	40,000	45,000	184,000
Total	273,000	293,000	304,000	325,000	346,000	1,541,000

SOURCES: CDW and PWD: data supplied to the Mission, and Mission estimate for sanitation services.

While provisionally accepting these figures for planning purposes the Mission would again stress its conviction that economic charges for water, sewerage and sanitation services should be introduced. On the assumption that such charges are introduced, the Mission would urge the Administration to review projected expenditures, particularly capital expenditures, as the effects of the higher charges on demand become apparent.

CHAPTER 8 *MONEY, BANKING, CREDIT AND PUBLIC REVENUE*

MONEY AND BANKING

Monetary and Banking System

The monetary and banking system of Papua and New Guinea is largely that of Australia. The Australian foreign exchange system is equally applicable to the Territory. The powers of Australia's central bank, the Reserve Bank of Australia, apply to Papua and New Guinea. All trading, savings and development finance facilities are provided by branch establishments of Australian banks.

Money Supply. Australian notes are legal tender in Papua and New Guinea under provisions of the Reserve Bank Act of 1959. Present legal tender currency circulating in New Guinea comprises British, Australian and New Guinea coinage under the provisions of the Currency, Coinage and Tokens Ordinance 1922–60. This ordinance also provides that in a certain area of the New Britain coast, gold-lip shell may be used in the place of legal tender. Shell money is still used in some parts of the Territory, largely for payments in connection with special ceremonies and marriages. The Administration, in at least one district, uses gold-lip shell to pay natives for land purchased, the natives not being willing to accept cash. New Guinea coins to the value of about £A482,000 were issued during the period 1935–42 and are still being used in both Papua and New Guinea, although they are not legal tender in Papua. A considerable number of the New Guinea coins have disappeared from circulation as a result of war, hoarding and souvenir hunters.

Due to the integration with the Australian system, no data are readily available on the total amount of currency (notes plus coins) circulating in the Territory. An unofficial estimate provided to the Mission by the Reserve Bank places the amount of notes and coins in the hands of the public by mid-1963 at about £A5 million. An unknown but substantial amount of currency has disappeared from circulation. The amount of currency hoarded by natives is reported to be very considerable.

Foreign Exchange. Foreign exchange needs of Territory residents are met through the central banking system of the Commonwealth; foreign exchange is made available through trading banks operating in the Territory. There are no exchange restrictions on payments between Papua, New Guinea and Australia and the only restrictions on exchange transactions with other countries are those which are applicable to similar transactions between Australia and such countries.

Reserve Bank of Australia. A branch of the Reserve Bank of Australia[1] has been established at Port Moresby. The Reserve Bank, as central bank, controls the Australian banking system. Besides this general function, the Reserve Bank is in charge of the issue of notes and coins in the Territory; acts as bank to the Administration, the offices of Commonwealth Departments and the Copra Marketing Board; administers a registry of inscribed stock (public debt) for the Administration; carries out research; and provides educational facilities for the purpose of educating the indigenous population in the concepts of savings and investment and the general requirements of a money economy.[2]

The Reserve Bank is, at present, training a small group of indigenes in various aspects of its operations. It is understood that this program was started first to give the Reserve Bank the advantage of having trained indigenes on its staff and secondly to form the nucleus of a well-trained group should the need for a separate central bank arise. The Mission was informed that this program is to be expanded when more qualified indigenous persons can be recruited.

The Question of an Independent Monetary and Banking System. In connection with the declared objective that the Territory is to become self-governing, the Mission considered whether there were economic factors which would suggest an independent monetary and banking system.

The most basic action to be taken to achieve an independent monetary and banking system would be the establishment of a separate central bank. The main implications of such a step would be that the Territory would acquire its own monetary unit, money supply, foreign exchange system and foreign exchange reserves and that it would be responsible for its own monetary policies, both internal and external.

---

[1] The Reserve Bank of Australia was established in 1959 (under the Reserve Bank Act 1959). It took over the central bank elements of its predecessor, the Commonwealth Bank of Australia, together with its Note Issue Department and Rural Credits Department.

[2] One of the most important aspects of the educational program of the Reserve Bank are its efforts to build up a system of savings and loan societies in the Territory (see page 377). This program was conceived and is directed by the Bank. Other forms of education are provided by such media as pamphlets, films and courses. On page 372 mention is made of the school savings program, undertaken by the savings banks. The Mission endorses these various activities as useful contributions to the major objective of advancing the indigene.

The Mission is of the opinion that at this time a separate monetary system would not be to the economic advantage of the Territory. The inclusion of the Territory in the Australian monetary area has the substantial advantages of unlimited access to foreign exchange (within the framework of the Australian regulations) and complete freedom of payments between the Territory and Australia. These factors are of paramount importance from the point of view of confidence of the foreign investor. Also, cost and effort of making payments between Australia and the Territory are reduced to a minimum.

The existence of a separate Territory central bank would, in principle, have the advantage of shielding the economy of the Territory from changes in monetary policy necessitated by internal economic conditions in Australia, not relevant to the Territory. It could be argued that changes in domestic monetary policy in Australia should not automatically apply to the Territory because economic conditions are, in some respects, basically very different. In the Mission's opinion, this argument is academic since the possibilities of stimulating economic development through variations in monetary policy in Papua and New Guinea are rather limited. Also, the present system does not exclude the possibility of some differentiation by the Reserve Bank in its policy directives between Australian and Territory branches of banks. The Mission was informed that in fact such differentiation has already been applied.[3]

The necessity for a separate central bank will only arise in case of political independence of the Territory and even then there may be advantages to a close relationship, if such could be arranged, between the Territory and Australia. In the light of these considerations, the establishment of a central bank is not an urgent issue.

It should be noted that Australia has adopted the decimal system of currency and in February 1966, the present Australian pound will be replaced by a dollar. All notes and coins in circulation in Australia and, of course, the Territory, will be replaced by the new currency. This has raised the specific question whether a separate Territory currency should be adopted to go into circulation at that time rather than the dollar. The question is largely political and the Mission has no suggestions.

Trading and Savings Banks

Four Australian banking institutions operate in the Territory besides the Reserve Bank. Within the framework of the Commonwealth Banking Corporation, there are the Commonwealth Trading Bank and the

---

[3] Admittedly such differentiation is subject to certain limitations since it could give rise to evasion or avoidance (especially if applied to interest rates).

TABLE 1: Trading Banks—Deposits and Advances

(annual averages in £A thousand)

Year Ending June	Deposits	Loans and Advances	Ratio of Loans and Advances to Deposits Percentage
1946 [a]	250	45	18.0
1947	791	47	5.9
1948	1,338	98	7.3
1949	2,107	146	6.9
1950	2,157	241	11.2
1951	2,682	438	16.3
1952	3,454	617	17.9
1953	4,329	591	13.7
1954	5,317	732	13.8
1955	5,404	1,253	23.2
1956	5,929	1,684	28.4
1957	6,376	1,966	30.8
1958	6,702	2,198	32.8
1959	6,918	2,290	33.1
1960	7,696	2,219	28.8
1961	7,913	2,589	32.7
1962	7,385	2,757	37.3
1963	8,095	3,318	41.0

[a] Ten months ending June 1946.

SOURCES: Commonwealth Statistician's "Finance" and "Banking and Currency" Bulletins.

Commonwealth Savings Bank.[4] The other three are the Bank of New South Wales, the Australia and New Zealand Bank and the National Bank of Australasia (they are privately owned and engaged in trading and savings bank activities only).

Trading Banks. By mid-1963 the four trading banks operated 21 branches and 10 agencies in the Territory. Their activities have grown markedly as is demonstrated by the rise of deposits and credits (see Table 1). Total deposits had reached an average of £A8.2 million during June 1963, whereas loans, advances and bills discounted stood at their highest level, almost £A3.7 million.

[4] The Commonwealth Banking Corporation, wholly owned by the Government, also was established in 1959 (under the Commonwealth Banks Act 1959). It took over all general banking functions of the Commonwealth Bank of Australia, excepting the Rural Credits Department. In addition to the trading and savings banks, the corporation comprises the Commonwealth Development Bank, discussed later.

Advances extended in the categories of agriculture and of finance, building construction and commerce have each been for more than one-third of the total in most recent years, except in 1962/63 when advances in the latter category rose sharply. Advances for manufacturing, transport and communications have together equalled less than 10 percent (see Table 2).

Rates of interest for bank deposits and advances are generally the same as those in Australia. Since April 1963, the maximum rate on bank advances has been 6½ percent; actual average charges, depending on the nature of the advance, are up to about 1 percent lower.[5]

Credits extended by the trading banks are, as in Australia, mostly overdrafts (i.e., a customer is allowed to draw funds up to a limit granted by his banker). The overdraft system allows for considerable flexibility in the terms of credits both with regard to periods of loans and security required. As a rule credits under the overdraft system are callable on demand, but in practice they are made available for periods ranging from very short-term (say one year and less) to long-term (up to seven or eight years, or more). Usually they are subject to periodic review for reduction. Security in the form of a first mortgage over land and buildings or chattels is normally required except in the case of very short-term advances. The term loan type of credit, which provides for credit for a fixed period, ranging generally from three to eight years, was introduced in April 1962; few term loans have been extended in the Territory.

The ratio of loans, advances and bills discounted to deposits has gone up in most recent years. For all trading banks it was mostly between 40–45 percent during 1962/63, against slightly more than 30 percent during most of the period 1955/56–1960/61. In earlier years this ratio had been still lower (see Table 1). These percentages do not include deposits of Territory residents with branches in Australia, nor advances by Australian branches for use in the Territory. Even with these limitations the loans/deposits ratio has been substantially lower than in Australia.

Although the trading banks have made a useful contribution to the financing of private investment, the credit volume has been limited by a number of factors which explain why the loans/deposits ratio has been substantially lower than in Australia. They require, in the case of lending against security of land, an individual recorded title. This, in practice, has meant no loans to indigenes. The banks do not, as a rule, lend for agricultural investments which involve real expansion or more development. There has been some caution exercised by the banks stemming

[5] In April 1964, the maximum permissible rate on overdrafts chargeable by trading banks was increased to 7 percent.

TABLE 2: Trading Banks—Classification of Advances

(£A thousand)

	1949	1951	1953	1955	1957	1958	1959	1960	1961	1962	1963
						(as at June 30)					
Agriculture, Livestock and Dairying	40	90	163	264	577	728	748	837	1,068	1,063	921
Manufacturing	—	11	10	357	275	222	103	96	106	175	141
Transport, Storage and Communications	2	65	32	77	83	129	83	74	141	106	171
Finance, Building Construction and Commerce	96	264	301	706	720	864	676	873	1,004	1,050	1,774
All Other	23	56	98	311	394	467	459	529	558	540	543
Total	161	486	604	1,716	2,049	2,410	2,068	2,410	2,877	2,934	3,550

SOURCE: Reserve Bank of Australia: data supplied to the Mission.

from the fact that there has been dispute over land titles and that land values have, in some cases, fallen considerably in recent years. The over-all question of confidence in the political future of the Territory has thus had an indirect effect on the volume of loans.

Unfortunately, no figures are available showing the volume of native deposits with trading banks or volume of credit extended to natives, but information available to the Mission indicates they comprise only a small fraction of the total. Lending to indigenes has, apart from the lack of title, been impeded by the smallness of the amounts involved and the lack of knowledge about a native or a group of natives as a credit risk.

To a limited extent the difficulties involved in making bank loans to natives were alleviated by the authority, granted in 1955 to the Admin-istrator, to guarantee the repayment of bank loans for approved purposes. (For sums in excess of £A20,000, the approval of the Minister of State for Territories of the Commonwealth Government is required.) By mid-1963, bank loans carrying the guarantee of the Administration totaled £A281,750. Of this amount, £A227,020 had been lent to Native Local Government Councils for the Tolai cocoa project and £A7,450 to indi-vidual indigenous borrowers for development of business activities and the purchase of vehicles to transport produce. [6]

Savings Banks. By mid-1963 the four savings banks operated 21 branches and 182 agencies in the Territory. Savings deposits have more than trebled during the last decade. At the end of June 1963, there were about 124,700 accounts with deposits of almost £A8.1 million (see Table 3). On June 30, 1962, native accounts numbered 87,100 and European 18,600, but native deposits totaled only £A1.8 million (average per account £A21), and European £A5.2 million (average per account £A280). Native deposits were 26 percent of all deposits. The number of native accounts almost doubled during the last ten years.

The savings banks have been active in promoting school savings, which are not an economic proposition for the banks, but have an important educational effect. School savings accounts numbered almost 18,100 at June 30, 1963, with total balances of about £A39,800 (average over £A2); some of these belonged to indigenous children.

Investment of the deposits of the savings banks takes place within the framework of the over-all investment policy and regulations applicable to Australia. Investments by the savings banks in the Territory, other than in their own office buildings, etc., are reported to equal only a small

---

[6] Guarantees may also be provided for bank loans to trustees of recreation reserves and sports fields for development of those facilities; associations for development of pre-school play centers; agricultural societies controlling show grounds and clubs, depending on the merit of the case.

TABLE 3: Savings Banks—Number of Accounts and Depositors' Balances

As at June 30	Indigenous		Non-indigenous		Total Indigenous and Non-indigenous	
	No. of Accounts (thousand)	Depositors' Balances (£A thousand)	No. of Accounts (thousand)	Depositors' Balances (£A thousand)	No. of Accounts (thousand)	Depositors' Balances (£A thousand)
1950	35.6	484.3	6.1	1,142.6	41.7	1,626.9
1951	38.3	612.4	6.6	1,348.4	44.9	1,960.7
1952	45.3	687.2	7.1	1,510.0	52.4	2,197.1
1953	48.4	761.2	7.8	1,781.6	56.3	2,542.7
1954	47.2	791.3	8.6	1,939.1	55.8	2,730.4
1955	46.8	735.6	8.8	2,189.9	55.6	2,925.6
1956	46.9	859.4	10.9	2,493.8	57.9	3,353.1
1957	50.1	1,066.9	12.1	2,901.3	62.2	3,968.2
1958	54.1	1,155.4	13.6	3,176.2	67.7	4,331.6
1959	57.6	1,190.1	14.8	3,773.1	72.4	4,963.2
1960	61.9	1,257.8	16.2	4,588.6	78.1	5,846.3
1961	72.3	1,499.7	17.6	4,831.6	89.9	6,331.3
1962	87.1	1,833.5	18.6	5,203.7	105.7	7,037.2
1963	n.a.	n.a.	n.a.	n.a.	124.7	8,066.5

SOURCE: Reserve Bank of Australia: data supplied to the Mission.

fraction of Territory deposits. The scope for investments by savings banks is limited by Australian banking legislation. Nevertheless, the banks have contributed to the borrowing program of the Administration and have done some lending for the financing of housing. As discussed elsewhere in this report, conditions have not been conducive to private home owner- ship, and the demand for private housing loans with the savings banks has been correspondingly small. Some of the banks have, in addition, lent limited sums to the Administration to provide finance for its housing loan scheme.

Local Participation in Banking—A Territory Bank

While it is generally recognized that the presence of the well-developed network of offices of Australian banks is a valuable asset to the Territory, nevertheless, efforts should be made to increase local participation in banking facilities and employment. Indigenous employment in banking, apart from the lowest ranks, is virtually non-existent. In discussing this question with several local bank managers, the Mission gained the impression that they were eager to employ more indigenes, also as trainees for higher positions, but that suitable candidates were very scarce. It is obvious that improvement initially depends on the further growth of education. With the prospect of a substantial expansion of secondary education, better educated indigenes will shortly be available for employment and training.

The idea of establishing a local bank with major local participation was brought to the attention of the Mission on several occasions. The Mission is rather skeptical about the idea. Since the amount of native business with the trading banks is very small, the major possibility would lie in the savings bank field. However, deposits of the indigenous sector with the savings banks at present total no more than about £A2 million, and a new savings bank could presumably attract only a small portion of these. There is no basis of estimating the volume of deposits the non- indigenous community would make in a new bank. To the extent that the establishment of a new local bank is advocated for reasons of more adequate credit facilities, the answer lies in the formation of a Territory Development Finance Company, as recommended below by the Mission.

Another possibility toward increased local participation which, in the Mission's view, may deserve serious consideration at some future date, would be the purchase, by local interests, of one of the existing institu- tions. Localization of part of the banking facilities would be a modest contribution toward increasing the element of economic independence of the Territory. In particular, the interests in the Territory of the Commonwealth Banking Corporation, owned by the Commonwealth Government, might be considered suitable for turning over to local interests. This could conceivably be done in stages as follows: establishment of a Papua and New Guinea Division of the Commonwealth Banking Corporation; segregation of the accounts; legalization of a separate institution; and finally, private interests or the Administration acquiring a controlling interest in this institution.

Commonwealth Development Bank

The Commonwealth Development Bank (CDB), a constituent of the Commonwealth Banking Corporation, commenced operations in January 1960 and as of June 30, 1963, 49 loans had been approved in the Territory totaling £A387,000; 45 of these were rural loans (total £A343,000) and 4 industrial loans (£A44,000). This is less than 1 percent of total loans granted by the CDB in Australia during this period.

The Development Bank's main function is to provide finance for primary production and for the establishment or development of industrial undertakings, particularly small undertakings, where, in the opinion of the CDB, the granting of assistance is desirable and the finance would not otherwise be available on reasonable and suitable terms and conditions. The CDB is authorized to provide advice and assistance with a view to promoting the efficient organization and conduct of primary production or of industrial undertakings.

Although the CDB's authority is defined rather widely, its lending operations are in practice subject to rather strict limitations. The CDB acts as a lender of last resort; it is only prepared to consider a loan application after a potential borrower has ascertained that a trading bank is unwilling to provide this loan. The CDB does not lend at less than 6 percent interest and generally requires security, preferably a first lien on land with recorded individual title. It has no staff in the Territory and the private banks act as its agent. All loans have to be approved by its main office in Sydney.

Ex-Servicemen's Credit Scheme

This scheme, for the provision of government credit, came into operation during November 1958. The primary purpose was to assist ex-servicemen, Australian and native, residing in the Territory since their discharge, to establish themselves as farmers, particularly of tree crops. The period for filing of applications for loans was initially three years; it was later extended by one year and ended in November 1962. No further loans can be made under this scheme.

The maximum amount of a loan was £A25,000 at 3¾ percent interest and not to exceed 25 years. The amount of the loan was determined on the basis of estimated amounts required for fixed improvements, plant and equipment, working capital, personal expenses and contingencies.

Loans were made for development of such crops as cocoa, coconuts, rubber, coffee and peanuts. Up to mid-1963, 269 loans had been made, 138 to Australian ex-servicemen totaling £A3,074,485 and 131 to native ex-servicemen totaling £A112,550. The averages of loans granted to Australian and native ex-servicemen were £A22,279 and £A859, respectively.

Native Loans Fund

This fund was established in 1955 to provide loans to natives or native organizations not able to obtain loans from the trading banks or other sources. Loans may be made for projects in primary and secondary industries or of a commercial nature, to further native welfare projects on a local government, community or group basis and for other approved purposes. Although loans can be made without security, the fund usually seeks some form of security. The majority of loans have been made to natives who were granted land under various land settlement schemes for the establishment of tree crops. Other loans have been made to purchase vehicles for the transport of produce to market; tractors and trailers for farming and for the transport of produce; outboard motors for canoes for transport and fishing; and for community development through local government councils and cooperative societies.

Originally, no loan could exceed £A5,000. This ceiling was removed in 1962. In the case of loans for business enterprises, the borrower must have an equity of at least 25 percent unless circumstances warrant consideration of a lesser amount. No uniform rules apply for the repayment of loans; terms vary considerably depending on the nature of the project. As a rule loans are made at 4¾ percent, but a few loans have been made at 3¾ percent, mainly to native local government councils for non-profit ventures.

The initial finance for the fund's operations was provided by the transfer of approximately £A56,700 from the Commonwealth Government. This amount represented profits of the Production Control Board earned from trading with indigenes during the Australia/New Guinea Administrative Unit (ANGAU) control of the Territory during the war period. In 1962/63, the fund was supplemented by an appropriation of

£A10,000 from the Administration. Interest earnings and repayment of loans have also contributed to resources, enabling financing on a revolving basis.

The fund started off very slowly. By the middle of 1963, a total of 372 loans had been approved in the amount of £A291,620 (average £A784, but the spread is very large). About two-thirds of the loans have been approved during the three most recent years. The record of service payments has generally been satisfactory although in some instances borrowers have found it necessary to dispose of their assets to repay their loan.

The native loans scheme is intended to associate credit and extension work. Extension officers of the Department of Agriculture and the Department of Trade and Industry are directly engaged in assisting in the preparation of loan applications and supervising the borrower's activities.

As indicated earlier, the Native Loans Fund makes loans to applicants who would not be considered a normal credit risk by established financial institutions. In some cases, however, the applicant may be considered near the normal credit standard and in such cases the applicant may be referred to a trading bank with a guarantee from the Administration for the loan given. Recently this has occurred in an increasing number of cases. The process contributes in bringing the indigenous population to a closer understanding of banking and commercial practices.

Other Sources of Finance

The commercial houses provide small-scale consumer credit and business credit of 30 days, as normally provided in Australia. In some cases they have extended credit to primary producers.

Hire-purchase credits are provided by some banks and Australian finance companies (the equity capital of the latter has in turn been provided in part by banks). The role of these credits is fairly important and has increased over time. Unfortunately, statistical information on total transactions is lacking and the Mission recommends that it be collected. Part of the hire-purchase financing is done by the CDB. Its credits during the period January 1960 to June 1963 totaled 185 in the amount of £A205,000.

The Reserve Bank is actively carrying on an education program to encourage the formation of savings and loan societies in the Territory. Such societies could become a source of credit of some importance to the indigenous sector. In fact, the opinion has been expressed that at a later stage the societies could also increase their lendable resources by borrowing from the trading banks; this might be one way of expanding the role of the trading banks as a source of credit for the indigenous sector.

Legislation providing for the formation of savings and loan societies came into operation only in May 1962. By June 1963, 52 savings clubs had been formed with total savings of about £A9,000 and four societies with total savings of £A3,000. A savings club is preliminary to the formation of a full society. It is an informal association which provides for members to save regularly in a common fund, but without the ability to lend the funds accumulated.

Little information exists on the financing of private investment as a whole. The sources mentioned in the preceding paragraphs have financed part of this investment. The larger part of private investment will have been financed, however, from reinvested profits and foreign capital. Against this, there has been an outflow of capital in recent years, perhaps of £A3 to £A5 million a year (see Chapter 1). On the assumption that confidence will be stabilized and that the Administration will adopt a positive development policy, Europeans and other non-indigenes with investments in the Territory should be prepared to reinvest locally a substantial portion of their future profits.

Inadequacy of Existing Credit Facilities

The credit facilities are not adequate to meet the credit requirements of the program recommended by the Mission. As already noted, the lending authority of the savings banks is limited. The Mission was impressed with the ability of the trading banks to provide the types of credit which are their responsibility. As the economy expands there will be an increasing need for the credit and services of both the trading and savings banks. The trading banks, however, are not organized or orientated to implementing an aggressive policy of development financing. They have a commercial banking outlook which is in keeping with their responsibilities. They require the security of land with recorded individual title, charge interest rates in line with those prevailing in Australia and finance only a relatively modest share of the total cost of new projects; also their period of lending is too limited. In general, they attempt to apply to the Territory the policies adapted for Australia. Nevertheless, the Mission believes that the trading banks should be able to take an increasing part, along with the Territory Development Finance Company recommended by the Mission, in financing sound development.

The officers and personnel of both the savings and trading banks are assigned from Australia, and assignments are generally limited to two or sometimes three years. The employee is dependent for promotion on progress in the Australian branches and can hardly afford the luxury of a longer assignment in the Territory. On the other hand, the normal two-year assignment is not long enough as it gives only enough time for the employee to acquire a good working knowledge of the people, conditions and opportunities in the Territory when the assignment comes to an end.

The Commonwealth Development Bank under its present operational policies cannot, as the circumstances of the Territory may require, follow a credit policy substantially at variance with that of its offices in Australia; in practice it requires the security of a recorded title; it covers under its present operating policies only a rather narrow margin of risk in addition to that assumed by the trading banks; it has no staff in the Territory, the private banks acting as its agent; and all loans and basic decisions have to be referred to headquarters in Australia.

The Ex-Servicemen's Credit Scheme is not a solution to the credit problem. It is restricted to ex-servicemen, from the economic point of view an irrelevant criterion, and in any event its authority to lend has expired.

The Native Loans Fund is authorized to make loans on terms and conditions which generally meet the requirements of the Territory. However, the original justification for limiting the criterion of eligibility for loans to the native and mixed race sectors (as noted above, the origin of the funds were profits from trading with natives) no longer has force. The restriction should be abolished; loans should not be made on the basis of race but credit should be available for development loans to all persons who meet the loan requirements. Also, the present direction of the fund by a group of civil servants already overloaded with other urgent tasks is not a desirable situation. As recommended later in this chapter, the Native Loans Fund should be transferred to and merged with the Territory Development Finance Company.

DEVELOPMENT CREDIT

Need for Development Credit

The five-year development program recommended by the Mission will require medium and long-term financing for productive investments in the private sector, as well as technical assistance to review, promote and develop investments.

The credit requirements estimated for each sector of the economy are summarized in Table 4. These estimates are subject to various assumptions and qualifications in addition to those mentioned in the footnotes and are only intended to indicate rough orders of magnitude. For forestry we were not able to give a satisfactory estimate, but it can be assumed that the exploitation of forest resources will require credit. Also, implementation of the program is bound to vary from the projections. Some activities will not keep pace with projections, others will exceed expectations and further, there will be a need for credit for new projects not considered by the Mission. We would also emphasize that there is only a limited experience in development lending and new credit facilities will take time to staff, organize and gain experience in sound and effective lending.

The Mission believes that the capital structure of the Territory Development Finance Company recommended in the next section should be based on the estimated credit requirements for the next five years as given in Table 4.

TABLE 4: Estimated Credit Requirements, 1964/65–1968/69

		(£A million)
Agriculture, Livestock, Forestry and Fisheries		
Coconut Plantings	2.30	
Cocoa Plantings	3.10	
Rubber Plantings	1.80	
Tea Plantings	1.20	
Livestock Expansion	0.60	
Forest Development		
		9.00
Secondary Industry and Tourism		
Processing of Agricultural Produce	1.75 [a]	
Other Secondary Industries	1.50 [b]	
Hotel Construction and Modernization	0.40	
		3.65
Transport		
Harbor Storage Facilities	0.80	
Coastal Shipping	4.00 [c]	
Air Transport	0.75 [d]	
Road Transport	1.80 [e]	
		7.35
		20.00

[a] Processing facilities for coconut, cocoa, coffee, etc., insofar as not included under Agriculture.

[b] Estimate based on survey of promising industrial ventures.

[c] Two-thirds of estimated investment expenditures in new and reconditioned ships and ancillary facilities.

[d] Estimated requirements of small operators and for airport cargo facilities.

[e] Estimated requirements for trucks and terminal and maintenance facilities.

Proposed Territory Development Finance Company

The Mission recommends that a Territory Development Finance Company should be organized to provide credit for the development program in amounts and on terms and conditions which meet the requirements of the Territory. The finance company could be organized as a private institution or as a government bank.

As the function of the finance company would be to provide long-term finance for the private sector, there could be advantages to having the ownership in private hands to assure that the operations would be directed by persons experienced in private investment. The Mission does not believe, however, that private sources, either in Australia or the Territory, could be expected to provide the capital estimated by the Mission to be needed by the bank over the next five to ten years. It would not be necessary, however, for private sources to provide all of the capital. Finance companies have been organized in other parts of the world on the basis that private sources subscribe the share capital and control the policy and operations with government and other sources supplying much larger sums of capital in the form of loans. Even so, it is not likely that private sources would be prepared to subscribe the share capital. The activities envisaged for the finance company in making, as example, many small agricultural loans to native farmers and in identifying, formulating and promoting investments will be expensive. With high overhead costs, the finance company can hardly be profitable enough to attract private investors without a large subsidy. The Mission assumes, therefore, that the Territory Development Finance Company will need to be organized as a government institution.

As a government institution, the finance company could be either an affiliate of the Commonwealth Banking Corporation or an independent bank organized under the laws of the Territory or in Australia.

A Territory Development Finance Company, as an affiliate of the Commonwealth Banking Corporation, should have a separate identity and authority and resources which would make it possible to develop policies and operations to fit the specific conditions of the Territory. Policies for Australia determined from the headquarters of the Commonwealth Banking Corporation in Sydney therefore should not *per se* be applicable to the Territory. To accomplish this, the organizational structure would need to be materially different from that of the Commonwealth Trading Bank, the Commonwealth Savings Bank and the Commonwealth Development Bank, the three existing units.

A finance company organized in the Territory would have the advantage of identity with the Territory. Its responsibility to finance sound development in the Territory would require that its policies would be directed to this end. Its board of directors, when composed of experienced persons both from the Territory and Australia and comprising representatives from Government as well as the private sector, would be able to draw on the experience in Australia.

However organized, the finance company should be able to draw on the extensive experience of the Commonwealth Banking Corporation, other government organizations and private banks. The Commonwealth Banking Corporation and other organizations should be prepared to second personnel to the finance company, at least in the early years, in order that it could have the benefit of such experienced staff.

In the organization and in the formulation of policies and procedures for a successful finance company, the following are important subjects to be taken into consideration:

Capital Structure. The capital structure of the finance company should be adequate to provide the volume of development credit needed to effectively implement the development program. It is assumed that most of the capital will be provided by the Commonwealth Government. If the finance company is organized in the Territory, there would be advantages in having the Commonwealth Government make the capital available through the Administration.

Management and Staff. The management should be experienced with an investment instead of a commercial banking outlook. Its investment decisions should take as much account of the economic and financial prospects of the enterprises being assisted as they do of purely credit security factors. From the beginning of operations, there should also be a sufficient quantity of skilled staff to carry out technical and financial appraisals and to follow up assisted projects. Both management and staff should live in the Territory and every effort should be made for their services to be extended over a period of years and not limited to the two-year assignments now in practice for the trading and savings banks.

Terms and Conditions. The terms and conditions for credit should, in addition to meeting the requirements of sound development lending, meet the particular requirements of the Territory. In agriculture, for example, funds will be needed to finance planting of tree crops such as coconuts, cocoa, rubber and perhaps even coffee; some of these do not come to full bearing for seven or eight years and for rubber and coconuts the period is about ten years. Other agricultural crops, cattle, exploitation and processing of timber, manufacturing, processing of agricultural produce, hotel construction and transport all will need financing. Thus, long as well as medium-term loans will be needed. The term of the loan should make it possible for the borrower to implement the project being financed with confidence that he will not have to take action to make payments or refinance the project to its disadvantage. In effect, the term of a loan should be for a sufficient period to permit the borrower to make the payments from the proceeds of the investment. Therefore, some loans could not be repaid in less than 15 years whereas most could be for shorter periods.

The payment of principal should normally be deferred until the income from the investment is sufficient to make such payments. On the other hand, where it is possible for the borrower to do so, interest payments should be required to be made from the beginning. It is particularly desirable that those borrowers with little or no experience in borrowing money should appreciate that the money has to be returned with interest. Under native custom, when borrowing involved gold-lip shell or other commodities, there was no interest, no time limit on the debt or schedule for repayment. The requirement that interest be paid as it falls due, without deferment, should be a useful technique in helping indigenous borrowers understand the meaning and operation of credit in a modern economy.

In many instances (especially in the case of tree crops) returns on investment are bound to be slow and risks considerable. This, combined with the desirability of creating special incentives, makes it important that credits will be available on suitable terms, including appropriate terms of repayment and rates of interest. Care should be taken that the terms should not open the way to uneconomic investments; proper screening and supervision of projects are the tools to prevent this.

In all loans the borrower should have a reasonable equity. Loans should not cover the full amounts of investment but the finance company should be prepared, as a matter of practice, to lend for more than 50 percent of a project. It will undoubtedly be necessary to use development credit as an incentive to interest entrepreneurs to invest in projects which can make a useful contribution to development. The percentage of the total investment covered by the loan may be the deciding factor.

The finance company may be expected to be called upon to provide, in particular, loan capital, but it should also have the power to take equity participation in suitable circumstances.

The finance company should be prepared to lend without the security of land. Land can only be security where there is a recorded title. The non-indigene will generally have a recorded title. The indigene, except in settlement areas, will be planting tree crops and raising cattle on lands to which he may have no more than a right of use and for which there is no recorded title. Mortgage loans would, therefore, be difficult or impossible. Chattels and the borrower may be the only security.

Technical Assistance Needs. It should be again noted that the indigene has had little or no experience in borrowing and repaying money with interest. Credits for expansion of native agriculture will undoubtedly raise many problems due to lack of knowledge about the background and general performance of the borrower. Preparing a farm plan will be a new experience for most native borrowers and if the lending requirements of a development-oriented financing institution are to be met, this type of borrower will need assistance. The finance company, in cooperation with the appropriate departments of the Administration, should organize to provide the necessary assistance. This should include in the case of an agricultural loan, for example, the preparation of a farm plan, the supervision of farm development in its use of the credit, and technical assistance in processing and marketing the product. The finance company could organize a staff to provide such services, but staffing is difficult under Territory conditions and takes time. The Mission, therefore, recommends that the staff of the Department of Agriculture, Stock and Fisheries be used to perform such services. Under the circumstances, this appears the only workable solution. The department has an extension service which is to be substantially expanded. The extension officers will be working closely with and providing technical guidance to the native farmer and, at least in the beginning, should be used by the finance company for appraisal and follow-up on credits. This will mean an indirect subsidy by the Administration to the finance company. The finance company will, of course, need a staff to review and approve agricultural loans and handle debt collection.

There is a scarcity of information and facts about investment opportunities. Promising investments need to be identified and technical advice and assistance should be available to review, formulate and promote investments. Management skills and experience which can be attracted to new investments are scarce and there is need to attract them from outside. The indigene has little experience and will need guidance in starting and operating small businesses. Enterprises too small to be able alone to attract capital and skills need help. Technical assistance could be helpful in stimulating foreign investments by acting as a channel through which Australian and foreign capital, management and skills can be brought into the Territory. The finance company will need a staff to handle such services but in doing so it should coordinate its activities with those of the Department of Trade and Industry.

One Institution Only. In view of the smallness of the economy of the Territory and the difficulties of staffing, the temptation should be resisted to establish more than one institution. A multiplicity of financial institutions each responsible for lending to a single sector—agriculture, industry, etc.—is not at this time justified, and development credit for both agricultural and non-agricultural purposes should be handled by the same institution. In making this recommendation, the Mission recognizes that it will be necessary to establish a strong agricultural credit department within the finance company. There will be a large volume of agricultural loans to indigenes which for the most part will be for small amounts. Such loans, in addition to the support given by the extension service, will be costly and perhaps difficult to service. The staff of the finance company must be organized accordingly.

The Ex-Servicemen's Credit Scheme and the Native Loans Fund should be transferred to the finance company and the Commonwealth Development ment Bank should discontinue its activities in the Territory when the new finance company is established.

Budgetary Requirements of the Credit Program

Special credit requirements were established earlier at a total of about £A20 million for the five-year period. For planning purposes, the Mission would suggest that £A3 million annually be set aside as the Commonwealth Government/Administration contribution to the financing of the finance company. When additional funds are needed, the Commonwealth Government or the Administration could make them available. Funds might also be obtained from the Commonwealth Banking Corporation or borrowed from other sources.

PUBLIC REVENUE

Internal Current Revenue

Structure and Level of Internal Current Revenue. The present tax system is to a considerable extent the result of basic changes in tax legislation introduced during 1959. In that year, an income tax was introduced for both individuals and companies. Existing export duties were abolished and the structure of import duties was changed; duties on foodstuffs, clothing and other items which enter into the cost-of-living or are considered essential for developmental purposes were abolished or reduced, and those on a number of other items, in particular luxuries and semi-luxuries, were raised.

Before the change, import and export duties were the preponderant sources of tax revenue, producing well over 90 percent of the total. Thereafter, the share of remaining customs duties (import duties) in total tax revenue has been less than one-half, whereas the income tax has provided less than one-half also (see Table 5). Other sources of tax

TABLE 5: Administration Revenue

(£A thousand)

	1951/52	1954/55	1957/58	1958/59	1959/60	1960/61	1961/62	1962/63	1963/64[a]
				(fiscal years ended June 30)					
INTERNAL CURRENT REVENUE									
Tax Revenue									
Income Tax, Individual[b]	—	—	—	—	942	1,226	1,355	1,535	1,750
Income Tax, Companies[b]	—	—	—	—	871	1,122	857	1,044	1,150
Personal Tax	—	—	103	154	175	147	111	95	85
Import Duties	951	1,344	2,134	2,142	1,956	2,258	2,497	2,760	2,950
Export Duties	495	708	535	1,142	313	—	—	—	—
Excise[c]	—	33	73	83	137	172	178	289	330
Stamp Duties[d]	11	32	87	68	82	86	123	120	110
Total Tax Revenue	1,457	2,117	2,932	3,589	4,476	5,011	5,121	5,843	6,375
Other Revenue									
Other Customs[e]	140	68	123	161	161	193	196	207	215
Licenses, Fees, Fines [f]	58	85	112	121	128	148	170	187	219
Postal	95	135	296	354	412	496	581	658	737
Lands[g]	48	121	199	115	102	131	117	152	141
Timber Leases and Permits	20	59	82	82	101	121	147	160	175
Agriculture[h]	76	58	62	83	129	104	181	146	151
Public Utilities [i]	72	200	454	553	591	633	673	788	235[j]
Miscellaneous[k]	424	311	466	547	494	614	520	884	2,282[l]
Total Other Revenue	933	1,037	1,794	2,016	2,118	2,440	2,585	3,182	4,155
Total Internal Current Revenue	2,391	3,154	4,726	5,605	6,594	7,452	7,706	9,024	10,530
COMMONWEALTH GRANT	5,285	7,126	10,796	11,479	12,808	14,797	17,293	20,000	25,250
LOANS	—	—	—	—	—	552	497	898	1,700
Grand Total	7,676	10,280	15,522	17,084	19,402	22,801	25,496	29,922	37,480

386

ᵃ Budget estimates.

ᵇ The amounts for income tax in this table are gross, i.e., before deduction of refunds (tax rebate); refunds for 1959/60–1962/63 were (in £A thousand) 13; 191; 332 and 379; and the estimate for 1963/64 is 400.

ᶜ Excise duties are levied on beer (since 1952/53) and on tobacco (since 1959/60).

ᵈ Probate, succession and general stamp duty.

ᵉ Harbor dues, storage, etc.

ᶠ Motor registration, liquor permits, trading permits, judicial fees, etc.

ᵍ Leases, sales of allotments, etc.

ʰ Mainly sale of crops and livestock.

ⁱ Electricity, water, sanitation, etc.

ʲ Decrease explained by establishment of Electricity Commission (revenue of Commission not included).

ᵏ Health, timber sales, mining royalties, rent of buildings, labor pools, general stores, government printer, motor transport, former years, etc.

ˡ Figure not comparable with previous years due to change in accounting procedure for general stores, government printer and motor transport.

SOURCES: Budget Papers and Department of Territories, Economic and Statistical Branch.

387

revenue of the Administration (together less than 10 percent of the total) are excise, stamp duties and the personal tax.[7]

Current non-tax revenues (other than the grant of the Commonwealth Government) have on a gross basis equalled about one-half of tax revenue or somewhat more. On a net basis, i.e., after deduction of related expenditures, their contribution would be substantially smaller. For instance, postal revenue, included in gross revenue, is estimated at £A737,000 for 1963/64, whereas in fact postal services are run at a loss. Due to difficulties in relating specific expenditures to specific revenues it is not possible to compute all revenue net on a consistent basis.

In the budget for 1963/64, a number of additional items have been included among revenue (for general stores, government printer and motor transport) which are in fact offsets of expenditures. Although this procedure may be desirable for accounting purposes, the Mission considers it a step backward from the point of view of showing in the budget meaningful revenue figures. Due to this accounting procedure, current internal revenue included in the budget was inflated to the extent of £A1.6 million. On the other hand, the exclusion from the budget of revenue from electricity due to the establishment of the Electricity Commission resulted in a decrease by more than £A0.5 million. The result therefore was a net increase by more than £A1 million out of a total of £A10.5 million.

Total tax revenue levied by the Administration in 1962/63 of £A5.62 million equalled about 10 percent of Gross Domestic Product (at market prices) in the monetized sector of the economy.[8] The corresponding percentage for total internal current revenue amounted to some 14 percent.[9]

Besides the Administration, local government councils are collecting current revenue directly. This revenue has risen from about £A20,000 during the calendar year 1952 to about £A310,000 in 1962. About three-quarters of the total is now derived from the council tax. Other small items of revenue differ from case to case and consist of proceeds from commercial operations (e.g., hire of trucks) and some license fees (e.g., dog licenses).

The contribution of the indigenous people to public revenues is small. The Administration probably collected by way of direct and indirect

[7] In addition, revenue from motor registration and licenses, included in Table 5 among *Other Revenue*, can be classified as tax revenue.

[8] Exclusive of tax rebates and inclusive of revenue from motor registration and licenses. The percentage is no more than a rough approximation in view of the global nature of Domestic Product estimates.

[9] After elimination of about £A750,000 on account of postal revenue and resale of cash crops, which should be regarded as direct offsets of current expenditures.

taxation from the indigenes about £A540,000 in 1962/63 or less than 10 percent of total tax receipts. Adding the taxes paid to the local government councils, approximating £A260,000 in 1962/63, the total tax burden was about £A800,000. This may be compared with indigenous incomes in the money economy estimated at £A16 million in 1962/63, giving a ratio of 5 percent. If the subsistence incomes of indigenes are also taken into account, this ratio is, of course, much smaller. Although, as indicated in Chapter 1, the average incomes of the indigenous people are small, the tax burden on them appears light by comparison with many other developing countries.

A new development since 1962 is the provision of grants-in-aid by the Administration to local government councils (prior to that, there had been little or no assistance of this kind). As yet the amounts involved have been quite small. The Department of Public Health provided £A4,330 in 1961/62 and £A20,000 in 1962/63 by way of subsidies for environmental sanitation, hospital buildings and salaries for health employees (on a varying scale, depending on the financial position of a council). Also, some councils have now been formed, in areas of low income, receiving a general subsidy from the Administration to permit the purchase of essential furniture and employment of key personnel (by mid-1963, four councils had benefited under this scheme to a total amount of £A1,500).[10]

Income, Personal and Council Taxes.

Income Tax. This tax, applicable to both individuals and companies, was introduced at the beginning of the fiscal year 1959/60. About 14,000 individuals and more than 400 companies pay income taxes. The key staff administering the tax includes a number of officers seconded by the Commonwealth Government. The legislation was based broadly on that of the Australian income tax. However, the rates are approximately half the corresponding rates in Australia and concessional deductions are about one-half higher than corresponding deductions.[11]

Salary and wage income is taxed at the source;[12] with respect to other sources of income (of individuals and companies) a system of provisional assessment exists.

[10] In addition, some of the relatively small amounts available to District Commissioners for road work have been allocated by the latter to contribute toward the cost of road projects started by councils.

[11] Income tax is levied in Australia solely by the Commonwealth Government.

[12] With respect to salaries and wages in excess of £A7/10/- a week.

Certain kinds of income benefit from exemptions from income tax. These include income of religious missions and income derived from gold mining.

Rates payable on taxable income of individuals are progressive. The scale starts with a tax liability of 1d per £A1 (0.4 percent) for taxable income up to £A150 and reaches a maximum of 6/8 per £A1 (33.3 percent) for taxable income in excess of £A12,000. For incomes of, for instance, £A2,000, £A4,000 and £A12,000, the tax rates are 9.3, 15 and 24.4 percent, respectively.

The rate payable by public companies is a flat 20 percent of taxable income. For private companies the rate is 12.5 percent of taxable income up to £A5,000 and 17.5 percent of remaining taxable income. A private company is liable to pay additional tax if it does not make a "sufficient distribution" of its taxable income by way of dividends.[13] This additional tax on the insufficient distribution is imposed at the rate of 33.3 percent.

In determining the tax base (taxable income), a series of deductions from gross income are applicable, including:

a. Expenses incurred in gaining or producing assessable income other than expenses of a capital, private or domestic nature. Depreciation rates allowed are generally higher than in Australia.

b. Special deductions, including a carry-forward of losses incurred during the previous seven years, deductions by primary producers for capital expenditure which will bring land into production or improve the productive qualities of land already in use and certain deductions for those engaged in the timber and mining industries.

c. Concessional deductions. These are family and personal allowances granted to resident taxpayers, as follows:
   i. personal allowance of £A286;
   ii. deductions for dependents: spouse, daughter-housekeeper and parent £A230; child less than 16 years of age, student child and invalid relative £A130;
   iii. certain domestic and private expenditure, such as medical and dental expenses, education expenses, life insurance premiums and leave fares (in the case of self-employed persons); these deductions are subject to certain maxima.

The Mission is in basic agreement with the Administration's policy of keeping the burden of the tax on the European sector light. A tax lower than in Australia is desirable to increase the attractiveness of private

[13] Sufficient distribution equals distributable income (i.e., taxable income minus tax payable at regular rate for private companies) minus retention allowance (50 percent of first £A2,000 of distributable income plus 40 percent of balance of distributable income—both with regard to non-property income—plus 10 percent of distributable income from property other than dividend from other private companies).

investment and to attract and retain badly needed European staff. Also, in Australia, a lower income tax applies for incentive reasons to Zone A which comprises the torrid northern part of the country, in particular the Northern Territory. The lower tax burden for Zone A is the result of higher deductions than those existing for Australia at large; tax rates applicable to taxable income are not lower in Zone A. As long as the large majority of taxpayers in Papua and New Guinea consists of Australians, it appears reasonable for them to pay a lower income tax than that applicable to their counterparts in the Northern Territory. Furthermore, residents of Papua and New Guinea do not enjoy the same level of social services and amenities as taxpayers in Australia.

The preceding arguments are in part not applicable to the income tax on companies, but incentive reasons plus the desirability of a certain balance in the rates for individuals and companies make a substantially lower tax burden than in Australia equally justifiable.

In view of the Mission's general endorsement of a light burden of income tax, it feels that no general increase should be made at this time. The Administration, however, may want to make some adjustments in the distribution of the burden among income groups and categories of taxpayers which together could produce some additional revenue.

Special tax concessions for incentive reasons with regard to secondary industry have already been discussed in Chapter 4. As mentioned there, the Mission advocates the introduction of an income tax holiday for pioneer industries and dividends paid by these industries,[14] provision for accelerated depreciation of new plant and equipment and more lenient treatment of undistributed profits of private companies. For reasons of revenue, additional concessions should be limited and selective. Apart from the concessions mentioned, the Administration should hold the line on further concessions, since the income tax rates themselves are concessional.

The Mission sees no justification for the complete exemption from tax of the income of missions. A number of missions are involved in economic activities on a substantial scale. We recommend that the income of missions derived from these activities be made subject to tax.

Almost no indigenes are as yet subject to income tax. This is primarily due to the low level of indigenous incomes, but also to the prevailing system of communal ownership and the adaptation to European standards of exemptions and deductions. The Mission believes that this latter situation has to be accepted since for a considerable time to come non-

[14] As indicated in Chapter 4, the Mission also suggests that, to make the tax holiday effective in respect of profits remitted to Australia, these profits be exempted from Australian taxation. This should also apply to dividends in appropriate cases.

indigenes will remain by far the most important contributors to income tax, both in numbers and size of income. For the indigenes, at this stage of development other forms of taxation should be developed, to be discussed below.

Personal and Council Taxes. A *personal tax* is levied by the Administration on all male persons 18 years of age or over; it was introduced at the beginning of 1958.[15] This tax is now raised almost entirely from indigenes. A person is not liable for the personal tax if he has paid income tax in an amount not less than the amount of the personal tax for which he would be otherwise liable.

The administration of the tax is flexible, both as regards rates and applicability. Rates are fixed annually and are based on ability to pay. The maximum rate of tax has been £A2, with lower rates for specified areas. The personal tax is levied only in areas with significant economic activity and where cash incomes are being earned by the indigenes.

Persons liable for local government council tax (to be discussed below) pay only that part of the personal tax, if any, which exceeds the council tax. Exemption or reduction of the tax may be granted according to personal circumstances such as lack of means or hardship. The personal tax is assessed and payment is made annually on demand, by cash only, to a patrol officer or Treasury official, who issues receipts to each individual taxpayer.

Native local government *council tax* is levied by and on behalf of councils within their area. The council tax is subject to the rules of the various councils. Here again, considerable flexibility regarding rates and applicability exists. In general, all males of 17 years and over are subject to the tax, unless they qualify for an exemption. Females of 17 years and over are taxed if they wish to be enrolled and must pay tax to be eligible to vote. Taxes for 1963 varied from 10/-d to £A5 for male persons and from 1/-d to £A2 for females. The importance of the council tax has grown with the increase in the number of councils and the higher cash income of the native sector.[16] As follows from the preceding remarks, the rise in revenue from council tax reduces collections of personal tax.

As emphasized throughout the report, the Mission attaches considerable importance to policies and measures that tend to foster and strengthen the sense of responsibility of the indigenous people. The personal and council taxes are particularly useful in this context. As in the case of other direct taxes, collection is felt directly by the individual and the two taxes

[15] Prior to World War II, a head tax for males had already been in existence in both Papua and New Guinea at the rate of 10/-d. There were a considerable number of exceptions to the general applicability of this tax.

[16] As mentioned in Chapter 1, the first councils were established in 1950, but most of them were set up only in recent years.

therefore have considerable educational value, apart from the revenue produced. As levied and collected they have shortcomings, however. Both taxes take account of the personal circumstances of the taxpayer to only a very limited extent; in particular, they leave virtually untaxed those natives with substantial cash incomes. In addition, the personal tax in urban areas, and in some rural areas as well, remains largely uncollected due to lack of adequate administrative machinery. Although these problems can only gradually be overcome, the personal and council taxes have a good potential and for a considerable time to come will offer the best prospects for taxing the indigene through direct taxation. This is confirmed in particular by experience in some of the African countries, where amounts collected from personal taxes are substantial.[17]

As the tax operates in these countries, persons (or, typically, adult males) are subject to a minimum tax. Those with higher incomes are assessed on a graduated scale, up to a maximum figure that is reached roughly at the level of income at which the income tax becomes effective. Assessment is usually made on a local basis, by a committee of county and village officials or non-officials who are familiar with local conditions. For employees, the tax is based on actual income; for the typical semi-subsistence farmer, it is based on external criteria of probable income such as acreage and number of cows. Non-indigenes are usually assessed at the maximum unless they file a return to demonstrate lower income.

The Mission recommends that the Administration close, to the extent possible, the gaps in collection and make it a long-term objective to raise more revenue from personal and council taxes, in particular by graduating the tax to take account of differences in income. Coordination with the income tax can be assured as at present. In case of levying of an export tax, as discussed later, an effort should be made to take this factor into account in levying the personal or council tax, although this will admittedly be difficult and at best be possible in only a global manner.

The objective should be to gradually transform the personal tax now levied into a local tax. This conforms to the Administration's present policy. When revenue is used for local expenditures, the educational effect and compliance may be expected to be largest. Nevertheless, where local government units do not yet exist or local administrative machinery is inadequate, the tax should be collected by the Administration, as at present.

While the Mission favors in principle the taxing of the income of natives through the personal tax (including the council tax), the poten-

---

[17] Due, John F., *Taxation and Economic Development in Tropical Africa*, Cambridge, Massachusetts, Massachusetts Institute of Technology Press, 1963; especially Chapter 5.

tials for increasing collections during the next five years appear quite limited. Levying of personal taxes in a more sophisticated form will require more elaborate machinery for collection than is available at present. To obtain satisfactory results, collection will have to be entrusted largely to educated indigenes. Also, efforts to subject the indigene to personal taxation in more advanced forms can hardly be successful as long as the indigene himself has not reached a higher level of education. Given the present status of education, these conditions will not be fulfilled in the short run. We therefore believe that in considering possibilities of making natives with cash incomes pay a reasonable share of the tax burden, it is appropriate to examine the opportunities in the fields of indirect taxation and direct payment for services. This approach is in accordance with the experience in other countries at an early stage of development, where invariably the expansion of direct taxation of an uneducated indigenous population has been found most difficult.

Import, Export, Excise and Stamp Duties.

Import Duties. Import duties are the most important single source of revenue. Specific duties apply to ales, wines, spirits, tobacco manufactures and petroleum products and now produce about 70 percent of total revenue from import duties. *Ad valorem* duties are levied on apparel, textiles, manufactured fibers, machinery and transport equipment and a group of miscellaneous items; they account for the remaining 30 percent. Originally Papua and New Guinea had separate tariffs but in October 1957, both were made subject to a single schedule of tariffs.

The primary purpose of tariff policy has been and still is the production of revenue. In addition, it has been the policy to apply or not apply duties in a manner which will assist in keeping down the cost-of-living, reducing the cost of imports conducive to development, including those of importance to new industries and protecting local industries.

As already mentioned, the structure of import duties was changed in connection with the introduction of the income tax on July 1, 1959. Tariff changes then introduced resulted, on the basis of the 1957/58 import structure, in reductions of £A360,000 versus increases of about £A140,000 (mainly for luxuries and semi-luxuries), leaving on balance a reduction of £A220,000.

In line with the general policy outlined, many consumer goods (food-stuffs, textiles, furniture, footwear, medicines, detergents, etc.) are now imported into the Territory duty free or are subject to low rates of 5 percent or 10 percent. The same is true for many capital goods and raw materials, such as machinery, tractors, building materials, cement, coal and coke, and agricultural and industrial chemicals. Examples of duties intended to protect specific industries are those on ale and beer (4/-d per gallon margin on excise), trade tobacco (3/9d per lb. margin on excise), plywood and paint (in both cases 15 percent tariff).

Import duties are applicable irrespective of the country of origin (including Australia). The major difference with Australian import duties (disregarding rates) is that the Territory operates a single column tariff (without preferences to any country), whereas Australia has a multi-column tariff providing for British preferential tariff, most favored nation treatment, general tariff and special tariff (preference), with substantial protective elements for the preservation of Australian industries.

The Mission is in basic agreement with the Administration's policy regarding import duties. It recognizes the importance of the argument that as long as the Territory is preponderantly dependent on Australia for technical and managerial staff it is important for incentive reasons to keep the cost-of-living in the main administrative centers roughly in line with that in Australia. This argument will become less important with the progressive taking over by indigenes of positions now occupied by Australians. However, as indicated throughout the report, this will take considerable time. The validity of keeping duties low on imports which affect the cost of production is obvious, although studies have shown that in the case of agricultural production the influence of this factor is quite small.

While the Mission is in general agreement with the Administration's tariff policy, it is necessary also to consider the budgetary prospects and the need for revenue. On balance, the Mission believes that an increase in import duties of about 15 percent, applied selectively, is justified and will not unduly affect the present main objectives of the Administration's policy.

In 1958, preceding the basic changes in the tax system, an extensive analysis was made of the then existing structure of import duties and subsequent changes were made in the light of that study. We recommend that another review of import duties be now undertaken on the basis that more revenue will be needed. Imported commodities sold preponderantly to indigenes should not be excluded from selective increases in import duties.

Export Duties. Export duties were already in existence prior to World War II. Separate and different legislation applied to Papua and New Guinea. Both Territories taxed the exports of copra and certain marine products such as shell. Papua and New Guinea taxed the export of gold and New Guinea had an export duty on certain types of feathers and sulfur (of little practical significance). Following the war, export duties were gradually made uniform. In 1951, uniform legislation was introduced for copra.[18] Rubber was subjected to duty in 1952 and cocoa in 1953.[19]

The system of export duty for the whole Territory consisted of a graduated scale of specific rates (i.e., a rising duty when the price per unit of weight increased), related to an assessed value declared on a monthly basis. If prices fell below a certain floor, no duty was levied. Most important in terms of revenue was the export duty on copra, which during 1955/56–1958/59 produced 75 to 85 percent of total revenue from export duties; in earlier years the percentage was over 90. In 1958/59, a year of high commodity prices, revenue from export duties reached a maximum of over £A1.1 million, more than one-fifth of all internal current revenue.

All export duties were abolished commencing July 1, 1959. The changes in the tax system at that time resulted, for the non-indigenous agricultural producers, in a substitution of export duties by income tax, although naturally not always in an equivalent amount. Indigenous producers of export crops, on the other hand, were exempted from export tax without, in practice, being subjected to a proper substitute. As a result indigenous producers will pay little or no tax on their expected rise in export production. Since the possibilities of taxing the indigenous farmers by direct rather than indirect taxation—in principle the preferable solution—will, as discussed before, be quite limited for a considerable period of time, the Mission believes serious consideration should be given to the possibility of the reintroduction of a system of export duties.

The Mission is not unaware of a number of disadvantages and difficulties inherent to this solution. Objections against export duties can be raised, *inter alia*, on the grounds that they can have disincentive effects, that they imply unequal treatment among different industries and among individual producers of the same crop (since duties are levied on gross sales and not on income) and that they are onerous in particular for new large-scale producers during the initial years when plantings have not yet reached full bearing. In addition, reintroduction would have to be accompanied by a system of rebates against income tax for European producers, either by allowing export duty paid as a deductible item, in full or in part, in determining taxable income, or by giving an outright rebate against the amount of income tax due. In the first case, the tax burden for the European producer would in fact remain higher than before the reintroduction of export duty and in both cases there would be

[18] In 1946/47, a levy to create a stabilization fund was imposed on all copra exported from Papua and New Guinea. Part of the duty collected on copra was paid to the fund to this end. The levy was discontinued together with the duty in 1959.

[19] The remaining export duties in the separate schedules were repealed in 1957; new legislation came into operation in 1957 for shell.

no relief for infant producers not yet subject to income tax who need it most. The latter problem might be relieved by temporary exemption from export duty above a certain minimum.

In spite of the various complications mentioned, the Mission believes that the budgetary situation requires that the possibility of reintroduction of export duties be seriously considered. The system, as past experience has demonstrated, is relatively easy to administer, although the complications raised by the income tax admittedly did not exist before 1959. Without such reintroduction, the Mission sees little hope for taxing, during the next five years, the growing income of indigenous farmers of perennial crops.

In order to limit the adverse effects, the Mission recommends that if duties were to be reintroduced, the level initially be kept modest, on the average equivalent to, say, not more than 5 percent of export value. Duties could be specific or *ad valorem*. The Administration should examine the best way of levying in respect of the main commodities and the system should allow for sufficient flexibility in case of major price fluctuations.

Indigenous output of export crops is now of the order of £A4 million and may be expected to go up to roughly double this amount by 1968/69. On the basis of an average levy of about 5 percent, this could produce revenue of the order of £A200,000 at present, rising to double this amount in five years. Total revenue over five years would be about £A1.5 million.

Excise Duties. The only existing excise duties are those on beer (levied since 1952 and at present 5/6d per gallon) and on trade tobacco (introduced in 1959 and now 2/9d per lb.). The original levies, after introduction, were 3/6d in the case of beer and 2/3d for trade tobacco. The duty on beer is the more important, particularly since the abolition of prohibition for indigenes. In 1963/64, £A240,000 is expected to be derived from the excise on beer against £A90,000 from that on trade tobacco.

Excise duties are a logical form of indirect taxation in respect of manufactures produced domestically for the local market; in this case no import duty is levied. In case of imported manufactures, levying of excise duties is unnecessary, since the produce can be taxed at the import stage. The Mission therefore recommends that, to the extent that imported manufactures subject to customs duty will be replaced by domestically produced commodities, levying of excise should as a rule be considered. There may be reason to deviate from this principle temporarily to provide a special incentive for new industries, as has been done for the newly established cigarette factory at Madang. Also, some measure of protection can be provided by keeping the level of the excise somewhat below that of the import duty.

General Stamp Duty, Probate and Succession Duty. These duties have been in existence since the early 1950s. Stamp duties are assessed at a fixed or ad valorem rate depending on the type of instrument. They are collected by sale of adhesive stamps, or cash when documents have to be impressed. Liable for duty are a series of documents, including bills of exchange, promissory notes, conveyances or transfers on sale of real property, leases, receipts, bills of lading, deeds of settlement or gift, memoranda and articles of association of companies, transfers of marketable securities, powers of attorney and certain policies of insurance.

Probate and succession duty is levied at rates lower than in Australia and produces less revenue than general stamp duty.

Legislation on stamp duties appears to the Mission outdated and therefore due for revision, a view shared in the Administration. Revision might also make possible the raising of some additional revenue.

Other Sources of Current Revenue. As already indicated, other sources of current revenue are rather important, having produced in recent years generally about one-third of total domestic current revenues (see Table 5). In the preceding chapters, suggestions have been made for raising more revenue from some of these sources.

Customs. Revenue from this item consists, apart from import and excise duties, almost entirely of harbor dues (including wharfage, berthage and pilotage). Revenue has grown over the years roughly in line with the increase in traffic. As indicated in Chapter 5, the Mission believes that with the establishment of a Harbors Board as a separate entity an effort should be made to raise more revenue from harbors, in particular from harbor concessions, rentals and land leases.

Licenses. About three-quarters of revenue raised from licenses comes from motor registration (vehicle registration and drivers' licenses). In Chapter 5, the Mission recommended consideration of a system of regional surcharges on vehicle license fees as a form of contribution to the cost of improvement and maintenance of regional roads. In addition, revenue from licenses is derived from arms permits, liquor permits and trading and business licenses. In many countries, revenue from licenses of this nature is considered in particular suited to fit local revenue needs. The Mission therefore recommends that, if urban governments were to be established, consideration should be given to the levying of licenses for this purpose. License fees should be reviewed periodically to take account of changing conditions.[20]

---

[20] In addition to license fees for specific activities, taxes on activities specifically concentrated in towns can be a useful source of revenue. The most important general example is a tax on amusements. Consideration might be given to the introduction of such a tax.

Lands and Other Property. Revenue from lands presently comprises largely that from leases (rents) by the Administration. Sales of allotments and survey fees are smaller items. Under legislation of 1962, all leases, rural and urban, are to be reviewed every ten years. This is a change from previous legislation which provided that urban leases had to be re-appraised only after 20 years. A lessee pays a tender price and an annual rental on the unimproved capital value, periodically re-appraised. Due to lack of staff and the need to cope with new valuations there is a large backlog of re-appraisals, and payments consequently often bear little relation to the current value of a property.

The Mission appreciates that the existing situation cannot be changed overnight, but urges that a serious effort be made to gradually improve it. As discussed in Annex I, the Mission believes that in case of establishment of urban governments, the proceeds from lease of land in the towns should become part of the revenue of the urban governments. The Mission also recommends the levying, in urban areas, of a tax on both freehold and native-owned land. A tax of this nature can only be levied in a satisfactory manner if there is a proper relationship to rents paid for leasehold prop-erties. Further, the Mission favors the levying of a property tax on buildings and improvements in urban areas, and recommends that the Administration aim at the gradual introduction of such a tax.

Forestry. Revenue from forestry is now derived from timber leases and permits. Revenue is no longer derived from the sale of government timber due to the recent ending of government milling operations. Royalty from timber leases has grown regularly and may be expected to rise rapidly in the future. As discussed in Chapter 3, the Mission estimates that if log output were to be increased from a level of about 80 million super feet in 1961/62 and 1962/63 to 300 million super feet in five years, and if the royalty charge on additional output were to be on average 7/-d per 100 super feet as against 5/-d at present, additional royalties would be £A1.22 million over the next five years and, assuming the same cutting rate, £A4.4 million during a ten-year period thereafter. This estimate is based on the assumption that additional roads, bridges and wharves for handling of the timber would be financed by the Administration. If financed by the operators themselves, royalty receipts should be expected to be substantially lower.

Public Utilities. The Mission believes that more revenue should be raised from public utilities. In relation to the establishment of urban government (see Annex I), it recommends that charges for water, sewerage and sanitation should be increased to make these services self-supporting or at least to reduce substantially the operating losses. In respect of electricity rates (the proceeds of which now accrue to the Electricity Commission), the Mission is of the opinion that total revenue is at a reasonable level considering local conditions, although it believes, as discussed in Chapter 4, that the existing rate structure needs review.

Summary of Revenue Prospects. In Chapter 2, we discussed the outlook for the Administration budget during the next five years and expressed the opinion that the Administration should aim, during this period, as a minimum, at the financing of 27.5 percent of projected budgetary expenditures from taxation and other internal current revenues. To reach this objective, the Administration would have to collect internal revenue in the average amount of £A13.8 million annually (see Chapter 2, Table 2), which figure compares with estimated revenue for 1963/64 of £A10.13 million (after tax rebates).

In the following tabulation we indicate roughly how this revenue target might be realized:

	Five Years	Annual Average
	(£A million)	
Normal Revenue on the Basis of 7.5 percent Growth per Annum	63.25	12.65
Tax Increases:		
Import Duties (15 percent)	2.70	0.54
Timber Royalties	1.22	0.24
Export Duties	1.50	0.30
Various Minor Increases	0.33	0.07
	69.00	13.80

We want to emphasize that these figures serve illustrative purposes only and should not be interpreted as precise forecasts. They would appear to confirm the opinion, expressed in Chapter 2, that the revenue target should be capable of achievement. However, it is fairly ambitious if the assumed normal growth of revenue would turn out to be slower and export duties would not be reintroduced.[21] The Mission therefore stresses once more the need for a determined revenue effort on the part of the Administration.

Public Borrowing

Public borrowing by the Administration has only in recent years become a source of revenue of importance in the Territory. All borrowing

---

[21] Also, no allowance has been made for likely delays in the introduction of some tax increases.

requires approval of the Australian Loan Council. This procedure also applies to the Commonwealth Government and the Australian States. The function of the loan council is to coordinate the competing demands of all public borrowers in Australia. To this end, the loan council examines annually the combined loan programs and determines the total amount to be borrowed during the year. In addition, the terms and conditions of each loan issue are subject to approval by the loan council. All loans issued by the Territory carry a guarantee of the Commonwealth Government for the repayment of principal and interest.

Amounts of approved borrowing and those actually raised are shown in Table 6.

TABLE 6: Borrowing by the Administration [a]

(£A)

	Amounts Approved	Amounts Raised [b]
1959/60	100,000	—
1960/61	450,000	551,665
1961/62	500,000	496,776
1962/63	900,000	898,397
1963/64	1,700,000	—

[a] Does not include amounts borrowed by the Administration from banks to provide loans for housing.

[b] Contributions to revenue from loan raisings.

The loan program for Papua and New Guinea has so far been achieved by the issue of three types of loans: savings certificates (mainly for indigenous subscribers); special bonds (Territory premium securities) and private treaty loans. Of total debt outstanding by mid-1963 over 70 percent was in the form of private treaty loans, about 20 percent of Territory premium securities and less than 10 percent of savings certificates. In addition to the raising of revenue, the program intends to serve educational purposes, notably with respect to the indigenous population.

Savings certificates have a maturity of five years, are negotiable and, after three months from the date of issue, can be cashed subject to one month's notice. The major part of subscriptions have come from co-operatives, individual natives and native local government councils. The issue of savings certificates is considered costly and only moderately successful; largely, it serves educational purposes.

Territory premium securities have a maximum maturity of somewhat over seven years: they also are negotiable and may be cashed subject to one month's notice after varying prescribed periods. Here subscriptions by Europeans, companies and official trust funds have accounted for 60 to 70 percent of the total, with cooperative societies accounting for most of the remainder.

Private treaty loans (also referred to as loans by agreement) are negotiated directly between the Administration and the lender: the major lender so far has been the Copra Stabilization Board; others were various public superannuation and retirement funds. These loans are mostly long term with periods up to 40 to 45 years.

Interest rates follow Australian conditions and are, depending on market conditions at time of issue and maturities, in the range of $4\frac{1}{2}$ percent to $5\frac{7}{8}$ percent.[22]

Subscriptions to loans issued by the Administration have come largely from investors in the Territory; the only exceptions are two loans in the total amount of £A180,000 subscribed to by Australian pension funds. In some instances, Europeans who subscribed in the Territory have returned to Australia, retaining their investments.

Two groups of Territory investors who would be in a position to lend considerably larger amounts in case the Administration would need the money are savings banks and insurance companies. As pointed out earlier in this chapter, total deposits of savings banks exceed £A8 million and only a small portion of this amount has so far been invested in the Territory.[23] No comprehensive data are available on amounts collected by insurance companies in the Territory, but they are known to be fairly substantial.[24] Savings banks and insurance companies have contributed on an increasing scale during the current year 1963/64 to the fulfillment of the Administration's borrowing target of £A1.7 million.

The views of the Mission concerning future borrowing by the Administration have already been expressed in Chapter 2. The Mission advocates a policy of moderation in contracting additional public debt on the grounds that borrowing on conventional terms on a substantial scale would tend to make the Territory increasingly dependent on foreign assistance to finance the debt service burden, even in respect of debt payments due domestically. The Mission, therefore, recommends that public borrowing be kept limited and, in practice, be applied mainly for the financing of projects that may themselves be expected to produce enough revenue to cover the debt service.

[22] In the case of savings certificates, interest is payable at maturity together with principal.

[23] Increased investments in Territory loans might require minor changes in Australian banking legislation governing the investments of savings banks.

[24] The Administration has a special scheme of deductions of premiums from salaries on behalf of civil servants insured with private companies.

ANNEXES

ANNEX I *URBAN GOVERNMENT*

With the growth of urban centers, the populations of the five largest towns are now approximately as follows: Port Moresby, 33,500 people; Rabaul, 8,500; Lae, 6,500; Madang, 4,000 and Goroka, 2,500.

The Administration from Port Moresby administers the towns. There are no urban governments. The town advisory councils, which exist in most urban areas, are purely advisory, have no executive authority and their members are appointed by the Administration. The residents and organizations having business interests in urban centers have no responsibility for, and cannot effectively participate in, the affairs of the centers.

The Administration devotes a great deal of attention and energy to the direction of urban affairs but the control of urban centers, scattered throughout the Territory, by officials located in Port Moresby has serious disadvantages. The Administration is subjected frequently to criticism by people who believe that they have a better knowledge of what should be done because they live, work and have interests in the centers.

The costs of running the urban centers are paid from the Administration budget. Charges are levied for water, sewerage and sanitation services in Port Moresby and for sanitation services in other centers, but substantial losses are incurred on all these services. No rates or taxes are levied on urban properties, and no revenues are obtained from freehold land, native land or Crown land in urban areas. This has given rise to anomalies such as freehold business properties paying no property tax of any kind, although the properties are valued at many thousands of pounds and they directly benefit from government expenditures.

The only direct income to the Administration from lands within the urban centers is derived from lands which the Administration leases. The lessee pays a tender price and an annual rental on the unimproved capital value which is re-appraised every ten years. In many cases the payments have little relationship to the current value of the property. At present, the identifiable rents of leasehold properties in urban areas are very small; in 1962/63, £A26,000 in Port Moresby, £A11,000 in Rabaul, £A8,000 in Lae and £A2,000 in Madang. The basis for determining rents in urban centers needs to be re-examined and re-appraisals should be sufficiently frequent to keep abreast of rapidly changing conditions.

Estimates of the total expenditures by the Administration in the centers are not available but the major costs of providing water, sewerage and sanitation services as well as the expenditures for road construction and maintenance for 1962/63 are as follows:

	Losses on Water, Sewerage and Sanitation Services	Expenditures on Road Maintenance and Construction
Port Moresby	£A186,000	£A302,000
Rabaul	13,000 [a]	74,000
Lae	19,000	61,000
Madang	7,000	28,000

[a] Excluding the sanitation service on which the loss was unknown but was probably substantial.

In addition to the above expenditures, the Administration pays the costs of general administration, health services, fire protection, police, town cleaning, cemeteries, etc.

Historically, there were good reasons for the Central Government to administer all parts of the Territory, there being no centers of sufficient size to justify a separate administration. However, the Mission believes that development has now reached the stage where it is advisable for the Administration to divest itself of responsibility for administering the larger urban centers and to transfer responsibility to such centers. All of the major centers have people capable of directing the affairs of the centers and of providing a substantial number of the staff needed to carry out the functions of urban government.

In making this recommendation, the Mission recognizes that there are complex issues to be resolved such as the form of urban government, election procedures, the responsibilities and powers to be vested in the urban governments, the formulation of a system of local taxation or payments of rents which will be equitable and reasonably comprehensive, as well as a formula for providing grants for those activities in the centers in which the Administration should share the burden or in some instances pay the total cost. Nevertheless, the Mission believes that it is important that local governments should be established both to relieve the Central Government of the very heavy burden of administering urban centers and to encourage the growth of local responsibility and initiative.

The Administration is the principal landowner in all urban areas and its policy is to lease, not sell, land it owns. Lessees benefit from the development of urban centers and they should contribute to the costs. The

Mission suggests that leased property should be taxed by the urban governments, or that the rentals paid on leased property be adjusted so that the payments would be comparable to taxes on freehold land; the rentals in whole or part should be transferred by the Administration (lessor) to the urban government.

In Port Moresby and some of the other urban centers, there are lands owned by natives who enjoy the benefits of community facilities. These lands should be taxed, but taxing native lands raises difficult problems. Ownership is hard to establish; more than one person (in some cases many) may claim rights in a given piece of land, and native owners will generally have few resources from which to pay taxes. However, with the development of the urban centers the native-owned land in the centers will become increasingly valuable and it would be inequitable if these lands were to be exempt from taxation. Moreover, the costs of providing town services such as roads, water supplies, sewerage services and electricity, will be more expensive if areas owned by natives and suitable for development are not developed by their owners and have to be by-passed, or if less well-located areas have to be developed instead. Careful consideration will need to be given to the system of taxation and to methods of collecting taxes on native-owned lands. An education program to explain the purpose and the need to tax these lands should be undertaken before the system is inaugurated. The restriction that natives can only sell to the Administration also should be re-examined.

The Mission believes that the financial position of the urban centers would be greatly strengthened if charges for the principal services to be provided more closely approximated costs. Such an adjustment of charges need not wait until urban governments are ready to assume responsibility for the services, and there would be a distinct advantage in transferring to the local governments responsibility for services which were more nearly, if not entirely, paying their way.

ANNEX II *PLANNING FOR ECONOMIC DEVELOPMENT*

The Territory should have an economic development plan which points the direction development is to take. At this stage of development, such a plan would be useful to the Commonwealth Government in spelling out the magnitude of the demands to be made upon it for both manpower and finances; to the Administration in establishing policies and priorities and also in organizing to accomplish the objectives; and to the indigenous and non-indigenous people by helping to bring about an understanding of the issues involved and what is required of them. It would also be useful to the United Nations, involved because of the Trust Territory of New Guinea, in understanding the magnitude and complexity of the task of bringing a primitive society into a modern economy.

A development plan will serve to stimulate discussion, interest and participation by the people. While many of the native people will not have the education and experience to enable them to comprehend all of the issues and objectives, those who can, coupled with the Europeans, Asians and mixed race people in the Territory, will provide an audience which can and should be reached.

A development plan will be of particular significance for the new House of Assembly scheduled to meet for the first time in 1964. The House will have a majority of indigenous members, many of whom will have had little or no experience in national politics or development. This body will consider requests from the Administration for financial resources and appropriate funds for development purposes. Intelligent and free discussion of the development issues and objectives will be enhanced if the House is presented with annual budgets based on a development plan which has been carefully and thoughtfully prepared.

The Mission's recommendation concerning planning should not lead to the inference that the Territory has been entirely without planning. In October 1961, the Minister of State for Territories made a statement describing five-year targets for educational, social and economic advancement in Papua and New Guinea. A considerable amount of detailed work was done in preparation of the announcement of these targets. Other statements on specific policies and targets have been made from time to time. A Central Policy and Planning Committee (the Planning Committee) was formed in 1961 to, among other activities, "ensure that forward planning is realistic and comprehensive," but no full-time staff has been assigned to the committee. A Budget Sub-Committee (consisting of representatives of the Departments of the Treasury, of the Administrator and of the Public Service Commissioner) has the responsibility of working with the departments to prepare annual estimates of budgetary requirements. A Works Consultative Committee considers the level of the works program and decides on the division of work between the constructing authorities. The Planning Committee is required to approve annual estimates before they are submitted to the Commonwealth Government for determination of the size of the annual grant. Following this determination by the Commonwealth Government the estimates are adjusted to the finances available. The Legislative Council—in the future the House of Assembly—considers the budget and authorizes the expenditure of funds.

The principal weakness in economic development planning has been the lack of a central staff. The estimates of requirements presented by the various departments are no doubt carefully prepared and represent the ideas originating in these departments. But there is no economic development planning staff responsible for review of the merits of the estimates of the individual departments, for analysis of alternative opportunities and for carrying out a continuous review to assure necessary flexibility. There is need for such a staff.

In the opinion of the Mission, planning should be kept simple and realistic. Elaborate and theoretical planning is not encouraged. The planning machinery need not be complicated.

The Mission recommends an economic development planning staff, to serve as the Secretariat of the Planning Committee, under the direction of a senior and experienced economic adviser. The planning staff should be small and the Mission believes that two good economists, in addition to the economic adviser, is all that is needed. Its main functions should be coordination and judgment. It can be small because most of the planning work should be done in the departments and in the districts.

At the present time, the membership of the Planning Committee consists of the Administrator, the two Assistant Administrators and the Treasurer. They are neutral officers, not advocates for or claimants of particular functions. The Mission suggests that the committee be expanded to include the heads of the major departments primarily concerned with action programs—the principal claimants on the resources to be allocated by the development program. The experience of such major operating departments can be most useful. At the same time, the heads of these departments would have the responsibility of objectively balancing the interests of the programs, for which they are directly responsible, with the over-all objectives of development. Experience in other countries suggests there are advantages to this form of membership. The planning committee, however, should not be large. The Mission suggests a committee of not more than seven or eight, including the administrator, one or both of the assistant administrators, the treasurer and the heads of, say, four of the major departments.

Another approach would be to have the planning function placed in a new department—for example, a Department of Economic Development. However, the Mission would not recommend a new department; already there are 16. Also, there are definite advantages to the location of the development planning function in the office of the administrator. He has the power and authority to shape the development plan. A planning staff in his office can be objective, will not be competitive with the departments of the Administration and under the cloak of the administrator will have the assurance of cooperation from the departments and agencies.

The planning committee should have the responsibility for formulating policies, establishing criteria, and determining the procedures to be followed by departments and districts in the preparation of their contribution to an economic development plan for the whole Territory and also for the preparation of the development plan and the periodic review and revisions thereof. Heads of departments, not members of the committee, should be invited to meet with the planning committee for discussions on matters affecting their department or on subjects in which they have a particular competence. The economic adviser should be in attendance at all meetings of the planning committee.

Under the direction of the planning committee, the planning staff should be responsible for:

a. assessing, (in cooperation with the departments), the availability of resources, both physical and financial, for development;

b. coordinating and stimulating the planning activities of departments and agencies, including the preparation of criteria and policies for development as well as the general procedures to be followed by the departments and agencies in the preparation of their contribution to the development plan, both annual and long-term;

c. evaluating projects and programs prepared by the various departments and agencies and recommending priorities for public investment within the framework of a coordinated program;

d. reviewing progress in the private sector and recommending ways and means for accelerating and strengthening private development;

e. reviewing and evaluating progress in the implementation of the development plan and recommending proper action and change.

It will be necessary to guard against both over-burdening the planning committee and its becoming too deeply involved in detailed evaluation of projects. Accordingly, the responsibility of evaluating projects could be assigned to a sub-committee of the planning committee or working party—perhaps identified as the Development Projects Working Party. The membership should be the next ranking staff member to the respective department heads represented on the planning committee with the economic adviser as chairman. The working party should establish and make known to the departments its criteria for evaluating projects.

To make development planning effective, there should be a flow of ideas to and from the various departments and agencies and the planning committee, and also to and from the private sector and the planning committee concerning, not only the use of public funds, but also policies and ways and means of stimulating private economic activity. The public could have a voice in development planning through advisory committees of farmers and businessmen, both indigenous and non-indigenous, appointed by the district commissioner in each district.

The principal sources of ideas and programs for public development spending are the departments and agencies in which are located the staff and technicians familiar with development possibilities. It is essential that the planning staff work closely with the technical staff in the departments, both at the center and in the 15 administrative districts throughout the Territory. The Mission wishes to stress that every effort should be made to have members of the staff familiar with the development possibilities contribute their experience and knowledge. This means that the staff in the district offices, as well as the staff in the departments in Port Moresby, should be made a part of the planning process. To date, there has been a tendency to minimize the contribution district officials can make to planning. This is a mistake. Unless each district plays a major part in preparing its contribution to the Territory plan, the latter is not likely to reflect problems in the district and the plan is not likely to be carried out effectively.

In the accomplishment of administrative objectives, economic development planning should have both the long and short view. The Mission considers that, in accordance with the experience in a good many other less developed areas, a period of about four or five years might be adopted for the first plan, giving the long view.[1] An annual plan should be prepared not later than six months before the annual budget procedure

---

[1] However, the time horizon for each of the sector plans does not necessarily have to be identical. For commercial agriculture a period of about ten years may be more appropriate in view of the predominance of tree crops, which do not come into full bearing until after a number of years.

begins, the annual plan being the basis for the annual budget estimates. It would be most desirable for the long-term plan to be revised each year and a new year added, thus keeping the long-term plan both flexible and adjusted to the progress made to date and to changing situations. We want to emphasize again that in our view the plans should be simple and straightforward with avoidance of elaborate and theoretical planning techniques.

Budgetary requirements under the annual plan should cover both current and capital expenditures, in effect all Administration expenditures. It is assumed that the Budget Sub-Committee, working closely with the planning staff, would continue to be responsible for the preparation of the annual budget. The economic adviser should *ex officio* be a member of the budget sub-committee.

Such a procedure would provide the necessary flexibility to adapt to changing estimates of financial resources, changes due to the rate of progress under existing programs and policies, and changes due to circumstances not taken into consideration.

The planning committee should prepare a statement of development criteria and general policies and the general procedures, including a time schedule, to be followed by the departments and agencies of the Administration in the preparation of plans covering the subject matter areas for which they have responsibility. The district commissioners should be asked to prepare plans for the districts within specified amounts. The technicians stationed in the districts, with the benefit of advice and guidance from their central offices, should assist in the preparation of the district plans. The district commissioner should justify the plan recommendations including the basis for priorities. It would be useful if the plans prepared in the districts were for both a minimum and maximum expenditure of funds. The departments and agencies at the center, taking into consideration the district plans, should prepare plans covering the subject matters for which they are responsible. The plans prepared by the departments and the districts should be reconciled and integrated into a development plan prepared by the planning staff for consideration of the planning committee. As soon as feasible, the draft of the long-term plan and subsequently its annual revisions should be considered by the Commonwealth Government.

Effective development planning will also require that attention be given to the availability of sufficient statistical data. There is a Bureau of Statistics in the Department of the Administrator. The Mission has considered whether this bureau should be merged with the proposed planning staff. We have arrived at the view that so long as the bureau and the planning staff work hand-in-hand there are no particular advantages to the merger of the two units. But the bureau needs to be strengthened to effectively perform its present duties and it will need some further strengthening to bring the flow of statistical information up to a level required for purposes of satisfactory planning. At the time of our visit we found the bureau seriously understaffed with eight vacancies out of a total establishment, including lower staff, of 22. These vacancies included the newly created positions for a principal and a senior research officer to be in charge of problems related to sampling, research and development.

The Mission recommends that as a first step adequate attention be paid, in consultation with the Commonwealth Bureau of Statistics, to its staffing with competent personnel within the approved establishment. Thereafter, some expansion should be considered. Quality will be more important than quantity and the addition of one or two staff members of the necessary caliber, supported by a modest increase in subordinate staff, would in our view be sufficient.

Our suggestion for strengthening the bureau of statistics is not intended to indicate that little useful statistical work has been done so far. In a number of important fields, adequate statistical information is already available, but there are some gaps. There is need for the development of adequate price statistics and for more data on demographic trends, subsistence agriculture and trade establishments. Above all, there is need for the publication of national accounts on a regular basis and development of the underlying statistics, including those mentioned.

The work of the bureau of statistics has to be coordinated not only with that of the planning staff, but also with that of other departments and of the Department of Territories in Canberra. Several departments, such as Health, Education and Labor collect statistics directly, and we see no need for change in this procedure as long as proper liaison is maintained with the planning staff and the bureau of statistics. The Department of Territories in Canberra has done useful work to increase statistical information about the Territory. We suggest that, with improved staffing in the Territory, sole responsibility for the work should be transferred to Port Moresby.

There are also some problems with respect to the budget that require attention in relation to development planning. The presently available documents relating to the budget (the Budget Papers, Appropriation Ordinance and Works Program) are almost exclusively adapted to administrative purposes. In the Mission's opinion, there is need for additional information in three respects.

First, information should be available, to the maximum extent possible, on total expenditures on behalf of each of the departments and autonomous agencies, not only with respect to current expenditures, but for maintenance and investment expenditures and purchase of capital

assets as well. At present, it is not possible to derive this information completely from the budget documents. The Mission recommends that the
structure of these documents be changed to show this information.
Second, the budget documents should be more detailed by providing
information about the total expenditures of divisions of departments. As an
example, for the Department of Education the budget should include all
proposed expenditures for administration, primary education, secondary
education, teacher-training and technical education separately for each
division. Third, we recommend that information be collected on the total
cost of the basic functions performed by the Administration, such as
agricultural services, transport, communications, health, education,
regulation of trade and industry, etc. If the other recommended changes
in the budget structure are made, information on the total cost of basic
functions will largely become available at the same time. A breakdown
of the budget by functional categories could be shown as an enclosure to
the budget documents. Additional information along these lines will be
required for purposes of planning, and will also be helpful in providing a
better understanding of the functions of the Administration and its costs.

Preparation and publication of the additional information, as suggested, should not necessarily result in a curtailment of the authority of
the Administration to make adjustments during the fiscal years among
items, although in the Mission's view this authority should not be too
extensive.

The Mission also noted that under present procedures a final budget
document is available only after two to three months of the budget year
have passed. This is not helpful to planning and administration and the
Mission suggests that the Commonwealth Government in consultation
with the Administration try to work out a change in procedures that will
solve this problem.

Finally, the Mission believes that a useful purpose could be served by
the publication of an annual progress report which would combine information on past and anticipated activities under the development plan,
and major economic and financial trends against the background of
national accounts. A report of this nature would be of particular value if
published shortly after the end of the period covered, say, not more than
three months. The planning staff should be given responsibility for this
economic survey, working, of course, in close contact with the bureau of
statistics and the various departments involved.[2] For internal purposes
we recommend in addition brief semi-annual progress reports, to be
available with a delay of not more than about one month.

[2] The economic survey might be a brief document, limited to essentials with some
enclosures. In this case, the voluminous reports on Papua and New Guinea could be
substantially curtailed as far as economic reporting is concerned and the budget speech
could be limited to budget developments proper.

ANNEX III *PROJECTION OF ADMINISTRATION EXPENDITURES AND REVENUES, 1964/65–1968/69*

To assess the implications of the Mission's program for the public finances of the Territory, the Mission made a projection of the budget of the Administration covering the five-year period 1964/65–1968/69. The results of this projection are given in Table A.1. For purposes of comparison, this table also includes the budget estimates for 1963/64.

Table A.1, which follows the main classification of the Administration budget, includes the estimates of expenditures by the Mission, mentioned in the chapters of the report. In addition, a projection has been made for other categories of expenditures not directly covered by our recommendations. For these latter expenditures, inevitably somewhat arbitrary assumptions had to be made; moreover, as indicated below, on the whole rather minimum assumptions have been adopted.

In view of the global nature of our projection, we have not made forecasts for each year and have projected broad categories of expenditures rather than individual items.

For *Departmental Expenditures*, which cover almost two-thirds of the budget total, and which are largely current in nature, our estimates for Agriculture, Stock and Fisheries, Forests, Trade and Industry, Public Health and Education follow directly from our sector programs. The Mission was not staffed to review and make projections of expenditures for activities not directly related to its sector programs. Other departments have therefore been presented as one item and we assumed for these departments a rise of 5 percent annually (cumulative).

In our projection of *General Maintenance* expenditures, the item *Roads and Bridges* is based on our program recommendations. Expenditures for *Other* items as a group have been assumed to rise by 5 percent annually (cumulative). The resulting total has been raised somewhat to take account of increased maintenance for minor airports, where the Mission proposes a rise of somewhat more than 5 percent.

Capital Works and Services in the Territory budget consists of *Building Construction and Engineering Works and Services*. Proposed spending on residences, hostels and quarters, and on hospitals, schools and ancillary buildings is in accordance with the proposals made in the respective chapters of the report. *Other Building Construction* has been projected

414

TABLE A.1: Territory Administration Expenditures and Revenues

(£A thousand)

	Projections 1964/65– 1968/69	Annual Average	Percent of Total	Budget Estimates 1963/64	Percent of Total
Expenditures					
1. Departmental Expenditures					
Agriculture, Stock and Fisheries	12,250	2,450	4.9	1,390	3.7
Forests	2,700	540	1.1	419	1.1
Trade and Industry	3,900	780	1.5	594	1.6
Public Health	20,900	4,180	8.3	3,643	9.7
Education	33,425	6,685	13.3	4,150	11.1
Other Departments	77,800	15,560	31.0	13,400	35.8
Total	150,975	30,195	60.1	23,605	63.0
2. General Maintenance					
Roads and Bridges	8,000	1,600	3.2	1,233	3.3
Other	10,750	2,150	4.3	1,826	4.9
Total	18,750	3,750	7.5	3,059	8.2
3. Capital Works and Services					
Building Construction					
Residences, Hostels and Quarters	8,000	1,600	3.2	1,236	3.2
Hospitals and Ancillary Buildings	1,800	360	0.7	617	1.6
Schools and Ancillary Buildings	2,000	400	0.8	1,589	4.2
Other	13,400	2,680	5.3	2,309	6.3
Total	25,200	5,040	10.0	5,751	15.3
Engineering Works and Services					
Roads and Bridges	9,000	1,800	3.6	765 [a]	2.0 [a]
Wharves and Beacons	2,250	450	0.9	192	0.5
Forestry Roads, etc.	4,200	840	1.6	—	—
Coastal Shipping	700	140	0.3	—	—
Aerodromes	800	160	0.3	70	0.2
Powerhouses and Elec. Reticul.	925	185	0.4	283	0.8
Electricity Commission	8,325	1,665	3.3	386	1.0
Water Supply and Sewerage	2,225	445	0.9	460	1.2
Other	900	180	0.4	594	1.6
Total	29,325	5,865	11.7	2,750	7.3
Total Capital Works and Services	54,525	10,905	21.7	8,501	22.6
4. Purchase of Capital Assets	9,400	1,880	3.7	1,617	4.3
5. Special Appropriations	2,425 [b]	485 [b]	1.0	697	1.9
6. Territory Development Finance Company	15,000	3,000	6.0	—	—
Grand Total Expenditures	251,075	50,215	100.0	37,479	100.0
Revenues					
7. Internal Revenue	69,050 [c]	13,810 [c]	27.5	10,530	28.1
8. Public Borrowing	182,025	36,405	72.5	1,700	4.5
9. Commonwealth Grant				25,250	67.4
Total Revenue	251,075	50,215	100.0	37,480	100.0

[a] Including special project Sepik District.

[b] Superannuation and principal and interest payments on public debt outstanding at the end of 1963/64.

[c] Excluding tax rebates.

SOURCES: 1964/65–1968/69, Mission estimates; 1963/64, Territory Administration budget papers.

to rise by 5 percent annually (cumulative). This item includes expenditures for the construction of a number of important buildings, endorsed or recommended by the Mission. Estimates for *Engineering Works and Services* follow directly from our recommendations almost completely.

The projection for *Purchase of Capital Assets* is based on an assumed cumulative rise of 5 percent per annum.

The estimate for *Special Appropriations* (superannuation and debt service) is based on estimates provided by the Administration. A lump sum requirement of £A3 million annually has been assumed for the recommended *Territory Development Finance Company*.

As the share of projected expenditures to be financed from *Internal Revenue* (taxes plus other current revenues), 27.5 percent of total expenditures has been taken. This target implies a rise by somewhat more than 10 percent annually over the 1963/64 estimate for Internal Revenue (£A10.13 million after deduction of £A0.4 million for tax rebates) and has to be judged in relation to the prospects for economic growth during the five-year period as discussed in Chapter 2.

On the basis of the assumption for Internal Revenue, £A36.4 million remains to be covered annually from the *Commonwealth Grant* plus *Public Borrowing*.

The increases in expenditures projected by the Mission have deliberately been kept on the low side in view of the desirability to limit the need for grant-aid and/or public borrowing. They contain a task-setting element and should, on the whole, be regarded as minimum estimates. The following comments are relevant in this context.

a. The projected rise in expenditures for *Other Departments* of 5 percent annually is substantially lower than the rise during 1958/59–1963/64 when it was of the order of 15 percent annually (after correction for a change in accounting procedures which caused a particularly steep rise in 1963/64).

b. Expenditures for *General Maintenance* (excluding roads and bridges and powerhouses, where figures are not comparable due to the establishment of the Electricity Commission) have roughly doubled since 1958/59.

c. Proposed expenditures for *Hospitals and Schools* reflect the Mission's recommendations to limit the construction of additional health establishments, to use simple construction standards and to have local communities and native local councils contribute to the cost of certain structures.

d. The Mission's projection for *Building Construction* leaves only limited scope for buildings other than those which it directly recommends or endorses.

e. No allowance has been made in the projection for service payments on additional public debt to be contracted after 1963/64, nor for the annual payment into the Territory Debt Sinking Fund (2 percent of the outstanding debt in excess of five years as at June 30 of the previous year). The Administration estimates that for each additional £A1 million to be borrowed annually during each of the next five years (on terms similar to those prevailing so far), total service payments during the five-year period will rise by about £A500,000, or £A100,000 annually.

f. No allowance has been made for some items which may give rise to expenditures during the five-year period but for which the Mission was not in a position to present estimates. Examples are adult education, higher education and housing for indigenes.

g. All estimates are presumed to be in constant prices. With rising prices, an effort will have to be made to remain within the assumed ceilings, but this may not be possible under all circumstances. On the other hand, some more local revenue may be expected in case of a rise in prices.

In addition to the projection summarized in Table A.1, the Mission has also attempted to assess the implications of this projection for the pattern of Administration expenditures by broad functional categories. This functional classification is shown in Table 2 of Chapter 2 (page 56). The reconciliation between the items shown in the functional classification and those shown in Table A.1 of this annex is given below:

	£A thousand	£A thousand
Agriculture, Stock and Fisheries		
Departmental Expenditures (Table A.1)	2,450	
Vocabulary Stores	260	
Capital Expenditures:		
Livestock	84	
Fisheries	20	
Various Buildings	220	
Agricultural Machinery	32	
	3,066	

The item for livestock is exclusive of the cattle freight subsidy (which is included among *Departmental Expenditures*) and land purchases (which is included among *Lands, Surveys and Mines*, see below). Allowing for expenditures for minor new works, total annual expenditures are estimated at   3,100

Forests	£A thousand	£A thousand
Departmental Expenditures (Table A.1)	540	
Vocabulary Stores	70	
Capital Expenditures:		
Roads, Bridges and Wharves (Table A.1)	840	
Various Buildings	70	
Plant, Machinery and Equipment	35	
	1,555	

Total annual expenditures, excluding those for purchase of timber rights and forest land (included among *Lands, Surveys and Mines*) are thus estimated at

1,550

Lands, Surveys and Mines

Expenditures of the department and those for *Purchase and Lease of Land* are roughly estimated at 800 and 250 annually, respectively, thus giving a total of

1,050

Trade and Industry

Departmental Expenditures (Table A.1)	780	

Deducting expenditures for *Administration Vessels and Stevedoring* (to be included in *General Administration*, see below) and adding a provision for *Vocabulary Stores* (which two items more or less compensate each other) total annual expenditures are estimated at

800

Territory Development Bank (Table A.1)		3,000

Roads and Bridges

General Maintenance (Table A.1)	1,600	
Capital Works and Services (Table A.1)	1,800	3,400

Ports

General Maintenance	50	
Capital Works and Services (Table A.1)	450	500

Coastal Shipping (Table A.1, rounded)		150

	£A thousand	£A thousand
Aerodromes		
General Maintenance	125	
Capital Works and Services (Table A.1, rounded)	175	300
Electric Power		
Capital Works and Services:		
Electricity Commission (Table A.1)	1,665	
Powerhouses and Electrical Reticulation (Table A.1)	185	1,850
Posts and Telegraphs		
Expenditures of the department and those for various capital items not included in the budget of the department are roughly estimated at a total of		1,750
Education		
Departmental Expenditures (Table A.1)	6,685	
Vocabulary Stores	416	
Library Books	20	
Capital Expenditures:		
Schools and Ancillary Buildings (Table A.1)	400	
Furniture and Equipment	15	
	7,536	
Disregarding teacher housing (which is included among *Housing*, see below), total annual expenditures are estimated at		7,500
Health		
Departmental Expenditures (Table A.1)	4,180	
Vocabulary Stores	700	
Hospital Engineering	76	
Capital Expenditures:		
Hospitals and Ancillary Buildings (Table A.1)	360	
Hospital and Medical Equipment	97	
	5,413	
Total (rounded)		5,400

Housing	£A thousand	£A thousand
Residences, Hostels and Quarters (Table A.1)	1,600	
Contingency (additional housing needs which cannot be specified at this moment)	400	
Domestic Furniture and Fittings	150	2,150

Water Supply and Sewerage

Capital Works and Services (Table A.1)	445	
Operation and Maintenance Expenditures	310	
Minor Works	20	
	775	
Total (rounded)		800

General Administration, Law and Order; Various Public Works and Miscellaneous

This is the residual item in the budget projection, amounting to		16,900

In view of the assertion that the existing level of overseas shipping rates prevailing in New Guinea trade is unreasonably high, it was considered useful to analyze briefly the general level and structure of shipping rates within the general context of the existing rate pattern.

The general level of in-bound shipping rates is illustrated in Table A.2.

TABLE A.2: General Cargo Rates

(£A)

	Rates[a]
To Port Moresby from:	
Sydney	12/10/–
Hong Kong	15/10/6
Tokyo	16/12/6
London	21/3/3
To Lae, Madang, Rabaul from:	
Sydney	13/10/–
Hong Kong	15/10/6
Tokyo	16/12/6
London	21/3/3

[a] Per cargo ton in weight (long tons) or measurement, whichever is the greater.

SOURCE: Information provided by shipping companies.

The figures in Table A.2 are subject to various qualifications and may not be strictly comparable.[1] However, they do provide a general indication of the rate levels. New Guinea rates do not appear out of line as compared with the general rate pattern, although Australia/New Guinea rates appear rather high.

For purposes of comparison, shipping rates from and to Fiji and between Australia and South Asia are shown in Table A.3.

[1] In assessing the real rate burden not only the standard general cargo rate but also specific commodity rates have to be considered. However, the general cargo rate does provide the basic point of reference.

421

TABLE A.3: General Cargo Rates

(£A)

	Rate
Suva (Fiji)–Sydney	8/7/6
Suva (Fiji)–Hong Kong	21/12/6
Suva (Fiji)–Tokyo	18/2/6
Suva (Fiji)–London	39/7/6
Sydney–Manila	13/2/6
Manila–Sydney	12/9/6
Sydney–Singapore	12/9/-
Singapore–Sydney	17/17/-
Sydney–Tokyo	13/2/6
Tokyo–Sydney	15/17/6
Sydney–Hong Kong	13/2/6
Hong Kong–Sydney	14/12/6

SOURCE: Information supplied by shipping companies.

In view of the importance of air transport services to the economy, the problem of airline rates deserves a brief analysis.

Unit rates are necessarily related to the length-of-haul. Short-haul operations decrease the effective speed (because of the time spent on landing, take-off, ascent to the cruising altitude and descent) and increase the relative ground-handling cost component. Most of the Territory operations are short-haul, and loads are small. Therefore, one can expect some very high unit rates. This is borne out by actual experience.

As a check on rates charged in the Territory, a comparison was made with rates actually charged elsewhere under similar situations, where the relationship between rates and costs is more direct and where operating conditions are similar. For the purpose of such a comparative analysis, rates charged by regional carriers in Northern Canada are used—these services can be considered as high-cost operations because of the isolated conditions and relatively low-traffic volumes. Only rates relating to routes where DC 3 equipment is used are included in the comparison—the rates based on the use of larger equipment, such as C 46s, F 27s, Heralds or DC 4s are lower.

The chart (with key) shows the results of these comparisons. It indicates that the two rate structures are roughly comparable; the detailed differences can be explained by different approaches to rate-making or different conditions prevailing.

It must be noted, of course, that the effective charter rates are considerably lower. The basic charter rates per hour are set out in Table A.4.

TABLE A.4: Charter Rates

Aircraft Type	Charter Rate (£A) per Hour	Aircraft Type	Charter Rate (£A) per Hour
Bristol Freighter	115	Otter	45
Catalina	97	Cessna 185	25
DC 3	75	Cessna 180	22
Piaggo	50		

Notes: The rates apply to time charter, i.e., actual time flown between point of departure to destination and return. Positioning flights are charged for.

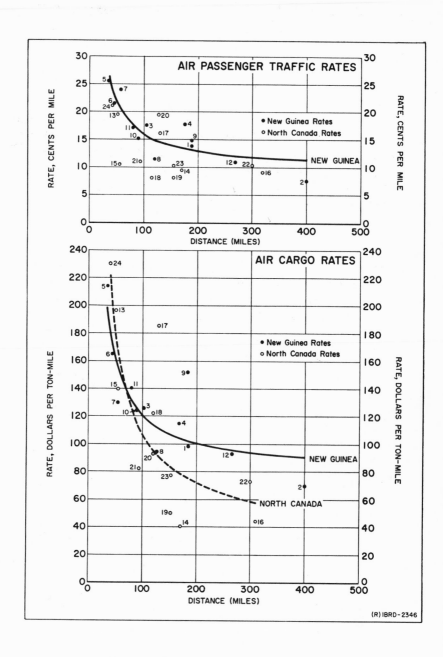

(R) IBRD-2346

KEY TO CHART

NEW GUINEA		NORTHERN CANADA	
1 Lae	—Port Moresby	13 Rimouski	—Baie Comeau
2	—Rabaul	14 Winnipeg	—Red Lake
3	—Goroka	15 The Pas	—Flin Flon
4	—Mt. Hagen	16 Winnipeg	—The Pas
5	—Bulolo	17 Prince Albert	—Lac La Ronge
6	—Wau	18 Mayo	—Dawson
7 Madang	—Goroka	19 Flin Flon	—Lynn Lake
8	—Mt. Hagen	20 Vancouver	—Port Hardy
9	—Wewak	21 Vancouver	—Comox
10	—Minj	22 Moncton	—Sept Iles
11	—Banz	23 Moncton	—Charlo
12	—Port Moresby	24 Matane	—Baie Comeau

On the basis of these rates and assuming full utilization of chartered capacity, the effective rate can be as low as 40 percent of the unit air-cargo rate on scheduled services.

A comparative analysis of direct operating costs of the same aircraft type in New Guinea, Alaska and Northern Canada is summarized in Table A.5.

TABLE A.5: Aircraft Operating Costs per Hour Flown, DC 3s

Item	New Guinea Carriers		Alaskan Carriers	Canadian Regional Carriers	
	£A	US$	US$	Can$	US$
Flying Operations	22/1/–	48.88	86.28	71.71	68.12
Direct Maintenance	n.a.	n.a.	35.63	30.93	29.39
Maintenance Burden	n.a.	n.a.	21.66	14.22	13.51
Total, Maintenance	22/1/–	48.88	57.29	45.15	42.90
Total, Maintenance and Flying Ops.	44/2/–	97.76	143.57	116.86	111.02
Depreciation, Flight Equipment	3/6/–	7.41	1.04	6.30	5.98
Total, Direct Operating Costs	47/8/–	104.62	144.61	123.26	117.00

Notes: 1. Period: New Guinea Carriers, 1962/63; Alaskan and Canadian Regional Carriers, 1962 (Calender Year).
2. Revenue and non-revenue hours.
3. Alaskan Carriers: Cordova & Wien Alaska.
4. Canadian Regional Carriers: Eastern Provincial Airways, M.C.A., Nordair, P.W.A., Quebecair, Transair. Most of the operations take place in the north under high-cost conditions.
5. Landing fees and navigation charges: landing fees are not included under flying operations classification of Alaskan carriers; they are included in the case of Canadian carriers; no navigation charges and landing fees are charged in New Guinea.
6. Insurance (loss, damage, public liability, etc.) is included with "Flying Operations."

SOURCES: Summary provided by Department of Civil Aviation, Commonwealth of Australia, and data provided by Patair; Air Transport Association of America, Airline Finance and Accounting Conference, comparative statement showing air carriers' direct operating costs; Air Transport Board (Canada), summary provided by Statistics Section, Economics Division.

This comparison reveals the following:

a. Total operating costs per hour are very similar, and in fact New Guinea operators enjoy a small cost advantage.

b. New Guinea operators enjoy the lowest flying costs, which is reasonable in view of lower salaries of flying personnel, lower quality of service and lower fuel costs.

c. New Guinea operators have somewhat higher depreciation costs than Canadian operators, and considerably higher than Alaskan carriers. However, these costs are only a minor item.

d. The relative burden of maintenance costs is much higher in New Guinea than in Alaska or Northern Canada (46.7 percent versus 39.6 and 36.7 percent).

No meaningful cost analysis of administrative overheads and traffic-handling operations could be made. These costs in this type of operation should amount to 30 percent of the total costs.

If the present equipment continues to be operated, the promising fields where cost reductions could be achieved are:

a. *Maintenance costs.* Here, some long-range improvements could be achieved by better training of indigenous personnel and gradual substitution of expatriate personnel by indigenous tradesmen and mechanics.

b. *Ground handling costs.* In this field some savings could be made consistent with improved quality of service by the more efficient use of ground facilities and more aggressive introduction of mechanical loading and unloading equipment.

However, the major improvements and cost reductions could be achieved by the partial replacement of DC 3s with larger aircraft. The prerequisite for such a change would be the concentration of internal terminal traffic-handling points at a few major centers served by an adequate system of local roads. On the basis of experience of other countries, working under similar circumstances, the probable cost and rate reductions should be substantial.

STATISTICAL APPENDIX

TABLE S.1: Indigenous and Non-indigenous Population, 1947–62

As at	Indigenous			Non-indigenous			
June 30	Enumerated	Estimated	Total	European	Asian	Other	Total
1947	n.a.	n.a.	n.a.	5,954	2,238	1,247	9,439
1950	991,984	447,680	1,439,664	10,541	2,199	n.a.	n.a.
1955	1,376,087	317,400	1,693,487	14,731	2,523	2,085	19,339
1960	1,716,786	163,540	1,880,326	n.a.	n.a.	n.a.	23,870
1961	1,815,391	131,640	1,947,031	19,962	2,651	2,717	25,330[a]
1962	1,902,346	95,830	1,998,176	n.a.	n.a.	n.a.	26,544

[a] Census of non-indigenous population.

SOURCE: Department of Territories: Statistical tabulations prepared for the Mission, June 1963.

Note: n.a., not available.

TABLE S.2: Indigenous Population by District, June 30, 1962

Territories and Districts	Enumerated	Estimated	Total	% of Total	Square Miles	Density Per Square Mile
PAPUA						
Western	46,636	22,100	68,736	3.4	40,000	1.72
Gulf	47,603	7,800	55,403	2.8	15,360	3.61
Central	105,056	—	105,056	5.3	12,000	8.75
Milne Bay	88,509	—	88,509	4.4	7,820	11.32
Northern	50,474	—	50,474	2.5	8,960	5.63
Southern Highlands	142,978	17,700	160,678	8.0	6,400	25.11
Total	481,256	47,600	528,856	26.4	90,540	5.61
NEW GUINEA						
Eastern Highlands	345,325	6,500	351,825	17.6	6,900	50.99
Western Highlands	267,246	13,000	280,246	14.0	9,600	29.19
Sepik	235,016	25,100	260,116	13.0	30,200	8.61
Madang	140,201	1,400	141,601	7.1	10,800	13.11
Morobe	199,998	1,800	201,798	10.1	12,700	15.89
New Britain	114,591	430	115,021	5.8	14,100	8.16
New Ireland	40,659	—	40,659	2.0	3,800	10.70
Bougainville	59,619	—	59,619	3.0	4,100	14.54
Manus	18,435	—	18,435	0.9	800	23.04
Total	1,421,090	48,230	1,469,320	73.5	93,000	15.80
Grand Total	1,902,346	95,830	1,998,176	100.0	183,540	10.89

SOURCES: Territory of Papua, Report for 1961/62; Territory of New Guinea, Report for 1961/62.

TABLE S.3: Import and Export Values, 1948/49–1962/63

(£A thousand; f.o.b. at port of shipment)

Year	Imports	Exports	Total Trade	Import Balance	Imports Covered by Exports (%)
1948/49	6,883	4,830	11,713	2,053	70.2
1949/50	8,614	6,101	14,715	2,513	70.9
1950/51	9,845	8,374	18,219	1,471	85.1
1951/52	12,738	10,479	23,217	2,259	82.3
1952/53	10,994	11,786	22,780	−792	107.2
1953/54	13,788	12,032	25,820	1,756	87.3
1954/55	17,048	12,887	29,935	4,161	75.6
1955/56	19,256	13,250	32,506	6,006	68.8
1956/57	19,580	13,079	32,659	6,501	66.8
1957/58	20,239	12,404	32,643	7,835	61.3
1958/59	20,068	16,297	36,365	3,771	81.2
1959/60	20,808	18,820	39,628	1,988	90.4
1960/61	26,464	16,606	43,070	9,858	62.7
1961/62	25,642	15,901	41,543	9,741	62.0
1962/63	28,268	18,142	46,410	10,126	64.2

SOURCES: Department of Territories: Statistical tabulations prepared for the Mission, June 1963; Territory of Papua and New Guinea, Overseas Trade Bulletin No. 8.

TABLE S.4: Export Values by Principal Commodity Groups, Selected Years

(£A thousand; f.o.b. at port of shipment)

	1950/51		1954/55		1959/60		1960/61		1961/62		1962/63	
	Value	% of Total	Value	% of Total	Value	% of Total	Value	% of Total	Value	% of Total	Value	% of Total
Copra and Copra Products	5,196	62.0	7,823	60.7	10,287	54.7	7,758	46.7	6,840	43.0	7,381	40.7
Cocoa	92	1.1	526	4.1	1,671	8.9	1,666	10.0	1,983	12.5	2,956	16.3
Coffee	8	0.1	75	0.6	717	3.8	1,106	6.7	1,557	9.8	2,014	11.1
Rubber	802	9.6	954	7.4	1,500	8.0	1,292	7.8	1,211	7.6	1,174	6.5
Timber and Timber Products	25	0.3	893	6.9	1,664	8.8	1,174	7.1	1,207	7.6	1,338	7.4
Gold	1,361	16.3	1,356	10.5	635	3.4	681	4.1	718	4.5	668	3.7
Other Produce	218	2.6	480	3.7	630	3.3	580	3.5	806	5.1	838	4.6
Total Territory Produce	7,702	92.0	12,107	94.0	17,104	90.9	14,257	85.9	14,322	90.1	16,369	90.2
Re-exports	672	8.0	779	6.0	1,716	9.1	2,349	14.1	1,579	9.9	1,773	9.8
Grand Total	8,374	100.0	12,886	100.0	18,820	100.0	16,606	100.0	15,901	100.0	18,142	100.0

SOURCES: Territory of Papua and New Guinea, Overseas Trade Bulletins, Nos. 3-8.

TABLE S.5: Quantities of Principal Exports, Selected Years

	Unit	1954/55	1959/60	1960/61	1961/62	1962/63
Copra	tons	79,582	65,396	76,524	74,839	72,499
Coconut Oil	tons	8,660	25,526	20,429	19,627	23,641
Cocoa	tons	1,106	5,870	7,291	10,014	14,071
Coffee	tons	107	1,488	2,295	3,444	4,845
Rubber	tons	3,592	4,399	4,373	4,680	4,760
Peanuts	tons	184	1,897	2,019	2,212	2,064
Timber: Logs	thousand super feet	2,519	1,453	1,396	1,980	14,766
Sawn	thousand super feet	2,750	4,836	3,413	2,734	3,746
Plywood	thousand square feet	20,717	30,511	21,862	26,358	17,161

SOURCES: Department of Territories: Statistical tabulations prepared for the Mission, June 1963; Territory of Papua and New Guinea, Overseas Trade Bulletin No. 8.

TABLE S.6: Export Values by Destination, Selected Years

(£A thousand; f.o.b. at port of shipment)

Country[a]	1954/55 Value	1954/55 % of Total	1959/60 Value	1959/60 % of Total	1960/61 Value	1960/61 % of Total	1961/62 Value	1961/62 % of Total	1962/63 Value	1962/63 % of Total
Commonwealth Countries										
Australia	6,570	51.0	9,253	49.2	8,389	50.5	7,973	50.1	8,702	48.0
United Kingdom	5,617	43.6	5,975	31.7	5,460	32.9	5,017	31.6	5,630	31.0
Canada	1	—	1,323	7.0	—	—	—	—	9	—
Other	27	0.2	142	0.8	197	1.2	198	1.2	246	1.4
Total	12,215	94.8	16,693	88.7	14,046	84.6	13,188	82.9	14,587	80.4
Other Countries										
Japan	86	0.7	1,033	5.5	736	4.4	610	3.8	615	3.4
U. S. A.	484	3.8	260	1.4	730	4.4	572	3.6	966	5.3
West Germany	49	0.4	407	2.2	627	3.8	627	4.0	696	3.8
Netherlands	16	0.1	268	1.4	360	2.2	477	3.0	791	4.4
Belgium	—	—	7	—	4	—	230	1.5	232	1.3
Other	37	0.3	142	0.7	91	0.5	163	1.0	251	1.4
Total	672	5.2	2,117	11.2	2,548	15.3	2,679	16.9	3,551	19.6
Unspecified	—	—	10	0.1	12	0.1	33	0.2	4	—
Grand Total	12,886	100.0	18,820	100.0	16,606	100.0	15,901	100.0	18,142	100.0

[a] Country of destination refers to country of consignment.

SOURCES: Territory of Papua and New Guinea, Overseas Trade Bulletins Nos. 3-8.

TABLE S.7: Import Values by Principal Commodity Groups, Selected Years

(£A thousand; f.o.b. at port of shipment)

Group	1954/55		1959/60		1960/61		1961/62		1962/63	
	Value	% of Total	Value	% of Total	Value	% of Total	Value	% of Total	Value	% of Total
Food	4,704	27.6	5,342	25.7	6,380	24.1	6,559	25.6	6,753	23.9
Drink	335	2.0	333	1.6	401	1.5	455	1.8	587	2.1
Tobacco	619	3.6	602	2.9	698	2.6	695	2.7	681	2.4
Drugs and Chemicals	1,100	6.5	1,357	6.5	1,646	6.2	1,799	7.0	1,930	6.8
Clothing and Textiles	1,439	8.4	2,001	9.6	2,565	9.7	2,433	9.5	2,450	8.7
Metals, Manufactures and Machinery	3,875	22.7	4,784	23.0	6,461	24.4	5,310	20.7	6,390	22.6
Transport Equipment	1,638	9.6	1,498	7.2	2,300	8.7	2,334	9.1	2,432	8.6
Petrol Products	911	5.3	1,140	5.5	1,242	4.7	1,252	4.9	1,496	5.3
Other Imports	2,427	14.2	3,751	18.0	4,771	18.0	4,805	18.7	5,549	19.6
Grand Total[a]	17,048	100.0	20,808	100.0	26,464	100.0	25,642	100.0	28,268	100.0

[a] Excludes outside packages.

SOURCES: Territory of Papua and New Guinea, Overseas Trade Bulletins Nos. 3-8.

TABLE S.8: Import Values by Origin, Selected Years [a]

(£A thousand; f.o.b. at port of shipment)

Country[b]	1954/55 Value	1954/55 % of Total	1959/60 Value	1959/60 % of Total	1960/61 Value	1960/61 % of Total	1961/62 Value	1961/62 % of Total	1962/63 Value	1962/63 % of Total
Commonwealth Countries										
Australia	11,007	64.5	13,275	63.1	16,239	60.7	14,782	57.0	16,515	57.9
United Kingdom	1,321	7.7	1,410	6.7	2,189	8.2	1,915	7.4	2,137	7.5
Hong Kong	670	3.9	1,024	4.8	1,386	5.2	1,470	5.7	1,420	5.0
India	165	1.0	185	0.9	311	1.2	171	0.6	188	0.6
New Zealand	—	—	11	0.1	82	0.3	256	1.0	265	0.9
Other	200[c]	1.3[c]	144	0.7	200	0.7	334	1.3	446	1.6
Total	13,363[c]	78.4[c]	16,049	76.3	20,407	76.3	18,928	73.0	20,971	73.5
Other Countries										
U. S. A.	1,777	10.4	1,443	6.9	1,663	6.2	1,819	7.0	1,804	6.3
Japan	565	3.3	1,354	6.4	1,750	6.6	1,930	7.4	1,819	6.4
Indonesia	525	3.1	995	4.7	1,121	4.2	970	3.7	1,227	4.3
West Germany	282	1.7	427	2.0	680	2.5	802	3.1	855	3.0
Netherlands	242	1.4	75	0.4	153	0.6	222	0.9	265	0.9
Other	294[c]	1.7[c]	454	2.2	650	2.4	931	3.6	1,076	3.8
Total	3,685[c]	21.6[c]	4,748	22.6	6,017	22.5	6,674	25.7	7,046	24.7
Unspecified	—	—	235	1.1	314	1.2	328	1.3	529	1.8
Grand Total	17,048	100.0	21,032	100.0	26,738	100.0	25,929	100.0	28,545	100.0

[a] Includes outside packages except in 1954/55.
[b] Country of origin refers to country of production (not necessarily to country from which actually imported).
[c] Approximate figures only.

SOURCES: Territory of Papua and New Guinea, Overseas Trade Bulletins Nos. 3-8.

TABLE S.9: Terms of Trade, 1948/49–1961/62

(1955/56 = 100)

Year	Index of Export Prices	Index of Import Prices	Index of Terms of Trade
1949	66.0	66.7	99.0
1950	76.1	82.1	92.7
1951	86.3	84.7	101.8
1952	94.5	105.0	90.0
1953	97.3	108.0	90.0
1954	97.7	102.5	95.3
1955	100.2	103.2	97.1
1956	100.0	100.0	100.0
1957	93.4	95.5	97.8
1958	84.9	96.7	87.9
1959	108.7	98.8	110.0
1960	115.9	98.9	117.2
1961	90.8	103.5	87.7
1962	82.1	99.1	82.9

SOURCE: Department of Territories: data supplied to the Mission.

TABLE S.10: Balance of Payments—Current Account, Selected Years

(£A thousand)

	1950/51	1956/57	1958/59	1960/61	1961/62	1962/63
CREDITS						
Goods and Services						
Exports (Territory Produce, f.o.b.)	7,380	11,810	14,467	14,257	14,322	16,359
Copra Fund Interest	—	91	119	144	140	153
Transfers						
Mission Finance	170	496	491	560	680	963
Commonwealth Grant	4,355	9,645	11,479	14,797	17,293	20,000
Net Direct Commonwealth Expenditure	1,320	2,078	2,429	3,922	4,775	4,759
Total Credits	13,225	24,120	28,985	33,680	37,210	42,234
DEBITS						
Goods and Services						
Imports (f.o.b.)	10,490	18,487	18,433	24,236	24,173	25,800
Net Freight and Insurance	a	1,482	1,520	3,086	2,878	3,011
Net Foreign Travel	450	1,255	1,685	2,055	2,014	2,069
External Cost of Management and Insurance	230	410	510	720	762	807
Other Services (Net)	1,000	1,410	1,760	1,875	2,139	2,572
Interest and Dividends Paid Abroad	n.a.	750	1,100	2,434	3,075	3,192
Total Debits	12,170	23,794	25,008	34,406	35,041	37,451
Balance on Current Account	1,055	326	3,977	—726	2,169	4,783
	13,225	24,120	28,985	33,680	37,210	42,234

a Included in import figure.

SOURCES: The Social Accounts of the New Guinea Market Economy for 1949/50 and 1950/51 by Prof. T. W. Swan; The Social Accounts for 1956/57–1960/61 by R. C. White; Department of Territories: National Income Estimates for 1960/61–1962/63.

TABLE S.11: Administration Receipts and Expenditures, Selected Years

(£A thousand)

	1952	1955	1959	1960	1961	1962	1963	1964 [a]
				(years ending June 30)				
RECEIPTS								
Import Duties	951	1,344	2,142	1,956	2,258	2,497	2,760	2,950
Export Duties	495	708	1,142	313	—	—	—	—
Excise Duty	—	33	83	137	172	178	289	330
Personal Tax	—	—	154	175	147	111	95	85
Income Tax: Individual	—	—	—	942	1,226	1,355	1,535	1,750
Companies	—	—	—	871	1,122	857	1,044	1,150
Postal	95	135	354	412	496	581	658	737
Public Utilities	72	200	553	591	633	673	788	235
Other Internal Revenue	778	734	1,177	1,197	1,398	1,454	1,855	3,293
Total Internal Revenue	2,391	3,154	5,605	6,594	7,452	7,706	9,024	10,530
Commonwealth Grant	5,285	7,126	11,479	12,808	14,797	17,293	20,000	25,250
Loan Fund	—	—	—	—	552	497	898	1,700
Total Receipts	7,676	10,280	17,084	19,402	22,801	25,496	29,922	37,480
EXPENDITURES								
Departmental:								
Public Health	1,469	1,829	1,967	2,349	2,649	3,010	3,403	3,643
Native Affairs	1,211	901	1,111	1,249	1,355	1,468	1,470	1,666
Agriculture, Stock and Fisheries	354	540	725	857	986	1,108	1,225	1,390
Education	438	562	1,226	1,546	2,040	2,473	3,135	4,150
Posts and Telegraphs	247	364	696	815	882	1,031	1,161	1,301
Public Works	[b]	29	396	412	517	445	593	776
Other Departments	1,355	1,677	4,568	5,151	6,156	6,815	7,723	10,679
Total Departmental	5,074	5,902	10,689	12,379	14,585	16,350	18,710	23,605
General Maintenance	850	1,192	1,741	2,067	2,345	2,804	3,135	3,059
Capital Works and Services	1,372	2,394	3,704	3,928	4,998	4,978	6,357	8,501
Purchase of Capital Assets	384	749	904	895	687	901	1,127	1,617
Special Appropriations	16	12	39	64	268	465	607	697
Total Expenditures	7,696	10,249	17,077	19,333	22,883	25,498	29,936	37,480

[a] Budget estimates.
[b] Included with *Other Departments*.

SOURCE: Department of Territories: Statistical tabulations prepared for the Mission.

TABLE S.12: Administration Current Expenditures, 1958/59–1963/64 (years ending June 30)

	1958/59 £A thousand	%	1959/60 £A thousand	%	1960/61 £A thousand	%	1961/62 £A thousand	%	1962/63 £A thousand	%	1963/64[a] £A thousand	%
Commodity Producing Sectors												
Agriculture, Stock and Fisheries	671	5.7	789	5.7	909	5.5	1,043	5.5	1,165	5.5	1,270	5.0
Forestry	280	2.4	314	2.3	355	2.2	367	1.9	324	1.5	384	1.5
Lands, Surveys and Mines	239	2.0	303	2.2	370	2.2	468	2.5	535	2.5	668	2.6
Trade and Industry	156	1.3	296	2.2	336	2.1	363	1.9	534	2.5	618	2.4
Total Commodity Producing Sectors	1,346	11.4	1,702	12.4	1,970	12.0	2,241	11.8	2,558	12.0	2,940	11.5
Economic Overheads												
Roads and Bridges	610	5.1	726	5.2	800	4.9	951	5.0	1,123	5.3	1,233	4.8
Ports and Harbors	33	0.3	62	0.4	36	0.2	55	0.3	34	0.1	46	0.2
Aerodromes	32	0.3	48	0.4	57	0.4	63	0.3	83	0.4	85	0.3
Electric Power	410	3.4	472	3.4	494	3.0	579	3.1	671	3.2	220	0.8
Posts and Telegraphs	532	4.5	632	4.6	709	4.3	849	4.5	900	4.2	930	3.6
Total Economic Overheads	1,617	13.6	1,940	14.0	2,096	12.8	2,497	13.2	2,811	13.2	2,514	9.7
Social Services												
Education	1,226	10.4	1,545	11.1	2,143	13.0	2,463	13.1	3,035	14.2	3,979	15.5
Health	2,000	16.9	2,376	17.2	2,687	16.4	3,065	16.2	3,446	16.2	3,699	14.4
Housing	—		—									
Water Supply and Sewerage	176	1.5	178	1.3	197	1.3	220	1.2	238	1.0	261	1.0
Total Social Services	3,402	28.8	4,099	29.6	5,027	30.7	5,748	30.5	6,719	31.4	7,939	30.9
General Administration, Law and Order												
Law, Order and Public Safety	990	8.4	1,295	9.4	1,376	8.4	1,737	9.2	1,904	8.9	2,121	8.3
Legislature	12	0.1	14	0.1	24	0.1	29	0.2	42	0.2	50	0.2
General Administrative Services	4,296	36.3	4,597	33.2	5,717	35.0	6,296	33.3	6,784	31.8	9,403	36.7
Total General Administration	5,298	44.8	5,906	42.7	7,117	43.5	8,062	42.6	8,730	41.0	11,574	45.2
Public Debt	—		—		4		49	0.3	126	0.6	377	1.5
Various Public Works	59	0.5	74	0.5	98	0.6	133	0.7	175	0.8	—	
Miscellaneous	124	1.0	121	0.9	117	0.7	200	1.1	227	1.1	315	1.2
Grand Total	11,846	100.0	13,843	100.0	16,428	100.0	18,930	100.0	21,346	100.0	25,660	100.0

[a] Budget.

SOURCE: Department of Territories: Economic and Functional Classification of Public Authorities Finances, 1958/59–1962/63.

TABLE S.13: Administration Capital Expenditures, 1958/59–1963/64 (years ending June 30)

	1958/59		1959/60		1960/61		1961/62		1962/63		1963/64[a]	
	£A thousand	%	£A thousand	%	£A thousand	%	£A thousand	%	£A thousand	%	£A thousand	%
Commodity Producing Sectors												
Agriculture, Stock and Fisheries	63	1.2	63	1.1	102	1.6	100	1.5	189	2.2	389	3.3
Forestry	12	0.2	14	0.3	12	0.2	11	0.2	66	0.8	35	0.3
Lands, Surveys and Mines	—	—	107	1.9	80	1.2	213	3.2	194	2.3	281	2.4
Trade and Industry	—	—	—	—	—	—	—	—	—	—	—	—
Total Commodity Producing Sectors	75	1.4	184	3.3	194	3.0	324	4.9	449	5.2	705	6.0
Economic Overheads												
Roads and Bridges	426	8.1	442	8.1	450	7.0	591	9.0	686	8.0	805	6.8
Ports and Harbors	42	0.8	52	0.9	21	0.3	100	1.5	78	0.9	192	1.6
Aerodromes	48	0.9	29	0.5	39	0.6	14	0.2	151	1.8	70	0.6
Electric Power	280	5.4	648	11.8	534	8.3	535	8.1	670	7.8	669	5.6
Posts and Telegraphs	194	3.7	199	3.6	202	3.1	206	3.1	283	3.3	443	3.7
Total Economic Overheads	990	18.9	1,370	25.0	1,246	19.3	1,446	22.0	1,868	21.7	2,179	18.3
Social Services												
Education	291	5.6	258	4.7	477	7.4	811	12.3	1,006	11.7	1,908	16.2
Health	767	14.7	795	14.5	887	13.7	492	7.5	691	8.0	771	6.5
Housing	1,271	24.3	1,292	23.5	2,018	31.3	1,653	25.2	2,165	25.2	1,993	16.9
Water Supply and Sewerage	410	7.8	169	3.1	133	2.1	135	2.1	128	1.5	460	3.9
Total Social Services	2,739	52.4	2,514	45.8	3,515	54.5	3,091	47.1	3,990	46.4	5,132	43.5
General Administration, Law and Order												
Law, Order and Public Safety	72	1.4	116	2.1	101	1.6	99	1.5	167	1.9	290	2.4
Legislature	—	—	—	—	—	—	—	—	—	—	—	—
General Administration Services	416	8.0	467	8.5	353	5.5	436	6.6	382	4.4	1,461	12.4
Total General Administration	488	9.3	583	10.6	454	7.0	535	8.1	549	6.4	1,751	14.8
Public Debt	—	—	—	—	—	—	—	—	—	—	—	—
Various Public Works	869	16.6	744	13.6	972	15.1	1,146	17.5	1,663	19.4	1,753	14.8
Miscellaneous	70	1.3	95	1.7	73	1.1	26	0.4	72	0.8	300	2.6
Grand Total	5,231	100.0	5,490	100.0	6,454	100.0	6,567	100.0	8,590	100.0	11,819	100.0

[a] Budget.

SOURCE: Department of Territories: Economic and Functional Classification of Public Authorities Finances, 1958/1959–1962/63.

TABLE S.14: Administration Current and Capital Expenditures, 1958/59–1963/64 (years ending June 30)

	1958/59 £A thousand	1958/59 %	1959/60 £A thousand	1959/60 %	1960/61 £A thousand	1960/61 %	1961/62 £A thousand	1961/62 %	1962/63 £A thousand	1962/63 %	1963/64[a] £A thousand	1963/64[a] %
Commodity Producing Sectors												
Agriculture, Stock and Fisheries	733	4.3	852	4.4	1,011	4.4	1,143	4.5	1,354	4.5	1,659	4.4
Forestry	292	1.7	328	1.7	367	1.6	378	1.5	391	1.3	419	1.1
Lands, Surveys and Mines	239	1.4	410	2.1	450	2.0	682	2.7	730	2.4	949	2.5
Trade and Industry	156	0.9	296	1.5	336	1.5	363	1.4	534	1.8	618	1.6
Total Commodity Producing Sectors	1,420	8.3	1,886	9.8	2,164	9.5	2,566	10.1	3,009	10.1	3,645	9.7
Economic Overheads												
Roads and Bridges	1,036	6.1	1,167	6.0	1,250	5.5	1,542	6.0	1,809	6.0	2,038	5.4
Ports and Harbors	75	0.4	114	0.6	57	0.2	156	0.6	111	0.4	238	0.6
Aerodromes	80	0.5	77	0.4	96	0.4	77	0.3	234	0.8	155	0.4
Electric Power	690	4.0	1,120	5.8	1,028	4.5	1,114	4.4	1,341	4.5	889	2.4
Posts and Telegraphs	726	4.3	831	4.3	911	4.0	1,056	4.1	1,182	3.9	1,373	3.7
Total Economic Overheads	2,607	15.3	3,309	17.1	3,342	14.6	3,945	15.4	4,677	15.6	4,693	12.5
Social Services												
Education	1,517	8.9	1,803	9.3	2,619	11.4	3,273	12.8	4,041	13.5	5,887	15.7
Health	2,767	16.2	3,171	16.4	3,575	15.6	3,557	13.9	4,137	13.8	4,470	11.9
Housing	1,271	7.4	1,292	6.7	2,018	8.8	1,653	6.5	2,165	7.2	1,993	5.3
Water Supply and Sewerage	586	3.4	348	1.8	330	1.4	355	1.4	366	1.2	721	1.9
Total Social Services	6,141	36.0	6,614	34.2	8,542	37.3	8,838	34.7	10,709	35.8	13,071	34.9
General Administration, Law and Order												
Law, Order and Public Safety	1,062	6.2	1,411	7.3	1,478	6.5	1,836	7.2	2,071	6.9	2,411	6.4
Legislature	12	0.1	14	0.1	24	0.1	29	0.1	42	0.1	50	0.1
General Administrative Services	4,712	27.6	5,064	26.2	6,070	26.5	6,732	26.4	7,166	23.9	10,864	29.0
Total General Administration	5,786	33.9	6,489	33.6	7,572	33.1	8,597	33.7	9,279	31.0	13,325	35.6
Public Debt	—	—	—	—	4	—	49	0.2	126	0.4	377	1.0
Various Public Works	928	5.4	818	4.2	1,069	4.7	1,279	5.0	1,837	6.1	1,753	4.7
Miscellaneous	195	1.1	216	1.1	190	0.8	225	0.9	299	1.0	615	1.6
Grand Total	17,077	100.0	19,333	100.0	22,883	100.0	25,498	100.0	29,936	100.0	37,479	100.0

[a] Budget.

SOURCE: Department of Territories: Economic and Functional Classification of Public Authorities Finances, 1958/59–1962/63.

TABLE S.15: Revenues and Expenditures of Native Local Government Councils, Selected Years

(£A thousand)

	1952	1956	1959	1960	1961	1962
REVENUES	22.7	44.2	145.7	182.8	209.7	312.8
EXPENDITURES						
Commodity Producing Sectors						
Agriculture	0.3	3.2	6.8	3.9	4.5	6.1
Forestry	—	0.6	—	—	—	—
Total Commodity Producing Sectors	0.3	3.8	6.8	3.9	4.5	6.1
Economic Overheads						
Roads and Bridges	0.3	1.5	3.5	2.4	2.8	9.1
Transport (incl. equipment)	—	11.9	19.5	32.5	33.3	48.7
Total Economic Overheads	0.3	13.4	23.0	34.9	36.1	57.8
Social Services						
Education	2.3	6.9	14.5	15.0	29.0	33.3
Health	2.6	7.4	18.6	18.9	25.0	33.6
Water Supply	0.3	3.4	4.4	5.8	9.8	19.2
Social Welfare	—	0.4	0.2	1.0	3.3	5.0
Total Social Services	5.2	18.1	37.7	40.7	67.1	91.1
Administration, Law and Order						
Council Administration	9.4	11.3	38.2	54.5	73.7	88.4
Law and Order	—	1.5	2.8	5.2	7.4	9.2
Total Administration	9.4	12.8	41.0	59.7	81.1	97.6
Loan Repayments	—	—	—	3.2	3.2	6.5
Miscellaneous	—	0.1	4.9	1.3	2.3	4.7
Total All Expenditures	15.2	48.2	113.4	143.6	194.3	263.8

SOURCE: Department of Native Affairs: data supplied to the Mission.

TABLE S.16: Expenditures of the Commonwealth Departments and Instrumentalities, 1958/59–1962/63 (years ending June 30)

	1958/59		1959/60		1960/61		1961/62		1962/63	
	£A thousand	%	£A thousand	%	£A thousand	%	£A thousand	%	£A thousand	%
Commodity Producing Sectors										
Agriculture, Stock and Fisheries	62	2.8	565	19.1	515	12.8	551	11.2	367	7.5
Forestry	—	—	—	—	—	—	—	—	—	—
Lands, Surveys and Mines	100	4.5	81	2.7	506	12.6	209	4.2	342	7.0
Trade and Industry	—	—	—	—	—	—	—	—	—	—
Total Commodity Producing Sectors	162	7.2	646	21.8	1,021	25.3	760	15.4	709	14.5
Economic Overheads										
Roads and Bridges	—	—	—	—	—	—	—	—	—	—
Ports and Harbors	—	—	—	—	—	—	—	—	—	—
Aerodromes	1,328	59.1	1,340	45.3	1,690	41.9	1,609	32.6	1,600	32.7
Electric Power	—	—	—	—	—	—	—	—	—	—
Posts and Telegraphs	84	3.7	112	3.8	103	2.6	350	7.1	507	10.4
Total Economic Overheads	1,412	62.9	1,452	49.1	1,793	44.5	1,959	39.7	2,107	43.1
Social Services										
Education	35	1.6	41	1.4	54	1.3	67	1.4	71	1.5
Health	—	—	—	—	—	—	—	—	—	—
Housing	—	—	—	—	—	—	—	—	—	—
Water Supply and Sewerage	—	—	—	—	—	—	—	—	—	—
Total Social Services	35	1.6	41	1.4	54	1.3	67	1.4	71	1.5
General Administration, Law and Order										
Law, Order and Public Safety	—	—	—	—	—	—	—	—	—	—
Legislature	—	—	—	—	—	—	—	—	—	—
General Administrative Services	235	10.5	240	8.1	239	5.9	265	5.4	342	7.0
Total General Administration	235	10.5	240	8.1	239	5.9	265	5.4	342	7.0
Public Debt										
Various Public Works	129	5.7	209	7.1	185	4.6	532	10.8	167	3.4
Miscellaneous	273	12.2	370	12.5	739	18.3	1,347	27.3	1,495	30.6
Grand Total	2,246	100.0	2,958	100.0	4,031	100.0	4,930	100.0	4,891	100.0

SOURCE: Department of Territories: Economic and Functional Classification of Public Authorities Finances, 1958/59–1962/63.

TABLE S.17: Expenditures of All Public Authorities, 1958/59–1962/63 (years ending June 30)

	1958/59 £A thousand	%	1959/60 £A thousand	%	1960/61 £A thousand	%	1961/62 £A thousand	%	1962/63 £A thousand	%
Commodity Producing Sectors										
Agriculture, Stock and Fisheries	801	4.1	1,422	6.3	1,531	5.7	1,700	5.5	1,730	4.9
Forestry	292	1.5	328	1.5	367	1.4	378	1.2	391	1.1
Lands, Surveys and Mines	339	1.7	491	2.2	956	3.5	891	2.9	1,072	3.0
Trade and Industry	156	.8	296	1.3	336	1.2	363	1.2	534	1.5
Total Commodity Producing Sectors	1,588	8.2	2,537	11.3	3,190	11.8	3,332	10.9	3,727	10.6
Economic Overheads										
Roads and Bridges	1,041	5.4	1,172	5.2	1,253	4.6	1,548	5.0	1,820	5.2
Ports and Harbors	75	.4	114	.5	57	.2	156	.5	111	.3
Aerodromes	1,408	7.2	1,417	6.3	1,786	6.6	1,686	5.5	1,834	5.2
Electric Power	690	3.6	1,120	5.0	1,028	3.8	1,114	3.6	1,341	3.8
Posts and Telegraphs	810	4.2	943	4.2	1,014	3.7	1,406	4.6	1,689	4.8
Total Economic Overheads	4,024	20.7	4,766	21.3	5,138	19.0	5,910	19.3	6,795	19.3
Social Services										
Education	1,566	8.1	1,860	8.3	2,695	10.0	3,371	11.0	4,158	11.8
Health	2,785	14.3	3,191	14.2	3,596	13.3	3,586	11.7	4,191	11.9
Housing	1,271	6.5	1,292	5.8	2,018	7.5	1,653	5.4	2,165	6.2
Water Supply and Sewerage	591	3.0	354	1.6	337	1.2	369	1.2	388	1.1
Total Social Services	6,213	32.0	6,697	29.9	8,646	31.9	8,979	29.3	10,902	31.0
General Administration, Law and Order										
Law, Order and Public Safety	1,065	5.5	1,416	6.3	1,484	5.5	1,844	6.0	2,080	5.9
Legislature	12	.1	14	.1	24	.1	29	.1	42	.1
General Administrative Services	4,986	25.7	5,355	23.9	6,377	23.5	7,085	23.1	7,624	21.7
Total General Administration	6,063	31.2	6,785	30.3	7,885	29.1	8,958	29.2	9,746	27.7
Public Debt	—		—		4		49	.2	126	.4
Various Public Works	1,057	5.4	1,027	4.6	1,254	4.6	1,812	5.9	2,004	5.7
Miscellaneous	490	2.5	613	2.7	965	3.6	1,618	5.3	1,875	5.3
Grand Total	19,435	100.0	22,425	100.0	27,082	100.0	30,658	100.0	35,172	100.0

SOURCE: Department of Territories: Economic and Functional Classification of Public Authorities Finances, 1958/59–1962/63.

TABLE S.18: Summary of Credit Needs under Agricultural and Livestock Programs, 1964/65–1973/74

(£A thousand)

Years	1	2	3	4	5	Sub-total	6	7	8	9	10	Sub-total	Total
COCONUT													
Indigenous at £A10/acre	115	135	175	175	175	775	175	175	175	175	175	875	1,650 [a]
Non-indigenous at £A26/acre	221	299	325	325	325	1,495	195	195	195	195	195	975	2,470
	336	434	500	500	500	2,270	370	370	370	370	370	1,850	4,120 [a]
COCOA													
Indigenous at £A22/acre	33	55	77	99	121	385	143	165	176	176	176	836	1,221
Additional at £A48/acre	—	—	—	—	—	120	—	—	—	—	—	218	338
Non-indigenous at £A60/acre	120	120	120	120	120	600	120	120	120	120	120	600	1,200
at £A70/acre	280	280	280	280	280	1,400	70	70	70	70	70	350	1,750
at £A120/acre	120	120	120	120	120	600	120	120	120	120	120	600	1,200
	553	575	597	619	641	3,105	453	475	486	486	486	2,604	5,709
RUBBER													
Indigenous at £A15/acre	6	7	9	12	15	49	18	22	30	30	30	130	179
Non-indigenous at £A75/acre	56	206	356	506	656	1,780	656	656	656	656	656	3,280	5,060
	62	213	365	518	671	1,829	674	678	686	686	686	3,410	5,239
CATTLE													
Indigenous at 2/3 of Costs [b]	43	43	66	86	108	346	130	151	173	216	281	951	1,297
Non-indigenous at 50% of Costs [b]	85	100	100	—	—	285	—	—	—	—	—	—	285
	128	143	166	86	108	631	130	151	173	216	281	951	1,582
TEA	240	240	240	240	240	1,200	—	—	—	—	—	—	1,200
Grand Total	1,319	1,605	1,868	1,963	2,160	9,035	1,627	1,674	1,715	1,758	1,823	8,815	17,850 [a]

[a] Does not include additional provision of £A350,000 for indigenous entrepreneurs (see text of Chapter 3 under Coconuts).
[b] See text of Chapter 3 under Livestock.